Keith Fennell was born in 1973. At the age of 21 he joined the elite Australian Special Air Service Regiment. He was deployed on many operations, including missions to Afghanistan, East Timor, the Solomon Islands and the southern Indian Ocean. Fennell also served on a medical deployment to East Africa, was a member of the boarding party in the controversial MV *Tampa* incident, and supported counter-terrorist operations for the 2002 Commonwealth Heads of Government Meeting (CHOGM) in Brisbane and the Sydney 2000 Olympic Games.

Fennell left the SAS in late 2002 and moved to the United Arab Emirates, where he was employed as a special operations adviser. In January 2004, Fennell accepted a position in Iraq, and he spent the next 30 months running operations there, in Afghanistan and in Banda Aceh. In June 2006 Fennell returned to Australia. He is now completing a double degree in Creative Arts and Arts at the University of Wollongong. Fennell is married and lives with his wife and three children on the South Coast of New South Wales.

KEITH FENNELL
TWO BOOKS IN ONE

WARRIOR BROTHERS &
WARRIOR TRAINING

BANTAM
SYDNEY AUCKLAND TORONTO NEW YORK LONDON

Note to readers: Underwater training can be extremely dangerous and should only be performed under competent and close supervision.

A Bantam book
Published by Random House Australia Pty Ltd
Level 3, 100 Pacific Highway, North Sydney NSW 2060
www.randomhouse.com.au

This edition published by Bantam in 2012
Warrior Brothers first published by Bantam in 2008, reprinted in 2009
Warrior Training first published by Bantam in 2009, reprinted in 2010

Copyright © Keith Fennell 2008, 2009

The moral right of the author has been asserted.

All rights reserved. No part of this book may be reproduced or transmitted by any person or entity, including internet search engines or retailers, in any form or by any means, electronic or mechanical, including photocopying (except under the statutory exceptions provisions of the Australian *Copyright Act 1968*), recording, scanning or by any information storage and retrieval system without the prior written permission of Random House Australia.

Addresses for companies within the Random House Group can be found at www.randomhouse.com.au/offices

A CiP catalogue for this book can be found at the National Library of Australia.

ISBN: 978 1 74275 9 616

Cover based on design by Christabella Designs
Photograph on page 198 of *Warrior Training* courtesy of Stephen Chu
Internal typesetting and design by Midland Typesetters, Australia
Printed in Australia by Griffin Press, an accredited ISO AS/NZS 14001:2004 Environmental Management System printer

Random House Australia uses papers that are natural, renewable and recyclable products and made from wood grown in sustainable forests. The logging and manufacturing processes are expected to conform to the environmental regulations of the country of origin.

WARRIOR BROTHERS

For Joe Bresler,
who, to me, personified the true meaning
of the word *warrior*.
RIP, old boy!

And for my wife, Colleen.
It is to you I owe the most.

CONTENTS

Prologue   xi

Part One: Heard Island   1

Part Two: East Timor   47

Part Three: Eastern Afghanistan   109

Part Four: Afghan Operations   169

Part Five: Haditha Dam, Iraq   241

Part Six: Banda Aceh   345

Abbreviations   383

Acknowledgements   385

PROLOGUE

Rounds are being exchanged in both directions. Little pieces of potential death are cutting through the air, searching for flesh. Ears are ringing. Eyes are large and round. Then there is silence.

'What happened?' asks Steve.

And Jimmy: 'Where are they?'

'There were six of them in the creek – I think I shot three of them,' I reply.

Suddenly there is frantic movement 50 metres to our front. The dense foliage is parted by men running for their lives. There is more shooting, then nothing. Just the sound of pounding, thumping hearts.

I move across the creek and then I see him. His motionless body is lying face-down in the dry, sandy riverbed. There is no movement, no life. His arms are stretched out in front of him, as if his last movements were to beg his friends to come back and make everything all right. His shoulder-length hair – thick, black and curly – is filled with dust, and his physique is strong. He is wearing shorts and a dark-coloured T-shirt. Four or five darker patches indicate the bullets that have entered his upper torso.

The image of this man's death remains seared in my long-term memory. I've tried to push it into the short-term, tried to lose it, but the picture is so deeply etched that I know it will stay in my mind forever.

≡

What was it like to be an SAS soldier?

When I reflect upon my experiences, my heart jumps into overdrive, beating harder and faster as I feel the blood whooshing through my veins like a runaway train. My military life made me feel alive and on the edge, and my body still craves this. Perhaps a person in a regular, nine-to-five job – excluding those who are addicted to extreme sports – would find an addiction to danger a little hard to fathom, but how could they be expected to understand? An SAS soldier's work is more than just exciting. Driving a fast car is exciting. But for me, this profession had become an addiction, a set of experiences comparable to nothing else.

I was accepted into the Australian Special Air Service Regiment in 1995, aged just 21. In the 11 years that followed I saw operational service and worked as a civilian security contractor around the world: from East Timor to Afghanistan, the southern Indian Ocean to Iraq. In 2006 I made the decision to come home for good. I needed to be with my wife, Colleen. I needed to be a father to my children.

I had always thought I'd be able to ease into a suburban existence, but this may not be the case. I am locked in my past, and when I look at my new life I feel like a ghost – an outsider looking in. One day I was in Iraq, locking eyes with a man who wanted to kill me, and the next I am at a mother's group with my kids, hanging out with a group of women I have never met, sipping lattes and talking about Tom Cruise.

I want to be able to enjoy the things that others enjoy and to feel content and complete with this. But my past does not make this possible. Things I enjoyed before I joined the SAS — adventure rides, fast cars, motorcycles, diving and parachuting — now appear bland. Have I been spoilt by my experiences or destroyed? I don't know.

It is hard for people to understand this, which only adds to the torment. Who can you talk to about such things? My friends in the Regiment were taking bets on how long it would be before I realised my destiny and came back. My new life as a husband and a dad hasn't been easy to accept, and sometimes the thought of returning to Afghanistan or Iraq seems the easier option. Closing my eyes results in an instant quickening of heartbeat and breathing, my palms begin to sweat and my right foot taps anxiously against the floor. Life in the SAS was all-consuming and I've struggled to let it go.

Some nights I dream of an explosion. The blast kills my friends but spares me. I am taken prisoner, placed in a cell with only a small, barred window to the outside world. With a growing sense of panic, I stand at the bars, trying to work out where I am. I can see a military convoy in the distance. Once I manage to free my hands, I begin to get my bearings. It looks like Fallujah.

Sometimes, in the dream, I manage to kill the guard who has been taunting me. Other nights I make it out of my cell and get all the way to the Euphrates. I jump in with my hands cuffed behind my back and watch while insurgent forces scour the banks for me. Once they work out where I'm hiding, they begin to pour lead into the river. Slowly I double back, desperate to escape, and lie hiding, moments from capture, almost under their feet in the reeds.

Other nights I find myself running through the familiar streets of Iraq's International Zone when a black van runs me down and breaks my legs. I am thrown in the back of the van and held down by the Iraqi workers inside. The van is hot and, no matter how hard I struggle, I can't move. I hear us pass through the military checkpoint while a hand covers my mouth and another squeezes my throat. Pinned to the floor, I can hear the US guard asking routine questions. He cannot hear my muffled screams. He cannot hear me thrashing in the back of the van. He lets us through the checkpoint. We drive on. That's it.

After my dreams leave me, I lie awake and confused, charged with exhilaration and anxiety amongst sodden and dishevelled sheets. In the Regiment, my fears had never been for my own wellbeing. Even when I was employed as a security operations manager working in Iraq and Afghanistan, my greatest anxiety was that a poor tactical decision could contribute to the death of a mate or colleague. In the context of operations, guilt, angst and fear were all tied up with supporting the guys. And yet when at home in New South Wales, with my family around me, inexplicably my dreams revolve around my own capture. The reason for this still eludes me.

Making a smooth transition from a life of adrenaline-charged experiences as an Australian SAS soldier to one of a civilian is near-impossible. The thirst for that moment of heightened senses, of racing pulse – caught in the moment, your entire body stretched tight with effort and adrenaline – leaves an indelible mark on your soul and psyche. Getting into the SAS was tough, but that was nothing compared to saying goodbye.

≡

Sometimes it appears as if your life is travelling smoothly: all the stars align, you are unstoppable, invincible. Then you can be hit by a pain that pierces your chest and leaves you numb: the news that someone you were close to, whom you respected and who touched your life, is no longer alive. I've felt this too many times, and never more than in 2007. Tapping away at my keyboard, I'm flooded with images. I see war zones and bomb victims. I see again the motionless body of the first man I ever killed, facedown in that dry, sandy riverbed in East Timor. I see the faces of friends who will never come home to hold their children. This is for them.

As this book has slowly taken shape, I've been struck by the realisation that the adrenaline rush, the challenge and the exhilaration – these aren't what I miss most from my old life. It is the men whom I was privileged to work beside. While my experiences were invigorating, it will always be the mateship that I cherish most, the camaraderie forged by sharing adventures with the most incredible men I'll ever meet in my life – my Warrior Brothers.

My Warrior Brothers
Who stand beside
Me

xvi WARRIOR BROTHERS

Who stands beside
Them
Who appear when trouble confronts
Me
Who runs forth to defend
Them
Whenever they need
Me
Or whenever I need
Them
To form the union of
Us
And those like
Us
Embrace in combined strength during adversity
And nothing, not even death, will ever sever this bond.

PART ONE

HEARD ISLAND, SOUTHERN INDIAN OCEAN

1998

ONE

My first operational deployment in the SAS was in early 1998, as a member of a four-man team. We had been deployed to join a naval mission near Heard Island, to help seize any vessels found fishing illegally within the Australian exclusion zone.

Heard Island lies deep in the southern Indian Ocean, approximately 4000 kilometres south-west of Perth and 1000 kilometres north of Antarctica. Alongside its immediate neighbour, the McDonald Islands, ownership of this uninhabited, desolate, sub-Antarctic patch of land was transferred from the UK to Australia in 1947, and it is now classified as a nature reserve.

To describe the conditions as rough would be putting it mildly. Heard is dominated by an active volcano, the Big Ben Massif, and its summit, Mawson Peak, claims the title as Australia's highest territorial point at 2745 metres. Eighty per cent of the island is covered in ice that can be up to 150 metres thick, and broad glacial fingers extend into the ocean where they are broken off by the brutal winds (gusts up to 210 kmh) and waves (up to 17 metres). The average daily maximum temperature is three degrees Celsius. With three out of four days being cloudy, Heard Island is far from an ideal tourist destination.

The wind chill is deadly, as is the icy water. A person who enters the water unprotected may only have a couple of minutes before falling into hypothermic unconsciousness. Even with an immersion suit, you wouldn't survive longer than about 30 minutes. The Patagonian toothfish, however, thrives in these deep, icy waters, growing up to 2.2 metres long and weighing up to 100 kilograms. A prized delicacy in the United States and Europe, the fish may only be caught by three authorised Australian vessels. Unfortunately, the 200-nautical-mile exclusion zone around the islands is frequently breached by long-line poachers who launch from numerous African ports. That's where we came in.

Heading towards Heard Island on the HMAS *Newcastle* in search of illegal fishing vessels was hardly counter-terrorism. It was a classic peacetime operation – we were using our expertise to save a fish we had never heard of. But our SAS training in medical, language and humanitarian skills would at least get a workout. And it was still a sensitive task: some years later, our deployment on the decks of the MV *Tampa* showed how easily the presence of soldiers in such a context could be politicised.

This operation didn't have the risk factor that some of our later deployments would, but we were all hungry to put our skills into practice. Negotiating the monstrous waves of the Indian Ocean presented our first real challenge. Within several days the weather had begun to deteriorate, and the seas rose accordingly. Even the most experienced amongst us, those with cast-iron stomachs, were lying flat on their backs, breathing deeply and trying to keep their rising nausea at bay. Most men were almost overdosing on sea-sickness tablets, which weren't much use in any case. We were barely holding on to the contents of our stomachs as it was, and the sickly taste and smell of the tablets were producing more waves of clammy retching. Not quite their intended purpose.

It made no difference that we had been at sea for more than 10 days. Waves broke relentlessly over the frigate, and there had been considerable movement on the vessel's metal bow. The hull had been displaced in some places by at least 30 centimetres, and the aft area was churning through the swell like a corkscrew. Monster swells continued to line up along the horizon. The windswept southern Indian Ocean offered no comfort and the heavy-clouded grey sky promised more of the same.

And yet, peering through the water-splattered window, feeling the floor rising up to meet me as nausea grappled with my stomach, I felt content. Finally, I was getting exactly what I'd signed up for. Finally, I had been deployed on a real task.

When I was young I never dreamed of joining the military. I thought the guys at school with shaved heads and camouflage pants had a screw loose and probably watched too many *Rambo* movies. Surrounded by strong and loving women, the first grandchild on my mother's side and the only grandson, little 'Keithy Boy' was being groomed to be a musician rather than an SAS soldier and adrenaline junkie.

As a boy I was far from being a stereotypical alpha-male. I watched *The Sound of Music* and *Grease*, I cried on my first day of school, I left others to play footy while I had organ lessons. I still remember sitting there, my back perfectly straight, as my music teacher asked me to turn up the volume for 'In the Mood'. As the pitch of my musical efforts increased, so did the heckling from my mates on the road below. The peanut gallery began to sing along, albeit out of tune and with slightly differing lyrics: 'In the Mood' became 'In the Loo'.

I have always had a special relationship with my mother and, although she was disappointed when I gave up music, I was never forced to do anything that I didn't want to do. She told me I would regret it and she was right. Who knows,

I may have moved on to the electric guitar. Now that would have been cool.

Our family was close. Ma was the driving force, both around the house and in the office of the family mechanical repair business. Through the early years growing up, my dad, a tough, loyal and honest man, worked his butt off to pay for family extras. My sisters and I were extremely fortunate children, given the opportunity to have a crack at any sport or activity we liked. While money was tight outside of the mortgage, food and general living expenses, extras included our sporting activities, as well as the odd trip to Pizza Hut or McDonald's.

At 11, after I saw the film *Kill or Be Killed*, I decided I wanted to pursue martial arts. Due to the outlay for uniforms, my parents made me wait six months – so they could be certain it wasn't just another passing fad. It wasn't. Something about the discipline needed, the energy it took and the sense of pride I got from practising was exactly what I'd been looking for. Rugby league, surfing, cricket and basketball all came a distant second to my love of kicking, punching and swinging dodgy homemade nunchakus.

I achieved my first black belt at 14. By 15 I had moved on to kung fu, and two years later I became a level one instructor. Running my own branch kept me busy, focused and healthy at a time when many of my friends were smoking a lot of pot. Training very quickly became my life. Dad wasn't overly fond of me kicking the hell out of the back of the house, so he looped some old car tyres around a tree in our backyard. I would flog those things, sometimes until my shins bled. The harder I kicked, the more it hurt – and the more driven I became to break through the pain threshold.

I loved the physical and mental challenges, but while the training gave me a powerful sense of drive, it failed to offer me a clear sense of purpose. It was, however, a welcome distraction from the other side of my life at that time: my apprenticeship as a motor mechanic. It had been a strange choice on leaving school, as I'd previously shown no mechanical aptitude whatsoever.

At 16 I had craved three things – challenges, excitement and sex. I weighed up my options. I could stay at school and double my girlfriend around on my pushbike, or complete a trade at my father's workshop and drive my girlfriend around in a shitty car. I chose the shitty car, but my heart wasn't in the work. I approached my apprenticeship as a stepping-stone to somewhere else.

Despite my father's patience and support, that time was more than a little stressful. He knew I hated the job but he did his best with what he had: a son who was bored mindless changing oil and completing 60,000-kilometre services on vans. The repetitiveness drove me mad, and my restlessness was only kept at bay by my rigorous training regime. If I knocked off at four o'clock, I'd be roaring down the road at a minute past.

While I somehow managed to finish my apprenticeship, settling into regular work as a qualified mechanic only heightened my sense of dissatisfaction. It took a colleague's idle comment to shake me out of my rut. We were sitting together having morning tea, staring at our cracked fingers and dirty nails, when he looked over at me and said, 'Dude, you are going to be working for your dad doing services for the rest of your life.'

Although his teasing comment was just standard banter

between us, it stayed in my mind. The more I thought about it, the more I hated the idea that my job as a motor mechanic was all the excitement I would ever be offered in life. I left within a couple of days. I applied for the police force but found it wasn't recruiting at the time, so I looked for another home for my training and obsessive determination. Suddenly the army didn't look that bad after all, especially if they would let me jump out of aeroplanes.

TWO

Was I passionate about saving the Patagonian toothfish? Not really. They weren't much to look at and, apparently, were rather oily to eat. But if protecting these unsightly fish offered me a little excitement, then count me in. Our patrol was joining an existing naval mission, lending the particular skills that we brought to bear as SAS-trained men – and before we'd even begun, the threat of missing out was dangled over our heads. In training and preparation our team had been made up of six, but Heard Island was strictly a four-man operation. Two of our number, the team leader and the second-in-command (2iC), were guaranteed positions. The rest of us, being in our mid-twenties, were notably younger than the average SAS team, and the knowledge that only two men could take part had us all a bit toey. Even a fishing expedition – a low-risk task – would give us some chance to put our training to use and was definitely better than shooting targets on the range.

Ultimately, the team leader chose Charlie and myself, the two soldiers who had not yet seen operational action. The men who missed out, Todd (ES) and Evo, were exceptional soldiers who had previously seen active service in

Somalia as members of the 1st Battalion, Royal Australian Regiment. The team was supported by JD, our witty troop sergeant, who provided the smooth link between us and the navy – a potentially fraught relationship.

The team leader was a man known as Buzz, and he was one of the most impressive and dynamic patrol commanders I've ever come across. He oozed confidence. His easygoing personality and quick sense of humour ensured a nice balance between work and play. Buzz could have been a movie star. In fact, I'm certain he's dreamt of such things.

Like many of the guys, Buzz joined the military almost by accident. After four long, fruitless days of having doors slammed in his face as an encyclopaedia salesman, Buzz decided to join the army as a steward. Can you imagine a mini version of The Rock being content to serve drinks in the officers' mess? This near-tragedy was averted by his roommate, who said, 'Fuck that! You're going to infantry.' The Regiment should track that guy down and thank him, as Buzz has now spent near on 20 years kicking arse in the unit.

A cool and engaging guy, Buzz loved his boys as much as they loved him. He was a man who led by example and was surprisingly patient when it came to handling his underlings' colourful egos. He would, however, occasionally bring us back to earth with a session on the bench press, where he was the undisputed master.

Our training for the Heard Island operation was carried out in Nowra. If we'd thought that the army had a knack for reducing fun activities to nothing but hard work, the navy quickly proved itself even more adept. Our team, along with two fisheries officers, were forced to carry out countless rehearsals, including routine fast rope slides, all the while decked out in the immersion suits and heavy woollen boots that we would be wearing on the operation.

What promised to be difficult in the Antarctic conditions of the southern Indian Ocean was murder in the sticky humidity of February in Nowra. After 30 minutes, our faces took on the same glow as our puffy orange suits. Luckily, the exercises themselves were ones we were well used to, so despite the heat we took them as an opportunity to torment our team leader.

Buzz had recently been trampled by our entire team when he lost his balance during counter-terrorism training in Townsville. Despite his considerable fitness – and the fact that he was the one leading the team – as second man onto the ground he was a little slow to depart the rope. Within seconds, the next man clipped his shoulder as he descended, knocking Buzz flat on his back. Each time he attempted to regain his balance the next man would arrive and knock him back to the ground. This occurred four times in total and, although our faces were hidden by gas masks, our squinting eyes no doubt revealed that we were pleased with our efforts. In contrast, Buzz's eyes were narrowed, his shaking head letting us know how furious he was with our immature antics. Buzz's solid reputation in the unit, and our growing respect for him, weren't enough to keep us from trying to destroy his larger-than-life ego by outgunning him. As it was, opportunities to show him up were scarce, as his moments of vulnerability were so few and far between.

Other parts of our training regimen for Heard Island were less extreme, although not without incident. We carried out close-quarter battle (CQB) range practices and the navy clearance divers were provided with some pistol training. One drizzly morning on the way to the live-fire range I was the designated bus driver. I was an advanced driving instructor and rather proud of my competence behind the wheel. I was also young and incredibly brash. Not only did I pride myself on my driving abilities, but I had a perfect accident-free record. What's more, I had completed the SAS fast driver and instructor modules, and had attended a three-week WA Police advanced driver's course — which involved me pushing a Gen III 350 Chev V8 Commodore to just under 200 kmh while chasing cop cars around a racetrack. Be it an assault vehicle or a 22-seater bus, there was no difference as far as I was concerned. Before long, I had the bus sliding through some corners in what I believed was a controlled manner. But in all the excitement I missed the entrance to the range road.

Desperately trying to keep my cool, I attempted to do a three-point turn on a fairly narrow stretch of road. It all happened very quickly: reverse, first, clutch, bang. I continued driving like everything was normal, trying to pretend that we hadn't all suffered a neck-snapping jolt, but a quick look in the rear-vision mirror confirmed the worst. A low-hanging branch of considerable girth had smashed in the rear window and a large section of the roof was partially crushed. There were also a couple of broken tail-lights for good measure.

Shock quickly gave way to ribbing and jeering. The navy guys didn't know whether to laugh or remain silent. My SAS mates didn't share their indecision: 'You were able to slide this little baby sideways without coming undone but can't manage a simple three-point turn without nearly writing off the bus!'

Buzz just gave me an unimpressed stare and said, 'I bet you're not really happy with that one.'

I tried not to let it faze me: 'I don't know what you're talking about. I hate the navy and if I want to scratch the back of one of their buses then I will.'

What else was there to say? We laughed, despite the knowledge that a paperwork nightmare would soon begin. I had not only fucked up, but had done so in front of a full complement of navy clearance divers. I would not be allowed to forget it.

After completing the training, our team returned to Perth and joined up with the HMAS *Westralia*, while the clearance divers departed from Sydney on the HMAS *Newcastle*. Weeks later, we would rendezvous in Rockingham before departing at last for the Indian Ocean and Heard Island.

THREE

I was stoked to be heading out to sea for my first deployment. Training for the water troop had thrown up a whole range of challenges and skills for me to embrace, and the prospect of putting them to use was nothing short of thrilling. Assault diving is physically and mentally taxing – but according to many SAS divers, it's little short of underwater sex. It is that good!

Water-work also includes diving and boating on and off submarines. Naturally, there is a downside. Having your bum bounced red-raw on the side of a small inflatable boat for six hours, all the while being buffeted by an icy spray, is something most of us are never nostalgic for. There is also no love lost on a night cache exercise where the boats and equipment are dragged up the beach and buried. This can take the best part of an entire evening, leaving you frozen, salted and covered in sand. Just the start you want to a two-week patrol.

It wasn't unusual for an assault diver to perspire profusely inside his facemask, such was the exertion of a force swim. In retrospect, all the sweating is hardly surprising: divers are fitted with an assault rig, primary and secondary weapon, ammunition, body armour, caving ladders, assault poles, sledgehammers, shotguns and demolition charges. Just a bit of extra baggage. Coupled with this, a re-breather (O2) dive set is more difficult to operate than a conventional air set. An operator must exhale hard into an O2 set, which in turn forces pure oxygen back into his lungs. It is almost the opposite of breathing. You breathe out hard and then air comes flowing back. If you try to do the reverse it is quite a struggle, and it's not unusual to feel a degree of claustrophobia from the restricted airflow. There are no bubbles and the exhaled breath is recycled, with the carbon dioxide being removed and absorbed into a granule-filled canister. A 1.5 kilogram bottle can provide a dive-time of three hours.

Considering that we are usually working flat-out and not just floating around looking at fish, this is an incredible piece of equipment. The O2 sets are designed for shallow-water assault diving – beyond a depth of 10 metres the oxygen becomes toxic to the human body. Additional care has to be taken when approaching the surface. It is imperative to 'breathe down' your set – to use up all the oxygen in the small bag without re-tripping the set. If this doesn't happen, bubbles will be expelled from what will have become full and bursting cheeks.

During a dive it is important to remain calm, especially for the compass operator, who must also concentrate on 'heading' (direction), depth and trying to lower his heart rate back to a workable level. He waits for a squeeze on his left arm and then on his right, to ensure that the team members are ready to continue, and then gradually accelerates towards the target. During a rapid descent, the sensation is quite similar to stuffing a piece of rag into your mouth and trying to go for a run – your lungs are pulling with all their might but only a trickle of air finds its way in. Given the dangers and the potential for oxygen deprivation, diving is not for everyone.

On top of these challenges, there is the added surge of adrenaline you get from having to negotiate four- to five-metre seas, sharks or both.

≡

Our dive training sites on the North West Shelf abounded with marine life, especially at night, when thousands of fish were attracted by the lights, and there was no shortage of 'top of the food chain' predators to add a little additional excitement. Prior to the Heard Island mission, our troop had been tasked to trial a shark-deterring pod that gives off an electromagnetic pulse. No water troop had previously carried out a night dive on the Shelf, and there was a perfectly good reason for this – there were far too many oversized, hungry, razor-toothed fish to worry about.

I was curious about what would happen if someone fell into the water at night, so on the evening before the night dive I moved to the vicinity of the boom (the large flame) and threw in several two-litre cartons of milk that I had punctured with my knife. Within moments of the cartons hitting the water, the area was awash with white frothy fluid mixed by a swish of shark fins and tails breaking the surface, almost like spoons that were stirring a broth on the boil. Whichever direction I looked in, there were small schools of sharks patrolling what was, apparently, their domain. We hoped these shark pods were everything they were cracked up to be, so we could dive without becoming dinner.

Before we carried out the drill, two of us entered the dark water to assess the currents. How did I manage to land such an unenviable task? Floating around on the surface was just a little too exhilarating, and I tried not to consider what was lurking beneath.

'Don't you dare do a piss,' I said to the team 2iC.

'Too late,' was his reply.

We didn't waste any time assessing the current and were quickly back in the twin 200-horsepower robust inflatable boats (RIBs), which began to approach our target. 'Prepare to turn, turn now, one, two, three, go,' was the call as we fell over the side and into the abyss of darkness and shadow.

'Mmm, the breathing sounds a little deeper than usual,' I thought.

As we entered the water, another diver's fin, which had the pulsing electromagnetic shark pod attached, glanced across the rear of my head. The jolt of electricity I received felt like being belted across the head with a rolled-up newspaper. Not a lean Tuesday paper but the Saturday version, heavy and busting with classifieds. The extra wordage gave me a headache.

With a squeeze of the compass operator's arm, the force began finning towards the dive platform. We were 600 metres away from our target but closed the gap in less than three minutes due to the strength of the current. The water was illuminated by several powerful lights, and dozens of shadows could be seen darting to and fro. Even worse, several much larger shadows could be seen in the depths below us. Heart rates were up.

With the task completed, we were all happy to scramble into the safety craft. I was one of the last men to board and had turned off my pod – until I noticed a shark circling only a few metres below me with its mouth wide open. This was all the encouragement I needed to turn it back on, and I also had no qualms about zapping one of my mates as I frantically swung my legs into the boat. As we were winched out of the water we saw a large dark shadow, a four- to five-metre hammerhead shark that was trailing one of the safety craft. Too late, buddy!

The next day, while we were conducting a day dive and were lined up on the tie-off line (eight metres from the surface), Buzz, in full team leader mode, gave the 'chop' – an indication to the end men (Todd and me) to head to the surface and fire the grappling gun in order to establish a line to ascend. We immediately followed his command, but later we learned that he was actually telling us to wait due to the presence of another large shark that was approaching. Some things are better left unknown.

≡

Diving in Bass Strait was, in many respects, even more challenging than evading rogue sharks on the North West Shelf. On a training exercise there, we learned the hard way that the crushing swell of the seas could be danger enough on its own. We saw evidence of Bass Strait's enormous power in the twisted and damaged metal grating of the nine-metre sea deck of a dive platform. The walkways were non-existent in some places – the metal had been buffeted with such force that the grates had folded like paper plates before being swept into the sea.

Attempting to secure a caving ladder to a dive platform is physically taxing. One method is to use a pole to position the ladder. In a strong current it can be impossible for the two operators to stay in position, so it is essential to develop a simple method to remain static. Two men attach a large tape sling (six metres long) between them and swim off with the pole in tow. The operators then swim around the opposite sides of a pylon. Although they are flung together with enormous force, they have the stability to begin attaching the ladder.

I was part of one such team with Mick, a supremely fit guy and a great mate. Mick had an enormous appetite for hard work and I enjoyed his sense of humour immensely. He was even more hilarious with a few beers under his belt. He also possessed uncanny hand–eye coordination, which made him a natural at any sport. Well, any sport except surfing. I am no Kelly Slater, but Mick looked about as comfortable sitting on a surfboard as a cat does having a bath.

Thankfully, Mick was a calm operator underwater, a necessary skill given that our objective, besides not drowning, was to extend the pole between us when we were at the surface. In calm water it would have been fairly straightforward, but with a four-metre swell washing over us it was hell. Rolling around underwater with aching ears was like being inside a giant washing machine as burning needles pierced our tympanic membranes. Tethered together, Mick and I were pushed from the surface to a depth of four or five metres in an instant. Our ears were close to bursting and breathing was impossible until we were able to hit the purge button on the front of our O2 sets and get a much-needed breath of oxygen. Remaining calm was a priority, because the swells continued to pound us over and over again.

At intervals during the battering we would pop up on the surface and push the pole, with ladder and hook attached, up the side of the pylon, which we were now becoming quite intimate with. The force with which we were slammed against it meant that our bodies would tangle together at times. If we had the chance we would stick out our fins and try to absorb the beating with our legs. If not, our bodies would be making love to the barnacles on the pylon. Despite the movement of the ocean, stillness was necessary, for to kick uncontrollably would only make things even more uncomfortable for your mate. Our heart rates were maxing at over 180 beats per minute as we struggled to push the pole, with a caving ladder attached, almost directly above our heads.

Our lungs were burning as much as our arms and legs, and we were breathing so powerfully that we constantly had to trip our re-breather sets and force excess air out of our swollen cheeks. After struggling for a good 20 minutes or so, we noticed another set of demoralising swells approaching. With one final lunge, we thrust the pole high above our heads. The effort pushed us both a metre or so underwater and another big swell swept over us. We had no idea if the hook had found its mark so we just held on and tried to remain calm.

At last the swell passed and we broke the surface, almost hyperventilating into our dive sets. I gave a thumbs-up signal to the others. The hook was attached to the railing. *Thank fuck for that*, I thought, before returning to depth to get away from the murderous surface conditions and to summon the energy for the strenuous ladder climb ahead.

The remaining team members took off their fins, placed them over their arms and climbed out of the nightmare. Mick and I took off our dive sets, attempting to lower our heart rates and rest our arms, which were already feeling the effects of lactic acid build-up.

One man had to remain on the bottom of the ladder to keep it taut, which would make the climb a little less taxing for the others. He would have to be the strongest climber, as there would be nobody to secure the bottom of the ladder for him. When he made the climb out of the water, his legs would be almost parallel to the water in front of his body, increasing the load on his upper extremities.

Mick, as per usual, had been assigned this unenviable job. He was the strongest climber in the troop. He typically had little trouble doing several sets of 25 to 30 chin-ups and regularly took part in insane workouts where we'd attempt to do 300 chin-ups and 300 push-ups in 32 minutes. He didn't do a lot of climbing but had a natural ability that could see him scale almost anything without so much as a strained facial expression.

While the weight of Mick below me kept the ladder taut, I clambered over the railing and began taking off my equipment. Looking back down, I suddenly noticed that the strength in Mick's arms was gone, with him still eight rungs from the top. His eyes were wide open as he gasped for air. Two of us went to his aid while the remainder of the team provided security.

Mick inched his way up, one rung at a time, locking his arms through the ladder at every step. He was too fatigued to crab his safety strap on to take a rest, and he was acutely aware that if he fell the almost 30 feet back into the water, without his fins on and with a heavy load of equipment, he would sink fast. He would also then have to start the agonising climb again. With all this in mind, he held on to that ladder for dear life.

Mick reached up to us – we were now dangling over the railing. We managed to grab a piece of his climbing harness, which provided just enough help for Mick to continue climbing. We pulled him over the railing and assisted him with his personal preparation for the assault. There was no need for him to be embarrassed. Everyone knew what an effort it had been with the pole and with climbing last, and besides, we knew that our team was the only group that had successfully established a ladder in such heavy seas.

Mick's effort made me stop and think. If this freak struggled, then it was fair to say that most of the other troop members would have failed. This was the first time I understood something that I would be reminded of again and again in the Regiment: the fitter operators take on an increased workload, which lightens the burden for members who may not be of the same physical standard.

Despite this knowledge, the troop still enjoyed paying out on Mick at the end of the day. We had to make the most of it, as seeing him struggle on a climb was a rare occurrence!

At times like this, or when we were battling the swell of the sea on the way to Heard Island, it wasn't hard to entertain the thought that maybe the freefall and vehicle-mounted operators were smart for choosing a less-demanding skill to maintain. But for me, a lung-burning dive in the heavy swells of Bass Strait, followed by a bicep-busting ladder-climb as a wild wind lashed your face with sea spray, was as good as it got. Although some of the freefall and vehicle-mounted operators were relieved that they weren't required to pull on a damp wetsuit in winter, their faces sometimes showed us that they knew they were missing out.

FOUR

I felt pumped to be heading in the direction of Heard Island and the toothfish poachers, but I quickly encountered difficulties to match those in training. My greatest obstacle early on in the operation was a severe bout of seasickness. The World Meteorological Organisation defines sea states in the following way:

0	= Calm (glassy)	0 m
1	= Calm (rippled)	0–0.1 m
2	= Smooth (wavelets)	0.1–0.5 m
3	= Slight	0.5–1.25 m
4	= Moderate	1.25–2.5 m
5	= Rough	2.5–4 m
6	= Very rough	4–6 m
7	= High	6–9 m
8	= Very high	9–14 m
9	= Phenomenal	Over 14 m

Heading towards Heard Island, we sat firmly within the upper limits of a sea state seven.

Just the thought of my bravado and confidence being punctured by seasickness cheered the other guys no end. Nobody else had succumbed yet – or they'd kept it well-hidden – and my friends appeared to be taking immense enjoyment in my Kermit-green face. With studied concentration and deliberate movements, I eased myself off the floor.

'Where are you going?' someone asked.

As I un-dogged the six clips that secured the door, I choked out my unconvincing reply: 'For a walk'.

I had been seasick before, but not like this. I had swallowed so many of those little pink tablets that I could taste them every time I burped. I re-dogged the latch before taking off quickly for the toilet, two locked chambers away.

I swear that the rumblings in my stomach could be heard over the mechanical drone of the ship. People who passed me in the corridor smiled good morning, but I couldn't reply. One foot after the other, hands out to steady myself, mouth clamped firmly shut. Walking up the hall was like running through a tunnel at rugby training, smashed from one side to the next. At times it felt like walking uphill, at others it was like being flung down a set of stairs.

As I reached the toilet door, I found myself violently regretting having eaten such a large fatty navy breakfast. I grabbed the handle, unable to wait any longer, my cheeks already filling with anticipation. The handle wouldn't open. Occupied. There were now several sailors looking at my panicked face and swollen cheeks. In desperation, I opened the nearby broom cupboard and jumped inside. The mop bucket was a welcome companion, and not a moment too soon.

I've rarely felt so wretched in my life. No sooner had I lowered my head than the violent contractions began. It was like I was drowning in reverse. The detritus of breakfast poured from my mouth and nose with the force of a fire hydrant, leaving me gasping for air before almost choking on the inevitable next wave.

After what felt like an age, I sat heavily on an upside-down bucket and tried to clear my head. My brain felt battered, like a pair of old shoes thumping around inside a washing machine. But I no longer cared. My stomach was empty and my only concern was that the mop bucket remained upright. I heard the toilet door open and close a couple of times, but it was some time before I had the strength to make a move to claim the bathroom for myself.

Having cleaned myself and the bucket, I began to feel remarkably human once more, even wondering what was on the menu for lunch. You just can't keep a good belly down. I bounced my way back to the aft stowage area and was met by at least a dozen mocking looks.

'Did you chuck, fucker?' asked one caring individual.

Another just laughed: 'If you spewed then I am never going to talk to you again, you weak fuck!'

I opted for a dignified but transparent lie: 'I just went for a walk to grab a brew.'

The laughter surrounding me as I lay back on the floor was short-lived. It wasn't long before the door was opened and another man scooted away 'for a quick coffee'. This continued for the next several hours but, as everyone was hit, sympathy levels remained non-existent.

While we were below decks enduring our own particular taste of the action, up top things had gone awry. Apparently a forward hatch had been left open, and the XO (the executive officer, second-in-command on the HMAS *Newcastle*) had ordered two men to hook on to a safety line and secure it. Waves were smashing over the bow of the vessel and, as they approached the hatch, they were hit by a wall of water so violent that it snapped one man's safety strap. Suddenly adrift, his body was thrown sharply against the superstructure several metres above the deck before his body fell limply back. It was miraculous that he wasn't washed overboard, and his mates soon came to his aid. Both men were rushed to the medical centre, where the doctor found that one had a suspected broken femur and would have to be evacuated. This meant that the ship would have to turn around and return to within 150–200 nautical miles of Rockingham before he could be flown to hospital. We were to head back the way we had come.

There were 11 illegal fishing vessels in the vicinity of Heard Island and we were only several days off arrival. Turning around would delay the prospect of any action for at least another two weeks. The raiding party groaned silently. We calculated how many games of cards that turn-around time would equate to. We tried not to think of how many more pink tablets we would swallow in order to save our stomachs and our dignity. But a broken femur was a serious injury and the commander had little choice. He did a 180 and we returned to Australian waters.

=

The second time around, we were met with calm seas and caressed by warm weather and gentle conditions. It didn't last, but while it did our days were filled with task-oriented training, physical training, eating and cards. Several range practices were carried out on the rear quarter-deck of the ship. Two target lines were erected and 16-centimetre circle targets were our victims. The training was excellent, as it was a rare opportunity to shoot from a moving platform. The vessel was gently rolling, so locking on to a target must have been similar to shooting while slightly intoxicated. Our queasy stomachs added to the realism.

We also enjoyed one or two sessions per day of physical training. Deck circuits or sessions on the punching bag were the most popular. The bench press and chin-up bar, however, were more of a laugh than anything else. When the ship rolled in a certain direction, the weight on the bar seemed to double instantly. As the roll continued, the bar would return to its true weight before suddenly becoming light as a feather. Chin-ups were the same. The downward roll would see you hanging on to the bar with arms at full extension and fingers straining, before you would be flung up towards the ceiling with little or no effort.

The other highlight of the day was eating. Most men refused to let seasickness ruin their appetites. We would stretch the mealtime out for as long as possible. Basically, we tried to be the first to sit down and the last to leave, just to fill in our monotonous days. The hours of nothing were squandered with the aid of several decks of cards, but there are only so many times a man can lust over the Queen of Hearts before going completely stir-crazy. But it was the standard navy wake-up call that pissed me off the most:

Call of hands, call of hands, call of hands, wakey, wakey, wakey . . .

It was such an annoying way to start the day.

The bunks were small and dark and our team was spread throughout the sailors' sleeping quarters. I had a particularly irritating roommate in the bunk above me. He was a very large man and he passed wind throughout the night. Whether he was breathing in or out, coughing or rolling over, the outcome was the same – a crescendo of flatulence. At the first crackle of the morning wake-up call he would clamber out of his bed, more often than not stepping on my arm or leg, before half-apologising and grabbing a can of the vilest deodorant ever invented. He would then lace his body from head to toe with it – it smelt more like insect spray than anything else. The fumes would waft into my face and I would pull my head into my sleeping bag while whispering to myself, 'Fuck, I hate the navy.'

I was beside myself with rage every time I had to cross paths with this overweight, flatulent, insect-spray-wearing motherfucker. I would seriously have loved to throw him overboard, but the opportunity never arose.

The final nail in the coffin of our relationship came when the sailor began masturbating in the middle of the night. I tried to cover my ears but the rhythmic sound would not abate. I was infuriated that I had to be so close to the man during his time of self-indulgence – our bodies were no more than 40 centimetres apart. I would roll over and make an obvious noise to indicate that I was awake, but the rhythmic noise continued. I eventually gave up and forced my head into my pillow and tried to ignore what was happening above me.

One morning, when I couldn't take it any more, I

summoned up the various forceful things I'd wanted to say and channelled them into something less homicidal:

'Hey, dude – we're neighbours, and you probably need to make a few subtle adjustments to ensure we remain friends. Your midnight dick-pulling has just gotta stop. Seeing as our genitals are less than half a metre apart, this is not conducive to a good night's sleep. It would be appreciated if you could flog yourself in the bathroom from now on. Any questions?'

The sailor looked at the floor and mumbled, 'Nah, man,' in a passive tone before slinking away. His wife must have loved him being away at sea.

My only reservation when I'd joined the army was an old prejudice: surely it would be full of people who didn't have the goods to get a real job. I was quickly proved wrong. Half the guys in my platoon had joined on a 12-month contract before continuing on to tertiary study. Notwithstanding the odd goose who drove the rest of us insane, the vast majority of the boys were humorous, intelligent and physically fit – a good bunch to be around. I was wondering where on earth the Rambo types from school were.

And then I found them, disguised as recruit instructors. Despite myself, I was impressed by their artistic use of profanity. They were gifted men who took great pride in their belittling talents, and I copped more than my fair share of abuse.

The problem was my flippant attitude towards dickheads. I couldn't help responding to any trouble with a wide, irreverent grin. I felt like telling them that it wasn't anything personal; what they saw as full-blown insubordination, my dad had endured as cheekiness for the past 20 years. I had no idea what a corporal was. Not a clue about the difference between a sergeant and an officer. Two stripes, three stripes, pips, I really didn't give a damn. I just called them all 'Sir' and happily completed the mandatory push-ups for referring to them in an inappropriate manner. 'Sir? My rank is corporal, fuckwit. I work for a living – get down and adopt the position.'

Looking back, perhaps I was cocky – a confident young smart-arse with heaps of drive – but in my gut I know I haven't changed that much. I just hide it a little better now. To me, respect is earned, and it flows both ways, irrespective of anything at all. It's that simple. In the years that followed I would come to recognise the extraordinary talent and strength of the men I served with in the Regiment. For them, I never had any trouble following orders, sharing risks or paying respect. They'd earned it. Showing respect purely because of someone's rank, on the other hand, didn't come so easy. At 20, full of the rush of excitement that comes from finding a sense of direction in life and driven to distraction by my need to excel, it was all I could do not to laugh at what I saw as the absurdity of protocol.

One night during basic training, I returned from the mess hall and noticed that I had neglected to lock my cupboard, an offence known as 'insecurity' and punishable by hours of mind-numbing drill on the parade ground. The theory, unbelievably, was that failing to lock your cupboard promoted – even encouraged – theft! My three roommates and I took some pleasure in mocking both the rule and the platoon staff whose job it was to police it.

'Look at this,' I laughed. 'I forgot to lock my padlock and those stupid fucks were too lazy to notice.'

The four of us were in hysterics as I opened the door to my locker, but our hilarity died in our throats. Our section commander, a rather large and aggressive man, sprang from the cupboard bellowing abuse in a fit of mock rage. Running through the Timorese jungle dodging militia bullets had nothing on the terror I felt at that moment.

I nearly fell over, but in an attempt to slow my heart rate and get my breath back, I couldn't help but laugh. I was resigned to a stint on the parade ground later that afternoon, for mouthing off as well as insecurity, but to my surprise and pleasure, my section commander joined us in laughing.

'Make sure you keep your cupboard locked next time, fuck-knuckle,' he taunted, before strolling out of the room, a broad smile on his face.

Another time, our entire platoon was lined up in the hallway being hauled over the coals for some perceived failing. Always one to take advantage of an opportunity for mischief-making, I managed to lock eyes with the man standing directly opposite me during the tirade. When I was sure I had his undivided attention, I discreetly crossed my eyes. Our silent battle of wills raged, with my facial contortions met by his increasingly obvious amusement.

Just as the rant reached a heightened point, my victim exploded into uncontrollable howls of laughter. After giving him a blast, the section commander launched himself across the hallway looking for the cause of the poor man's hysteria. As he reached my part of the line, several of us now shared the battle to remain straight-faced. The chief suspect was the completely innocent soldier to my immediate left, and he received a savage verbal attack.

Within moments, however, I lost my fight against laughter in response to the words 'disgusting fat fucking slug'. Closed eyes were not enough to stop my shaking shoulders or bursts of laughter. The section commander's next round of abuse was all I needed to descend into hysterics, which earned me even more brutal abuse. As he barked and spat at me, I was marched down the hall to a mirror, to 'take a good hard look at myself'. The sight of my own grinning mug, tears streaming down my cheeks, only made things worse.

Through fits of laughter, with the sound of my mates' own amusement ringing in my ears, I attempted an apology: 'I'm really sorry, I'm trying to stop laughing but I just can't.'

That night, completing some thankless, mundane punishment, I felt a million miles away from changing oil in a van for my dad. I had a lot to learn, but the one thing I already knew was that I'd found a place where I belonged. Behind all the bullshit, I felt a rush at the potential of my situation. This was the life I'd hoped for: one with the promise of excitement and the opportunity to see some real action.

Far from being surrounded by Rambo nuts and dropouts, my army mates soon meant just as much to me as Al, Cully, Pricey and Luke (my closest bros from school). I couldn't wait to see where my new life took me. I couldn't wait to get started.

FIVE

As the HMAS *Newcastle* negotiated the heavy seas towards Heard Island for the second time, we received intelligence that there was now just one possible illegal fishing vessel within Australian territorial waters – a boat that had breached the Heard Island exclusion zone of 200 nautical miles. The assault team was instructed to launch a raid on the vessel.

As we prepared for the task, the weight of the situation hit me properly for the first time. After nearly three weeks at sea, the day had arrived. Finally, we were being given the opportunity to put our years of training into practice. Looking around at the faces of the boys, I could see that they felt it too. For many of us, this was the first time that we had loaded our magazines with live rounds for a live operation. We didn't expect that we would be forced to use them, but we were armed with pistols and submachine guns as a deterrent to acts of aggression.

Our team, Zulu One (Z1), was the lead water troop assault team. In a counter-terrorism assault, we would secure those areas most likely to be housing the command element of a terrorist group. Team members of Zulu Three

(Z3), on the other hand, would more often than not find themselves allocated to an area of lower priority, which could include the toilets. While this was just the luck of the draw and in no way reflected our relative abilities, it was always a source of considerable ribbing.

We donned our equipment. There would be two initial sorties to deliver the raiding party. Our first concern was that the rough seas would prevent the helicopters from taking off, since a roll of more than 30 degrees was considered too dangerous for rotary-wing-assisted operations. We were fortunate that it wasn't raining – in the freezing air, raindrops would turn into tiny shards of glassy ice, which would also have grounded the helicopters.

Z1 was split into two assault teams and augmented with a contingent of navy clearance divers. For us, this was not ideal, but the navy was also keen to gain experience. The first assault team boarded a helicopter that was still strapped to the rear of the HMAS *Newcastle*. With the team aboard, the straps were removed and the bird gingerly lifted off the rolling deck. Watching these pilots in action was truly impressive. Their skilful manoeuvring when taking off from the tight, rolling confines of the frigate's deck was awesome. The bird thumped towards the fishing vessel, the thin, harsh air stinging the men's semi-protected faces.

When the helicopter reached the vessel, Buzz was the first man down the rope. His feet had barely touched the ground when he began running towards the bridge, his submachine gun held directly out to his front. His aim was to prevent the crew from throwing any documentary evidence overboard. The remaining team members were not far behind.

With the first team safely aboard it was time for the bird to pick up the second sortie of eagerly waiting men, myself included. The bird had barely touched the deck when we were loaded and ready to go. It was my turn at last.

In the distance, a speck of dark colour bobbed in and out of view, sometimes hidden by the enormous swell. It was a desolate image, a tiny shape surrounded by the grey and angry sea. As we edged closer it became clearer. The Japanese-constructed fishing boat appeared to be handling the conditions remarkably well. We approached it from the rear, the helicopter ducking and weaving to get within boarding distance, and the heavy winds muffling the roar of the rotors.

Although we were excited, we knew that an operator must keep his exuberance in check. We were like children who were given a shot of red cordial but were expected to refrain from running amok. To think clearly, one must remain calm, no matter how much adrenaline is running through your veins.

If the fast rope was not properly on the deck of the target vessel before we took the plunge, the consequences could be dire. Sliding into the icy waters could well prove fatal. The rope was kicked out of the aircraft and landed in a large exhaust stack. I looked at the naval safety officer and decided to go anyway. As far as I was concerned, the party had already started. Now was not the time to procrastinate over a melting rope. I slid down it and straddled the stack, avoiding its hot black fumes. Kicking off the side, I dragged the rope with me before landing on the deck. The remaining team members were quickly on deck and, after touching base with Buzz, the clearance began.

We worked in pairs during the assault. Each team wove its way through the accommodation areas, locating crew-members – there were 43. A comprehensive search of the vessel also took place. The boat's crew came from a mixture of African and South American countries, and they were distinctly unhappy to see us. They had all been at sea for nearly three months and were soon to depart for home with a full catch. They were paid only a percentage of the catch so, with the booty of Patagonian toothfish now being confiscated, they were very aware that the past several months of hard work would result in no monetary reward. These were hardly the terrorists my training had prepared me for.

One of the navy steaming party helped me secure this motley crew in the galley. It is hard to look intimidating when you're dressed in a bright-orange immersion suit. I maintained a faceless image by wearing my Oakley facemask, which provided a dehumanising barrier between me and our captives.

My naval companion was increasingly uncomfortable with the situation, recoiling as the angry mob blew cigarette smoke towards us and barked insults in Spanish. 'They're staring at me,' he quavered. I swallowed my impatience with his pathetic tone and sent him out to assist another member of our team in securing six more crew-members in the engine room.

This was not the place to show weakness. I would not let myself be intimidated by this seedy bunch. Their gritted teeth and angry snarls exposed less than full complements of yellow decaying teeth. In contrast, I had a Heckler & Koch MP5 submachine gun in my hands, with thirty

9-mm deterrents. I focused on my training: remain neutral – firm and fair; remain alert – don't engage in conversation beyond simple instructions. No swearing, no insults. Despite the rush of adrenaline I was getting, this felt a long way from the joking and mucking around of training. *Sorry, boys, this is just business.*

Several members of the crew tried to intimidate us. One guy had a large scar running from his left eye to his chin – like a James Bond villain. Each time I turned my attention from him to one of his crewmates, he would loudly bark what sounded like instructions to the others. When I focused on him again he would stand stock-still, glaring at me without a word. I was reluctant to break eye contact. Why should he win? The best solution was to shine the torch on the front of my weapon directly into his eyes. The blinding light helped me regain authority and, with a fresh set of batteries in my torch, I was confident these games could go on for hours.

Another crew-member stepped forward, holding a picture of his family in front of him and yelling, *'Bambino, bambino, bambino.'* The weight of the fear these men were feeling suddenly hit me. I slowly nodded my head before giving him a non-threatening thumbs-up. This reassured the group, as they seemed to understand that the operation was a formality rather than a life-threatening situation for them. The tone of the room quickly changed and one of their chefs offered me a couple of pancakes. I thanked him but waved him away.

The remaining members of the assault team were scouring the ship for weapons and other personnel. Buzz was working with two fisheries officers who had joined the assault team. Their role was to find enough evidence to support the confiscation of the ship and enable charges to be laid against its skipper. After a little while, a triumphant shout rang out from the hold. There was $2 million worth of oversized, big-toothed fish buried in the freezers – these would do the trick nicely.

SIX

After the initial rush of the assault, I felt the adrenaline drain from my body. I could still taste the exhilaration of action at the back of my mouth, and I tried to savour the moment for as long as I could. It was a sensation I would grow very used to in the years to come.

A two-man security team, Buzz and I, remained on the vessel to provide armed protection for the navy steaming party of seven men. The remaining members of our assault team returned to the HMAS *Newcastle* to support subsequent tasks.

Our packs, filled with food and sleeping equipment, did not arrive on the first night as planned. The robust inflatable boat that was ferrying the equipment across overturned in the huge swell: the wind got underneath the hull and the crew was thrown into the icy waters. A second boat was dispatched to recover them. The navy managed to retrieve all our packs, which was quite an effort. Righting the upside-down vessel, however, proved a lot more difficult. A pair of navy clearance divers donned arctic wetsuits before attempting to attach a winch from a helicopter to the bottom of the overturned craft. It took four hours in the gale-force winds to retrieve the vessel, and all the men who spent time in the water were taken to the medical facility aboard HMAS *Newcastle* suffering hypothermia.

Buzz and I decided to do six-hour security piquet rotations that would be manned from the bridge. Six hours on, six hours off. Our initial 60 minutes of fun quickly turned into 12 days of tiresome shiftwork. We shared a sleeping bag in a forward stowage area with a cardboard box as our mattress. The area was covered in fish blood and guts, and even after we ordered the crew to scrub and disinfect the area the smell of rotting fish still filled the room. After several days, that and the sound of the sea bashing the hull where we slept had us feeling far from fresh.

Each morning our SAS obsessiveness would kick in and Buzz and I would have a workout on the roof above the bridge during shift handover. The Namibian members of the boat's crew often watched and made gestures with their dark, muscled arms – as if to indicate that they would like to join in. The workouts ranged from chin-ups off the side of the superstructure to exercises using pieces of pipe as gym equipment.

The navy steaming party was unarmed, with the exception of the watch officer, a man whom Buzz and I quickly grew to dislike. At one point, this man approached me – I was the more junior SAS operator – and confessed that he had lost his pistol. I was horrified, both that it was missing and at his visible lack of concern. I instructed him to find his pistol immediately before it was picked up by a member of the crew. It took almost 30 minutes before the man returned with his holster filled. Part of the problem was his enormously fat stomach, which made wearing the appropriate military belt difficult. When he attempted to wear the belt above his stomach, his pistol sat just underneath his armpit. The alternative, a low-slung position where the pistol was buried under several rolls of his stomach, was hardly an improvement. This was surely an example of a man being 'too fat to fight'.

If losing his pistol wasn't a big enough reason to dislike him, the watch officer was also obsessed with receiving a medal for his actions in the operation. We found this quite amusing: 'What, you want a medal for hanging out on a fishing boat?' We would just shake our heads in disgust. He was career-oriented in an utterly self-serving fashion, with little capacity for leadership. His indiscriminate and regular abuse of his subordinates would not wash with Buzz and me, whose SAS training had placed very little importance on questions of rank. The arrogance of his constant berating of his staff was particularly galling given the professional and diligent nature of his team. They deserved a leader of their standard, not this clown.

One evening during the security shift handover, I showered and changed into a clean set of overalls. I felt invigorated and returned to the bridge in a good mood to say goodnight to Buzz. Although I disliked the watch officer, who was there with him, I remained civil. I would generally just keep to myself when we were on shift together. With both my arms cradling dirty clothes and supplies, I turned to leave the bridge and return to my stinky fish-box bed. As I reached for the door handle that led outside, the watch officer spoke up: 'I wouldn't go that way. That's the sea side. You'll get wet.'

His condescending tone grated immediately, and

I promptly decided that I knew best so I disregarded the advice from Mr Obnoxious. No sooner had I opened the door than a tremendous wave broke over the ship's side – directly into my face. The freezing-cold salty water took my breath away. This was rapidly followed by a two-foot wave that swept straight into the bridge.

My cheery disposition was gone. The naval officer, surprisingly, kept quiet and I walked past Buzz offering nothing more than a roll of the eyes. I was soaked from head to foot, my boots squelching with salty water. Back at my fishy sleeping quarters I changed back into my dirty overalls before burying my shivering body deep inside my sleeping bag, all the while reflecting that even wankers can be right from time to time.

≡

The middle of the operation might not have been the ideal time for tomfoolery, but when I was bored my irreverence always came out to play. During heavy seas, the skipper of the fishing vessel would wind down the speed to no more than seven knots. After doing a quick calculation I realised we would take another seven days to get home: a speed of 12 knots would literally take days off the journey.

I waited until the skipper went for a trip to the toilet and sneaked over to the controls. Looking around, I wound the vessel up to 13 knots. When he returned, the skipper was initially oblivious that our speed had virtually doubled. As I watched him from the other side of the bridge, I saw him give a double-take, looking at his GPS. His surprise was obvious and the look he shot me left no doubt that he knew who was to blame. He chuckled before winding back the speed to five knots. It was going to be a slow trip home.

After 12 days the vessel entered the vicinity of Garden Island, Rockingham, and was boarded by the Australian Federal Police, who detained the crew. We were extracted from the vessel and returned home, bleary-eyed and smelling like a tin of sardines. We wouldn't be racing out for fish and chips any time soon. As a first taste of active duty, it hadn't quite been the adrenaline-charged test of our training that I'd hoped for, but that was to come soon enough.

PART TWO

RECONNAISSANCE PATROL, EAST TIMOR

OCTOBER 1999

ONE

My time in East Timor was a baptism of fire.

The International Force for East Timor was deployed under the banner of Operation Warden on 20 September 1999, after violence erupted following the referendum for East Timorese independence from Indonesia. On 30 August, 344,580 people – 78.5 per cent of those who voted – sanctioned the move towards independence. In response, pro-Indonesian militias were executing a scorched-earth policy, wrapping the country in a blanket of brutality.

Hundreds, possibly thousands of East Timorese were killed. A further 500,000 were displaced – many of them transported against their will to camps across the border in Indonesian West Timor. There were also reports that soldiers from the Indonesian Special Forces – Kopassus – were orchestrating the violence. In the Regiment this was a touchy subject, as many SAS soldiers had been involved in training teams with Kopassus.

The first task for the Australian Special Forces was to secure Komoro Airfield before moving on to the port in the capital city, Dili. This security preparation enabled the International Force to rapidly infiltrate the city and establish it as a base for taskforce operations.

I was deployed as a member of a six-man patrol to reconnoitre a village just 15 kilometres from the border with West Timor. The district was a hive of activity, with intelligence reports indicating that over 100 armed militiamen were causing havoc in the area. Despite the threat, squadron headquarters wanted to insert a patrol in the area to ascertain if this information was correct. If the patrol identified armed militants, a squadron-level assault (by up to 60 SAS soldiers) would take place.

I was relieved to be included in this patrol, as there had been a chance I would be left out. After returning from a medical detachment to East Africa, I had ruptured my anterior cruciate ligament in an accident. I had already participated in a six-month Indonesian language course, and with the possible East Timor deployment in the winds, I was beside myself with anxiety about missing out on potential action.

Within three weeks of my knee reconstruction I was, against the advice of the Regiment's physiotherapist, tearing around the street on my pushbike, desperately trying to regain the strength in my leg. All was going well until I ran into my dog – who was fine, but not overly impressed. I flew over my handlebars and into the bitumen. Hobbling into physio the following morning, I was not only missing a fair bit of skin, but had torn a hamstring that had already been weakened by the removal of a tendon graft.

Despite this, and true to impatient form, I continued to push the limits of my training, determined not to miss out, and 10 days later I was back to squatting 100 kilograms in the gym. I'm surprised those pins held my new ligament in place, and although I did stretch the graft considerably,

I quickly began to regain function and strength. I held off from running until 11 weeks after the operation, but soon after that I was hitting the cross-country course.

Two weeks prior to the deployment I went to see the regimental medical officer (RMO), hoping to be cleared for operational deployments. I was 'med class three' – no parachuting, no deployments. I wanted med class two – no parachuting, but able to deploy.

Despite my pleading, the RMO laughed at my request. Her diagnosis was brutal: I would remain med class three for a minimum of 12 months.

Never one to take no for an answer, I waited a week and went to see a civilian doctor who worked for the Regiment on a part-time basis. He had less to lose, and when I told him what I was achieving in the gym he asked me one question: 'Can you duck-walk?'

I had no idea what he meant.

'Can you walk like a duck?' he said. 'If you have regained enough flexibility in your knee to duck-walk, I'll give you med class two.'

I was so excited by this that I squatted and waddled around his office for a good minute, even throwing in a couple of quacks for effect. True to his word, he lifted my rating to med class two.

But his parting words were cautionary: 'Look after that bloody knee of yours. I've gone out on a limb to upgrade you this early, so don't let me down.'

Within six weeks I was stomping around the mountainous jungles of East Timor with nearly 50 kilograms on my back. My balance was not great, especially at night, but I was deployed. Life was good.

That wasn't the first time an injury had almost shattered my dreams of service. The first time had been during the ordeals of training for the SAS.

While I had, in a sense, fallen into the army by accident, my decision to join the Regiment had been a calculated obsession. Midway through my basic training I'd made up my mind that the regular army just wasn't for me. As good as hiding in cupboards and screaming abuse at people probably was, I knew I needed more.

A former commanding officer explained to me that the SAS selects above-average soldiers and each year makes them a little more above-average. Unlike the typical guard duties fulfilled by most infantry soldiers, in the SAS you work alongside the most highly trained soldiers in the country, and you're given the most challenging tasks. As far as I was concerned, the guys in the Regiment had the best job in the world and I wanted in. I wanted to join the SAS.

I was halfway through basic training when I informed my platoon staff that I wanted to be an SAS soldier. I wasn't sure what to expect so battened down the hatches and braced myself for a cyclone of abuse. But the weather remained pleasant – no gale-force 'Fuck you!' and no pounding of the parade ground. To my surprise, they actually took my request seriously! My drive and determination, it seemed, were enough to overcome concerns about my age and lack of experience. I was interviewed and my details were passed up the ranks during Infantry Employment Training (IET). I passed the basic requirements and found myself empanelled for the next selection course, due to begin in eight months' time.

Although I attempted to find out everything I could about the SAS selection course, not many guys seemed to know too much about it. I knew that the course was approximately three weeks long and was incredibly taxing, but everyone who passed selection was soon swallowed by the 'special forces serpent' and never seen or heard of again. There were those in the Battalion who had attempted the course and failed, but really, how credible was their advice? They were still in the Battalion.

Finding the time to train for SAS selection was always going to be difficult, but my section commander generously offered his experience in helping me and Jack, a brother I met during basic training, to prepare. We enjoyed the challenge. Before going out for a night on the town I would often con some poor soul into doing a 10- or 15-kilometre pack march with me. There was no time to waste, and weekends that should have been spent recovering from hangovers were instead filled with gruelling training sessions.

Some of the more senior soldiers in my battalion, especially those who had either never attempted selection or had previously failed, were less than thrilled that two guys still undergoing IET had made it onto selection. My physical training instructor at the Basic Training Centre in Kapooka told me that aspiring to be an SAS soldier was a great goal but I should wait three or four years before having a go. When he had attempted selection he'd made it to day seven – a third of the way through. A guy from the reconnaissance platoon questioned my navigational experience. I think he'd made day four. I knew where I wanted to go, so I wasn't going to be dissuaded by anyone, no matter how senior or experienced they were.

But sometimes a sense of purpose and determination isn't enough. Halfway through selection training, disaster struck. While on exercise, I was running with an injured soldier draped across my shoulders (a weight of 90 to 95 kilograms). Pushing through the pain and effort, I failed to spot a small pothole on the track ahead, and before I knew it my left ankle rolled and gave way beneath me.

I fell heavily, shocked at the sudden pain. It was the first time I had ever rolled my ankle, and I couldn't believe that one piss-weak joint could pack it in so utterly. SAS selection was looming and my ankle couldn't support my weight. I had less than four weeks to recover.

I was extracted from the field for physiotherapy and rehabilitation. After seven days the discolouration began to fade and the swelling had gone down. While the swift improvement to my ankle was a marked relief, the enforced time off from training had allowed my feet to soften. While stomping up Enoggera Hill with 35 kilograms on my back, the full implication of this hit me. My feet blistered and wept, huge chunks of skin rubbing away to leave me frustrated once again.

But I would not let a bunch of blisters stop me, especially

with the selection course so close. With gritted teeth, I taped my feet up and continued to pound the mountain tracks and nearby roads over the next two weeks. I felt I was almost back on track.

Then, with eight days to go, the nightmare returned. On a stifling day, with a heavily laden pack, I had spent the best part of an hour clambering up the side of Enoggera Hill. After reaching the summit I was impatient to make it back to the mess for lunch, so I decided to run down the access road. As if in slow-motion, with sweat obscuring my vision and the Brisbane heat burning my skin, my left foot glanced the side of a hole before buckling under the weight of my body and pack. I didn't even have time to raise my hands as my body slid face-first into the bitumen.

I can still feel the disappointment and rage that welled up in me. Justifications sprang to mind: I was fatigued; I was trying to protect my wounded feet. They made no difference. Lying flat on my back, tears pricking my eyes, I screamed into the air at the top of my voice: 'Fuck!' I wasn't screaming from the pain, excruciating as it was, but because my dream of being an SAS soldier – for that year at least – was over.

After the shock had subsided, I shook myself free of self-pity. I wasn't accustomed to giving up and this seemed like a bad time to start. Looking around, it seemed that there was no-one within earshot, so I rolled my pack off, steadied myself and hopped the remaining 3.5 kilometres to the regimental aid post.

By the time I got there my body was shaking. I was dehydrated and, bravado aside, I was dreading what the doctor was going to say to me. A civilian, he took one look at my inflamed ankle and red-raw feet and offered his diagnosis in a dispassionate voice: 'Your feet are a complete mess. They'll never heal in time for SAS selection. And this is the second time you have damaged your ankle in less than a month. I'm going to recommend that you be discharged from the army.'

I had joined the army on a 12-month contract and so his recommendation alone would be enough to finish me. Dispiriting as this was, it was the doctor's next words that cut the deepest: 'It's not fair on you and better for the army if you just call it a day. Once you damage an ankle like this it'll be a recurring injury.'

Horrified that this bespectacled clown wanted to fuck with my dreams of service, I quickly switched to salesman mode. I told him how hard I had trained for this, that becoming an SAS soldier was something I wanted more than anything else, that if he didn't get in the way of my chance for selection, I'd do everything I could to show I was worth it.

He squinted at me and pursed his lips. It felt like an age passed before he spoke again. 'Well, I can't make you discharge early . . .' he began.

The colour returned to my face.

'Okay. I'll refer you to the military hospital for X-rays. Provided there is no fracture, I'll recommend that you receive daily physiotherapy. Prior to departing, your ankle should be thoroughly strapped. Good luck.'

I could have kissed him. Three days before the selection course began, I threw away my crutches and tried to walk. The next day I went for a jog, and the day after that I ran. I also hardened up my feet with regular soakings in Condy's Crystals and by spraying them with methylated spirits.

I decided to approach the selection course in stages, one day at a time. I had no idea if I would be there at the end. If

I wasn't good enough, fine – I'd try again the following year, and then the year after that. What I did know was that I would never quit.

On the day of departure, my company commander called me into his office and offered some last-minute advice: 'Look, son, you are going for the SAS with only a year of army experience under your belt. Big call. But I guess the SAS are after guys who make big calls. Just remember, when your morale is down, pull out your brush and polish your boots. It will help.'

I left his office in two minds. I was inspired by his support but perplexed that polishing one's boots was seen as a morale-boosting activity. Now I really wanted to pass selection. Surely SAS soldiers didn't have to polish their boots to feel good about themselves!

When the Hercules aircraft landed at RAAF Base Pearce, I was extremely apprehensive. An SAS warrant officer boarded the aircraft, and the aura that surrounded him convinced me that I was making the right choice. I felt inspired and, more importantly, I felt ready. This was my chance at selection. I thought about how much I wanted it and considered my options: doing oil changes in my dad's workshop or polishing my boots back in the Battalion. No thanks. I wanted to be the best soldier I could be. I wanted to be an SAS soldier.

TWO

From the very beginning it was clear that all the best training we'd had in the SAS would be put to use in East Timor. The patrol that I was part of was brimming with talent and confidence. There were no weak links. Even though our operation in the border region was fact-finding rather than offensive, we were expected to be able to handle ourselves if we encountered a sizeable enemy force. The squadron commander had great trust in not only the ability of our patrol commander, Steve, but also in the men he'd selected for this patrol.

Steve was an SAS soldier with 12 years of experience. His personal skills and cool persona set a standard not only in our troop but also within the broader squadron. He was well known for his capacity to get even the most difficult jobs done. As a water troop sergeant, he had achieved notoriety for his high expectations of his men and for his gruelling sand sessions around an eight-kilometre cross-country track at Campbell Barracks in Western Australia.

Steve looked like your stereotypical SAS soldier, oozing confidence and a steely resolve that intimidated many. This was helped by his good looks, which were perpetually camouflaged behind a pair of Oakleys. There wasn't a sergeant in the entire troop who didn't fear Steve's wrath if they failed to deliver the required standard of excellence, but his effect on me was inspiring. He was a man of strength. No matter what the challenges facing us, there was no apprehension if Steve was running the show.

The patrol 2iC was a sergeant from the British Special Boat Service (SBS) who was on a two-year posting to Australia. Buster had a terrific sense of humour and could always be relied upon to lighten a situation by making himself the clown. Normally, a soldier of his standing would command his own patrol, but because this was the first decent operation for some time, there were too many Australian patrol commanders who needed the experience. Luckily, Buster was content at the rear of this talented patrol, offering advice when appropriate. In recognition of his rank, on this operation he wasn't lumbered with the patrol's administrative duties; I had previously been our patrol's 2iC so I took on the responsibilities of administration, the number two scout position and was also the patrol translator.

Buster was initially a little on the heavy side — he must have been horrified the first time he walked into our troop office and saw that it was filled with guys who loved to train hard. He often spoke about his induction 'jog', a cross-country thrashing that he had hated. As hard as it was on him — and it was probably made harder by his typical British breakfast of bacon, eggs and beans — I wasn't surprised to hear that he'd completed it strongly nevertheless.

Even at his least fit, Buster was incredibly robust and was never afraid to push himself. He was always strong underwater but running wasn't really his thing. That said, he did manage to show up his fair share of other soldiers around the cross-country track during his two-year posting. He also wasn't shy of getting his shirt off during drunken sessions up at the Gratwick Club, the Friday afternoon SAS bar we frequented. It was not an unusual sight to see Buster, shirtless in the bar, challenging someone to a few chin-ups. His best was 15. He soon began to drop clothes sizes too, and within 12 months even his wetsuit was falling off him.

Charlie and I were the two patrol scouts and had worked together for several years, including the lead-up to the Heard Island operation. If any man was too nice to be in the SAS, then it was Charlie. It was a pleasure to be working alongside him again. Charlie was one of the most morally astute men I've ever met, a man who nearly always looked for, or brought out, the good in people. His work ethic, self-discipline and integrity were inspirational. In a sense, Charlie epitomised many of the traits that SAS soldiers are selected for. But he was never in your face with any of it. You could talk to him for ages without suspecting that this man was bordering on the elite in fitness and other respects. He was a fantastic bush soldier, one of the best, and this was largely due to his self-discipline. He was the perfect choice for lead scout.

The patrol medic, G, was a fiery individual with a big heart. After growing up in Melbourne, he had led an interesting life – he was street-savvy but wild. G was close to 30 when he passed the SAS selection, but by the end of his first year in the troop he had been identified as a hard-charger, an energetic soldier with balls the size of basketballs. G prided himself on his medical skills, and rightly so: he topped his patrol medic's course during his first year in the Regiment. He was fitter than most men, but the thing I loved about him was his steely determination. Not many things in life are certain, especially not when it comes to human beings, but G's mettle under fire was never in doubt. If we found trouble, he would not only stand up and deliver, but having done that, he would no doubt deliver some more.

The final member of the patrol was Jimmy, our signaller. This man had forearms that made Popeye look like he was suffering from a spinach shortage. His enormous reputation for moral and physical strength preceded him. Like many SAS soldiers, Jimmy was a paradox: at once a warrior but at the same time incredibly kind and gentle. Although I'm sure he would never have admitted it, beneath his tough exterior he was a big softie, especially when it came to his wife and children. For me, that mix of compassion and physical power is what true strength is about, and it was there in all the best soldiers I've ever known.

Our team was stacked with men who were at the upper echelons of their experience levels. We were close-knit, high-performing and keen to see some action. We were so secure in each other's ability that we felt confident to storm the gates of hell. Once again, it was the waiting that was the problem! All six of us were acutely aware of how close we were to finally seeing some action. The more experienced members of the team had come close on other operations – we'd all had our own Heard Island-style dry runs – but we still hadn't tasted the real thing. It was almost like an ache, not a bloodlust, just a need to use all that training. And as we waited, our sense of camaraderie, of brotherhood, only grew.

=

Two weeks before the East Timor deployment, our troop, the water troop, went on a training trip south of Perth. I had been detached from the troop on my six-month language course and was rather anxious to return and work with the boys again. It was an excellent chance for us to get back to basics and rehearse our core insertion skills — which is a whole lot less dirty than it sounds! Our days were full of diving, boating and canoeing, topped off by physical training sessions that included beach runs and boxing circuits. Throw in a few nights on the piss and it was the perfect week — working, training and playing hard. Weeks like that are what I miss most since departing the Regiment.

We were accommodated in an army reserve barracks for the week, so naturally we were respectful of our surroundings. Unfortunately, there was one notable exception. The walls of most barracks are lined with military artefacts, pictures and plaques. This particular base even had a couple of Japanese swords captured during World War II. It also had something extra: a life-size mannequin named Private Lonely. Private Lonely had been a member of this army reserve unit for years, possibly decades, and he had become its mascot. Lonely was an iconic figure — some might even say a legend.

After a hard day's training, it was decided that the guys would have a few beers before getting an early night. It didn't take long for this theory to break down and it was Buster who led the charge. Obviously not prepared to wait for dinner, the big man took the cap off the biggest jar of pasta sauce available and proceeded to skol the entire contents. It was probably the greediest thing I have ever witnessed, and he devoured the lot without spilling a single drop.

And he didn't stop there. Obviously famished, and egged on by our laughs, he grabbed a second bottle of sauce – a smaller one – and gulped that down as well. I was intrigued by how the litre-plus of sauce, mixed with several litres of beer, was sitting inside that stomach of his. If he'd been able to keep it down, it would have been both gross and strangely impressive. As it was, it was pretty much just gross. His body's rejection of the rich cocktail was truly disgusting to behold, but the fact that he didn't let it affect his appetite for more beers made us laugh all the harder.

It was at about this time that Private Lonely joined the party. In full ceremonial uniform he was obviously overdressed for the occasion, and the constant dumb smile on his face seemed to us like a provocation from the start. After some discussion, we agreed that Lonely looked uptight, so the boys encouraged him to relax a little by removing his tie, unbuttoning his collar and strapping a can of VB to his right hand. It was definitely an improvement. Jimmy pointed out that Lonely had a large cavity in the centre of his back and we quickly adopted it as a place to store our empty beer cans. Lonely didn't appear overly concerned and just kept on smiling.

Over the next few hours Lonely really came out of his shell. He became the life of the party. He also sported several new tattoos, courtesy of a whiteboard marker that someone found. There was much hilarity, but at this point Lonely could still have been transformed back to his old, pristine self in a couple of minutes. This would soon not be the case.

My recollection is that Private Lonely became increasingly boisterous under the influence of alcohol and began to pick fights. I'm pretty sure the boys would back me up on that. It's all a bit hazy, but at some point in the ensuing altercations, Lonely's nose was bitten off. We had now passed the point of no return. How in the hell do you replace a mannequin's nose? We couldn't even find the bloody thing. Perhaps Buster found it lying on the floor and ate it?

It was then that I noticed all these cool swords hanging on the wall. I stood on a stool and eased one out of its scabbard. As I applied the tip to Lonely's neck and straightened my arm, poised to strike, one of the boys placed a restraining hand on my soldier.

'Give it here, mate,' he said. 'If I'm going to lose my job over this, then at least let me have the satisfaction of taking the prick's head off.'

The warrior calmly draws his sword behind his head and strengthens his grip around the handle. The sword does not waver and is held upright, while the elbow of the lower arm points directly at the target — the neck of the enemy. The warrior, whose body is at 45 degrees to his prey, draws in one final breath and focuses all of his energy onto the point of impact. Then, in an instant, the blade slices the air in deathly silence and removes the head in one clean motion.

If this was the way a samurai warrior beheaded an

opponent, then I guess it is fair to say that I've witnessed the complete opposite.

This guy took his place behind Private Lonely and looked a little off-balance from the start. I'm not even certain that both of his eyes were open, let alone focused on where he wanted the blade to strike. He drew back and then swung with all his might. The sword slammed into the top of Lonely's back, missing his neck by a good six inches.

As we all cheered, Lonely toppled over and his head fell off after connecting with a table on the way down. The sword fared no better. Having been wielded more like a prehistoric club than a precision killing device, it now looked like a banana.

As the night drew to a close, we decided to clean the barracks and fix up the poor dishevelled private before heading off to bed. Beer cans and tattoos were removed from Lonely's body and a new uniform was found. We even ironed it in an attempt to restore some of his lost pride.

But the fact that he was headless posed a greater problem. Even if we managed to stick the old one back on, it was missing most of its nose. Luckily, a replacement head was found in the store. We convinced each other and ourselves that the unit's members wouldn't notice the difference. The shoulder-length blonde hair and definite female features wouldn't matter too much. Lonely, supporting his/her new head, was returned to the back of the store and we all agreed to admit to nothing.

The following evening the army reserve unit was having a formal event in the dining area. We didn't take much notice as the tables were readied for the festivities, but a more dangerous question started floating around the gathering: 'Does anyone know where Private Lonely is?' A few of us who were still feeling quite seedy from the previous night looked at each other and raised our eyebrows, committed to our denial of any knowledge.

Fearing that their mascot had gone AWOL, a search was conducted. Before long, and to our relief, we heard hysterical laughs when Lonely was found sporting his new female head. One of the reservists said that their platoon sergeant, who had recently gone overseas, had probably taken the head to get some photos of Lonely on his travels. This sounded plausible. It looked like we were in the clear. After all, surely a troop of SAS soldiers wouldn't do such a thing. But after several hours' investigation, the web around us was tightening. The company sergeant-major approached one of the boys and asked if we knew where Private Lonely's head was. Always cool under pressure, he responded quickly: 'Who's Private Lonely?'

There was now no going back. Lonely's head, which was hidden in one of our bags, was definitely returning to Perth with us. We were as thick as thieves, and operational deployments would only strengthen this bond.

THREE

Even when our squadron was deployed to East Timor, the wait for real action still wasn't over. We were sent out in smaller operations to raid militia-occupied villages, tasks which more often than not turned out to be fruitless and frustrating exercises. We later learned that one of our raids had been announced on ABC Radio the day before we went in. And then things changed.

Our squadron raided a village 138 kilometres southwest of Dili. There were several small skirmishes, and then an SAS convoy escorting over 100 militiamen to the West Timor border was ambushed. In the ensuing firefight two SAS soldiers were shot, one through the neck and the other through the wrist and leg.

In a true display of style, the operator who was shot through the neck stayed upright and checked his own wounds before firing off a full magazine from his weapon. This man was one of the more senior soldiers I had completed selection with and had been a great support to me during training. We saw a picture in the paper of him being stretchered into the rear of a medical transport aircraft while casually holding his own IV drip bag. This made us laugh. He had very nearly had his head blown off and yet was still holding his own IV like it was just another medical training scenario.

We found out later that the round had split in two: one piece exited the side of his neck and the other the front. Surgeons informed him that the round missed his carotid artery by only a millimetre or two. When a tattoo artist offered to cover up his scar by adding to the already impressive artwork on his back, his response was far from ambiguous. 'No you fucking won't,' he snarled.

The second soldier was less fortunate. He did himself proud, as he was shot through the arm but jumped back onto the vehicle-mounted machine gun and kept firing. Unfortunately, however, it wasn't long before his leg was blown from under him and that was that. His calf muscle was blown off and the bones in his lower leg were completely shattered. Half of his abdominal muscles were later inserted into the calf area, but they didn't take so the surgeons cut out the other side and tried again.

One soldier that day had a bullet cut through a pocket in his trouser leg, and another had one of his webbing straps severed and a hole through his headrest. Four militants were killed in the action. These accounts filled us with mixed and complex feelings: sympathy, excitement, even envy at having missed out. As it was, we wouldn't have to wait long for our turn.

=

Squadron HQ gained intelligence that a militia leader and a contingent of his men were operating out of the main village of our target region near the border with West Timor. Our team was tasked to locate the militants and send a detailed plan to HQ for a squadron-level assault. We were soon packed, briefed and raring to go, frustrated at having to wait until nightfall for the helicopter insertion to take place. After carrying out several rehearsals, we boarded the aircraft – three men on each side – and leant up against our heavy packs. The squadron commander (who would later command the SAS Regiment) came and shook our hands before telling us to be careful. Intelligence had just come through that the area was crawling with armed militia. All this did was make us even more impatient for the bird to take off.

The rotors began to turn and the internal whine increased until the blades were neatly cutting the air with a rapid thumping sound. The vibrations travelled into our bodies, making us feel as one. We lifted into the darkness before angling west and picking up speed. Our heavily camouflaged faces were hidden in the blackened aircraft but a casual cheeky grin would reveal an eerie set of white teeth, glowing like a fluorescent road-marker touched by a vehicle's headlight. Banking left then right, the bird roared through the night, dancing from mountain shadow to shadow. It was an exhilarating ride.

After 30 minutes we were told that the first dummy landing would take place in five minutes. The pilot hovered low over the ground before pulling hard into the air and continuing on towards the insertion point. We were given a three-minute call: we switched on our night-vision goggles and tightened our pack straps. The next call was 30 seconds. We readied our weapons.

As the bird touched the blackened landscape, we stumbled out into the darkness, flung ourselves to the ground and immediately adopted the firing positions we had rehearsed so many times. Within seconds there was a tremendous downdraught that pushed us into the earth and pelted us with dust and foliage. Then we were alone. All that could be heard was the faint sound of the helicopter gradually fading into nothingness. We quickly moved away from the landing zone and went through our all-round-defence procedures. The orchestra of cicadas returned to full song as we began to move. The village was eight kilometres away.

The air was thick and humid, and the vegetation seemed impenetrable. Charlie, as lead scout, forced his way through the undergrowth for several metres at a time before stopping and listening. Our shoulders were aching within minutes but we were aware that we'd be walking for the best part of the night. Charlie and I took turns at the front, bearing the brunt of tangled vines and spikes, tree branches and mammoth spider webs blocking our way. We tried not to think about the tropical-sized eight-legged creatures that, having created such enormous webs, lurked in the darkness.

With each step the vines wrapped themselves around our necks, limbs and packs. We felt choked by the foliage, and fearful about the deep holes that swallowed our feet, causing us to twist and roll before being belted in the back of the head by the frames of our packs. Throughout, it was critical to maintain stealth. If it were just a matter of blazing away and cutting a path, movement through this area would have been relatively easy. But the aim was to part the vegetation calmly and without destroying it. We needed to minimise any sign of the patrol's presence. And so we continued on our slow jungle dance.

After about two kilometres we reached the primary north–south river. The banks resembled small cliffs and Steve decided that the patrol should locate an area to sleep (a 'lying-up place') and then search for a crossing-point before first light.

Sleeping in the tropics is a bit of a contradiction in terms. Attracted by the carbon dioxide of our breathing, a relentless swarm of mosquitoes swooped in to feast upon our exposed skin. Necks, cheeks and hands were fair game, and in the hush of the night, the whine of mosquitoes ebbed and flowed incessantly. The problem ran deeper than mere irritation. One sting from these pint-sized vampires could result in a recurring legacy of fever. Many of the men, me included, didn't bother with the anti-malarial prophylaxis, a drug called doxycycline. The side-effects, including nausea and sensitivity to light, were probably a small price to pay in comparison to a life of malaria, but the mentality of 'it won't happen to me' often won out.

Despite the mosquitoes, we managed to get some rest before G, who was on security piquet, gently woke us just as the dark skies slowly began to turn grey. We sat silently, making the transition from deep sleep to total alertness. Steve instructed us to take turns packing away our sleeping gear. We did this slowly and silently.

There is a real art to being silent, and it comes with practice and discipline. Even opening or closing a zip on a sleeping bag is a painstaking task when absolute silence is necessary. You have to cradle the zipper in between your thumb and forefinger to muffle the sound, so it may take 30 seconds or more to complete. The same principle applies to the Fastex clips on the enormous packs we carried. Allowing your clip to click would have been showing a lack of respect for the patrol's security. Being a good bush soldier is all about having this sort of self-discipline and patience. I definitely needed all my self-discipline as I was never known for my patience.

By the steep banks of the river, as the pre-dawn light began to filter through the skies, our time had arrived. We were a small, isolated group of men moving into a hostile area. SAS soldiers thrive on such opportunities. All the tedious and unglamorous training had led to this very moment. We had proved ourselves in training – now it was time to see how we fared when the stakes were considerably higher.

I had learned a valuable lesson about stealth on my patrol course. Being assessed while you are trying to silently have a meal is nerve-racking. All you want to do is throw the meagre rations into your grumbling stomach but no, it all has to be painfully slow.

Slowly angle the spoon into the ration bag. Meanwhile, diligently scan the foliage to your front. Conceal the spoon deep inside your hand. Scan the foliage to the sides. Slowly deliver the food to your mouth. Return the spoon to the green bag containing the breakfast mush. Chew, pause, listen, scan, chew, pause, listen, scan.

God, the army makes everything such hard work. I was nearing the end of my slop when my spoon caught on the side of the green bag and fell from my fingers. Everything happened in slow-motion. With eyes wide open I saw the spoon plummeting towards my rifle with the precision of a skydiver before making the loudest *clunk* I have ever heard.

I slowly picked up the spoon before looking at my assessor, who was just shaking his head. His scowl clearly told me that if I did something like that again then I might as well pack my bags and head back to the Battalion.

I didn't enjoy the last part of my meal and, with my confidence blown to pieces, there was no way I was going to attempt to make a brew. I just sat in silence and hoped that someone else would fuck up – but no-one did.

For these practical reasons, all the bits and pieces of the bush soldier's life are selected with great care. Metal spoons are a no-no. Velcro, which might be great on a set of board shorts, has no place in an SAS bush patrol. Some men persisted with velcro seals for their map covers, but a piece of duct tape provides a far better seal and can be removed and reapplied numerous times in complete silence. Camelback water bladders are a great invention for the disciplined soldier, as they allow him to take a couple of sips of water without the noisy rigmarole of removing a water bottle from his pack. There is a downside, of course: because the fluid is so easy to access, you can easily drink far more than you otherwise would. Water is a scarce resource on a patrol, so not a drop can be wasted.

Applying camouflage-cream was another prime example of the army's tortuous routine. A soldier usually signals to a mate that he is going to reapply cam-cream by dragging his open fingers down the front of his face. The acknowledgement comes in the form of a single controlled nod or a wink, meaning that you'll be covered while you do it. There is no excessive movement. You reach into your breast pocket to retrieve the little box of dark colours. With great care to prevent any clicking noise, you open the cover, keeping the lid over the top of your fingers as you insert them into the neapolitan contents below. Sadly there is no chocolate, strawberry or vanilla here – just brown, light-green and dark-green.

You then apply the 'hide-me cream' in stripes, checking the coverage in the mirror, which you cradle in your hand to prevent any glare escaping. At regular intervals your eyes should shift to the foliage in front of you. No bare skin is left unattended – not the backs of your hands, the sides of your neck, inside your ears, even on your eyelids. The cream tastes like clay, but if they ever manage to make it a little more pleasant then you'd probably see some over-exuberant soldiers applying it to their teeth. Most men just content themselves with never smiling. When a soldier finally finishes, he lets the man who was helping to cover his arc of responsibility know that he can go back to his primary area of concern. In other words, he can go back to staring at the bush while dreaming about food or sex.

I don't really want to go into the process for taking a shit, but whether it is the first or fiftieth time, there is always something very personal about it. I do recall one particularly embarrassing moment during the early stages of the deployment, before our patrol had separated from the rest of the squadron. At the helipad, the toilet was a tent that housed a tree branch which sat over a large ditch. Unfortunately, this branch was able to accommodate two bums at once. One morning I was adopting the position when the unit doctor – a woman – strolled in. She made herself ready and planted her arse on the log beside mine. 'What the . . .' I was so taken aback that I thought I'd fall into the contents below. There was no way I was letting anything go with her sitting there.

Apparently, however, I was alone in my misgivings. She initiated some idle chitchat before farting and pushing out something that landed on the pile below with quite a thud. I was embarrassed for her and even more embarrassed for myself. But she was just so damn cool about it all. She wiped herself clean, pulled up her pants and left. I wondered if I was dreaming but the drone of the blowflies made it real enough and so did the filth below. Her spot on the log was quickly filled by another bum – one that shared my gender – and I was able to continue.

FOUR

With the benefit of the early morning light, a three-man recce team – Charlie, Steve and I – moved closer to the river to look for a possible crossing-point. The area was extremely exposed; any error in making our crossing could lead to our patrol being compromised. Steve decided to set up an observation post (OP) over a small village nearby to get a feel for the area. We would hold our position for the day and make our move prior to last light. G and I were given the task of maintaining eyes on the village, and things remained quiet. We spent the day crawling from shadow to shadow in an attempt to dodge the burning sun.

As night approached, our patrol set off again, paralleling the river. It was a calm, stagnant evening and our progress was relatively swift and unremarkable, until we became aware of a low, droning sound. We proceeded cautiously as it slowly increased in decibels, eventually surrounding us. It appeared that our safe passage was being jeopardised by a beehive! But it was no ordinary hive. There were scores of underground chambers that continued for more than 50 metres. We pressed on, and as the sound intensified, so too did the numbers of bees thudding against our bodies. Swarms were diving in and out of the holed earth but, fortunately, they didn't appear overly concerned by our presence. We breathed a sigh of relief when we exited this noisy little cyclone of black and yellow.

As if large tropical bees weren't intimidating enough, we soon came across a creek filled with deep mud. Steve indicated that this would be a 'hasty crossing', where we would bump through one at a time, so Charlie identified a crossing-point and stepped into the mud. He promptly sank to the full depth of his boot and took some time and effort to extricate himself.

As second scout, I smirked silently and thought I would try my luck somewhere else. I didn't sink up to my boot – I managed to go down to over my knees. The pack on my back helped to pin me to the very bottom and it took all my effort not to have my boots sucked right off my feet. I didn't bother looking back at the guys as I made my away across the sludge pit; I could sense their silent laughter and there was no need to confirm it. The remainder of the patrol followed the direction Charlie had taken.

As darkness fell across the landscape, our heaving bodies were rewarded with a short rest. The feeling of elation when the weight of our packs was rested on the ground was pure ecstasy. My numb shoulders began to return to life as the ache slowly receded. But we weren't able to rest for long. Within moments Steve made his trademark clicking noise to indicate that we were moving again. We all made last-minute adjustments to our packs before heaving ourselves back to our feet and continuing.

The next stage of our long walk south took us through

countless fields of rice paddies, which was a welcome relief after the tangled web of vines and lantana. In the early hours of the morning Steve identified an area of thicket where we would snatch a couple of hours of sleep. We positioned two command-detonated Claymore directional mines at the most likely enemy approaches, established a spot for the security piquet, and then the other five of us collapsed onto the earth, soaked by our own sweat. So total was our exhaustion that we didn't even bother getting into our sleeping bags. We just nestled into the heavily dewed soil.

Pre-dawn, we were up again. We retrieved the mines and set off for the nearby river, which we also had to cross. Traversing it was more difficult than we anticipated, as the current was fast and the bottom deep. Charlie dropped into the river and was soon up to his armpits in the streaming current. We couldn't see his eyes but they must have been pretty wide at that moment. He was laden with 50 kilograms of equipment, so swimming was not an option. He later told us that if the current had taken him another couple of inches he would have ditched his pack. As it was, he kept going and made the other side.

I was keen to regain some credibility from the previous mud crossing and managed to locate a point that was no more than waist deep. Although shallow, the river here was at least 80 metres wide so we had to cross slowly. Mindful that the rising sun was rapidly exposing our position, we took advantage of the thick blanket of fog and crawled up the banks on the other side.

Weaving through the vegetation, we were suddenly confronted by an alarming sight. There, in the clearing ahead, were several saddled ponies. We faded back into the bushes and waited, the sound of voices distinct and close. Quietly consulting the map, it was clear that while the major village was still some way off, between here and there was an almost constant track of smaller hamlets. The other noises we were hearing now made sense – a melodic group of goats, roosters and chickens on the well-populated path ahead of us. Remaining concealed would prove almost impossible.

We continued as far as we could to the south-west before we saw that the village was coming to life. Tracks surrounded us on either side. We decided to try to seek shelter closer to the river but even that offered no respite. After narrowly avoiding being seen by a woman washing clothes in the river's shallows, we had to veer off again. At last we decided to bury ourselves in a small thicket, sitting tight while trying to remain concealed for the day. It was nerve-racking, lying so close to human activity, in constant danger of being exposed by the numerous village dogs that wandered across our path.

As the sunlight grew stronger, our hiding place was closely passed by dozens of locals. Lying there watching their feet passing to and fro throughout the day was tense but also amusing. Despite our close proximity, the villagers remained completely oblivious to our presence.

By midday the sun was splashing against our shoulders like torrents of hot water. Most of us were able to find some token level of shade but Jimmy, as signaller, was continually occupied sending and receiving messages. We all felt sorry for him, sort of, as we spied his increasingly red and sweaty face throughout the day.

Through a series of signals G asked me how much water I had left. I held up my fingers to indicate that I still had about 9 or 10 litres. G furrowed his brow and held up four in response.

The sun continued to scorch us, and streams of people passed by, singing, talking and laughing. We were compromised several times by goats, pigs and dogs. One pig meandered into the centre of our position, raised his head and locked eyes with me. Little piggy nearly shit himself and took off squealing. At another point, Steve was taking a piss when a dog crept in for a look. A carefully aimed rock was enough to get the message through that we didn't want any extra attention.

As the day cooled and things began to quieten down again, I asked G in a hushed voice how he was travelling for water. Through parched lips he gave me a grin: 'Cool – I still have four litres left.' He had spent the day baking in the sun and hadn't consumed a single drop. I was concerned about his hydration levels, but we didn't have the time to address it then.

Jimmy had received word from the squadron that we had to 'get eyes' on our target by the next morning or a raid would take place. This seemed a little backward to us. The whole point of our operation was to obtain information that would make a raid safe and effective. Their impatience would force us to compromise our security in order to reach the target by first light. As time was short, we would need to pass directly through the villages ahead. We readied our night-vision goggles and waited for the sky to fall completely black.

=

We had just entered a small clearing when Charlie and I froze. At a range of no more than 25 metres, and directly in front of us, were two hunters with spears. We stood stock-still – not moving, not breathing – until they had passed by and it was safe to go on. With the coast clear, we signalled to the others and continued through the village.

A little further along this happened again, but with an added difficulty. Charlie and I were well ahead of the rest of the patrol when our night-vision goggles flared. A bright ray of light was coming towards us. We didn't have time to signal the other guys so we just squeezed off the side of the path. With our weapons poised we crouched in the shadows and remained perfectly still. There was no time to take cover in the foliage and we were well aware that any noise or movement would draw unwanted attention to ourselves.

We held our breath as several men carrying spears and torches walked within two metres of our position. Fortunately, the other patrol members had seen us dart left and crouch, so they, trained as they were, had followed suit. At one point the hunters' torch-beam had rested less than twelve inches away from Jimmy's boot.

We pressed deeper into the village, silently passing within metres of groups of men around campfires, skirting thatched dwellings where we could hear the occupants chatting amongst themselves. They had no idea what was lurking so close to them. We crept through a maze of huts and tracks throughout the night. At one point, a dog – perhaps the one we'd pelted with rocks earlier – started going berserk. Luckily, barking dogs were obviously not out of the ordinary and no-one came to investigate.

Further on towards the end of the village, I almost found myself in deep shit. Out of the blue, the ground disappeared from under me. One leg and then the other slid into a black abyss and soon my body followed. I had fallen into some type of hole. Judging from the smell, it was probably a toilet. Luckily, my heavy pack wedged me tight against the earthen walls with my legs dangling in midair. It stopped me from falling all the way to the bottom, but was hardly the most becoming position for an SAS soldier! Even with extensive wriggling I was unable to free myself. I could see Steve's white teeth glowing in the darkness as he helped me out of the stinky hole. His amusement wasn't contagious but his assistance was appreciated.

The incessant barking of several dogs shadowed our patrol as we wove our way through the final lanes of the village. Miraculously, we made it without being compromised.

With a silent sigh of relief, we listened to the barking fade into the distance as we re-entered thick vegetation. Not long afterwards, during a brief navigational stop, G began pressing Steve as to how long we would remain there. When he was told it would be about 10 minutes, G began ripping open his shirt and panting like a dog, his tongue lapping at the air. At first, Steve and I just laughed at his antics. Either G was clowning around or he was being bitten by ants. We continued to consult the map and GPS in order to ascertain our precise location.

But G still seemed disoriented. The problem soon became clear when he told us that he had never been that hot in his entire life. He was without doubt experiencing heat exhaustion. He guzzled a decent quantity of water and slowly regained focus. G was a warrior and carried both the patrol medical kit and the light machine gun. Even a slight increase in temperature can have a profound effect on a soldier over the duration of a patrol.

With G back to normal, we continued a little further before locating a suitable position to sleep for the night. We were now only a couple of hundred metres shy of the creek that ran into our target village. The sun would be rising soon, and should the squadron raid take place, we were well placed to block any militants who attempted to flee into West Timor.

FIVE

In the morning we received a message that the raid had been postponed and we had another day to assess the area for the presence of armed militants. The information we gathered would be utilised to plan the raid.

As we made our way towards the creek that ran between us and the village, I turned and whispered to Steve: 'Fuck, I hope we get hit today.'

'You say that every day,' he grinned, falling back so that his patrol scouts could go ahead.

Charlie and I cleared the ridge and looked down at the dry riverbed in front of us. Our path was incredibly exposed, the high banks leaving little opportunity for cover as we crossed. We propped just short of the crest and signalled back to the other four members of the patrol that we had reached the creek. Steve slowly approached our position while the other patrol members each dropped to one knee and scanned the bush for signs of movement.

Buster and Jimmy were pretty low on water, so they signalled to ask us whether the creek might quench their thirst. I couldn't resist. With one eye on its dusty, dry banks I turned back to them with a large smile and hearty thumbs-up. When both their faces broke into relieved smiles I turned my thumb upside-down again with a grin. Their hand signals sent an unmistakable message back.

Looking at the exposed nature of the crossing, Steve decided we should carry out a 'deliberate obstacle crossing'. The entire team would take firing positions to cover Charlie and myself as we crossed first. Once we were established on the far side of the creek, we would give the all-clear for the remainder of the patrol to join us. Charlie slid down the bank first, doing his best not to leave tracks across the sandy bottom. As he hit the base of the bank, he quickly moved into a sideways walk, making sure that any prints he did end up making would appear to be pointed down the creek, not across it.

The creek was between 15 and 20 metres wide, and the banks were three or four metres high. As Charlie moved across the riverbed it was obvious that he would have trouble scaling the bank on the far side unassisted. I signalled back to the others and slid in after him. Under the watchful eyes of the rest of the team, we located a suitable point to exit the creek, all the while treading carefully to minimise our tracks. I assisted Charlie up the bank and he silently scanned the foliage before turning around and providing a helping hand for me. Once up safely, we spread out and vanished into the undergrowth.

Steve watched anxiously as our camouflaged fatigues were swallowed up by the maze of green on the opposite bank. We didn't have to be told what to do. The standard procedure was as straightforward as it was effective. The key thing was finding the balance between stealth and haste. Move too slowly and the remainder of our team could be compromised. Too fast and we could find ourselves in contact with the enemy and isolated from our mates. Our constant training and retraining had prepared us to adapt our skills and knowledge to the terrain and situation.

In silence, we both began to clear the terrain, moving through the bush in a large figure eight. As our eyes scanned the area around us, we kept our mouths slightly open to achieve optimal hearing. I tried to shut out the sound of my racing heartbeat and ignore the weight of my pack and the rush of adrenaline coursing through me.

Each movement was slow and precise. We edged forward only a couple of metres at a time, before pausing to scan and listen once again. There was no whispering and only the odd hand signal, which was always carried out with the non-master hand. Your master hand grips your rifle's pistol grip, the pointer finger parallel to the trigger, the thumb gently caressing the safety catch, ready to disengage the safety mechanism at the first sign of danger. Despite our soaring pulse rates, our senses were operating at maximum efficiency. I'd never felt so alive.

We cleared our way to a small track approximately 35 metres into the foliage, before returning to the creek bed. Charlie stayed in the undergrowth as far back as he could while remaining visible to me. I moved to the edge and signalled to Steve that it was safe for the team to cross. Steve replied with a slow thumbs-up before ordering the remainder of the team across the gap, one man at a time. The creek bed was always covered in both directions, as was the direction we travelled from and where we were heading. The whole procedure took place without words; it was exactly like the drills we had practised so many times before.

Buster was the last man across the creek and he covered all footprints and signs of our presence swiftly behind him. Steve immediately ordered the patrol to adopt a defensive position approximately 15 metres into the foliage. I dropped to my stomach further along in the undergrowth so I could take in the full view from our potential new OP, while the rest of the patrol remained in a defensive circle, seated with packs on.

The OP site was alive with ants, like most of East Timor, and the little bastards wasted no time running up my arms and into my collar, where they savagely bit my neck. After wiggling my back slightly in the vain hope that the ants might leave me alone, I tested the site's suitability as a vantage point. The frame of my pack pressed hard up against the rear of my neck and I signalled to Steve that I was going to remove it to make it easier to shoot if necessary. Another encouraging thumbs-up came my way. After further assessment I gave the nod and Steve signalled to the patrol that my position would indeed be the location of the OP. It was now my job to clear the area and remove the noisy foliage that littered the ground.

Carefully climbing to my feet, I painstakingly began dragging aside the rotting palm fronds that covered the area. Even with extreme care, the foliage was extremely dry and any movement was going to be noisy. The branches were also entwined with vines, making them even harder to remove. Scanning the creek bed, I had my weapon in my right arm while with my left I attempted to drag the fronds free. I signalled to Steve that I required some assistance and he set about informing one of the others to begin clearing a path to the OP which would allow me to maintain a visual on the creek.

I felt vulnerable standing with my back towards our point of maximum exposure so, as I worked, I glanced over my shoulder to take in the creek bed more fully. I wasn't expecting what I saw. There were six men no more than 20 metres away. All had weapons and all were walking up the creek towards my position. We'd confirmed the presence of armed militia in the area, and they were headed straight towards me.

SIX

The sandy bottom must have silenced the militiamen's movement. The lead man held his weapon to his shoulder and stared intently into the foliage about 10 metres further down the bank from where I stood. For a second I could see the white sections in the right corners of his eyes. I knew that any movement would draw his attention straight to me. His professional stance and the way he held his weapon suggested he was far from just an average militiaman; this looked like a man with comprehensive military training. There were others, possibly two who were like him and three who appeared more of a ragtag bunch. They continued to move towards me and it was clear that there was no way out. In an instant I would be locking eyes with the lead man.

There was no time to think.

I instinctively flicked off my safety catch, raised my weapon towards the group of men and squeezed the trigger. My first round, fired from the hip, crashed into the lead man's shoulder, a cloud of blood and dust exploding as the bullet found its mark. I continued to fire, pulling my weapon up to my shoulder and dropping to one knee.

I fired another five or six rounds into the direction of the group as the militia began to return fire and scatter for cover. For every bullet I fired, three or four were fired in my direction, most travelling high. Without the time to turn on my aim point – the red dot inside my sight – I levelled my foresight onto the second man, fired several rounds and moved quickly on to another. It all went so fast. I was vaguely aware of one of the militia staggering as the rounds entered his torso, and I briefly thought that I must have been hitting his legs instead. But the militia only had to move four metres to the side before they disappeared around the corner of the bank, and within a blink they were gone.

As the dust cleared, Steve jumped beside me and delivered a 40-millimetre grenade into the creek. Jimmy took up a firing position on the other side of me. We stood shoulder to shoulder. It was a surreal moment – complete silence as Steve, Jimmy and I stood facing an empty creek bed. There was no sign of the militia at all.

Steve scanned the scene ahead of us, poised for further action. 'What happened?'

'Where are they?' asked Jimmy.

'There were six of them in the creek,' I replied, determined to keep focused. 'I think I shot three of them.'

Just as I spoke, there was frantic movement 50 metres ahead. The dense foliage parted and the clearing was filled again with men running for their lives, shooting back at us as they ran. Steve, Jimmy and I responded promptly to this second burst of fire, exchanging several more rounds and sending several 40-millimetre grenades whistling through the air in their direction. With every shot from Steve's rifle next to my head I could feel the shock-wave cutting into my eardrums. My hearing was now so distorted that my ears were pulsating with a loud and incessant ringing.

Steve made the decision to hold ground and assess the situation. After a brief discussion, he told us he wanted a better idea of what was happening further down the creek. I promptly volunteered to cross to the opposite bank, requesting the support of G and his trusty light machine gun, the Para Minimi. Steve arranged the other three remaining men into a defensive perimeter, providing support on the bank to cover our movement as much as possible, and I moved down the bank and darted across the open creek.

With every step I expected a volley of fire to rattle past me or worse, but the adrenaline pumping through my body gave me the strength to scale the opposite bank of the creek in a couple of quick lunges. I then adopted a position ready to fire and covered G as he followed me across. Once again we braced ourselves for the distinctive crack of rifle fire. None came. We both attempted to slow our breathing, taking turns to hold our breath while listening for signs of enemy movement. From my new position I could see the motionless body of one of the militiamen, face-down in the creek. He appeared to have been shot at least four times in the upper chest and abdomen during our initial confrontation. Following the routine from training exercises, I dispassionately informed Steve that there was 'one dead enemy'.

G and I began to traverse the bank. As we were relatively exposed, G remained in a fire position, offering clear lines of sight and fire down the creek. I propped myself on the bank to his left, scanning the close vegetation to his front. Before long G attempted to attract my attention. Eighty metres to our front, two militiamen were edging up the creek towards us. With my ears still ringing from the earlier assault, I didn't respond to G's whispers, but I had no problem hearing the burst from his light machine gun, which kicked into life with a high-pitched rattle as he poured rounds in the direction of the enemy. Why not? He was carrying 1000 of them, so he might as well put them to good use.

I adopted a firing position and got off several rounds before lobbing a 40-millimetre grenade into the dust storm that G's rounds were creating. G then delivered a perfect target indication and I responded with another 40-millimetre grenade. It was like clockwork. Then it was their turn.

After a brief moment of silence, we began to take fire from our left flank. The rounds cracked over our heads and we could hear several coordinating voices. We took stock of our situation and swiftly realised that there were possibly militiamen across the other side of the creek, another group further down the creek on their side of the river, and yet another flanking our position from the left. We were very nearly surrounded.

I informed Steve of our situation and he ordered us to wait while he positioned some fire support to cover our path back across the creek. We were all too aware that the open creek was now a prominent fire lane and by re-crossing we would most likely draw some heat. With Steve initiating fire support, I was first to cross. G provided his own covering fire, which he did with a brilliant burst into the vegetation while

I dropped back into the creek and broke across the open ground.

I was sure that there would be militiamen lining the banks, ready to pour some lead into my direction. My first thought as I began my run was how much I dreaded being shot in the arse. Being wounded is fair enough, but just not in the arse. G must have poured at least 50 rounds into the vegetation in quick time before following my progress across the open ground. His eyes were wild – his initiation in contact had started very well.

In those few minutes, G and I formed a significant bond. Relying on one another in a fight for life and death produces a tight brotherhood. We had both passed the other's test. Just as importantly, so too had our fellow patrol members, who had remained a calm and controlled support throughout the contact.

We joined our mates and Steve immediately reorganised his defensive perimeter. Jimmy attempted to establish communications with squadron HQ, informing them that the patrol was in contact and required the assistance of the rapid-reaction force (RRF). It seemed fair to say that we were in no doubt that armed militiamen were operating in the area.

Due to our split patrol, the encircling militia were unsure of our exact location and composition. They could be heard moving through the dense foliage but, especially with several of us now suffering a degree of hearing loss from the gunfire, it was impossible to identify their precise position or the direction they were moving. We would slowly glance at each other and indicate that we could hear noise somewhere to our front but would point to our ears before giving a slight shrug of the shoulders. The enemy continued to search and before long had managed to encircle us in a loose cordon.

Our nervous energy was at a peak, but despite ourselves G and I occasionally made eye contact and grinned at each other. Jimmy was having difficulty sending off the message, as there was an error at the base station that was preventing transmissions from being received.

From the rear of the patrol, Buster and Jimmy began to hear movement. Unfortunately, their signal could not be passed to the other patrol members as the dense foliage prevented us from maintaining eye contact. Charlie was located near the creek on the opposite side of the defensive perimeter. Buster heard rustling through the vegetation that increased in clarity and intensity as the enemy probed towards our position. His heart was pounding in anticipation of imminent contact. How many of them were coming? Would his weapon work?

While outwardly he remained calm, Buster later commented that he could 'feel his chest bouncing off the earth below him'. He was lying in the prone position, scanning the vegetation to his front, when two militiamen came into view – no more than seven metres away. With his breath held, Buster fired two rapid rounds into the chest of the first man before adjusting onto the second, who was diving for cover.

In response, there was then a volley of fire in Buster's direction; an extended line of attackers, maybe seven to nine men, was attempting to sweep through our position. There were also men to the rear carrying ammunition and organising the assault. Rounds were now cracking around the entire patrol, slicing the branches above our heads, sending a shower of leaves to slowly blanket us where we lay.

The marauding militia were taking fire positions. This was all the motivation we needed to remain low and calm, only opening fire when targets presented themselves. Battle in close country is similar to night operations. The aim is to prevent signalling your precise location until the last possible moment. Otherwise you are likely to find a flurry of grenades hurled in your general direction.

Jimmy placed his palmtop keyboard down and fired several carefully aimed shots into the moving vegetation, while Steve offered additional support. Several bullets flicked into the dirt mound within a foot of Buster, so he decided to take cover and deliver a grenade in the direction of an enemy he could hear moaning. Buster quickly sourced a grenade from his pouch and peeled off the safety tape. With a sharp pull he dislodged the safety pin before calling 'grenade' and delivering the little ball of death to our attackers. The fragmentation grenade exploded, showering the patrol with dirt and debris. The moaning ceased but Buster delivered one more grenade into the same location for good measure.

Steve decided it was time to break contact. The attack had been interrupted, providing us with enough room to manoeuvre. I asked if we were taking packs. Steve's reply was immediate and decisive: 'No. Remove all mission essential stores from your packs and leave the rest behind.' This offered us a greater range of mobility and stealth. Rations, water, sleeping equipment and miscellaneous stores would only hinder us in our attempt to break from contact.

Steve then ordered me back into the creek to observe the bank from the direction of the most recent exchange of fire. My time in the creek felt like an eternity as my back was now completely exposed. Charlie assisted Jimmy in clearing the packs. Each grabbed a patrol radio, which could not be left for the enemy. Charlie then dropped into the creek beside me – we were now able to cover both directions.

With the patrol ready to move, Steve ordered the withdrawal. Charlie didn't hesitate and darted across the creek with the speed that was expected from his athletic frame, and I followed suit. Now, with the two scouts securing the opposite bank, the remainder of the patrol broke across the creek one at a time. There was some sporadic shooting from the vegetation on the opposite bank but we disappeared into the undergrowth.

Once we were clear, I looked Steve in the eye. 'Goddamn, what a rush!' I whispered, quoting a line from the movie *Broken Arrow*. Steve laughed and the tension eased somewhat.

No longer encumbered by our packs, we worked our way through the vegetation with a new level of mobility. *This is how an SAS patrol should be,* I thought, finally able to crawl, weave and slide through the lantana and vines with relative ease and stealth. We'd travelled about 300 metres when Steve ordered another attempt to communicate with the squadron.

I was tasked to put the men into a defensive perimeter while Steve and Jimmy set up the satellite communications. G and his light machine gun were positioned to cover the most likely enemy approach route, alongside Buster at the six o'clock position. Charlie remained at twelve o'clock with Steve and Jimmy in the centre covering three o'clock. I covered a small opening in the vegetation at the nine o'clock position. Voice communications were established with squadron HQ and they were re-informed of the situation moments before the second radio failed too.

Although the majority of the squadron were conducting a raid some 15 kilometres away, a 12-man rapid-reaction force was sent to our aid from Dili. The RRF boarded two helicopters and thundered towards us. They didn't know what to expect on the ground, but they were aware that their mates were in trouble, and that was enough. If they could have made those flying machines go any faster from sheer commitment and exuberance then they no doubt would have. In the meantime, we lay low and waited.

Within 20 minutes we identified the distinctive shapes of two Blackhawk helicopters in the distance. The members of the RRF couldn't see us against the background of parched vegetation. On Steve's orders I prepared a smoke grenade to signal our location. The birds continued past us towards the creek, before looping back and landing in a small open area of lantana in the centre of our position. This was some of the best flying we had seen. It was evident that the pilots didn't mind pushing the limits during a time of need.

Six men scrambled off the helicopter with eyes and fingers ready for action. We could not have hoped for a more reliable band of brothers to come to our aid, and we scrambled aboard before the pilots launched the bird hard into the sky. The six men who got off were relocated on the second helicopter, before the two Blackhawks circled back to the contact area so we could retrieve our packs. The terrain looked vastly different from above.

One helicopter hovered over the vicinity of the creek, ready to provide fire support, while the helicopter carrying us landed in a clearing approximately 40 metres from the contact location. Steve ordered Buster, Jimmy and G to secure the landing zone while he, Charlie and I were to head for the undergrowth to locate our packs. This was a vulnerable time for the helicopters, so we wasted no time, running in the direction of our packs with eyes wide open, half-expecting to run into another group of militia.

Immediately, I nearly tripped over the twisted and mangled body of a dead militiaman. His eyes were open but lifeless. His bloodstained mouth was also ajar, but there was no breathing, no rise and fall from his damaged chest. The fragmentation grenades had twisted his lower torso and the blast had bent one of his lower limbs into an impossible position.

Steve put a hand on my shoulder and told me to keep going. I didn't look back.

The first packs were only about seven metres from the dead man. We quickly rolled them over to ensure that they were not booby-trapped with grenades before attempting to throw one over each shoulder. Weighed down by two packs each, as well as an enemy resupply bag and weapon we had found, we trudged back towards the whining rotors. We piled aboard the Blackhawk with heaving chests, holding on as the bird pulled hard into the blue sky above. The helicopters circled the village one last time before heading east towards Dili.

SEVEN

We were on a high like no other. The enemy weapon was unloaded and a 7.62-millimetre round was handed to each of us as we slapped one another on the shoulders, relieved that we had all come through this close call unscathed. Up front, the pilots were chattering to themselves. I heard one load master comment over the radio that we were pumped. The pilot's response made me smile: 'Yeah, you would be too if you had just shot some cunts that were trying to take you down.'

The birds glided home, filled with operators still high on adrenaline. Dishevelled and putrid, we were unloaded onto the helipad in Dili and welcomed by our mates. We were debriefed and it was later confirmed that five militiamen were killed, with a further three wounded. Various intelligence sources let us know that the Kopassus who were orchestrating and organising the militiamen had associated the helicopter buzzing over the area three days prior with the insertion of a small reconnaissance patrol. There had been at least 60 armed militia and another 40 unarmed men who were sent to search for our patrol. In three 20-man groups, further broken down into squads of six men, they had scoured the countryside for us. Unbeknownst to us, we were actually overlooked because we were positioned within the confines of the village; the hunting militiamen did not think that an SAS patrol would be audacious or silly enough to hide so close to a major population centre.

≡

Most of our patrol had a couple of restless nights of sleep as we came to terms with what had occurred during those 90 minutes in October 1999. In my mind I was back in the moment, reliving those minutes of ringing silence after a barrage of bullets. My thoughts linger on that motionless body, lying face-down in the dry, sandy riverbed.

Torturing myself, I have tried repeatedly to imagine what the injured militiaman must have been thinking during his final moments. When I talk to others about it, one of the first things they ask is: 'How can you know what he was thinking?' But in my mind's eye it seems as clear as day. Our eyes met and in that moment he appeared just as shocked to see me as I was to see him. His face told me that he too was overwhelmed by the little pieces of lead flying through the air. He and his five friends panicked. They ran from me while randomly firing their weapons in my general direction.

I have never been shot but I am acutely aware of the havoc a bullet can do to a body. Travelling at 930 metres per second, the bullet would have ripped into his flesh with a sickening thump. If he was lucky, the bullets that struck him would have kept going on their course; but if this didn't happen, they would have bounced around his chest like a pinball machine. He was shot in the lungs, which might be a bit like taking in water in heavy surf when you are not expecting it. Your lungs fill with fluid and you cough and gasp for air. He didn't die instantly, but managed to scamper out of view before dropping to the ground some 10 metres away. His friends left him, so he would have felt alone and scared.

In my mind I write lines of dialogue for him, things I imagine might have run through his mind as he felt his life begin to slip away: *'I was the hunter, I was looking for them, and now I am feeling cold and I see my friends running further and further away. My vision is becoming blurred and I feel like I'm drowning. Here I am, lying alone in the dust, no longer able to move or breathe. I think I'm dying.'*

I would love to hate him. This might relieve the sickening feeling that envelops my stomach when I think about the incident in detail. But I don't. Nor can I respect the mayhem that he might have been part of. I do, however, respect the fact that he had the courage to come after us. Unlike dated World War II films, where enemy soldiers are depicted as faceless automatons, these men, just like us, had lived, laughed and cried. They were human. I wasn't the victor in this battle. There is no gloating or glory. I just get the chance to keep on living.

=

We had, as a team, performed exceptionally well. Some of these men would go on to see significant action in other theatres of war, and some would not. It is sad when SAS soldiers leave the Regiment before their time. Sometimes life works out and sometimes it doesn't. You can analyse why things go wrong until you go insane, but there comes a time when you have to make a decision to move forward – to remain shackled in the past is a burden on your soul.

The five Australian SAS soldiers of this patrol would all be out of the green machine within four years. But that morning, on the helipad in Dili, it was all adrenaline and euphoria. The squadron quartermaster, Steve (a great guy), snapped a black-and-white image of the patrol which – with its caption, *Baptised* – captures our ragged elation perfectly.

Charlie was attempting to smile but was unable to fully open his eyes. The camouflage-cream that had served him so well during the previous few days had liquefied and run into his eyes. That stuff really burns! Holding the ammo pouch of the dead militiaman, he looks composed, his trigger finger extended outside his trigger guard.

Jimmy, rifle cradled in his right arm, appears exhausted and his face remains blackened from the strenuous patrol. His torso is twisted by the heavy pack slung over his left shoulder. If you look carefully, his relief at being part of the patrol is oozing out of him. He would have hated Steve, one of his closest friends, to have had this experience without him.

Buster is still on a high, relaxed and smiling. Although he had been a member of the British Special Forces for some 15 years, this was the first time he had been involved in contact at close range. His right trouser-leg is no longer bloused but is draped over his boot, and he is missing his right nomex glove, which he removed during the contact. Buster would later serve with great distinction in Afghanistan and would be awarded the Military Cross. Looking at him in this photo and remembering how he was under fire, I am not surprised.

Like Jimmy, I appear gaunt. My lower limbs have thinned over the three days of action. A sense of deep satisfaction has spread across my face – I knew I would see some action – and I am grasping an SKS rifle retrieved from the dead militiaman. The cam-cream has run from my face thanks to hours of adrenaline-induced sweating, and my clothing is still muddied from one of the creek crossings.

Steve carries the same steely resolve that he held throughout the contact. He is radiating not only pride in himself but pride in his men. His head is covered with a bandanna, while his M4 rifle is held firmly across his body. He has a shell dressing attached to the upper-left section of his web vest. Steve was awarded the Medal for Gallantry for his strong leadership under fire.

G is facing Steve, whom he held in high regard, while the christened light machine gun is cupped in his arms. His eyes are still wide with fire and he is radiating an even greater level of confidence than usual. His large pack no longer looks like a burden but the trophy of a hard patrol. The coconut trees and wooded forest that tower above us in the background provide a reminder both of the tropical climate and the foreign terrain. And the dusty ground underfoot is our path back to headquarters.

We had proved ourselves under fire, and our smiles in that photo are a celebration of life. We may now have scattered and moved on with our lives, but that was one hell of a patrol.

EIGHT

In late August 2001, images of Australian SAS soldiers preparing to board a Norwegian cargo ship, the MV *Tampa*, were beamed around the world. Four hundred and thirty-eight refugees, or illegal immigrants, depending on which side of the argument one sits, had been rescued by the *Tampa* in the Indian Ocean after the boat taking them from Indonesia to Australia began to sink. Our deployment quickly became highly politicised. The fact that a complete SAS squadron was being used to secure the *Tampa* initiated a debate that divided not only Australians but people around the world as well.

Shortly after arriving at work on 27 August, we were told that we were heading to Christmas Island, an Australian territory located 500 kilometres south of Jakarta, for an interception task. Later that day, my wife received a telephone call informing her that I had been deployed for a maximum of three months. This was not the first time I had gone to work and failed to come home, so she wasn't stressed out. When Colleen turned on the evening news, there we were, unloading pallets of equipment on Christmas Island.

We spent that evening preparing our equipment while being updated on the situation. The Indonesian authorities had refused to allow the *Tampa* to dock, so the freighter's skipper, under the influence of some refugees who had occupied the bridge, began steaming towards Christmas Island. The Australian Government denied the *Tampa* access to Australian territorial waters and, when this order was ignored, Prime Minister John Howard ordered our squadron to board the vessel.

Our team led the assault and secured the bridge while the remaining water-assault teams cordoned off the refugees. Committing highly trained SAS soldiers to such a banal task was, no doubt, an excessive display of force, but in fact our medical and linguistic skills, as well as our ability to secure the vessel, quickly lowered the tension level on board considerably.

After accounting for all personnel and conducting a thorough search of the vessel, we began to improve the sanitary conditions of the refugees. We emptied waste buckets into the ocean and were sprayed with urine and faecal matter as the wind blew them back in our faces, and we dry-retched as we scraped turds off the floor of a cargo container. It was an afternoon I would like to forget. Other soldiers prepared hot meals for the refugees, and some days later they were moved to an Australian transport vessel, the HMAS *Manoora*. Several SAS teams deployed to the *Manoora* to provide assistance and security.

The vast majority of the people on the boat were young men. Some were from Afghanistan but several groups I spoke to claimed to be from Pakistan. One Afghani who spoke English told me how he had fought with the

Mujahideen and shot down 12 Soviet helicopters during the USSR's occupation of Afghanistan in the 1980s. There was another man who wore a gold watch and paraded around in a leather jacket, and we discovered several who were carrying large sums of US currency. Elsewhere on the vessel, I felt compelled to intervene when a father began to beat his daughter, who'd had an altercation with the jewel of the family – the prized son.

One Afghani man spent every moment caring for his wife and cradling his children. I made sure that his family, along with several others who had been relegated to the most uncomfortable part of the ship, were repositioned to an area of greater ventilation and comfort. This man reminded me of some of my friends from Kabul, and I recalled the great importance Afghanis place on family.

Several days later, the *Manoora* drew alongside another people-smuggling vessel; this one was carrying around 150 people from Iraq. They, too, were brought on board, but we had to search their bags before loading their possessions onto the ship. One lady lashed out and scratched my face, yelling in perfect English, 'I hate you, I hate you, I hate you,' as I tried to search her handbag. It was jammed with packets of cigarettes, and her possible addiction to nicotine may have caused her outburst. But she later proved to be most helpful and influential when it came to organising the group and informing it of what was going on. She was a tough woman and I respected that.

The following day, several Australian Federal Police officers boarded the *Manoora* and detained the Indonesian crew of the second boat for people-smuggling. I acted as the interpreter and although these guys knew what they were doing, they still appeared genuinely naïve. The true beneficiaries of the racket – the men who actually took the asylum-seekers' money and employed the crew – may never be identified. We later learnt that many more vessels loaded with asylum-seekers had been ready to travel from Indonesia to Australia but, due to the Australian Government's hardline approach, had all turned around.

As our squadron was needed for another task, we were replaced six days later and sent home to Australia. Then came September 11.

PART THREE

RECONNAISSANCE PATROL, EASTERN AFGHANISTAN

APRIL 2002

ONE

When the planes slammed into the Twin Towers in New York and burst into flames on 11 September 2001 we were in no doubt that our skills would soon be in demand. The increased threat of terrorist attacks led to the Australian SAS doubling its counter-terrorism commitments. 'Sabre squadrons' were positioned on both the west and east coasts. The troop office on 12 September was tense and alert, packed with elite soldiers all fully aware of the realities of this situation. A dozen sets of eyes were glued to the small television set, and the only noises that could be heard were the strained sounds of reporters' voices crackling out of the set's single speaker. It was the type of silence and sombre intensity that accompanies a funeral procession.

The men were, as usual, sitting on the multicoloured sofas — but things were different. No-one was leaning back, half-swallowed by chairs that had lost their springs at least a decade prior. Instead, all sat perched on the edge of their seats like they were watching a close football match. I squeezed through the crowd and onto the dusty brown lounge, joining my brothers as we observed the same images over and over again. Together we watched the surreal loss of life as if it were some kind of big-budget action film. With each replay I hoped that the plane would miraculously miss the tower. With each replay I hoped for something different.

The political fallout from these events left the Regiment abuzz with speculation. Would Australia commit troops? If so, how many? Osama bin Laden, the director of this film, quickly became a household name and it soon became clear that the Regiment would deploy troops to Afghanistan. But as the online counter-terrorist squadron, we would be staying put in Australia, at least for the time being.

It would be an understatement to say we were disappointed at missing out on the first deployment. Nursing our dented morale while watching another squadron prepare for war wasn't easy – but we all had mates who were heading out, so we wished them well. Although I attempted to be genuine with my support, I was gutted not to be amongst them. The only thing that provided some solace was the fact that I was not alone. Two complete SAS squadrons would share the dubious privilege of remaining in Australia on domestic counter-terrorism duties. We could all be frustrated and pissed off together.

Our squadron was to support the Commonwealth Heads of Government Meeting (CHOGM), therefore Brisbane became our base. Right from the outset we knew that the vigorous physical training in the sweltering Queensland heat was going to be gruelling. Enoggera Hill was the obvious location for our hideous team-building sessions. The primary objective was always the same – to reach the tower at the summit – but as the troop's fitness levels improved, it was not uncommon to drag metal bars along for a little extra fun.

As we pushed ourselves to the limits in and around Brisbane, we were aware that the next time we would be truly tested would be in the mountains of Afghanistan. The placenames in the newspaper reports and the mountains we glimpsed on TV would soon be very familiar to us all. I had spent the last seven years preparing myself for such an opportunity. It felt like the SAS selection process all over again.

My eagerness to join the SAS and the determination with which I launched myself into achieving that goal were almost not enough. The 20 days of selection would have been incredibly tough under any circumstances, but I was inexperienced and young and had no thought for self-preservation. I saw every march, run or physical training session as an opportunity to prove myself. I would push myself to the very limit in my desire to come first. I was usually up the front but never first. There were obviously some sick bastards who had trained harder than me!

Midway through the course, an SAS warrant officer gave me a pep talk before I set off on a night navigation activity. The directing staff were meant to be neutral, providing no negative or positive feedback. So when this man showed his human side, it gave me strength.

'Okay, mate,' he said. 'It's imperative that you complete at least one night checkpoint. This leg is just over five kilometres. My advice to you is to run as hard as you can until it begins to get dark. You should be able to get halfway there. Then I want you to rest. Just relax and let it get dark. Once you have calmed down, follow that compass of yours to the checkpoint. The vegetation will be pretty thick all the way along, but trust your compass and paces. Just before you get to the checkpoint gather your composure.' He paused, looking at me. 'You are doing really well – keep it up. Any questions?'

I felt completely pumped that this man liked me enough to offer some friendly motivation. I wasn't going to let him or myself down.

Physically and mentally, we were being pushed to our limits, so this was fairly typical of the support offered by the guys running the show. Some were bastards, but we were soon to learn that these guys were generally the average Joes whom no-one respected. The best of them had nothing to prove and remained firm but fair. Two days later, the senior instructor in charge of the course bailed me up for a few questions. He pulled in beside me during the closing stages of the 20-kilometre pack march endurance test, a hardcore run that was taxing enough without pausing for conversation.

'Are you leading the group, trainee Fennell?'

What I wanted to say was, 'How in the hell do you know my name?' but I held my tongue. 'No sir, I was in the ninth group to leave,' I said. 'I think there are at least four guys in front of me.'

Nine teams had departed the start line at 60-second intervals, and I was feeling pretty proud of my effort at getting up to this position. But I knew there was no point pumping myself up. I kept things matter-of-fact with him.

'How old are you, son?'

'Old enough to join the SAS, sir. I'm 21,' I replied confidently.

'The average age of soldiers who pass selection is several

years older than that, but I think you're old enough. How are you finding the course so far?'

'Extremely challenging, sir.'

He laughed. 'You can expect plenty more of that. We're only just getting started.'

I smiled back. 'Thank you, sir, I'm sure you're right, but please excuse me – I'm going to double-time.' My impatience to pick up the pace amused him further.

'Don't let me hold you back,' he said with a smirk on his face.

Exactly as he said, the course only became increasingly arduous. We were regularly woken in the middle of the night and tested while still disoriented. At 02:00 in the morning we were instructed on Morse code. The following evening we were woken at 23:00 and tested. The night after that, we were woken at 02:00 again, this time made to write an essay about our life.

There was obviously a plan to this madness. They were attempting to weed out those soldiers who had the physical ability but lacked the aptitude required to be an SAS soldier. Those who passed selection needed to be mentally astute as well as physically robust. They had to be capable of absorbing an enormous amount of information in a relatively short period of time. It was an intense training schedule with a lot to learn: from demolitions to foreign languages, medical and communication skills, driving and diving, boating, parachuting, survival, patrolling, close protection and room combat. It was a lot to take in, especially when you were worn down by physical demands at the same time.

On the evening of day 10 we were crammed into the rear of a blacked-out truck and dropped off in Lancelin, a military training area 120 kilometres north of Perth. This was the beginning of an individual four-day navigational exercise. A look at my diary from the time reminds me that my hands, shins and knees had been scratched raw by the thick, bristly vegetation. I vaguely remember the sand dunes, but one thing that I can recall as clearly as if it were yesterday was the constant annoyance of the flies. Dozens of the little bastards swarmed to my bleeding hands. What felt like hundreds more incessantly danced and clung to my perspiration-drenched face. I would swipe viciously at them and be left with nothing more than a stinging face. I always seemed to miss. So persistent were they at driving me insane that during one scorching afternoon I dedicated the best part of 20 minutes to killing as many of them as possible.

I was aware of my navigational limitations so didn't try anything fancy. More experience might have shown me how to skirt around the thickest vegetation by utilising map-to-ground techniques, which involved assessing the terrain by examining its appearance in relation to a map. I kept it simple, relying on my bearings and keeping track of paces only. This didn't make for easy progress and forced me to drive headlong through the spiky saltbush, but by day 14 I'd covered just under 70 kilometres.

Day 15 was a roping day. Apart from the opportunity it offered us to squeeze the dozens of thorns from our shins, I'm sure that those guys who were afraid of heights would have preferred the slog of the previous days. We abseiled and climbed, even traversed a rope suspended between two 10-storey towers. It was exhilarating and, predictably, I loved it, but it required every ounce of our strength and focus.

With that completed, we progressed to the final and most challenging phase of the course – lucky dip.

During lucky dip things were made as difficult for us as possible. We were given just one meal – fish-heads and rice – over four and a half days. This was combined with very little sleep, as well as enormously taxing physical activity. I had wanted to be challenged. But this exceeded all my expectations. I was pushed beyond the realms of my physical capabilities and then pushed some more.

By the end of the course, fatigue was beginning to break my body down. I began selection at a very lean 79 kilograms. Twenty days later I weighed in at no more than 66, a drop of 13 kilograms in less than three weeks. My body was a mess. It would be several months before I would regain total feeling in my shoulders and the soles of my feet.

The last two days of the course were murder. It should not have come as a surprise when I collapsed from hypoglycaemia (low blood-sugar levels). I was young, inexperienced and physically spent. Several men who were in their mid-twenties or older handled the latter stages of the course much better than I did. By pacing themselves, they'd kept their reserves of energy for the final push. But despite my levels of exhaustion, I was still there at the end.

Before the course, I had said to myself that I would attempt selection as many times as it would take. Thank God I was accepted on my first attempt. I had reached my goal. I was now in the best job in the world. But the price it would take to hold it, and to be the best I could possibly be, would be considerable.

Standing there reflecting at the end of selection, I realised that my endurance levels were barely adequate. I never wanted to feel that weak again. As soon as my body recovered, I began to rectify the shortfall. The next time I would be severely tested would be on operations – and I was determined to be physically and mentally robust for them. A brutal training regime would help me achieve this. If my determination had been obsessive before, now it was all-consuming. Selfishly, I began to put it ahead of everything else in my life. Including my family.

TWO

As East Timor had taught me, there was a huge difference between training and operations. During our domestic counter-terrorism duties, the patrols had been re-arranged, leaving each team with a sense of edginess and uncertainty. There were unspoken questions. Who could be relied upon if the situation became dire? How do you teach a man to be brave? A soldier may be highly skilled, but that is only half of what's required. The other element is courage. Shooting a practice target is easy. The real test is if you can still perform when your heart is pounding inside your chest, when numbness and nausea envelop your body and your senses are completely overloaded. On operations, the decisions whether to fire or not, to break contact or hold ground, must be made in a split second.

Our patrol had a mixed history. Some of the guys had been tested under fire previously. Others had not. Due to the nature of training in the Regiment, you have a fairly good indication as to how a soldier will perform in battle, but until judgement day arrives nothing is guaranteed. I've seen soldiers who were expected to do well stumble, and others who were unlikely candidates for bravery awards display extraordinary courage. Our patrol looked good on paper, but would it be able to live up to these high expectations?

I felt confident about the team, thanks to the inclusion of one of my closest friends in the service. Kane, our patrol scout, was a highly skilled and respected operator with the strength and fitness of an Olympic athlete. At 28, he was exactly a year younger than me – we shared a birthday, 8 April – and since I'd met him, in the lead-up to the Timor operation, he'd become like a brother to me. He was also the toughest training partner I'd ever known. Alongside my family and Al, my best mate from school, I respect Kane more than any other person. He has stood beside me and covered my arse in situations where we both were severely vulnerable.

He was actually diagnosed with an abnormally large heart from the years of pushing himself. Our own Phar Lap was not one to shy away from a fight, and his passion for pushing the limits was often the subject of widespread awe. With his muscular and athletic frame and perpetually straight back, he was a walking advertisement for perfect posture.

Kane was the SAS pinnacle. He could outrun, outlift and outshoot nearly everyone he encountered. To the frustration of many, mainly me, he would effortlessly win the majority of troop pistol-shooting competitions and offer nothing more than a grin. No gobbing off, no self-glorifying praise. He knew he was good and that was all that mattered. Sometimes those who barely knew him mistook his quietness and single-mindedness for arrogance. Despite my competitive instincts, with Kane there was no jealousy, just deep admiration for his ability. If he beat me to the top of a sandhill or managed one more chin-up or an extra rep on the bench press, there was no angst. We had some epic battles over the years, but I didn't mind having my arse kicked by this guy. The prospect of fighting alongside him was inspiring.

Our patrol commander, whom we called 'the Boss', was also the troop commander. He was a natural leader and, like Hector in the Trojan War, had an air of nobility and an instinct for command. Like most of the troop, the Boss was incredibly fit. He had completed the Australian Ironman Triathlon at Forster–Tuncurry. A 3.8-kilometre swim, 180-kilometre ride and 42-kilometre run was his idea of a bit of escapism.

Although aged in his mid-twenties, the Boss carried himself with the maturity of a much older man. He was highly intelligent and possessed a rare trait for an officer: common sense! Officers may be outstanding at delivering a set of orders and planning complicated tasks, but if there was a member of a troop who would lose his facemask or a fin, or carry a pack that appeared to be organised by a five-year-old, it was usually the troop commander. Thank God, this guy was different. He came from quite the family of service over-achievers. His father was a former helicopter pilot and commanding officer of 5 Aviation Squadron, and his brother was an army medical doctor. The Boss was a caring man and would later prove himself under fire. An eloquent, dedicated man who could also fight: what a great combo!

Our patrol signaller, Grant – the oldest member of the team in his mid-thirties – had a background as a navy clearance diver. Grant was a relatively new addition to the troop, and his wry sense of humour and tireless work ethic were warmly welcomed. He'd also spent time as a member of the sniper troop and was well-trained in the technical tools of the trade. Put the man in front of patrol radios, observation devices or image capture and transfer equipment and he was in his element.

Known as 'a bit of a computer geek', Grant didn't possess the same demented drive for pushing himself as other patrol members. Despite this, his fitness was acceptable and he more than held his own when required. He also had the ability to offer a satirical comment at the most opportune moments. Grant was not overly concerned with personal looks, a fact made eminently clear when, during a brief sojourn on a vehicle-mounted patrol, he decided to trim his ginger-matted fringe with a pair of trauma scissors. He was amazingly proud of his repugnant new look and this self-inflicted barbarism lightened the mood.

Grant's closest mate in the group was arguably the most experienced amongst us. K-man held the rank of sergeant and had performed well on previous operations. There were only so many command positions, so on operations it was not unusual for senior members to be attached to a patrol to make up numbers. They generally took a back seat and left all administration to the team 2iC – in this case, me – but they would be available to offer advice during challenging operations. K-man was physically strong, aggressive and vociferous but also had a humorous side that could turn a lacklustre office meeting into a raging inferno of laughter. Grant and K-man became known as 'the Lion Brothers'. Even their scruffy beards grew in unison.

The final man in our patrol was Ry, who was posted to the troop only weeks before we commenced combat operations. Ry was a 'beret-qualified' corps signaller, indicating that he had passed the SAS selection course. He was a highly skilled communications specialist. On top of that, Ry was an intelligent man, like most from the signal corps, and an able soldier. The regular sabre squadron operators were generally a cut above when it came to soldiering skills, but Ry was well-suited to perform and support a range of roles.

Ry also had great taste in music. He often supplied the guys — mainly me — with quality tunes when we weren't on patrol. The others were particularly appreciative of this, because if I was listening to music then it meant that I wasn't trying to play it. Every chance I got, I borrowed the Boss's guitar. I had become obsessed with learning the Metallica classic 'Nothing Else Matters'.

Even Kane had a go at me: 'Look, dude, it's starting to sound pretty good, but for fuck's sake, can you *please* play something else?'

I wasn't one to acknowledge criticism and neglected to absorb the real meaning of his comment. I practised even harder. Always in denial, I still wonder why my stretcher was sometimes placed outside our sleeping quarters.

=

Many historians describe Afghanistan as the Soviet equivalent of the US foreign policy debacle in Vietnam. The Soviets established infrastructure — hospitals, schools, government buildings and roads – but this was brought undone by countless acts of barbarism. Soviet weapons, ammunition and equipment were left in abundance when their final troops withdrew on 2 February 1989. The greatest tragedy of the era was the estimated 5 to 7 million landmines that would lie dormant, sometimes for years, before breaking their silence with a limb-shredding roar.

When the news came that the first squadron deployed to Afghanistan had performed well, our patrol was ready and waiting to join them. Operation Anaconda had begun in March 2002. A US-led coalition battled against over 1000 well-entrenched al-Qaeda and Taliban forces in the Shahi-Kot Valley and Arma Mountains. For us in Brisbane, the frequent intelligence and country briefs had definitely lost their novelty.

Before we deployed, the commanding officer of the Regiment briefed our squadron. Although I can't recall exactly what he said, he did manage to grab everyone's attention: 'Men, I must be honest – operations in Afghanistan are dangerous. We expect casualties and there is a chance that some of you will be killed . . .'

His speech was strong and honest. He didn't hype things up or play them down. But we were confident in our ability and wanted nothing more than to deploy to Afghanistan and get out on patrol. At last our squadron got the call. It was our turn to join the action.

THREE

As usual, our initial rush of excitement and elation proved to be premature. After a couple of weeks in Kuwait, we boarded a C130 Hercules aircraft bound for Bagram Airbase in Afghanistan, pumped to finally be on our way. A five-month wait for someone who has never been known for his patience is an acute form of torture. Under the cover of darkness, the aircraft circled high above Bagram but severe weather conditions forced us to return to Oman in the Arabian peninsula.

I was like a child who, after a sleepless Christmas Eve, has been told that Santa's sleigh couldn't make it due to inclement weather. Suffice it to say, Corporal Patience was well and truly pissed off.

The following night we again boarded the aircraft and departed for Bagram. Several hours later, like a scene from *Groundhog Day*, we were once more circling the airfield. *Those pussies had better take us down this time*, I thought to myself. There was considerable shifting in seats and shuffling of feet as we watched the load masters busily walking up and down the aircraft. After what seemed like forever they turned to us, thumbs firmly up: 'We're going in!' they yelled. Finally, our time had arrived.

We exited via the rear ramp and were confronted with a night so cold that it stung our eyes and sucked away our breath. The air carried the thick, distinctive aroma of recent rain. There were no lights and we were herded off the runway to a tent to have our details recorded. It began to rain as we trudged towards the dank building that was to be our home for the next five months. The mud stuck to the soles of our boots like toffee in your teeth.

The squadron sergeant-major (SSM) gave us a quick brief on what to do in the event of an incident during the night and then told us to get some sleep. It was surreal. Who wanted to freaking sleep? We were in Afghanistan. There was plenty of time to sleep when we returned home. I found a piece of muddy carpet, pulled out my sleeping bag and shut my eyes. Sleep? No chance. Lying flat on my back with my eyes closed would have to be close enough.

=

We rose early the next morning but were not permitted to explore our surrounds. Bagram Airbase is located about 47 kilometres north-east of Kabul. It has a long history in serving the military and played a key role during the Soviet occupation of Afghanistan from 1980 to 1989. It's like a mini city in its own right, with many large hangars, a control tower and numerous support buildings to house equipment and thousands of soldiers. That morning, my first in Afghanistan, we assembled outside our sleeping quarters and took in the clear day and the cold, distant sun, which provided light but little warmth. A magnificent ring of snow-capped mountains framed the base to the north, east and south. The distant peaks radiated strength and beauty; their sheer size was imposing, while a blanket of snow softened the image. The contrast was breathtaking.

My attention shifted from the mountains back to the SSM, who had begun speaking. He informed us that we'd soon be deploying to the mountainous eastern region of Afghanistan. Our task was to establish an observation corridor to look for signs of enemy infiltration into the country. The SSM also provided a thorough orientation of our compound, with particular emphasis on the mined areas. Bagram was the most heavily mined location in Afghanistan. Tragically, most days a silent killer screamed to life and claimed another victim. Sometimes they were soldiers, but sometimes they were children. We paid extra attention to this warning as an SAS soldier from a previous rotation had stepped on a landmine. Can you imagine what he must have felt? Not the way any of us wanted to be sent home.

Establishing an observation corridor in Eastern Afghanistan sounded like a straightforward, if dangerous, mission. We were to fly from Bagram to Forward Operating Base (FOB) Khost, located approximately 150 kilometres southeast of Kabul and 100 kilometres from Gardez, in the Paktia province of Eastern Afghanistan. During initial assaults in Afghanistan, the Soviets had used Khost Airfield as a base for inserting troops into the combat zone. History was now repeating itself. Once we arrived in Khost, we would make final preparations before deploying into the mountains.

The aim of our operation was to move progressively closer to the Pakistan–Afghanistan border and gather intelligence. We were to log all 'pertinent' information and relay the intelligence to squadron HQ via high-frequency communications. As with many similar patrols, we knew in advance that there would be a lot of sitting around, minimal conversation, thirst, heat and food rationing. But if we'd wanted lives of comfort then we would have chosen different careers.

With the operation parameters made clear, there was no more waiting around. A British C130 Aircraft Special Forces crew were to provide our ride into south-eastern Afghanistan and by all accounts they were a highly proficient team. As a forward operating base, Khost Airfield regularly came under rocket and small-arms attack. This meant that, on arrival, we would have to unload swiftly so the plane could slip away into the relative safety of the moonless night. Seatbelts were left unclasped and we sat silently in our blacked-out aircraft as it felt its way through the rugged valleys. It was a flawless piece of flying, low and fast, gliding across the terrain with the confidence of an eagle searching for prey. At touchdown the ground staff moved about with an air of urgency. Chains were removed and vehicles rolled onto the airfield under the protection of darkness. Within seconds the aircraft roared down the blackened runway and launched back into the night.

On the ground we kept noise to a minimum, a task made easier by the use of night-vision goggles (NVGs). After positioning our vehicles, the Boss delivered a brief set of orders covering 'actions on' – these included which bunker to run to should we come under indirect fire attack. We then found a place to sleep. It was like a scene from a Hollywood movie, but without the directors, actors or the ability to call 'cut' if things didn't go according to plan. Together yet alone, we lay listening to the unfamiliar night sounds, grateful that the blanket of darkness was masking our apprehension about what lay ahead.

FOUR

We were now a long way from Brisbane, Kuwait and Bagram Airbase. After months of waiting, we had finally arrived in the wild frontier of Eastern Afghanistan. We were fit, alert and excited, like a team of salivating greyhounds before an evening meet. That little hare didn't stand a chance. One of the better vehicle-mounted patrols in the squadron was responsible for our insertion. It was also filled with some of our closest friends. As we squeezed into the patrol vehicles, I looked around with a sense of contentment. It didn't get much better than this.

The vehicles wove their way along the tracks, while on the horizon, lightning and tracer fire could be seen. In the evening light the rugged beauty of Afghanistan was somewhat masked, but the jagged, barren countryside still gleamed with contrasting shapes and colours. Darkness made the distant mountains even more imposing; masses of muscled granite lined the road ahead – shoulder to shoulder, like the All Blacks glaring down at those with the gall to approach them. The lightning may have been the mountain's version of a haka.

Not a single word was spoken and all that could be heard were the gentle rumblings of the engines. The crisp breeze forced us deep into our Goretex jackets, but I'm not sure if the occasional shiver was from the cold or excitement. As is common on night operations, most of the men retreated into their own thoughts. By night, whether preparing to enter the water on a midnight dive or leap from the back of a blackened aircraft, there is rarely bravado, no idle chatter, no emotion. Our training and our basic instincts left us locked in separate worlds of deep concentration, ready to instantly snap back to life the moment the task began. Operations provided a smorgasbord of adrenaline shots, and I already knew how addictive I found them. I liked not knowing what danger lay moments away. I liked the pounding inside my chest.

The insertion took longer than expected and we reached our drop-off point with just one hour remaining before first light. There was no time to waste. A series of handshakes and slaps on the shoulders saw our patrol and the mobility guys part company. Without hesitation, we stumbled into the darkness and began to make our way up the rocky incline. A couple of minutes later the gentle rumblings of the vehicles had faded. We were alone. We were racing the night. We could see our security blanket being peeled across the sky as we desperately attempted to gain altitude and find a place to hide.

≡

Each man was weighed down by over 60 kilograms of equipment. The load was made even heavier by the severity of the gradient, not to mention all the unstable broken rock underfoot. NVGs were both beneficial and a hindrance. As useful as they were, they inevitably fogged up as the cold breeze met the steam and sweat that our exertion produced. Fresh no longer, our lower limbs, backs and shoulders were heaving with fatigue, yet despite the pain, for some of us this was pure ecstasy. A vigorous workout in treacherous conditions? The possibility of the distinctive crack of rifle fire as we cleared the summit? What more could we ask for? This was the definition of exhilaration.

But things didn't run quite as smoothly as they had in Timor. No sooner had we reached our destination and begun to settle in to our OP than a couple of young boys and a dozen grazing cattle meandered up a track to within 50 metres of our position. Something about our desert-pattern fatigues gave the game away; possibly the white glow of the uniforms against the lush green background of the local vegetation. The area, usually dry and barren, had received recent rain. We were as noticeable as someone at a funeral in a white tuxedo. The youths promptly ran in the direction of their village to raise the alarm. Great! While the engine noise and movement may have alerted the villagers to our presence, they now had confirmation.

Even the most adventurous adrenaline junkie feels a little nauseous in the moments after a patrol compromise. The anticipation, the fear of the unknown, can destroy a soldier. It was possible that we could soon be fighting dozens, even hundreds, of Taliban. When things go bad it is essential to think clearly, as to make a poor decision, to lose one's nerve, can be fatal. I remember glancing at my light machine gun and feeling confident in myself – the same type of confidence that I had observed in G back in Timor.

We were well-trained, well-armed and motivated to keep on living. If we were to be overrun, then we would make it as difficult and costly for the enemy as possible.

The Boss immediately conferred with the patrol and we decided to carry out standard deceptive procedures, feigning a move in one direction before looping back to a more elevated position on the same part of the slope. We located a shallow ridge on the side of the mountain that offered excellent fields of view and limited protection. We now had a perfect vantage point, so we kept ourselves amused watching the villagers scour the slopes below for signs of an Australian SAS patrol that appeared to have vanished.

Village life in Afghanistan is a tough existence. The country has been ravaged by decades of war, and these experiences are etched into its people's bodies. The men are heavily bearded, hard-eyed and lean. The leathery creases on their faces speak of lives of hardship; not just the indelible legacy of their torn past but also the wearing pressures of an exacting climate. Their strong, calloused hands indicate that they are no strangers to rigorous physical work.

Inadequate nourishment has left Afghani children undersized, and their eyes suggest that their innocence has been torn from them far too early in life. The trademark cheeky grin of well-fed Western children is infrequent. These children stare back at us with an air of vagueness and distance that unsettles even the most hardened soldier. Perhaps detachment provides the only peace from their constantly hungry bellies, from bodies overrun by parasites. Their mothers and sisters were inevitably denied access to education, ostracised from the public sphere and otherwise oppressed under the Taliban. We rarely saw women without full body coverings. In the time we spent monitoring the local population, one observation came up again and again: living in a remote Afghan village is a gruelling existence.

=

For the next two days we remained in the OP undetected. The days were stifling. The weather had shifted from the chill of our arrival in Afghanistan; nestled amongst the rocks, we found no solace from the sun's brutal rays. We were hoping to remain secure in our reconnaissance for at least 10 days before requiring resupply, and this could only be achieved by extreme rationing of our water supplies. Trying to survive on 800 millilitres per day when staying largely immobile and exposed to the elements left the patrol severely dehydrated.

Before long we were no longer able to urinate. Attempts to sleep did nothing to ease the torturous thirst. Our night demons became water sprites and giant sprinklers running amok in the parched desert. There was no respite and even our daytime thoughts came to be dominated by visions of guzzling water. A couple of mouthfuls of our carefully rationed supply would provide moments of delightful relief. Who would have thought there were such pleasures in drinking hot water from a bottle that had spent hours baking in the sun?

Each patrol member had been tested many times before, in the ordeals of SAS selection if nowhere else, and as a group we were resilient, but there are no training manuals describing how to cope with the experience of severe thirst. In just days, our faces began to age and wrinkle as the water drained from our skin. We were left with a tired, creased appearance, our eyes glazed, like an elderly dog's. Coupled with a lack of proper sleep, it's fair to say that foot patrols in the mountains of Afghanistan were challenging.

But the hardship did not detract from our patrol's ability to observe and record information. Each man ignored the pain and covered his arc of responsibility as diligently as the day before. Thirst is one thing, but a rogue bullet ripping through one's stomach is another. Patrol security remains first and foremost even in the most uncomfortable circumstances.

Despite our thirst and massive loads, our patrol was looking forward to being on the move again. We were to advance several kilometres towards the Pakistan border. After last light we wound our way down from the position that had been our home for two long days. Walking down a mountain at night with over 60 kilograms on your back is even less fun than walking up it. Each man managed accidentally to create moments of amusement for the rest of the patrol by losing his footing and toppling a metre or two into an array of jagged rocks. We all became familiar with the unstable surface and its stony traps. The sporadic groans of bruised bodies would bring a smile to the faces of those who were still upright, but the satisfaction was short-lived. Every man suffered the embarrassment of these painful stumbles.

Once at the bottom, we crept carefully along a river before finding a small stream of running water. This seemed too good to be true. After drinking our fill and replenishing our water supplies it was now time to ascend another mountain. With our freshly quenched thirst and swollen bellies sloshing with litres of cool water we felt unreasonably optimistic. How hard could it be? The slope didn't look too daunting from where we stood and Grant claimed that there was only 500 metres to go.

But looks can be deceiving. Grant's calculations didn't take into consideration the evil number of contour lines that might have given some clue of how ghastly the climb really was. Within 30 metres we were struggling: panting and heaving like a pack of hunting dogs. Another two hours had passed before we reached the summit. As I crouched at the top, letting my breath return and my heart rate slow once more, Kane approached me and shook my hand.

'Well done, gangster,' he said. 'That was one bad-ass climb.'

I grinned. 'Thanks, bro,' I replied. 'But why in the hell do you still look so bloody fresh?'

I thought I had coped well but in Kane I saw a man who had thrived on the challenge of the climb, in spite of its brutality. He was an excellent choice for lead scout, as he was composed, sharp and still able to operate.

Others in the patrol hadn't fared so well. During the climb there were several redistributions of stores as some of the guys were virtually unable to go on with the combination of their heavy loads and the severity of the climb. Our preparation back in Brisbane seemed painless in comparison. Those of us with a passion for training had pulled up okay, relieved to still be coherent and physically (and mentally) capable of facing any action. We knew we were in the badlands and would rarely, if ever, get a clearer example of how our dedication to training back in Australia was connected to our own survival. Adrenaline will only carry a soldier so far. Maintaining a high level of fitness at all times was about more than obsessiveness and drive. Our lives depended on it.

Although some members of the patrol had struggled more than others, the hike had been lightened by hushed banter. At one point Grant seemed like he might pass out, only to pipe up and ask, 'Do you think army pants make my bum look big?' I nearly laughed out loud.

Once atop the mountain, we established a piquet and changed out of our soaking wet clothes before drifting off to sleep. Sleep on patrol is cherished, and usually interrupted. We managed to grab three hours before the security piquet gently woke us just prior to first light. The disorientation and nausea associated with being woken for your turn on sentry is without doubt the lowest point of a patrol day. No-one gets excited about sentry duty, but there is no point in complaining – it is part and parcel of patrol security. It is better to suffer the burden of a little sleep deprivation than run the risk of a never-ending siesta, compliments of a lead sleeping pill fired into the side of your brain.

That morning it was essential that the OP be established before the villagers began to stir. We did not want any accidental detection this time around. Unfortunately, in an area so densely populated, Lady Luck didn't appear to be by our side. It was not long before the distinctive sound of goats could be heard coming in our direction. I looked up to see an elderly woman traversing the top of the mountain. She was dressed in a dark local dress but her face was completely exposed.

Her pace was slow and her eyes downcast, as if she were depressed. She hadn't seen us yet. As we sat stock-still, her tired eyes lazily scanned the hill in our direction. We were close, perhaps only three metres away from her, and I could see right into her hollow stare. In those dark eyes I thought I could see years of struggle, the flickers of deep grief and weariness.

Time froze. So did we. For a brief second even our breathing ceased and the only movement came from our hammering hearts. Surely she would focus and see what was ahead of her at any moment. Surely we were compromised – again. But, with a sigh, the woman turned her head and her hunched shoulders to continue on her unhappy journey, utterly lost in her thoughts. This time our camouflage had been more effective. With a collective but unspoken feeling of relief, we went on with our task.

FIVE

We now had approximately two days' rations remaining but – in one of the perennial frustrations of operations – had to conserve our supplies to last an additional four to five days. Breakfast consisted of two dry biscuits smeared with peanut butter. There was no room for luxuries as our packs were already overflowing with necessities. The list was as straightforward as it was heavy:

- 16 litres of water (minimum)
- seven days' worth of rations
- lightweight sleeping equipment
- warm and wet-weather clothing
- personal medical kits and radios
- batteries
- ammunition
- grenades
- signalling equipment
- camouflage nets
- optical viewing devices
- night-vision goggles
- helmets
- survival kits

This didn't include the equipment carried as part of the patrol stores: a further supply of patrol and satellite radio sets, advanced trauma medical kits, intravenous fluids, Claymore mines and task-specific equipment. Generally, the bigger the pack, the more that you'd pile into it. Our patrol attempted to limit our total weight to no more than 65 kilograms per man. Anything more would prove counter-productive and result in excessive water consumption. Where's a good donkey when you need one?

Setting up a patrol base and then staying there for days on end bears no resemblance to the glamorised Hollywood version of war. Those in the OP have to remain alert, constantly gathering information and maintaining security. The other patrol members have plenty of time to reflect or drift off. The quality of one's journey is dependent on the strength of one's imagination. There is very little conversation as noise must always be kept to a minimum. Some men write in small notepads. Others just sit back and contemplate life.

I had discovered years earlier that I liked to write poetry, finding in the structure of these little creations a calm, secure way to order my thoughts and channel my emotional responses. I would sit scribbling away, quite content to write about the experience of being on operations, about my family back home, about the dreams and fears that drove me.

Whenever we got back to base, we would inevitably talk in depth about what had occupied our minds over those silent days. Some members spoke of daydreaming about home, others about their families, their childhood, food or travel. Each man had his own recurring themes.

Depending on the intensity or length of the trip there was another topic that always came to mind: sex. The sexual torment of a lengthy trip could prove almost unbearable. 'Be thirsty, hungry, fatigued and sexless' – not the kind of things that you would highlight in a recruitment program!

=

If writing didn't alleviate the boredom (or satisfy the itch), then we looked to the locals to provide unwitting moments of hilarity. Such moments were so rare that even sleeping patrol members would be woken if something entertaining was afoot. Early one morning we noticed a young Afghani male escorting two donkeys up a track about 300 metres from our position. He met another youth who looked about 15, handed over one of the donkeys and then headed back down the track. All fairly unremarkable until, with a furtive glance, the first youth pushed up a creek and stopped in a shadowy spot mostly hidden from view. From our vantage point he was still visible, however, and with the help of a 60x zoom scope I was able to trace his movement. The view that greeted me was unmistakable.

It was like something out of a cheap porn movie. Now we knew where all the donkeys were! I quickly let the others see what was going on and, more than a little horrified, we gathered around the scope to watch the action. Despite our moral outrage we were elated to have something interesting to observe. As I said, we were bored and no patrol member, no matter how righteous, was ever going to pass up the opportunity to view this surreal live sex show. As word passed around the entire patrol, there was a rapid reallocation of all the viewing equipment.

It was now very obvious that this 15-year-old kid considered himself to be the Afghan equivalent of Hugh Hefner: his steadying hand on his arse as he enjoyed quality time with his ass was quite a nice touch. We were mesmerised by the show and were somewhat tempted to fire a couple of warning shots in the youth's direction to scare him or at least save the donkey's reputation. But we remained controlled and let him finish his business. We were divided when it came to scoring his performance. Choreography, originality and backdrop scored highly but a lack of hygiene and excessive brutality did detract from the overall score. He didn't score a perfect 10. From that moment on we would cringe whenever a donkey could be heard belching in the distance.

Eventful distractions weren't always so trivial. Later that same afternoon, the appearance of a red tractor further down the hill caught our attention. The tractor, a trailer in tow, appeared to be carrying only a light load of thatch. Despite this seemingly insubstantial load, the trailer was oddly close to the ground, and the tractor was struggling to climb only a slight hill. There were also four men trailing the tractor, adding to our suspicions that something was not quite right. We reported the event immediately and later learned that the US military had been very close to targetting the tractor with an air-strike. It trundled away up the hill unawares.

At another point, a stray goat wandered from its herd and walked straight through the middle of our OP. Goats are an essential component of village life. They provide milk and meat for the villagers and are integral to sustaining life in this harsh environment. A young goatherd will spot a missing goat within seconds. He simply cannot afford not to. Knowing this, our patrol became edgy when the goat skipped close by. Freaking rogue goats. Where there were goats, it was guaranteed there would be little rock-wielding boys not too far behind. Our anxieties proved correct.

A ragged little boy aged no more than 12 came stumbling across the rocks. He was watching his footing and so came to within four metres of our patrol before looking up into the gaze of six grubby white men with weapons poised. Thank God he didn't have a heart condition. He recovered quickly from his frozen terror and sped off like a hare running for its life. We saw him waste no time in joining his friends and excitedly sharing what he had just seen. The three boys then split and ran to several villages to spread the word.

We were utterly compromised. It was time to move or dominate. Attempting to vanish off the side of such a prominent feature would see our patrol left extremely vulnerable, so it was decided to secure the high ground, establish radio communications with squadron HQ and wait.

We were confident that it would take a sizeable or lucky force to overrun our patrol; we were spread along a ridgeline that offered commanding fields of fire. But our course of action was not without its anxieties. We had six hours to wait it out before we could escape into the valleys of darkness. Early in the afternoon a curious contingent of villagers came to investigate. Our proficiency in Pashtu was equally as poor as the villagers' grasp of English, so communication was pretty much non-existent. We were scrutinised from a distance, but all we could do was hope they would get bored and leave. The villagers were obviously experienced and decided to descend the mountain before darkness engulfed the rugged slopes. We had little choice but to wait for nightfall before resuming our downhill acrobatics.

We scaled several ridgelines as we continued towards the border. The strain of seven hours of walking in trying conditions resulted in all of us consuming far more water than anticipated. Each patrol member now had only four to six litres remaining. If the patrol's resupply was delayed then there would be a couple of very thirsty days ahead. We snatched four hours of sleep before once again going through the ritual of attempting to find a suitable place to hide.

It was Anzac Day, and the Boss had thoughtfully packed a hip flask of rum to celebrate. The alcohol stung our cracked lips and parched mouths but it was a nice touch and enabled us to pay our respects to those generations of soldiers who had come before us. We all knew that their experiences – the carnage of the Somme, or the malaria and dysentery that plagued the Kokoda Trail – made our trip look like a holiday.

The Boss decided to split the patrol during the day, since the most suitable position for observing the primary border track would only accommodate two people. That meant that the remainder of the patrol would remain concealed 100 metres further back, receiving communications via handheld radios. Once the OP was set, there would be only one relief in place, as any movement during daylight would greatly increase the chances of further compromise.

In the middle of the afternoon we observed two thickset men walking towards the Pakistan border. The duo was about 1300 metres from the OP, but my swift-zoom enabled me to establish that they were notably different from the villagers in the area. They were tall and strong in stature and appeared to be Arabic. While they had no visible weapons, one of the men was holding his arm peculiarly still. Upon further examination a magazine was seen protruding from under his arm, which then moved to reveal an AK-47 gleaming proudly in the sun. It took another two minutes of observation to locate the second man's weapon, slung underneath a black duffel bag. The men were attempting to conceal their weapons, and the way they dragged their feet along the track suggested they had been walking a considerable distance. We held our position and watched them pass without incident.

There were many shepherds tending to their herds on the lower slopes throughout the afternoon but our patrol remained undetected. Being a shepherd seemed to be a complex life: they didn't just rise in the morning, grab their goats and amiably follow them around for the next 10 hours. Afghanistan is an inhospitable landscape with limited resources. The shepherds would strategically cover different slopes on alternating days. No area would be overgrazed and no pasture, no matter how high or difficult to get to, would be left untouched. This is why remaining undetected was such a difficult feat to achieve.

With our water and rations now almost gone, we had no choice but to contact the base for a rotary-wing resupply, thus greatly increasing the possibility of yet another compromise. We sent the request through and settled down to wait.

SIX

After last light we departed for a small volcano-like feature that appeared suitable for accommodating a Chinook resupply helicopter (or helo). The aircraft arrived 45 minutes early and we identified our location with infra-red strobes. After circling our position, the helo dropped its rear ramp on the side of the mountain to allow our patrol to offload supplies, which included 140 litres of water, 14 days of rations for each man and spare radio batteries. Within two minutes the helo was thundering into the valley below, and within three there was nothing but silence.

We knew this was a vulnerable time for our patrol. The local villagers and any potential enemies would now be aware that something had taken place. The night was as dark as a murderer's soul. For 15 tense minutes we hugged the stony earth and listened. Then, working in pairs, we each took turns filling water bottles before strapping ration-filled sandbags and empty jerry cans to the outside of our bursting packs. Finally, as an emergency supply, we cached 40 litres of water (two jerry cans) underground.

With each man now carrying in excess of 70 kilograms, it was time to move — what fun this would be! Just standing up required another man's assistance. The enthusiasm that had accompanied previous night marches was now well and truly dissipated; this was nothing more than a punishing five-hour grind. One comfort was the fact that we were now traversing a series of ridgelines; although most of the movement was uphill, it was nowhere near the severity of previous gradients.

We heaved our murderous packs throughout the night. Shoulder aches soon dissolved from sheer numbness caused by lack of circulation. Thighs and lower backs quivered increasingly, straining at and strained by our debilitating burdens. Our energy levels were low — we had not eaten a significant meal in nearly 48 hours. We were running on empty but somehow managed to keep going. Some of the patrol members who had struggled earlier clearly found this one just as torturous. But, to their tenacious credit, they still managed to crack the odd joke on the few occasions they were able to gather enough oxygen.

We marched for most of the night and then spent 40 minutes reorganising our rations and packs before snatching two hours of sleep. It felt like only five minutes after crawling into our sleeping bags that we had to move again, but with daylight approaching it was time to face a new day. As the darkness dissolved around us, it became evident that there were half a dozen artificial caves 480 metres south of our position. The openings were significant; it was well worth monitoring the area to ascertain whether they were occupied.

Suitable locations to remain concealed were limited, so we were forced to spend the day balancing on a rocky crag. Having your legs pulled up beside your body with no ability to stretch out bordered on complete hell. This was easily our most uncomfortable day. We set up palm fronds to help camouflage our precarious position. A yodelling shepherd and his herd of 30 goats walked within 40 metres of the OP that morning, and in the afternoon a hunter with an old .303 bolt-action rifle draped over his shoulder had come a tad closer. Clinging to the side of a rock ledge in the scorching sun was as much fun as resistance-to-interrogation (RTI) training. I'm sure every man would have gladly suffered a swift kick to the groin for the chance to stretch out and end this aching balancing act.

The sinking sun, exhausted from a day of incessant illumination, was just about to knock off as it kissed the western ridgeline goodnight. This was a welcome relief and an indication that it would not be long before we could establish a piquet and find somewhere to retire for the night. A more comfortable OP and patrol base would finally allow us to stretch out our legs. The valley was teeming with shepherds. Surely our good fortune was not going to last.

Just before nightfall, a shepherd who was running down the mountain in a race against the fading light came face-to-face with Ry in the OP. The rest of us held back and listened cautiously. A short conversation ensued; the shepherd must have been surprised to see one man lying in a hide on his own with observation equipment. The remainder of the patrol remained concealed and the anxious shepherd left. Regardless of the compromise, we still had a job to do. Our mission was to continue towards the border, a further five kilometres east of our current position, to reconnoitre a significant cave complex.

Within hours the sun had disappeared completely, leaving the darkest of nights. There was no ambient light at all, as the lazy moon seemed to be having a sleep-in, and descending into the valley was always going to be a dangerous move. The contour lines on the map appeared to be smeared together, such was the drastic drop in elevation. A heavily laden hike down a mountain, a surface of loose stones and boulders, and a landscape shrouded in total darkness: what a recipe for disaster!

We were stumbling blindly into the murky depths of the valley below. Each step was taken with more dread than the last. Countless times my foot would roll off the side of a rock and I'd be faced by the split-second realisation that it was time to pay my respects to the mountain with an agonising stumble, scrape or slide. For 90 minutes we wove our way down the side of the mountain with the elegance of charging elephants. We may have had aching backs and bruised bodies, but this had now become a personal struggle: us versus the mountain. Our mental fortitude was pitted against the unforgiving and emotionless feature, and if something were to break it would have to be one of our bodies. Never our minds. Unfortunately, that would prove to be correct.

Just as we entered a creek at the base of the mountain, finally feeling that we had conquered this most inhospitable landscape, the sickening sound of a body and rifle smashing into river-rock reverberated through the darkness. Ry had taken a severe fall and this time there was no thought of laughing: his distinctive grimace indicated that this was serious. In addition to my 2iC responsibilities, I was also the patrol medic, so the patrol was immediately placed in all-round defence while I assessed his injuries.

Ry had damaged his ankle badly and was unable to bear weight. Rolling one's ankle on the football field or when jogging is painful enough; throw more than 65 kilograms onto a man's back and the damage can be greatly increased. We had all been there.

Ry's ankle immediately became warm and swollen as fluid poured into the joint; discolouration would come later. I took some comfort from the fact that he didn't appear to have broken a bone. What I was concerned with now was patrol security. All mission-essential stores were removed from Ry's pack and the majority of his water was redistributed amongst the other patrol members. I then applied a compression bandage to the injured joint. This was a common injury, so the bandaging was almost second nature, even in the dark shadows of a lifeless creek.

While I treated Ry's injury, the Boss and Kane located a place to hide – an elevated position that was protected by considerable vegetation. With an injured man who would not be able to move anywhere in a hurry, we knew that if we were confronted by an enemy force we would have to stand and deliver. Concealment was now our best form of defence. We had been rendered vulnerable and immobile.

We requested a casualty evacuation but due to our close proximity to the Pakistan border it was rejected. Such procedures were only available for troops who were in enemy contact. It would have to be Plan B: assist Ry back up the mountain and rendezvous (RV) with a vehicle-mounted patrol. This would allow our patrol to extract Ry and resupply again before continuing with our task. An RV was arranged for the early hours of the following morning.

We departed just before last light. There was a lot of debate as to what would be the best way to reach the ridgeline above, but a work team in the centre of the patrol seemed most efficient. Ry was stripped of everything except his web belt and weapon. Two patrol members would either drag Ry's pack between them or they would take turns carrying two packs – their own on their back and the other on their front. Whenever a patrol member carried two packs he would be escorted by another member who would carry both their rifles. Security was always maintained at the front and rear of the patrol and the majority of the gut-wrenching effort was carried out in the middle.

The patrol really lifted during the move and no-one was working harder than the bustling team in the centre, a role that was rotated amongst the non-injured five. After several hours we reached a trail that traversed the ridge leading to the RV. Ry was struggling to keep going and attempts were made to carry him during the less elevated stretches of the journey. We soon realised that this achieved little more than destroying the back of the man who was attempting the murderous lift.

Towards the end of the march, one of the guys placed Ry's pack on a rock ledge while having a breather. We all glanced at the pack, noticing its precarious position, but due to our fatigue we all thought, *She'll be right*. We were taking our time to regain our breath when, out of the corner of our eyes, we saw the pack begin to tilt and then roll. In a moment it was gone.

As if it were excited to have some newfound freedom, the pack rapidly gained momentum down the ravine.

With mouths wide open, we all looked on in horror. The sounds of the tearaway pack grew fainter and fainter but did not abate, and the rolling appeared to continue on and on and on. The cheeky pack finally settled at the very bottom of the re-entrant. 'Fuck,' the Boss exclaimed. What more was there to say? Kane and the Boss began the descent to retrieve the pack while we showed our sympathy by laughing.

We were reunited an hour later and immediately continued towards the RV. We observed the area from a distance for several hours before the vehicle-mounted patrol arrived. The patrol marry-up was initiated via hand-held communications after we had established a secure perimeter. After 10 days by ourselves, it was great to see the smart-arse faces of the VM guys, who were a great crew and could definitely be relied upon in a time of need. Still, whispers were kept to a minimum as we boosted Ry onto one of the vehicles. Our reconfigured team of five quickly resupplied our water bottles and disappeared back into the darkness.

Although we were now one man down, I was still confident that, should we contact the enemy, our incessant training and ability to shoot straight would keep us alive.

I have never been a gun nut. In all honesty, firing a weapon has never really excited me. During my time in the SAS, I spent countless hours improving my marksmanship skills not because it gave me great enjoyment but because, as a soldier, they were skills that could well save my life. I also hated not being the best at something. The hard work did pay dividends, and although I usually struggled to outshoot Kane, which wasn't through a lack of trying, my time on the range firing tens of thousands of rounds into targets was to prove invaluable in combat.

I vividly recall the first time I fired a weapon. At the time I had no concern for the furry little rabbit that I planned to blow away. I was more consumed with the awareness that to miss from a range of less than 10 metres would be somewhat embarrassing. I was 17 and accompanying my girlfriend (now wife) to a family property in New South Wales. My brother-in-law Ian, a man 16 years my senior, had asked me to go shooting. I said yes and I'm sure I appeared genuinely enthused, but after 30 minutes of driving around the scrub in a beat-up four-wheel drive looking for vermin, I was getting pretty bored. Just as the sounds of outback radio drove me to within an inch of insanity, Ian spotted a rabbit.

Thank fuck for that, I thought. Not because I lusted over sending that furry little bastard to the big warren in the sky, but because it was an opportunity for me to escape the heat of the car and the monotony of that music.

I grabbed the rifle, and although Ian told me to fire a shot through the open window, I jumped out of the car. After much fumbling around I managed to cock the weapon, a bolt-action rifle, and slide a round into the chamber.

I first moved to the other side of the car, where I could rest my elbows on the bonnet. Although this provided me with a stable platform to fire from, I reckoned that the additional three metres would severely erode my chances of success. So I moved to the front of the vehicle, pulled the rifle up to my shoulder, held my breath, and attempted to line up the target with my front and rear sights.

After a minute or two of stuffing around I was perplexed – why wasn't I able to maintain my sights on the rabbit? I wasn't frightened but for some reason my rifle was shaking wildly. I didn't realise that my Hulk-like strangling of the weapon was the cause of my unsteadiness. I decided that I must be too far away so I crept several metres closer. It's fair to say that Bugs was an excellent sport for not running away. I was now only about five metres and one trigger-pull away from glory, but I still had trouble locking on to the target.

The longer I waited, the more pressure I put on myself to make the shot, the tighter I squeezed the weapon and the more my sights rocked and rolled. I decided to steady myself against a tree, although it was another metre or two further away.

After several minutes a voice bellowed at me from the vehicle: 'Just shoot the thing! Are you waiting for the bastard to run away?'

Fearing failure, I gritted my teeth, snarled and snatched the shot. The firing pin sprung forward, striking the percussion cap on the base of the round, which in turn ignited the propellant behind the bullet. The bullet accelerated as it rotated to the right and spiralled out of the barrel, gaining momentum. The round cut through the air and hit the dusty earth moments before the rabbit would have heard the shot.

Flinching from the recoil and sound of the weapon, it was a moment before I opened my eyes and scanned the scene ahead nervously for success. There was none. To my complete and utter horror, I saw the rabbit darting through the bush while a roar of laughter crash-tackled me from behind. I could make no reply.

I uncocked the rifle and got back in the car. Ian was one of the most patient and laid-back guys in the world. I'm sure that his heart only beats because it is an involuntary action that he cannot control. Sporting a smirk that made me furious, he asked if I was ready to head back to the house. My reply was characteristic: 'We are going to stay out here until I learn to shoot straight.'

Ian gave me a few tips and allowed me to stand on the rear tray as we searched for rabbits and kangaroos. The roos were in abundance and had taken a fancy to the crops, so Ian was happy for me to have a crack at them. I didn't care about the crops; I didn't care about the roos either. All I gave a damn about was restoring my pride.

And then my chance came. A large red roo stood proudly

at the base of a small hill. I listened to Ian's instructions carefully before propping my elbows on the roof and aligning my sights. This time I felt steady and pulled the trigger with a greater level of determination and confidence. The bullet burst out of the weapon and struck the roo in the middle of the chest with a tremendous thud. Not content with this, I nailed another two roos that afternoon.

Later that night I reflected on the fact that I had killed three animals. It didn't sit well. The roos were destroying the livelihood of the local farmers, so I had no problems with pulling the trigger, but to kill for fun made no sense to me. I'd rather go for a surf.

Many years later, in the final weeks prior to our deployment to Afghanistan, our troop was carrying out a live-fire practice on a rifle range outside Brisbane. We had completed several live-fire serials when a large kangaroo hopped onto the range. At a range of 150 metres, we were initially excited to have a live target, so half a dozen of us began to fire at the fleeing marsupial. I saw rounds striking the ground around the animal before it bounded onto the road and fell. Then it limped into the bush.

A sick feeling enveloped my stomach. I halted the range practice and ran down the road, where I followed the blood trail for 30 metres into the bush. At last I came across the wounded animal. The kangaroo's left paw was shattered and it had also been shot through the right thigh. Without hesitating, I approached the animal, lowered my rifle and shot it in the head.

While walking out of the bush I met Kane, who asked if I had put the roo out of its misery. I nodded. He could see how much it unsettled me, and I felt the need to explain: 'Hey, bro

– two minutes ago that roo was very much alive and now it's dead. Its life was ended for no good reason at all.'

Kane agreed. 'What's the point in killing something that can't fight back?'

At that moment I made a decision that, unless a situation demanded it, I would never shoot an animal again. Engaging enemy troops in combat was one thing. I'd reflected about the death of the Timorese militiaman, but I wouldn't hesitate to go out and do the same thing again. I've thought long and hard about why this is so. Why does the slaying of an animal disturb me, yet taking an adversary's life, a human life, affects me less?

In the end, it comes down to choices. The enemy combatant has made his own choices. The kangaroo and the rabbit have not. If I were to take a bullet on the hills of Afghanistan, far from home and those I love, it'd be because of a choice I made.

SEVEN

We had a couple of options for how to proceed as a smaller patrol. We could head back down the mountain towards the border and spend another fruitless day in a creek before continuing on our way the following evening. Alternatively, we could stay where we were and locate a position from which to observe the nearby villages. None of us had forgotten the two armed men we had seen several days previously. Keeping an eye out for them seemed like it might be a better use of our time.

There were only two hours of darkness remaining, so we decided to gain some altitude and see if anything was going on in this area. Our party of five moved onto the forward slope and located an adequate OP position in the middle of a cluster of small palms and bushes. We collected additional vegetation to provide us with a greater depth of cover. Having established the OP by first light, those of us who were not required were able to grab some much-needed rest. Our decision to stay put was to pay dividends, and quickly.

At 07:50 I identified four armed men standing at an intersection on the track below. They were too low to observe with the swift-zoom but it was not long before they began moving along the track. From the OP we could use the optics and examine the four suspects closely. One of the men was of athletic build, square-jawed and possibly an Arab. He stood with his shoulders pulled back, oozing confidence as he brandished his RPD 7.62-millimetre machine gun and 150-round drum magazine. He was an impressive individual, dressed in brown fatigues and a Russian-style webbing vest – a far cry from the average lean Afghani farmers we had been observing. The other three men were armed with AK-47 assault rifles and were also wearing webbing vests. There was no time to report the information back to base as the men were heading along a track that wound its way back towards the border.

The Boss quickly commanded Grant, the patrol sniper, to initiate contact. I was to follow with my Para Minimi – a 5.56-millimetre light machine gun with a high rate of fire and 150-round pouch attached. The patrol M4 assault rifles – 5.56-millimetre modular rifle system – would supplement the attack, despite the fact that they would be far less effective due to the distances involved. While Grant was moving into position, I took the time to lightly oil the bolt of the machine gun to decrease the risk of the weapon jamming.

Kane, aided by a laser range-finder, reported the distance of the targets to us at regular intervals. Tension was beginning to build. In a sense, this was 'the calm before the storm'. The hard treks of the previous days had affected the accuracy of Grant's sniper rifle, so caution and preparation were vital. As Kane gave the enemy's last range as 740 metres, Grant checked his breathing and squeezed off a round in the direction of our intended targets. It missed.

The four men turned around just as I released a 15-round burst from my Para Minimi. The rounds thumped slightly low and left of the enemy but flicked up into the man carrying the RPD machine gun, who staggered and fell backwards near a small palm tree. The enemy were on the crest of a small rise and quickly disappeared from view. Within seconds bullets were being returned from the thickets to the right side of the track. Grant began to adjust his fall of shot while I plunged 10- to 15-round bursts into the area.

With that, the sleepy, seemingly innocent valley was awake and boiling with aggression. The Boss was dynamic and quickly moved to establish the tactical satellite communications to report the incident and request air support. We were all very, very aware that a rapid-reaction force would take at least two hours to reach our position. I continued to pour long bursts of automatic fire into the crest of the small knoll 700 metres in front of us. There was now little chance of hitting anyone, but this strategy meant that the enemy would be unable to return fire.

I don't recall the enemy RPD machine gun kicking into life, and the roar of our weapons reverberating through the valley and bouncing back up the mountain made it impossible to be certain. Within minutes, however, we began to receive increasingly accurate fire from three separate locations. Grant concentrated on the initial contact site and managed to successfully adjust his fire and subdue another combatant atop a small knoll to the right of the initial contact location.

I scanned the terrain with a pair of binoculars and fired the odd burst of automatic fire. We were taking fire not just from these guys on the track, but also from a small village to our direct front. I was focusing on the initial contact area and on a couple of huts to our left. But there was also movement further along the ridge to my extreme left. Two men would pop up and yell directions to those down the hill. But I couldn't identify any weapons, so I had to treat the men as non-combatants. This is the etiquette of warfare.

We all had our targets, agreed on instinctively: the Boss remained calm and was attempting to source air support; Grant was hitting the knoll; Kane covered the village to the right; K-man covered our rear. We found that one of the fighting tactics in this area was to send unarmed men to vector in enemy fire, which meant our left flank was vulnerable.

I was having trouble observing both the ridgeline and the hostile village. My body was completely exposed and while I concentrated on the village to my front, I was half-expecting a round to kick into my ribs from the two jokers to my left. For now there was nothing I could do about it other than sit it out and keep firing.

Kane noticed my vulnerability and took up a fire position behind me so he could maintain a visual on the left ridgeline. He was now in an exposed position and could have been killed for his troubles. I knew I liked this guy for a good reason. There were some worried faces amongst the patrol, but not from him. He was sporting a larger-than-life smile while chewing a piece of gum. In a brief lull in the firefight, he sent me a wink that said, *I got your back covered, bro. You nail those fuckers in the village.* Kane was with me: he was calm and even jovial, but more than anything else he was there by my side regardless of the outcome. I turned my eyes and weapon back to the village.

The enemy fire was generally high, cracking above our heads. The odd enemy round began to make things a little more exciting – at times they landed only metres from us. A round thumped into the ground near Kane. Incoming fire from three directions intensified; the Boss was now in contact with the squadron HQ and had requested air support. He had not been under enemy fire before, but I remember looking at his face while he calmly passed on our grid coordinates to a close-support aircraft. I doubt his heart rate even broke 100 beats per minute.

Our left flank was still exposed and it was time to seek cover. We were outnumbered and it was only a matter of time before a lucky enemy bullet found its mark. The patrol carefully covered each man and pulled back in pairs to a position that offered cover from fire and view. The incoming rounds didn't abate, but we weren't overly concerned as we had the benefits of high ground, superior weapons and training. The locals had the advantage of knowing the terrain, and their numbers were beginning to swell. Even so, we decided to find a defendable location and fight it out.

We moved into dead ground – a position that could not be observed by the enemy – and Kane and I cleared higher ground 120 metres further up the mountain. We crept up with weapons ready and fingers poised. With squinted eyes, we carefully scanned the high ground. We knew that if the ground to our front was occupied, we would have no choice but to take it by force. Securing the top of the feature was vital. Kane and I worked as a team and trusted each other. The thought that we or the rest of the patrol could be taken down in this hazardous situation simply did not arise.

Once we had secured the crest, the Boss, Grant and K-man made their way to join us and establish all-round defence. I positioned the Para Minimi to cover the slope that led to the contact area, Grant and his sniper rifle lay further to the rear of the mountain where targets of greater distance might present themselves, the Boss coordinated air support from the middle of the position, and the two remaining patrol members, Kane and K-man, were allocated arcs of responsibility on the opposite side of the feature. Enemy fire could still be heard but we were well-positioned and ready to face anything.

The VM troop was only five kilometres away from our location and could hear the gunfire echoing through the valleys. One patrol commander commented that the rate of fire sounded like an SAS patrol in contact, and the VM call-signs established radio communications and identified that we were. The VM troop wasted no time and bounced their vehicles along the potholed tracks to reach our position in less than 75 minutes.

By this time all firing had ceased and we began to descend towards the VM troop under the cover of the two F18s carrying out low passes – an impressive deterrent. Five men in the middle of the badlands can be pretty light-on in the event that something goes wrong. The arrival of a full complement of eager VM operators eased the tension considerably.

We were relieved to see the boys on the track below, but

we'd never admit it and still claim that we only called in the VM support so they could 'pick up our brass' – referring to the empty brass cartridges left behind at the completion of a practice session on the firing range. The VM troop actually damaged one of their beloved vehicles in their haste to lend support. Many of the guys were involved in a similar situation two years earlier during the early stages of the East Timor deployment. There were striking similarities and the ribbing began almost immediately: 'We're tired of bailing you guys out of the shit!'

Despite the banter, we were all aware of the gravity of the situation and recognised that the military language we used – terms like 'subdue' and 'contact' – was designed to draw attention away from the intensity of our situation. There was little doubt that we had left several of our antagonists dead on the mountain behind us.

But in a situation like this, the taking of a life is nothing personal. There is no joy or celebration, no anger or hatred. It is a neutral feeling. Few of us have been in an incident where we felt happy about what had to be done. The simple fact is that two sides, due to whatever circumstances, are pitted against each other and the fight is one of survival. It is about instinct. The fight stays on the field. They were doing their job. And we were trying to do ours.

We were two groups of men who may have been more similar than we realised. We were all soldiers who were fighting alongside our mates, and both sides were determined to end up on the winning team. To lose this game was to lose the gift of life. Sure, we were relieved to have come out unscathed, but we were still charged with adrenaline. Reflection would come later.

The US military command told us that two companies of the US 10th Mountain Division were being dispatched in five Chinook helicopters, and that a clearance of the surrounding villages would be carried out. We were to secure the landing zones and hand over responsibility to the US commander on the ground. It was several hours before the Americans began to arrive, and it took at least another two hours before the search commenced.

The VM troop maintained security of the east–west track while our patrol tagged along with the mountain division, which was searching two of the villages. A series of tunnels leading into the mountains was found underneath several stone huts close to our previous OP position. The Americans decided that the most effective way to ensure they were clear was to toss in a couple of grenades. Two ammunition caches were found containing 80 boxes of 50-calibre ammunition, mortar rounds, grenades, landmines, detonators and rifles. The contact area was examined almost seven hours after the initial event. Traces of blood were found but all the dwellings were empty. Funny that. A track disappearing towards the Pakistan border was the likely escape route. The enemy were either watching the search from afar or were already long gone.

The VM troop departed in the late hours of the afternoon and our patrol returned to Bagram Airbase with the American soldiers. The air passing through the helicopter was crisp and seemed to cut deep into our souls. With the adrenaline gone, we began to feel the effects of the previous 11 days. Our heads were still filled with the recent events but, for now, we pushed those thoughts aside and relaxed. A sense of calm swept over our patrol as we dozed on the two-hour return flight to the airbase.

Upon arrival, things appeared no different than before. It was hard to think it had been almost a fortnight. Aircraft were taking off and landing, support crews were busy unloading pallets of stores, and soldiers from an array of nations were strolling along the primary dusty track, Disney Parade. What we'd just been through was nothing special – just part of operations in Afghanistan. Today it was our turn, tomorrow it would be someone else.

Yet the thrill we had felt during the action – the hit of adrenaline – was unforgettable, something that some of us would hunger for over years to come. Is it normal to want to experience this again? I have no bloodlust or desire to take life. The very thought sickens me, but to be tested in battle, to experience the rush of combat and the fight to stay alive, is addictive. How much is too much? That's difficult to know. Every man seems to have a unique threshold for this kind of action. But one thing was clear: our work in Afghanistan was far from over.

Negotiating an obstacle during basic training at Kapooka.

Providing live-fire support for Indonesian special forces soldiers while on training exercises.

Physical training on board the captured illegal fishing vessel in the southern Indian Ocean.

Sleeping quarters in the forward fish-stowage area.

The majority of asylum-seekers picked up by the MV *Tampa* were men, and conditions on the cargo ship were cramped.

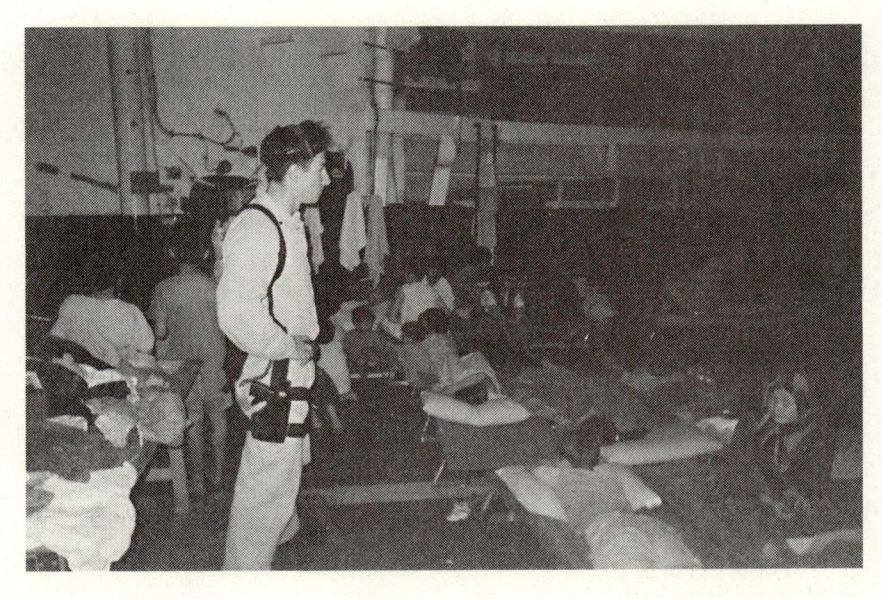

On the HMAS *Manoora*, we ensured that the women and children were set up in the best-ventilated area of the ship.

G observing a village in East Timor.

Baptised. Our patrol photo taken at the helipad after our 90-minute contact in East Timor.

A distraught East Timorese woman lunges out of the crowd and strikes a captured militiaman.

Providing 'close personal protection' for East Timorese President Xanana Gusmão. *Photo by Andrew Meares/Fairfaxphotos*

Securing the high ground during a contact in Eastern Afghanistan.

Kane after a sleepless night.

Mick mans a 50-calibre machine gun on a vehicle-mounted patrol in Eastern Afghanistan.

The view looking north from the roof of Bagram Airbase. To the right is a mined track where a young Afghani girl was tragically killed.

Writing my diary in Afghanistan while curious locals look on.

Steely-eyed Afghani men drinking chai.

Baking in the sun. A mountain OP in Eastern Afghanistan.

The mountainous and beautiful landscape of Eastern Afghanistan.

Haditha Dam, Iraq.

Chatting with Joe near Haditha Dam, while waiting for helicopters to arrive.

Lucky to survive. An IED attack in western Iraq.

The result of an IED on a non-armoured vehicle.

Joe and Si manning the rapid-reaction force office in Baghdad.

Going for help. We returned to our accommodation to fetch medics to assist in treating several US marines who were injured by this roadside bomb and small-arms attack near Haditha Dam.

Escorting an American civilian engineer – a wonderful and selfless man – during the second phase of our reconnaissance of Haditha Dam.

A US military Humvee destroyed by an anti-tank mine. Haditha Dam, Iraq.

The after-effects of a vehicle bomb detonated outside the International Zone in Baghdad.

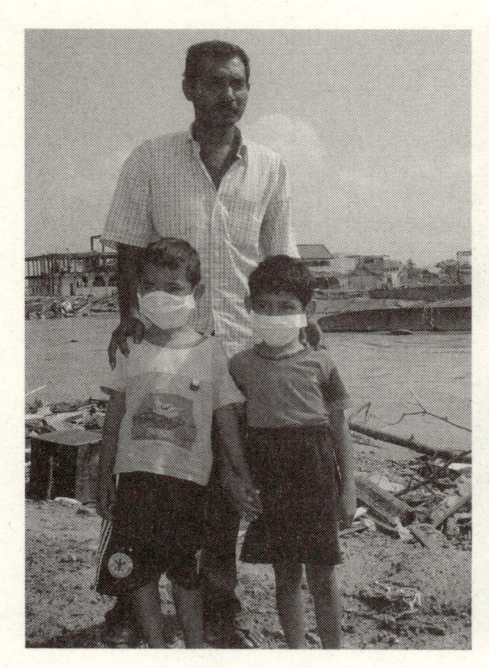

Left: A father and his two sons in Banda Aceh.
Top right: A damaged clock lying amid the mud and debris.
Bottom right: Human remains four weeks after the tsunami.

The destruction in Banda Aceh some 800 metres from the ocean.

Above and below: Scenes of incredible devastation in Banda Aceh after the tsunami struck.

Security team members Harps and Si in Banda Aceh.

Surfing and writing have been salves to my soul. After the death of several close friends, Kane arranged for my 'Warrior Brothers' poem to be scribed onto this custom board.

PART FOUR
AFGHAN OPERATIONS
JUNE 2002

ONE

It was 08:30 and our patrol had been up since 04:00, perched at an altitude of 10,000 feet while overlooking the village of Ali Kehl. We had been in Afghanistan for several months now, and this would prove to be our last reconnaissance/foot patrol. Thank God for that! I swear my butt was as calloused as a baboon's. An uncomfortable reminder of the hours, days and weeks spent sitting in various OPs.

As a group we were proud of the fact that we had not been compromised during our last two patrols, a combined period of 23 days in the field. At times, shepherds had walked within 30 metres of our position, but a combination of good fortune and well-selected OP sites allowed our patrol to remain undetected.

We had been in our current OP for nearly 10 days and were running low on supplies. I had already devoured my fudge brownie so there was very little to look forward to for the rest of the day. Usually a lack of water was a problem on foot patrols but for this task we had carried in several additional jerry cans. Food, or the lack thereof, was now the issue. The incessant rumbling in our stomachs had been replaced by a feeling of nausea from lack of sustenance.

We were to be extracted the following morning. We collapsed the OP after last light and headed towards the extraction landing zone. There were a couple of trees that had to be felled before we could snuggle into the cold earth and attempt to steal some sleep. It was a cool night, but waking was not difficult the next morning: the glow of the rising sun looks all the more pleasant on the morning of a patrol extraction. We were looking forward to a warm shower and a meal, hot or cold – it didn't matter, as long as it filled the ache in our shrunken stomachs.

Within two hours an Apache gunship appeared out of nowhere. It completed a quick search of the area before the extraction Blackhawk came into view. We identified our position with a smoke grenade and within seconds the bird swooped in and gathered our band of weary bodies. Our leg muscles had deteriorated during the last 11 days of the task and quivered under the weight of our packs. We clambered rather than climbed aboard, and were grateful to the pilot for giving it plenty of stick on the way back.

We unpacked our equipment and were debriefed before dinner. Three of us were joined in the mess tent by Lieutenant General Peter Cosgrove. The lieutenant general was a charismatic man whom I had met previously – I had provided close protection and translation assistance for him during the initial stages of the East Timor campaign several years prior. A man of his standing and rank is generally followed around by a high-ranking entourage, and we were interrupted by many willing candidates who really just wanted to kiss the big man's arse.

This type of thing always annoyed the hell out of me.

Some people, either because of their education or their positions of power, took great joy in setting themselves above others. These individuals used to turn into top-shelf grovellers when in the company of someone of higher rank or standing.

To our amusement, Cossie was obviously no fan of sycophants, and in a subtle way basically told one senior officer to piss off and let him enjoy his dinner with a few guys who had just got back from patrol. Cossie was a soldier's soldier, always keen to hear what it was like from the men on the ground. He was a good man who had been there and done it himself. We all liked him. We spoke with the lieutenant general for 45 minutes before excusing ourselves and letting the kiss-arse entourage resume their humiliating antics.

≡

The next day I pulled myself out of bed and went for an eight-kilometre run with a former operator who was now a support staff member (he became a computer guru after injuring his back in a parachuting accident). The first 25 minutes of this first run back from patrol were fine, but then the lack of endurance in my legs became frustratingly obvious. It was always good to get that initial run out of the way. In the afternoon a couple of us had a gym workout and our efforts were also far from peak performance.

This was fairly standard for patrol members. Operators would return from patrol with heavily fatigued bodies and face a race against time to build up their strength and endurance before the next patrol. Some guys didn't bother doing any training but over the months they deteriorated physically at a much faster rate. In essence, what this meant was that the physical capabilities of some men could really hamper a patrol's overall efficiency. One such man was an American forward air controller (FAC) who was attached to our patrol. He looked robust enough but was rendered inoperable on the very first ascent. On several occasions he just sat down and refused to continue until he was rested. This was frustrating. How do you coax a man with no sense of self-respect or fortitude to keep going?

Added to this, he was probably the most poorly disciplined field soldier I had worked with. He was incapable of remaining silent while in OP, so the rest of us decided that we would let him sleep in each morning for as long as possible. At least if he remained concealed within the depths of his heavy green sleeping bag there was less chance of him making noise or creating excessive movement.

He would wake, sometimes hours after the rest of us, and while wiping the sleep out of his eyes would noisily comment, 'It must be nearly midday. Why didn't you guys wake me?'

'You looked tired and could do with the extra rest,' we'd whisper in reply.

This man was unable to fathom the concept that a small team's chances of survival were directly related to stealth and concealment. Being forced to work with him made me realise afresh how fortunate I'd been to work with such high-quality operators. The difference it made to an operation having a patrol member you couldn't rely on was profound. And there was little that the more valuable members of the team could do to make up for the liability. We couldn't just leave him or kick the hell out of him, for his skills might come in handy later. We just had to lighten his load and make certain that he was never again permitted to deploy on a foot patrol.

Back at Bagram Airbase, finished with reconnaissance missions for the time being, our lives settled into a rhythm of sorts: training to get our fitness levels up, interspersed with bouts of impatience to be put to good use again. They weren't the worst conditions to live under for a while, but if there was one thing that would add to the frustration of operations, it was the occasional bout of food poisoning.

Many guys in the squadron had fallen ill with what appeared to be a 48-hour virus. I was not immune and one evening after a meal, my stomach began to feel unsettled. I was actually watching the film *Blackhawk Down* with at least a dozen other soldiers when my stomach cramps intensified. I grabbed the bin just as, onscreen, a US ranger was writhing in pain from a femoral arterial bleed. I began vomiting rather violently and the boys laughed, no doubt thinking that I had lost my nerve and was no longer capable of watching a gory battle scene.

But the vomiting wouldn't stop. By the time the film was finished I was completely incapacitated. I would have loved to crawl back to my stretcher but the most I could manage was to rest my forehead on the rim of the bin. Before long, my undignified appearance included a thick red crease just below my hairline.

One of my closest mates, Mick, finally noticed that all was not well and fetched a medic. A quick assessment led to three litres of Hartman's fluid being pumped into my system via the cubital fossa vein in the crook of my right arm. The medic then threw a blanket over my semi-comatose body.

And there I lay for the evening ahead, curled around my new best buddy, the bin.

But after a few hours things got interesting. Lying in a semi-alert yet vegetative state, my eyes suddenly snapped open. The cramps were worse, and this time they were situated much lower down. The feeling was unmistakable. I realised that it didn't matter how hard I tried to clench my body, there was a strong possibility that I was going to shit myself. As if all the vomiting wasn't bad enough!

I struggled to my feet and scrambled outside, managing to turn on my head torch as I stumbled into the cold darkness. Even the 40-metre walk to the portaloos was too much of a challenge. Midway through my very restricted, bum-cheekclutching journey, my stomach gave way. Even in my weakened state I was thoroughly disgusted with myself.

Once I made the toilet it was on for young and old, from both ends. I felt like I had been turned inside out and just sat there trying to recover some semblance of control. When I could safely bring my head up for air I looked around to grab a roll of toilet paper. I was going to need every single sheet. There was none. 'Great,' I spluttered.

I took off my pants and began to walk to the next toilet, but not before the cycle began all over again. I now felt too miserable to care how I looked and only just managed to get the door open before falling inside. This toilet was another bad choice – there was only enough toilet paper to do half the job. I spent five minutes recovering before moving to a third toilet. What a freaking epic this was turning into. Ignoring the icy cold wind, I grabbed my pants and walked, semi-naked, to the wash point, the light from my head torch shining down on my filth-smeared, dishevelled form.

I was beyond caring how pathetic I looked to the gate sentry. I had far more pressing issues to worry about. After lathering up my lower limbs and washing myself clean, I threw my underwear into the bin before trudging back to the stretcher in the regimental aid post. I didn't bother putting my pants back on. There was no point – they were probably splashed with faeces and it would only delay me if I urgently required the loo again. I pulled a blanket over my shivering body and rested my throbbing head on the stretcher. *Tomorrow is a new day*, I consoled myself, before drifting off to sleep.

The next several days were composed of general admin and rest, with the exception of an unfortunate trip to the range (10 kilometres from Bagram Airbase). Not my finest hour. I was driving the lead car when I felt that familiar bloated feeling in my lower stomach. I immediately pulled over to the right side of the road while remaining on the sealed surface, before darting around to the front of the car. The sides of the road were lined with red and white rocks, indicating that we were surrounded by landmines. Bagram was one of the most heavily mined areas in Afghanistan and it was not a danger to be taken lightly. I was not going to risk blowing off my foot just so I could suffer from the squirts in privacy.

I held on to the bullbar with one hand while my body let go once again. I kept things as quick and as tidy as humanly possible. The man who reappeared from in front of the car must have looked different from the man who had disappeared there two minutes before. I was several shades paler and I fastened the buckle to secure my pants rather gingerly. To my surprise and gratitude, no-one said a word.

The convoy continued and had travelled several kilometres when a brief message burst over the radio: 'Did anyone see the cat shit on the road back there? That is the most pathetic attempt at a shit I have ever seen.'

I laughed but secretly prayed for rain to wash away the evidence before our return journey.

=

The next morning, with a largely recovered constitution on my part, the Boss and I went for an 11-kilometre run around the dusty track that circumnavigated the airfield. We were all too aware of the threat of mines, so there would be no shortcuts. Enormous sections of the airfield had not been cleared. (Four years later, when I returned as a civilian contractor, not much appeared to have changed.) As we were running we noticed a significant puff of what could have been either smoke or dust rising from the mountainous ridges to the south.

We stopped and watched it for a couple of moments, idly trading speculation as to what it could have been. Within 30 or 40 seconds a rocket slammed into the ground just 100 metres from our position. Two US soldiers on a quad motorbike came tearing towards us like startled rabbits. They had no idea what the explosion was so we pointed out to them where we suspected it had been fired from, and they went to report the incident. There wasn't much else we could do about it, so we decided to continue with our run.

The dangers facing us out on operations were many and varied. But landmines presented perhaps the greatest threat to our safety in Afghanistan. Along with Cambodia, the country is one of the most heavily mined in the world. Estimates have suggested there are more than 7 million mines spread throughout the country.

During our time in Afghanistan we received daily reports of landmine incidents in the vicinity of our airfield base. Soldiers, civilians and, even more sadly, children had their limbs blown off and bodies shredded by the deadly mines, which were a lasting legacy of the former Soviet Union. One unfortunate child was blinded, lost all four limbs and his penis in an anti-personnel mine blast. You steel yourself for the idea that soldiers may be killed or maimed, but hearing of children being torn apart was sickening, especially for those of us who have children of our own.

Unfortunately, the Regiment has lost far more soldiers in training accidents than on operations. In the years since I completed selection, such tragic losses touched my life on a number of occasions, each more senseless than the last. A close friend, Marty, who had organised my buck's night, was killed in a parachuting incident. He was a gregarious and charismatic man who loved life with every ounce of his enormous heart. I don't recall ever seeing him unhappy. We were presenting a parachute/dive demonstration to a salary review panel who were assessing if our skill-sets and workloads warranted a pay rise. Marty's arm was pinned when he exited the aircraft, preventing him from being able to steer his parachute. Fate was unkind as he drifted into a clump of trees and struck his head on a branch. I couldn't believe that he was gone. His parents' house was rapidly turned into a shrine, crammed with dozens of photographs of his cheeky face.

Shortly afterwards, many more families were equally devastated when two Blackhawk helicopters collided in Townsville. The crash killed 15 SAS soldiers and three members of 5 Aviation Squadron. Safety standards are impeccable in the unit but the work is dangerous. The very same excitement that drew me and countless others to the Regiment – to be part of a unit that is able to achieve things that are beyond the capabilities of conventional units – can be perilous.

That year 16 young SAS soldiers had their names added to the rock at Campbell Barracks which commemorates the fallen. It was hard not to make that moment of grief personal: watching young children cry for a father who is never coming home; viewing Anzac Day with eyes that can actually picture the faces of friends who have been killed. Knowing Marty as I did, I picture him laughing to himself and boasting that it was his efforts that secured the boys a significant pay rise. Thanks, Marty, but I'm positive Skip, Evo, Craig and the rest of your mates would rather watch you making a goose of yourself on a Friday night, dancing on the speakers and drinking tequila laybacks at the Duck Inn.

The tragic passing of another three SAS brothers in a Victorian vehicle accident was equally heartbreaking. I knew one of these warriors well. Sergeant Craig 'Crackers' Linacre was the husband of his beloved Taryn and a devoted father to Asha. He was an incredibly gifted soldier, one of the best. I will remember Craig for his infectiously enthusiastic personality, his love of being a water operator, and his smart-arse grin and mesmerising vocals that were capable of shivering an audience's soul. And as for bravery, well, Crackers' actions in Afghanistan spoke louder than words.

TWO

Our patrol was informed that we would be placed on the evening security piquet of the SAS compound. This was not an unusual or particularly arduous task and there were always three men on at any one time. One soldier would secure the front gate, one would man a machine gun on the roof to monitor the rear perimeter, and a third would rove around the inner perimeter. Two hours after last light, I was woken to begin my shift.

The security piquet was generally a pretty boring way to spend two hours. I was in a pair of shorts and just threw on a wind-stopper jacket, my webbing vest, helmet and night-vision goggles before grabbing my Para Minimi light machine gun. I also opted for a set of double-plugger thongs rather than my boots – a decision I would come to regret.

I walked to the northern building and silently scaled the ladder. It is always fun to sneak up on the man who is manning the gun piquet, never more so than when, as in this case, the unsuspecting victim was a support staff soldier (non-SAS personnel). I crept onto the roof, but all my plans of surprise were stopped when I noticed the soldier on duty diligently scanning the rear of the compound with a thermal viewing device.

I was impressed with the professionalism of the man and approached him, asking what he was looking at.

'I'm watching a couple of Americans lying down in the grass outside the perimeter,' he replied matter-of-factly.

I thought this was a little odd and quizzed the man as to how long they had been there and what they were doing.

With the aid of my NVGs I began to watch these supposed 'Americans', who were no more than 100 metres in front of us. Far from just 'lying down in the grass', they were moving in a very military manner. It was a dark night and I had trouble picking up detail. The figures were hazy but I noticed that the men would move 10 to 15 metres before appearing to prop. To say I was rather suspicious of their motives would be an understatement.

I asked for the thermal sight, and when I focused on the men it was clear that they were probing towards the rear of our compound. They were obviously trained in military tactics, as they moved one at a time while the other knelt with weapon poised. Furthermore, they were armed with rifles that were pulled into their shoulders and held parallel to the ground. Just before they disappeared behind a large sea container, I could see they were wearing turbans. Americans, my arse!

I told the security piquet to inform Ops that a couple of guys were probing our rear perimeter. In hindsight, we should have opened fire. I didn't initiate contact due to the initial claim that they were American. To this day I regret that decision. Had I not hesitated, it might have saved a young girl's life.

The squadron commander and Ops team assessed the situation and observed the two men casually walking away from our perimeter before disappearing into a hole-riddled building some 200 metres away. After reporting the incident, a decision was made to send out a five-man team to contact the enemy. I was in, as were four others: the squadron sergeant-major (SSM), the squadron 2iC, and an operator from both the mobility and water troops, Thommo and Big Dave. Selection was down to nothing more than finding three guys who could be ready to join the hunt in less than no time. The SSM and 2iC were in the squadron command group, which meant they rarely got to leave Bagram, so nobody resented them being part of the team. In any case, the SSM was a great shot and had the fortitude to back it up.

There was only one thing undermining my own enthusiasm for the job ahead: my footwear was completely inappropriate! I couldn't risk returning to my accommodation to throw on my boots as I didn't want to lose my spot. If the Vietcong could march through the jungles of Vietnam in battered pairs of homemade sandals, then I was more than capable of running around in a pair of thongs. Besides, if they gave me grief I could always kick them off and go barefoot.

We assembled near the front gate for a snap set of orders, and it was clear that the squadron 2iC was going to be in charge. Without any further talk, we wove our way through the wire and disappeared into the darkness in search of our prey. While we were fairly sure that we were the hunters, we could not discount the strong possibility that we were stumbling into an ambush. To counter this, spacing and silence were emphatically maintained.

There was no denying it – this was exciting. We were tracking two armed men who, from what I'd seen, possessed some degree of military training. We crept along a narrow track in single file to more easily thread our way through the heavily mined area. About 50 metres from the stone building, we stopped. Ahead, we briefly saw the shadowy movement of two figures passing across the doorway. The 2iC signalled to me and the SSM to find a place from which to provide fire support. We looked at each other and could read the other's thoughts: who wants to fire from a distance when there is an opportunity to get up close and personal? I was regretting my choice to take a light machine gun and not my rifle.

We moved off to the flank where, due to the two-foot-high grass, we had to adopt a kneeling firing position. I was painting the building with my laser while using my NVGs to identify signs of movement. The SSM kept a vigil on the three-man assault team and provided commentary to me as to their precise position. The assault team had just disappeared from view when the silence was broken by the sound of three rapid shots.

I couldn't see our guys at all, and had to wait until I had their current location before I could follow my instincts and pour fire into the building. The SSM quickly let me know that they were somewhere to the right of the building so I was free to 'get into it'. I placed the dot from my laser in the doorway before squeezing the trigger. I planned to fire several bursts into the open door, however my weapon had other ideas and fired a single round before a cartridge became wedged under the bolt and prevented any further firing. I quickly cocked my weapon and attempted to refire but – nothing. I opened the feed cover and removed the belt, feeling inside the weapon for signs of anything unfamiliar. Even in the pitch-darkness, I managed to clear the weapon and find the offending obstacle. I pulled out the mangled cartridge and threw it into my breast pocket.

As I straightened up with my gun again there was deathly silence. We had no idea who had fired the three rounds. We called out to our mates. There was no reply. We waited a moment, listening and watching carefully, before trying again. Silence. Three shots, three of our guys. Surely the enemy weren't capable of achieving that in the dark.

I turned to the SSM: 'Let's head back to the track and see what's going on.'

He nodded firmly in response. 'Right on, tuffy.'

There was no point in procrastinating any longer, so we crept up the track, almost side by side so we could deploy both our weapons. Our safety catches were disengaged and our fingers were comfortably poised on our triggers. Our lasers were flashing past the window of the building and our NVGs turned the darkness into a depthless shade of green. We were ready for anything.

There was nothing but an eerie silence and slight breeze that touched our perspiring necks and faces. We were not carrying a lot of weight and had been relatively still on this cool night. As I was dressed more for the beach than a military contact, it would be fair to say that any perspiration could be attributed to the adrenaline pumping around my body. The two of us were poised in anticipation, bracing ourselves, at any moment, for a volley of fire.

Despite my concern for the welfare of my mates, I felt more alive than ever before. Parachuting, diving, driving fast – none of these things come close to the feeling and apprehension of combat. Especially at that moment of calm, just before things go loud. Once things really swing into action, most guys with any decent training just react instinctively. Waiting for the unknown is far more intimidating – and exciting!

We took up fire positions and called out once again to the other three assault team members. There was still no reply. I informed the SSM that I had my radio in my vest and would turn it on to attempt to establish communications while he covered me. My webbing was prepared for a reconnaissance patrol so the radio was well secured. I quickly attached the antenna and within seconds of turning on my personal radio I heard the 2iC's familiar voice. I established contact and was informed that they were chasing the two combatants towards a village. I asked if the buildings had been cleared – they had not.

Reassured that the assault team were all okay, I requested approval from Ops to clear the uninhabited buildings with grenades. The squadron commander's answer was an immediate and emphatic refusal.

The SSM just laughed. 'Serves you right for asking. You should have just done it.'

We lined up outside a window and, despite my offer to enter first, the SSM took the initiative, withdrew his pistol and dived inside. Cursing silently, I followed him. We moved swiftly through the first room, sweeping for any human presence before moving on.

Before long, there was one room remaining and as we entered the doorway we half-expected a burst of 7.62-millimetre rifle fire. As a defensive precaution, I took up the slack on my trigger as we carried out a partition drill. This time I took the lead, leaving the SSM to 'carry the drinks' from behind.

The two of us had established a bond many months before when training on Enoggera Hill, but at that moment, making our way through a deserted and pitch-black building in Afghanistan, our respect for each other cemented the friendship. I was impressed with the SSM's courage, even if it did piss me off to be sharked into the dwelling by a man who was 12 years my senior. Several years later we would catch up in Afghanistan while working as private contractors. The SSM enticed me to run a half-marathon with him at Bagram. For a man who wakes up, opens a packet of chips and washes it down with a durry and a can of Coke ... well, it impresses me that he is able to run so well.

I informed the 2iC that the building had been cleared and that we would move to their location. We patrolled some 150 to 200 metres along a small bank, and joined the other three members just as the moon illuminated a series of mine markers: we had stumbled into the middle of a minefield. We instantly froze. Assessing our options, we decided to retrace our exact steps and exit the minefield along the same bank we had so casually traversed just moments before.

We maintained spacing and moved gingerly along the darkened mound of earth. At such a perilous moment, many things go through your mind. I wondered just how much it would hurt to have my foot blown from my body. Thommo told me later that he had refused to look down. His logic was that losing the lower half of a limb is bad enough, but being blinded was an even greater cause for concern.

Worse still was the fear of having the blast rip into your groin and remove your manhood. Mines are nasty. We had already been deployed for several months and the idea that my sexual frustration could be a permanent state due to my genitals being pulverised wasn't worth thinking about. Give me two bullets in the stomach any day. Some of our team took bigger steps to minimise the amount of contact they had with the ground. Others appeared to be stepping softly to reduce their impact. An anti-personnel mine will go off if the corner of one's boot initiates the slightest downward pressure, so this last tactic was more a bit of comical relief than anything else.

With each step, our feet would sink into the soft earth below as we dreaded the thundering blast that could instantly destroy a person's life. This was the wrong kind of excitement. Not knowing what's around the corner is one thing, but making our way through a minefield was a situation none of us ever wanted to be in again. Being shot by an adversary is no soldier's idea of a desirable outcome of battle, but it is something that you think you could deal with. If the enemy manages to shoot faster or straighter or is luckier than you, then fair enough. But having your lower limbs shredded by a small Russian device planted over 20 years ago was not something that anyone would request from Santa. There is just something so damn offensive about being taken out by such impersonal means.

We made it in one piece back to the path and moved about 400 metres to the north-north-west, bypassing several derelict buildings on our way. Our aim was to cut the enemy off before they got too far. SAS operators on the roof of a building inside the perimeter were vectoring our team onto the enemy. They informed us that we were walking parallel to them.

Due to the vegetation, each group was unaware of the other's precise location. The men in the compound were attempting to identify the enemy position with lasers but the splash deflected off numerous surfaces, making it difficult for us to know exactly where they were. We knew we were close but we still didn't have visual confirmation. We circled around the minefield and were now 500 or 600 metres from our compound. We were informed that the two men were walking towards us, so we took up firing positions, with my light machine gun taking pole position on the track.

We scanned feverishly through our NVGs, eyes straining for any sign of movement. The enemy moved to within 50 metres of us before entering the last clump of vegetation. We knew they would soon be exposed. Minutes passed – our every muscle was coiled in anticipation. But another report came through from the compound. Our targets had changed direction. They were continuing away from us to the north.

After several minutes the 2iC ordered the team to continue. We located another small path leading in the enemy's direction to a single dwelling some 200 metres away. Was it possible that we had them cornered? The 2iC took the lead, with me, as the light machine gun operator, right on his tail. There was then a 15-metre gap back to the SSM and a further 15 metres to Thommo and Big Dave.

This move was the most nerve-racking of the entire

event. Once again, we were expecting the flash of muzzles followed by rounds zinging through the air. Our unseen adversaries could have been anywhere. The 2iC and I carried out small silent bounds towards the last dwelling, while the remaining members adopted a position to provide fire support.

I edged forward, determined not to let the distinct flip-flop of my inappropriate footwear make any noise. We painted the dark entrance with our lasers and got to within a metre of the doorway when the 2iC decided that enough was enough. He ordered a retreat. I still wonder if those two men were in that building, but he made a decision and that was that. He probably saved two men's lives that night. Whether they were our lives or theirs, we'll never know.

We retreated to the other patrol members and then, as a group, patrolled back to the squadron perimeter. The boys on the roof, aided by numerous thermal imagers, watched over us, providing support for our return trip. As we neared the compound, Thommo leaned in and whispered to me that we had 'the two squadron HQ minesweepers' out the front. We both chuckled to ourselves before dropping back and covering the rear of the patrol.

It had been an interesting night. When we returned to the compound we were debriefed and, once that was done, we headed back to bed – my shift had finished some 30 minutes earlier. *If only all evening piquet duties were like that one*, I reflected. The next morning we went to the range and I test fired my light machine gun with two 25-round belts of ammunition. The weapon fired the first belt and then the second without so much as a stutter.

That'd be right, I thought, shaking my head. Some would

nod in the direction of Murphy's Law – after all, my weapon's stoppage had only occurred at a time of need. But I don't believe in Murphy's pessimistic worldview. Weapon stoppages aren't personal and can occur just as easily in battle as in training.

That afternoon, I learned that three children had been playing about 150 metres up the track that we had patrolled the night before. A six-year-old girl tripped a mine and had one of her legs blown off. The two boys with her fled and the young girl spent her final moments alone, no doubt scared and in agony before she died.

The squadron sentry observed the tragedy and reported the incident immediately. The little girl died before her distraught family could reach her. The American military carried out an assessment of the site and ascertained that the mine had been laid the night before. The two men we had observed lying on the track – the two men we had spent a couple of hours pursuing – had planted that mine. They had then patrolled towards the perimeter, possibly in an attempt to lure a clearance team out onto the track. It is a miracle that our five-man team patrolled along a path (twice) that was no more than seven feet wide and missed the mine.

At that time I already had two young daughters – Tahlie, aged two, and Sian, who was fast approaching 12 months old. As hard as it was, I tried not to let myself think about them too often, as I couldn't afford to lose my focus. I was physically present in Afghanistan and it was imperative that my mind was also. But the thought of that little girl writhing in pain sickened us all to the very pits of our stomachs. A mixture of emotions, including guilt, affected us as we tried to face our regular routine that evening. We had been the mine's targets, not a small child who was just trying to have some fun. Those of us with young children will carry this image for a very long time. Perhaps forever.

It was a relief when, not long afterwards, squadron HQ issued the Boss with another 'warning order' outlining our patrol's next task. We were to leave Bagram Airbase and head back to Eastern Afghanistan.

THREE

The Boss, Grant and I felt like Russian dolls, strapped into our seats inside our vehicle, which was inside a C130 Hercules aircraft. We were en route to FOB Khost and the ride had been relatively uneventful. But suddenly, things changed.

The aircraft banked hard to the left, then to the right, then appeared to fall through the sky. Through our NVGs the green haze was sharply disturbed by a series of brilliant white flashes from the cabin windows. We were under fire. My stomach felt as though a thousand butterflies had begun to flutter their wings simultaneously. The bird roared towards the ground, and we braced ourselves and instinctively sucked in a gulp of air.

It was like a fireworks display, but there was no sense of awe or innocent wonder. Everyone was aware that tracer fire generally has a visibility ratio of 5:1 – for each little glow of light there were possibly four more large chunks of lead heading our way.

The plan had been for the aircraft to touch the runway at Khost, where we'd roll off the rear ramp in our vehicles as quickly as possible. Someone was obviously attempting to make this a little more challenging. The flashes of light were streams of tracer fire that were being hurled towards the aircraft from two positions, creating an interlocking arc of criss-cross fire. The SAS operators who were already located at FOB Khost watched the show as the British Special Ops pilots rapidly lowered the aircraft in an attempt to prevent their baby from being punctured by the large-calibre bullets flying towards us.

The aircraft hit the runway hard, violently throwing our heads back and forth. The ramp was lowered, the chains were removed and we began to move our vehicle off under the cover of darkness. No sooner were we off than the aircraft taxied into position, the engines screamed to life and the C130 was once again thrust into the sky.

Only half of our patrol was inserted; the other vehicle, carrying K-man and Kane, was due to arrive in 30 minutes. After our somewhat fiery greeting we were informed that no fixed-wing aircraft would be granted permission to land until the situation improved. The three of us moved quickly towards the vehicle-mounted troop, who ran us through what they had seen.

After we were briefed we found ourselves some stretchers, where we sat and chatted with our mates for a couple of hours before calling it a day and drifting off to sleep. In the early hours of the morning we were woken by an explosion. Then we heard a rocket zinging directly overhead. Someone yelled out: 'Incoming!'

Even amongst the tension, the high-pitched scream was met with a flurry of imitations; mocking cries of 'Incoming!' and laughter filling the air. What a time to take the piss out of someone! The zinging motors could be heard propelling the 107-millimetre rocket through the blackened sky.

When something like this occurs it takes a couple of moments to gather your bearings. One minute we were sound asleep, the next we were scrambling out of our sleeping bags, grabbing our weapons and helmets (with NVGs attached), pulling on our boots and making our way to the bunker that we had been allocated during the evening briefing only hours earlier. The enemy fired a total of five rockets and, although they were straight, they all either fell short or overshot our position.

We were not responsible for the security of the airfield, so just chatted for half an hour before we were stood down and allowed to return to the relative comfort of our stretchers. We slept well, excited by the fact that Khost appeared to be hotting up.

On a subsequent mobility patrol, our alarm clock, once again, was a 107-millimetre rocket. I had not been asleep long when I heard a *crump* sound burst out of the darkness. I opened my eyes to see a bright flash, which was accompanied by the *zing* of a rocket directly overhead. It continued before detonating further up the hill with a tremendous explosion.

I had rehearsed this over and over in my mind. In a state of disorientation, you react quicker if you have established a routine. I always positioned my weapon on my right side with my helmet draped over my sight. I grabbed my helmet, fastened my chinstrap and rotated my NVGs down over my eyes. They switched on automatically. I scanned the night while throwing on my web vest and lying down behind my weapon, and then disengaged my safety catch. The other 10 SAS soldiers did the same. Were we about to be attacked? By how many? Or was this just a random rocket attack? Either way, for 20 minutes we remained silent and composed, staring into the darkness, waiting for the unknown.

≡

A US Delta Force operator was killed the following day when his team went to investigate reports that a Yemeni al-Qaeda member was in a compound just outside Khost. These reports are common. More often than not, a village dispute led to the incident being reported to coalition forces — with the extra spark of a hollow accusation of terrorism. Regardless, each report had to be taken seriously.

The Delta operators, with regular US army personnel in support, cordoned off the compound while the Afghani interpreter attempted to coax those inside to allow entry into the compound. The interpreter was instructed to correspond with those inside by verbal communication only and not to attempt to scale the wall. The two Delta operators who were with him moved back to their vehicle, and as they turned around they saw that the interpreter had failed to follow their instructions and had foolishly climbed the wall. Before they could yell at him to get down, he was met with a burst of 7.62-millimetre gunfire that ripped into his upper torso, flinging him back to the ground. The Delta operators didn't hesitate — they withdrew their pistols and ran to the man's aid, dragging him away from the door while they unloaded full clips from their pistols into the metal gate.

We found out later that the interpreter was dead. His body had ceased living before he hit the dusty earth.

The cordon then retreated and targetted the compound with an air-strike. Two 500-pound bombs were dropped, while two Apache gunships raked the compound with 40-millimetre cannon fire. The latter had very little effect but the bombs would have sent percussion waves so severe that anyone inside would surely have had their insides turned to jelly.

The Delta operators prepared themselves to assault the compound. Prior to entering, one man removed his helmet, since it was unlikely that anyone inside would be left alive. The team had just breached the compound via an area of wall that had been destroyed when a 'pineapple' grenade landed behind them. A chunk of metal fragged the operator in the rear of the head, and he fell as his mates detained the man responsible. The Yemeni al-Qaeda man had been killed, and so too had several other combatants, but the young man who'd managed to throw the grenade had a fist-sized hole in his chest. He was detained but, although severely injured, he remained defiant and refused to talk. I don't know if he survived. Sadly, the Delta operator did not.

During that same period, another US soldier was killed when the vehicle he was travelling in was ambushed. The men were riding in a convoy of six unarmoured four-wheel drives, when an Afghani male on the side of the road waved to them with a broad and seemingly genuine smile. The soldiers waved back and exchanged friendly expressions. The temperature was close to 50 degrees Celsius so the team had draped their body armour over the doors of the vehicles and the car's windows remained open.

The Afghani man, still smiling, approached the last

vehicle, unslung his rifle and jammed its barrel through the open window. He forced it into the lap of an American, who had been waving at him just moments earlier, and fired half a clip of AK-47 ammunition into his stomach and chest. The man then fled into the crowd.

In the confusion of the ambush that followed, several vehicles were lost. Needless to say, military tactics soon changed. The smiling assassin had been able to carry out such a brazen attack because none of the vehicles had mounted machine guns or men positioned where they could immediately return fire. Bouncing around in the back of a four-wheel drive means it is extremely difficult to return fire with any real degree of effectiveness. Many private security operators in Iraq would later experience similar problems.

≡

The three troops that comprised the squadron on the Khost operation – the water, freefall and vehicle-mounted troops – were already remarkably tight: a kin of extended brothers, a second family. Despite the ever-present jovial banter, we in the water troop shared a conviction that we were the hardest, comfortably atop the food chain. We delighted in dismissing the freefall troop, of which one of my mates, Craig, was a patrol 2iC, as nothing more than a pride of weak 'gaylords'. Our two troops came together, however, in dismissing the vehicle-mounted troop, whom we stereotyped as a bunch of cake-eating, beer-swilling, doughnut-munching, McDonald's, KFC and pizza-loving fat boys.

Our claim to superiority lay in our having passed two exhilarating and strenuous selection courses – for the SAS and as assault divers. In reality, these provided us with nothing more than swollen ankles and a lower level of hearing. But we wouldn't admit this to the other troops! Over the following weeks, the majority of the squadron (including squadron HQ) deployed to FOB Khost to carry out operations in the volatile Paktia, Paktika and Nangarhar provinces. As an upside, HQ brought with them mail from home.

This is something that is a great morale-booster. Some soldiers receive heaps, while others receive nothing. Soldiers often share their letters from home with mates who are repeatedly missed at mail-call. With the deployment now well into its third month, one soldier had not received a single email or letter from his family or girlfriend. His mates eventually got together and wrote him a couple of letters and stuck them in the mailbag. He was quite surprised when his name was called out not once, but twice. There was no shortage of smart-arse one-liners to brighten up his day.

It is always nice to hear what is going on at home and men are sent magazines, old papers and articles about significant events. Some men are sent enormous food parcels, which are always shared with their mates. Army rations are not that exciting, so a bit of variety is always greatly appreciated.

My family were incredibly generous, even a little over-zealous in regards to sending food. My wife, mother, sisters and nan obviously didn't want me coming home malnourished. Being the only son and grandson has its advantages. Furthermore, my family were all enthusiastic and interesting writers, so the letters arrived thick and fast. During basic training I sometimes received up to five letters per day.

One of my 'top-shelf' brothers, Mick, who was from another patrol, had a father who knew what it was like to be deployed on operations. He was a former Vietnam veteran and knew how to bypass inspections by sending a few cans of beer hidden in a tube. Mick ensured that all his mates got at least one sip of VB. Besides being generous with his beer, Mick had a tremendous work ethic. There were times when he would spend hours helping us to prepare our patrol vehicles until well after midnight.

More recently, I gave Mick a call to see if he could fly to Sydney to give me a hand on a motivational seminar. His answer was immediate and unquestioning: 'Yeah, I have heaps on but tell me what day you need me and I'll be there.' That was it. For a mate, Mick would drop everything at a moment's notice. On a poignant note, Mick's father passed away recently. Like so many Vietnam vets, he made it home but had his life cut short some 30 years later, one of many victims of the cancerous Agent Orange.

If mail was important, then sleep, or the lack of it, was similarly so. Intelligence suggested that FOB Khost would be attacked by rocket-propelled grenade (RPG) fire during the evening, so the Canadians, who were responsible for base security, decided they would send up 60-millimetre mortar illumination throughout the night. And luckily for us, the base plate (the mortar firing position) was only 50 metres from where we were sleeping. Just when we began to settle we would be startled by the *doonk* sound of an illum round being punched into the sky. The burning flare would then turn night into day.

In the age of night-vision goggles and thermal sights, it didn't make too much sense to be firing illumination. Perhaps we were biased and hated the fact that they were messing with our beauty sleep. Regardless, illuminating the perimeter was a double-edged sword. While the outer perimeter may have been lit up, the light didn't just stop at the perimeter gun pickets. It danced well into the base itself, so any possible RPG firing team would have little trouble aiming their weapon in the right direction. The following morning the sun jumped out of bed and stabbed my swollen eyes over and over again – burning and stinging without remorse. With the constant noise and light display of the previous evening, it was little wonder that we looked ragged.

Things were moving fast and squadron HQ issued the Boss with a warning order for our next task. The Boss wasted no time in gathering his patrol together and issuing a comprehensive set of verbal orders. He always kept his men meticulously well informed. He outlined a plan – a six-man mobility patrol would escort our six-man reconnaissance patrol into a valley and through a suspect village. The vehicles would remain north of the village until after last light, when our patrol would climb into the mountains, establish an OP and observe the village for signs of enemy movement.

This subterfuge would be aided by the mobility guys travelling back to base through the same village. Hopefully, this course of action would give the impression that our vehicles had simply moved up the valley and then left again. A second contingent would carry out a similar operation and insert another patrol on the other side of the mountain. Both reconnaissance patrols needed to secure a position that enabled them to overlook the suspect village while also being no more than 1000 metres apart. This positioning was strategically necessary. Each patrol had to be in a position where they could support the other should an 'incident' arise.

There was, of course, a high probability of an incident occurring. In the minutes before we departed, a US intelligence officer told us that the area we were headed for was dotted with caves and enemy positions. The combination of the late intelligence and the look of concern on the face of the US officer had us all approaching the task with a high degree of apprehension. The task was initially formulated as an attempt to confirm or deny enemy presence in the area of operations (AO), and an overt vehicle move sounded more than feasible. However, with the confirmation of enemy positions, a two-vehicle convoy driving through a suspect village in the middle of the day had upped the ante somewhat.

Before departing, the two reconnaissance patrols shook hands. The banter and sledging was fairly standard, with casual comments like 'Don't toss off in the OP because we'll be watching you' bandied back and forth. Misgivings about an operation are all well and good, but the opportunity to be competitive with the other troops was too good to pass up.

My mate Craig, the team 2iC of the other patrol, was an outstanding soldier and made a beeline for me. I was his counterpart in the water recon patrol. We had completed selection together and were part of a close-knit group of men. Our entire reinforcement cycle had been posted to the same squadron many years before. We shook hands, each trying to suppress a strange sense of foreboding about the task we faced. We were not to know that one of us would later be surrounded by around 80 men trying to kill him.

FOUR

I've worked with so many men and so many teams. When out on patrol, and particularly on patrols as dangerous as those in Afghanistan, we were all mates relying on each other's tenacity and skill. In reality, all testosterone aside, each troop brought different skills to the table, and each contained its own impressive cross-section of talented, impressive soldiers. Even just the briefest assessment of the men who supported the Khost operation reveals what an extraordinary team it was.

One freefall soldier, who is now studying medicine, was unmistakably one of the toughest men going. He was nicknamed 'Weapons Platform' due to a physique that bordered on the hyper-masculine. This man was rarely seen in the gym – in fact, he was regularly observed (by jealous eyes) gorging himself on a bacon and cheese pie and washing it down with a big smile and a Coke. He would then take off his shirt to show off a muscular and chiselled mesomorph frame that would shame most bodybuilders. For every pie he consumed, his biceps seemed to grow an extra centimetre. For every can of soft drink, his abs became increasingly defined.

You couldn't hate him for this unnatural gift, since he was one of the nicest guys in the Regiment. He was a gentle giant who was as honest as the days are long, but could turn that little switch inside his brain at will to transform himself into something that would terrify even the most ardent enemy soldier. He was just a freak. To top it off, he was blessed with a super-sized brain that after six years of hellish study will see him employed as a medical practitioner. His one fault was that his vocal range was pretty limited, only ever reverberating around the lower octaves. But besides singing, he was good at almost everything he attempted. The 'gaylords' were rightly proud of this man.

The vehicle-mounted troop had their own share of talent, whose existence proved our worst prejudices wrong. One of their team, who was responsible for the insertion of our recon patrol, was Thommo, my partner from the evening saunter around Bagram Airbase. He had joined the Regiment at the same time as me and was a well-liked and valuable member of any team. Thommo loved to gamble and was perhaps one of the most skilled bush soldiers of the era, with a satirical personality well-equipped to make a light moment out of the most dire of situations.

But to many, Thommo will always be remembered for the dining equipment he used during the patrol course. We were required to source our own eating utensils and most operators purchased a large plastic plate or something similar. Thommo, on the other hand, waited until a crowded mealtime before retrieving an enormous blue cat bowl out of his bag. Well aware of the effect his choice was having on the men around him, he stood in the messing line with his bowl cradled in front of him. It was so bloody huge he needed two hands to carry it. His explanation was that the cat bowl could fit more food in it. Personally, I think he liked to shock, and the constant meows that were thrown his way were lapped up like a kitten purring over a bowl of milk.

Another character and gifted soldier, who had proved himself in numerous contacts in Somalia, East Timor and Afghanistan, was Steve (known around the squadron as 'High Level'). The man was an icon. He was always raring to go. During a counter-terrorism exercise he refused to remove his body armour even during an allocated time of rest. He was determined not to let anything prevent him from being the first man kitted up and ready to take part in an assault. He was brash, aggressive and covered in black tattoos that suited his stocky frame. Many of the operators' wives loved him and couldn't believe that such a catch was still single.

The truth of it was that, despite being preternaturally cool under fire, High Level was a jibbering wreck when in the presence of the opposite sex. His charm with other operators' wives was only possible because there was no pressure. He dated many women but the true love of his life was the Regiment. He will probably go on to be the regimental sergeant-major (RSM). High Level had asked the army if she would become his wife and, naturally, she said yes. It is a match made in heaven – till death do them part.

But once again, the SAS was nothing if not an exercise in contrasts. Another legendary member of the team, known as 'House', was far from a stereotypical SAS soldier. At my wedding, several of my civilian friends refused to believe that this man, who looked 18, was an SAS soldier. He weighed in at no more than 65 kilograms and had been a biochemist before joining the Regiment.

House had a love of explosives and, during the basic demolitions course, answered questions that bewildered even veteran instructors with 20 years' experience. He was a tenacious little bastard, and how he managed to carry some of those weights during selection still astounds me. He finished selection weighing no more than 55 kilograms but from the very first day the smile on his face was ever-present. He wore glasses but his accuracy on the 50-calibre vehicle-mounted machine gun was exemplary. With the lightweight House in the turret, the boys knew that in the event of an incident, 50-calibre chunks of death would be slamming towards the enemy in no time at all. He practically required both arms just to cock the heavy gun, but once rounds were chambered – look out!

It was an extraordinary and diverse group of patrols in Afghanistan, and any doubt we might have had about particular operations paled when held up against our faith in the men we were working with. Those soldiers, those warrior brothers, did each other proud, and that knowledge was a more powerful motivator, a more compelling drug than all the adrenaline in the world.

※

Our four-vehicle convoy headed out, passing through the chicanes of barbed wire that lined the departure gate. A sense of danger about what lay ahead enveloped the men. It was early afternoon and our vehicles bounced and shuddered their way along the dusty, potholed tracks for an hour before the convoy split and both patrols continued towards their designated tasks. As we parted ways, the men casually raised an unsentimental middle finger to their mates who were heading off in another direction. There would be some interesting stories to swap the next time we met.

Our recon patrol rattled down the road, the men balanced precariously on storage bins. In an attempt to limit the bruising to our tailbones we placed pieces of foam under our behinds, but with every bump the foam would shift. Finally we resigned ourselves to the discomfort, squinting and growling as we winced at each pothole the driver skilfully found.

As our two vehicles entered a village, several Afghanis tried to attract our attention. They held their hands out in front of them as if cradling a weapon before pointing towards the mountains in the distance. The mountains were still a long way away, but as we drove closer, they felt ever more ominous.

The vehicles slowly crept into a deep *wadi* (gully) at the foot of the mountains. Realising that it was a classic place for an ambush, we gripped our weapons and scanned the opposite banks for any sign of danger. This intuition seemed confirmed when our lead vehicle stopped abruptly. The gunner, Brans, had noticed a significant defensive position to his front, which appeared to be unoccupied.

Our vehicle had only just entered the *wadi*, so we reversed a little and remained still. The Boss, Kane and Grant moved up the *wadi* on foot and identified a platoon-level defensive position that had been carved into the earth and reinforced with rock. The Boss requested the digital camera to capture images of the position, so a vehicle-mounted operator ran towards the men with a 12 megapixel camera. At the time, this was light years ahead of anything else on the market.

I was armed with my trusty Para Minimi light machine gun and told the rest of the guys in the vehicle that I was going to move up the bank of the *wadi* to find some high ground to observe from. I slung a set of binoculars around my neck and headed up the semi-vegetated, rocky bank. I was glad of the chance to stretch my legs and let the blood return to my still rather tender bum cheeks.

At the crest of the *wadi*, I located a weapons pit constructed of rock, and a range card that had been etched into a piece of stone with directions and prominent landmarks. This was interesting. There was no doubt that this spot had been occupied and used by people who knew what they were doing. K-man joined me and we signalled to the rear vehicle for the video camera. Our newest patrol member, Dave, arrived with the camera and while he and K-man worked out how to turn the thing on, I continued along the side of the bank.

I clambered across the broken rock for another 15 metres to investigate a rustling sound – probably nothing more than an animal that had managed to stay one step ahead of the Afghani hunters (no mean feat in poverty-stricken Afghanistan). I saw several other defensive pits in the area, and was just placing my light machine gun on the ground to get the lay of the land with my binoculars when an unmistakable crack rang out.

A bullet whizzed past the top of my head and continued past K-man and Dave, who were still struggling with the video camera. We were fortunate our unseen shooter was not a more competent marksman, as the sound had indicated that he'd fired the shot from no more than 200 metres away.

I grabbed my weapon and quickly moved to the base of a nearby tree, where I took up a firing position. 'You sneaky little prick,' I muttered as I scanned the *wadi* with my binoculars. A bullet slamming into my head or body would have been a very bad start to the patrol.

K-man soon joined me, thumping keen to lend a hand. Dave, showing early signs that he'd fit in well with the rest of the patrol, also fell into line and adopted a firing position on the top of the *wadi*. Our minds were racing. Was an attack imminent? The men on the opposite side of the *wadi* also took up firing positions.

The patrol commander of the vehicle-mounted patrol, Grizz, thought he had located the person responsible for firing the shot, but thankfully Kane corrected him – it was me he was pointing his weapon at! We remained quiet for several long minutes. Confident that a major attack was not immediately pending, the Boss set up the tactical satellite (tacsat) communications and attempted to source some air support overhead. But none would arrive for at least 60 minutes. Moving forward through the steep-banked *wadi* would be a reckless decision, so the senior members of the two patrols discussed the situation and the Boss ordered the vehicles to retreat and observe the *wadi* from a distance while he formulated another plan.

Our two patrols retreated 800 metres into the valley and located some 'hull down positions' – areas of dead ground where only the vehicle weapon systems were visible. We quickly sourced every piece of optical equipment at our disposal and began to scan the features to our front. An operator on the swift-zoom picked up movement and countless other defensive positions scattered through the mountains to the north. The decision to sit back and observe had been a sound one.

The men occupying the defensive positions were armed and carried handheld radios. We quickly dubbed one defensive position 'Hilltop' and noted with alarm that there were half a dozen armed men peering towards our patrol location. A second position was nicknamed 'Pillbox' and an additional four armed men were observed there. There was also a heavily sandbagged bunker in this location. Two other significant defensive positions were identified, and all of them were well equipped to support each other.

In the minutes before last light, our patrols pulled back an additional 800 metres and informed squadron HQ of the find. Coalition forces were yet to operate in this region, so it was possible that there were hundreds of enemy hiding in the area. The Boss advised squadron HQ that a battalion-sized group would be required to conduct a thorough cordon and search operation. Several messages later the response came through. Our patrol was to ascend one of the mountain features that overlooked the defensive positions and gather intelligence. The vehicle-mounted patrol was to remain in location until first light and then return to FOB Khost.

We looked up at the ominous mountain that rose out of the valley to our north-west. From there we would have a commanding view not only of the two villages to our front but also of the ring of defensive positions that straddled the ridgeline. From an intelligence-gathering perspective, it would be perfect. But in terms of our own safety, we were going into the lion's den.

FIVE

Even the most daring members of the patrol were apprehensive about the latest variation to our task. Something didn't feel right. But there was no point wasting time. We were acutely aware that we had one hell of a stomp before us. There was no need to check our maps or GPS. The mammoth shadow of the mountain to the north-west was more than identifiable. We knew it was potentially dangerous, as it dominated the area and could have accommodated dozens of armed men in defensive positions covering all the major approach routes.

We decided to scale a less obvious section of the mountain – in all likelihood a much safer route, but agonisingly steep. We donned our packs but, to begin with, didn't really notice the weight due to the adrenaline that was already pumping through our bodies. We headed into the darkness, not knowing who or what was ahead.

We walked for about a kilometre before we came to a significant *wadi* with banks at least eight metres high. This was a dangerous descent. We established a sentry and attempted to locate a suitable location from which to drop into the dry riverbed. We balanced our way down the precarious, jagged banks and each man passed his pack down to the man on the rock ledge below. Our heart rates had increased significantly with the effort and we had still not yet entered the *wadi*, let alone scale the bank on the other side or tackle the mountain.

Waiting for my turn to cross the *wadi* was torturous. I covered Grant across the open area as an annoying rock ground into my right knee. This did, however, take my mind off my aching shoulders, which were being squeezed lifeless by the straps of my pack. Increasing the burden on one shoulder by elevating it above the other provided some relief, but this game of shrugs was really a short-term fix. The shoulder that was burdened with the extra weight would quickly begin to numb and circulation to the corresponding arm would be restricted.

After a tense and careful crossing we located an appropriate spot to scale the opposite bank. Kane secured the top while the remaining patrol members assisted one another up the bank. While our arms and legs quivered from the strain, climbing up was actually a little easier than climbing down, and within five minutes we were perched atop the *wadi*, ready to assault the mountain.

Distantly in the east, we heard the distinctive sound of a large-calibre machine gun. The deep-thudding slow rate of fire indicated it was probably a 14.5-millimetre DSHK. The enemy were also known to have 82-millimetre mortars and 107-millimetre rockets. Since the firing was not directed at us, we began the murderous climb.

Movement was difficult from the outset, as the severity of the gradient was physically exacting and the knowledge that any moment could reveal an enemy with weapon poised heightened the mental anxiety. We had constant reminders that this was a formidable force we were facing, not a ragtag group of dissidents. At one point, we walked directly into a well-organised, but thankfully empty, defensive position. It was secured with overhead protection – serious fighting bays designed to protect the occupants from indirect fire and air attack.

Several members of our troop had been in numerous engagements, but the level of anxiety on that climb was greater than any we'd experienced before. Our nerves were as strained as our bodies as we heaved and pushed our way up the mountain.

We were wearing NVGs, which require an enormous amount of concentration as your depth perception is severely limited. The NVGs were attached to our lightweight helmets, a far more comfortable configuration than the classic face bracket, but the old problem of sweaty steam and goggles reared its ugly head again. Our eyes stung but we wiped them clear and continued to scan for movement, light or anything resembling a human figure. Our ears were also straining, like those of a guard dog that has been startled in the middle of the night. With each step our anxiety rose. We approached another false crest, and this time climbed directly into a second defensive position that was large enough to accommodate an entire platoon. Thankfully, it was also empty.

With aching backs and tense minds, we were now close to the summit. We decided to get our heads down and find a suitable spot for an OP before the sun rose, which was just over four hours away. In the military, sleep is obviously overrated, so we threw in a bleary-eyed 80-minute piquet to enjoy. An enemy defensive position was as safe a place as any to spend the night. We had spent the best part of five hours walking, so wasted no time in readying ourselves for bed. A sleeping bag nestled into the side of a rocky slope felt near enough to luxury. We were happy to grab sleep anywhere, but not before changing out of our soaking-wet military fatigues.

In the end, it was a fraught sleep anyway, interrupted by the whooshing sound of a 107-millimetre rocket being fired across the valley. We established communications with our vehicles and, after receiving the all-clear, passed out under the glow of a starlit night. I lay awake for a while, waiting for sleep to take me. Looking into the sky, we could have been anywhere. We might as well, I realised with a disoriented start, have been camping back in Australia. Only the absence of the Southern Cross provided the reminder of the reality — that we were lying on the side of a mountain, trying to grab a few hours sleep without being shot, in the rugged terrain that was Eastern Afghanistan.

≡

Too soon it was 'nudge, nudge' time. Being woken for your turn on piquet after being asleep for less than an hour is almost cruel, but the piquet list is rotated — everyone shares the most unpleasant shifts. We got moving quickly, and just before first light our recon patrol crested the feature. There, at the top of the mountain, we found a comprehensive bunker system that was clearly designed to accommodate up to 30 men, with crawl-trenches and overhead protection. There was no doubt that whoever put in this amount of effort knew what they were doing.

With this added incentive, we moved onto the forward slope of the feature and found a suitable location for our new OP – a thinly wooded re-entrant, from which we could easily observe the villages and defensive positions to our front.

Our nerves were still strained, and we remained silent and focused while we prepared our new home. The sense of misgiving about our task was palpable; our stomachs swung between feeling knotted one moment and fluttering the next as we waited for dawn to break. The vehicle-mounted patrol had now departed for Khost and we were once again isolated in a volatile region of Afghanistan, utterly in charge of our own destinies.

We were a small contingent, so our security was closely tied to our ability to remain concealed. Support was anywhere from two to four hours away, if we were lucky. Noise and movement-discipline were emphatically maintained. We were all too aware that this was a long time for a small band of six to be in contact, especially if the patrol began to suffer casualties.

Life in the Regiment isn't always so serious. Although a gas mask may hide a grin, it has also been the subject of many practical jokes over the years. On one training exercise our team was kitted up in our assault vehicles waiting for Buzz to give the orders for an emergency action (EA) assault to take place. The exercise involved the use of CS gas – tear gas – so a mask was imperative, unless you wanted to become a dribbling wreck halfway through the assault.

I was Buzz's driver. While he stood in front of the troop vehicles, I took the filter off his gas mask and hid it in the glove box. Buzz came racing back to the car with his trademark grin, yelling, 'Let's go, tool!' He feverishly fitted his gas mask, followed by earmuffs and helmet.

Our vehicles were soon roaring towards the target. As we drove, Buzz placed his hand over his filter as part of the standard confirmatory check to ensure he had a seal. He froze in his seat when he noticed he was lacking that one crucial piece of equipment. Without it he would lose all credibility, running out of the stronghold in tears.

I couldn't conceal my joy and was almost in hysterics as I tried to control the vehicle, which was screaming around the bend on the way to the target building. I regained my composure and, with full concentration, I steered the vehicle – with the three assaulters standing on the back – around the sweeping left-hander while also shouting 'glove box' to my very pissed-off team leader.

Buzz frantically tried to screw on his filter. He cursed me, but I was again having difficulty concentrating, unable to suppress a series of debilitating belly laughs. Mr Cool was in a somewhat flustered state as the vehicle came to an abrupt stop. Our team blew in a window before scaling a ladder and launching into the first floor, but Buzz was the second-last man up the ladder, a position that he was not familiar with. He kept this little incident in his memory bank.

In another assault Buzz ordered that there would be no CS gas, and so team Z3 had taken the soft option and decided to go in with Oakley facemasks rather than the vision-restricting gas masks. Our team, Z1, were playing enemy and decided to teach Z3 a lesson by taking in a shotgun filled with CS gas.

I heard Z3 make entry so I pumped three or four CS rounds into the room I was hiding in. It wasn't long before two members of the assault team entered, and the sound of them choking on the gas, as cruel as it sounds in retrospect, was hilarious to our entire team. The Z3 assaulters lost all composure and ran for the exit.

I sprang out of hiding and shot the two fleeing men in the arse with paint rounds that would often draw blood if they hit exposed skin. The two men would be sporting a couple of cherries on their tender bum cheeks for the next few days.

Needless to say, they had their revenge. The team grabbed their gas masks before re-entering the stronghold. They located the individual who had caused them so much embarrassment and managed to shoot me several dozen times from a range that was probably well below the minimum safety distance for training purposes. I had bleeding fingers and split skin all over my arms, shoulders and thighs.

Later that evening, I groaned as the hot water of the shower touched my welting skin. A member of Z3 just laughed and asked if I thought it had been worth it. I was in no doubt. 'Absolutely!'

Nearer to our deployment in Afghanistan, our troop commander (the Boss) managed to secure the boys a ride on the training fighter aircraft – a PC9. These were like little sports cars and were capable of pulling over four Gs.

I approached the pilots before we left and told them that they looked like a 'bunch of pussies'. They were shocked at first, but then looked at each other with a smile. I am no mind-reader but I had no trouble working out that they were going to make me pay for such frivolous comments. This was all the motivation these pilots needed to make an SAS guy vomit.

The flight began violently. Even on take-off the pilot was throwing the high-performance machine to the left and right. As we gained altitude, he threw the aircraft into some serious aerobatics. I was now regretting my little taunt but the bravado continued, although with a little less conviction.

The pilot held the aircraft in a continuous loop-the-loop which seemed to last an eternity. *Shit*, I thought, as the sickening feeling that had taken control of my stomach moved upward. The pilot pulled back hard on the joystick until alarm bells began to signal – the aircraft stalled and then plummeted back towards the earth in a death roll that a saltwater crocodile would have been proud of.

The aircraft spiralled no fewer than seven times before being pulled back into the sky for another round of gut-wrenching torture. I was now totally over being a smart-arse and realised that a hugely embarrassing moment, a violent vomit, was only minutes away. I did everything I could not to vomit inside my oxygen mask as the pilot threw the trainer into a valley. The contours were the last thing my screaming, heaving stomach was craving.

The pilot asked me a series of questions before holding the aircraft in a four-G turn. I was unable to speak. The G-suit contracted around my thighs, squeezing the blood back up towards my torso and brain. I looked briefly at the ejection handle and contemplated how much trouble I would get in if I just bailed out of this sickening ride, but I just tensed my stomach and held on.

I was massively relieved when the pilot allowed me to take control of the aircraft, which gave me some much-needed recovery time. The pilot encouraged me to perform a few aerobatics – with his guidance, of course – but I had no intention of doing anything but flying with as little sideways and up-and-down movement as possible.

The pilot soon realised what I was doing and took control of the aircraft for another sickening set of aeros. As we finally approached the runway to land, I ripped off my oxygen mask and began dry-retching. The vomit entered my mouth but I forced it back down into my stomach. I simply refused to give the pilot the satisfaction of knowing that he had won.

At last the trainer touched the ground – not a moment too soon, as far as I was concerned. The pilot wasted no time in searching for some evidence of weakness, and my pale face showed a man who was clearly defeated.

'You'll pay for that,' I spluttered as I stumbled out of the aircraft.

It wasn't long before I had my revenge. That afternoon, the SAS soldiers took the pilots for some pistol training and I had Mr Top Gun in my sights – not literally! My pilot was actually a natural and easily outperformed his colleagues. He was hyper-competitive and winning was everything to him.

I decided to run a shooting competition, a prospect about which he was orgasmically excited. This was a chance for him to outshine his peers. Little did he know that I was setting him up for a dramatic fall from grace. The course required the pilots to fit their gas masks and helmets, run 100 metres, then load their pistols and shoot at a target. Each missed round would result in a two-second penalty.

Top Gun was confident that he would destroy his less coordinated peers. He'd had no trouble in nailing the bullseye during the practice. Having recovered from my near-death experience at his hands earlier in the day, I wanted revenge. I inserted a little piece of cloth inside the filter of his gas mask. When I tested it, the lack of suction did not appear sufficient, so I inserted another piece of cloth. I had now severely restricted the amount of air that could be inhaled through his mask.

The men were lined up and Top Gun began to struggle from the outset. He had never worn a gas mask before, so thought that his difficulty in breathing was normal. With each breath the gas mask was sucked hard against his face and his eyes looked like they were going to be sucked from their sockets. I tried to contain my glee.

His colleagues were off and running while he was gasping for air and yelling, 'I can't breathe! I can't breathe!' As the pilots ran, Top Gun slid further and further behind the group. His peers had reached the firing point and released all of their rounds before he had even completed the run. When he attempted to fire his weapon he couldn't land a single round on the target – he had lost all composure and appeared to be entering an oxygen-depleted panic.

He was horrified by his pathetic performance, while all of his mates were in hysterics. Top Gun was shattered, with his confidence left somewhere around the 100-metre circuit.

As the pilots unloaded their weapons, I unscrewed Top Gun's filter in front of the group, before apologising to him that I might have 'accidentally' left a couple of pieces of cloth in the filter. Top Gun was distraught that he didn't get the chance to show off his shooting prowess. We both had a good laugh and considered our little battle a draw.

SIX

Special forces operations are very different from larger conventional army operations. As a small team operating in the badlands, there was always the risk that an entire patrol could be overrun and annihilated. In the rugged mountains and valleys of Eastern Afghanistan, this felt very possible. Forlornly, a small US special forces team of four discovered this some time later. One man, severely wounded, managed to escape. His three mates were less fortunate. Their bullet-ridden corpses were stripped and kicked before their degradation was completed – images of them were flashed around the world via the internet. In Iraq, several US sniper teams, all four-man teams, suffered the same fate.

If men go into an offensive battle as part of a company or battalion, they can have confidence that if they are wounded, they will be treated. If they are killed, their bodies will be bagged and sent home to their families. Operating in small groups of four to six men does not offer this luxury. If a man is seriously injured and the terrain does not allow an assisted withdrawal, then the patrol may have to hold ground against overwhelming odds and risk being wiped out.

In a contact there would, initially, be no-one to rely on other than the men by your side. Air support could be up to an hour away, and a rapid-reaction force (RRF) could take many hours. Our patrol discussed this and we agreed on a 'one in, all in' mentality. The last man, if all remaining patrol members were confirmed dead, must fend for himself and attempt to escape. If someone was killed outright, their body would be left to the ravenous dogs that were chasing. Kane and I agreed that, if possible, each would rip something personal from the other's body, like a watch, which he would later present to the other's family.

But we didn't let such pessimistic thoughts overwhelm us. We had an OP to defend and intelligence to gather. As patrol 2iC, I was placed to the rear; the Para Minimi was also the most suitable weapon to cover the high ground behind us, which was the most likely direction of enemy approach. Dave and Kane were ahead of me, then Grant, and the Boss and K-man were on the leading slope.

The OP was located on the forward edge of the patrol position and the watch shift would be rotated at hourly intervals. The rear position would also be manned during daylight hours. After the entire patrol was familiar with the valley and defensive positions to our front, we attempted to minimise movement. The three rear men covered the high ground behind the patrol, while the three front men rotated through the OP. This was changed periodically. Staring at the back of the wooded hill offered little or no stimulation in comparison to watching the movements in the village below.

Anxiety was quickly replaced by discomfort and boredom. The re-entrant was lined with small scrubby trees that had one very annoying feature – their thistle-like leaves had four or five small spikes that repeatedly stabbed us in our backsides and hands. We spent considerable time sweeping the thick blanket of leaves away from our positions. This meant we could creep around the patrol location in relative stealth, but more importantly, we would only be stabbed by these evil little leaves a hundred times a day rather than every second of every minute of every day. Whenever a stiff breeze swept across our position, another blanket of leafy spikes littered the ground. Sweeping the position was a relentless but necessary task.

Our desert fatigues proved unsuitable for the scrubby surroundings, so we wore our dark brown or camouflaged T-shirts over the top of our lighter-coloured shirts. We rubbed dirt into our pants and sleeves, all too often moving a hand only to be pierced through the fingertips by one of the dreaded little leaves. The days were stifling and the sparse vegetation at least offered some relief from the grilling sun. It was an uncomfortable OP.

The tacsat communication set was established in the middle of our position, with the patrol signaller to call in a rapid air-strike if we were compromised and attacked by a numerically superior force. We were well aware of the threat, so we maintained an extra level of diligence. The sun made it near-impossible to sleep during the day, so if you weren't on piquet, you would fill in your time by scanning the vegetation to the front.

Occasionally the silence was broken by an unfamiliar voice drifting from behind our location. We'd slowly lower ourselves to the ground while our hearts began to thump. Our eyes, groggy just moments before, were now sharp and able to focus with brilliant clarity. Adrenaline is a wonderful drug and within moments our weary bodies would be primed for action, like thoroughbred racehorses gated for a big race.

One time a man crested the feature and moved down the forward slope and across the front of our position. I clicked softly to alert the patrol before taking up a firing position with my Para Minimi. The others froze, remaining perfectly still with their rifles cradled across their legs. The slightest movement from any patrol member could compromise us. But the man, dressed in traditional white Afghani clothing, continued down the slope none the wiser to our presence.

Our bloodshot eyes observed the village, fixed, intense, straining and scanning – like those of a hawk searching for prey. The light reflecting off our subjects was captured and scrutinised without consent. We were thieves, taking images without remorse. The light that was previously bouncing so freely off the subject, flickering like a butterfly, was suddenly bound to an image. The image was dragged up the mountain and sucked into the large round lens on the front of the scope and swallowed in reverse. Information was immediately sorted, unwanted images discarded, and those of more sinister intent remained captive, subject to further visual interrogation.

The village stirred. A man moved from one house to another. Women tended the fields. Finally, something of interest: there was a man with a mortar round cradled in his arms. From our vantage point we watched the man passing mortar rounds to his friend and storing them under the rear balcony of his mudbrick residence. The location was 'lased' – mapped with the aid of a laser rangefinder and GPS device – and the event and precise grid coordinates were scribbled into the patrol diary.

We were enlivened by this first catch of the day. The sound of a military helicopter in the distance encouraged the village men to scale their roofs with binoculars, all the while talking feverishly into their handheld radios. We spotted a high-frequency radio antenna, as well as numerous bunker systems and men with weapons. It was very Orwellian, *Big Brother Afghanistan* – our eyes captured everything. Secure the image, analyse it, write it down; image, analyse, transcribe. This procedure carried on without interruption. Our OP's task required it to be manned 24 hours a day. The village would get no reprieve from our prying and spying.

Surprisingly, there were no children. This was definitely a concern. Was this a village of enemy fighters?

With our high-powered scopes we continued to scour the village, searching for anything that resembled militant activity. The OP was briefly disturbed by two thunderous explosions that reverberated through the valley, delivering shockwaves into the mountains and cliffs. The muffled sound could be heard in the distance and grew in intensity as it echoed through the valley, like the roar of an angry lion. Birds scattered and heads turned in the direction of the blasts. With the aid of a compass, the direction, distance and time of the explosions were recorded in the patrol diary.

We recorded the reactions both of those in the village below and of the sentries in the mountains opposite. We were there to build up a picture and with each new piece the puzzle began to take form. Our impression was not of joy or happiness. There were no children laughing at play, no scenes of domestic routine and simple contentment. The picture we captured was one of darkness, sinister intent and rocket-propelled grenades. It was unsettling – something was not right.

SEVEN

In the early afternoon, at approximately 13:35, we received a message that the other reconnaissance patrol was in enemy contact. Although they were only 15 kilometres from our position, the ring of mountains made it impossible to hear the firing that was taking place. Over the radio, however, the sound was unmistakable. The patrol commander could also be heard, although his voice was regularly drowned out by the sound of firing in the background.

The patrol was isolated, in heavy contact and dealing with it. We knew how they felt. We later learnt more about their predicament in countless stories – it was all too easy to imagine. Craig initiated the contact, forced to shoot an enemy combatant at a range of 7 to 10 metres. After an initial few moments of calm, the air became thick with the sharp cracking noise of rifle fire, and pieces of lead flew around them. The sniper got busy and managed to land a large-calibre bullet on the chin of the man who was trying to kill him. The man was decapitated and his dog licked at his remains. The sniper, a compassionate and caring man, later commented that he 'felt really sorry for the guy's dog'.

The sniper was almost killed himself – a 50-calibre bullet slammed into the tree beside his head and exploded into shards of splinters. Trees were being cut to pieces around the patrol's position as the incoming fire intensified. Another militant managed to fire a rocket-propelled grenade at the patrol's position, but it thundered over the top of the men and detonated into the mountain behind them. The enemy was not fortunate enough to fire a second rocket. He was cut down by a burst of 5.56-millimetre fire.

The enemy manoeuvred into cut-off positions and occupied the ground above and below the patrol. Up to 80 men had now joined the fight and the patrol had to remain composed in order to avoid total annihilation. The squadron, several hours away at FOB Khost, quickly assembled a nine-vehicle RRF. The squadron commander led the convoy and within minutes a force the size of half the squadron was roaring towards the surrounded patrol.

Our patrol was sickened that we were not in a position to lend support. The initial plan had been for our two patrols to be located no more than 1000 metres apart – so we could provide back-up for each other. A second group of men opening fire would have confused the enemy and might have helped the stricken patrol to break contact. Instead we were stuck up a mountain, hearing their plight but able to offer nothing.

The afternoon progressed and the men under fire moved across the mountain, trying to stay out of sight of the enemy, who were vigorously hunting them. Night could not come soon enough, as the Australians' ability to don night-fighting equipment would allow them to fade into the darkness.

The ridge of the mountaintop slowly devoured the shimmering sun. Still the patrol desperately attempted to evade the probing enemy. It was a highly stressful situation but one that SAS men are trained to deal with. It was especially tough, however, on the patrol's young signaller, who was only there to make up numbers. He survived the day but, perhaps tortured by nightmarish recollections of his experiences, committed suicide several years later.

Within 45 minutes the coloured landscape began to fade, the bright pastel colours soon replaced by a lifeless grey that darkened with each passing moment. The men were tense but knew that the coming darkness enhanced their chances of survival. They didn't have long to wait before they could attempt to break free.

As night arrived, the typical nocturnal sounds – the occasional howl of a dog, the drone of insects in the cool air – had been replaced by the voices of the scores of men who were moving through the darkness, above and below the patrol, searching for them. They stayed absolutely silent. With NVGs providing a significant tactical advantage, the patrol traversed the mountain before descending into a re-entrant in their bid to escape. They had been dodging the enemy for six hours. This is a long time to be on edge, but they were aware that their mates were on the way.

The convoy roared along the dusty tracks, the vehicles bouncing towards the valley. The squadron commander was well aware that his men were involved in one hell of a firefight and that time was crucial. NVGs scoured the slopes while laser illuminators took large sections of the mountainside from impenetrable night into a lime-green day. The convoy had barely entered the gorge when thick streams of red tracer were flung towards their vehicles. The zinging fireflies skimmed over the top of the convoy but the men returned fire and continued. They would worry about the enemy later. They had a few of their own boys to collect first.

Meanwhile, our recon patrol was still suffering from the spiky leaves – this was as close as we could get to the action. We were in pole position to observe the enemy defensive positions, and we could admire the arrival of a C130 Spectre gunship that was trawling overhead. The aircraft's drone produced a feeling of elation in us. This devastating weapon could be called upon to silence the enemy, thus taking some heat off our mates.

The Boss efficiently rattled off the coordinates of the four enemy positions. Spectre illuminated one of the features with a large infrared spotlight that was invisible to the naked eye. We adjusted the beam until the light covered the defensive position which accommodated the machine gun that was raking the road below with automatic fire. The gunship released a shower of 105-millimetre rounds that peppered the defensive position, but the red tracer fire stopped only momentarily.

The aircraft delivered another salvo of fire. The enemy gunman foolishly (or bravely) decided to shoot in the direction of the growling aircraft above. Tracer fire spat into the dark sky towards the aircraft, but to no effect. The gunship would deliver another salvo, there would be a short pause in the enemy fire and then it would continue. At last the bunker received a direct hit. We subsequently learned that the man operating the gun had several RPG rockets attached to his back and was vaporised. The DSHK

14.5-millimetre machine gun he was so valiantly firing was found over 100 metres away. The combatant was responsible for pouring rounds down towards the convoy and, even under extreme duress, he courageously continued in his quest to kill Australian soldiers. He was an enemy combatant but he was also tenacious and brave – you can't hate a guy who possesses such fine qualities.

The convoy continued roaring towards the desperate patrol. As the eyes in the sky, Spectre informed the convoy that there were up to 30 men lying in ambush ahead. The US forward air controllers (FACs) who were in the vehicles called in a 'danger close' fire mission. The aircraft obliterated the enemy positions with 105-millimetre bombs, and large pieces of jagged metal burst in every direction. The vehicles were less than 60 metres from the blasts and so several large chunks of steel struck them. With enemy fire and friendly fragmentation raining from the sky, you would expect the operators to be ducking for cover, but one man, Brans, seemed to grow even taller as he continued to thump 50-calibre bullets towards the enemy positions.

Back at the US command centre at Bagram Airbase, a surgical officer deployed to the operations room and asked for an update so he could prepare the emergency ward. 'Who is in contact?'

'The Australian special forces task group,' he was told.

'How long have they been in contact?'

'Over six hours.'

'What sort of weaponry is being used against them?'

'14.5-millimetre machine guns and RPGs.'

'Has an RRF been deployed to assist?'

'No – they sent out their own force from FOB Khost.'

'How many friendly killed and wounded are we looking at?'

'None.'

There was a pause. 'What, no casualties?'

'Not yet,' came the reply.

The convoy dodged the streams of bullets and established radio communication with the isolated patrol. The patrol heard the rumblings of the vehicles and collectively thought, *We might actually get out of this.* The vehicles continued and had propped just before the re-entrant where the patrol was hiding, when an RPG and all of its fury sailed towards the lead car and skimmed over the bonnet before detonating on the ground a mere 10 metres away. An RPG is a basic but extremely lethal piece of equipment. The warhead is a shaped charge that detonates on impact and shoots a molten metal slug through its target. Its blast and fragmentation are similarly fearsome.

The men of the isolated patrol were just about to move when they saw the rocket narrowly miss the lead vehicle. It doesn't get much closer than that. One of the men thought, *God, this nightmare is never going to end.* The operators in the convoy were a resilient and valiant bunch – a great attitude in such a situation, as they certainly had more of the same treatment to look forward to on the way out.

Perched atop the large feature, our patrol continued to obliterate the remaining enemy positions. A total of four were silenced. The convoy received only sporadic resistance on their return and continued out of the valley to an area of open ground, where they adopted a defensive perimeter and prepared themselves for the much-anticipated light show.

The Boss was attempting to gain permission to drop J-dam missiles – 2000-pound laser-guided bombs – on the remaining defensive positions. Permission was denied, then approved, then denied, and when it was all too late, approved. The gunship informed our patrol that there was a group of 50 armed militants to the rear of the defensive positions. We were not granted permission to take them out as there were no longer friendly troops in contact.

One of the US FACs who was located with the convoy established comms and argued with US higher command to be allowed to bomb the enemy. The request was denied, and the FAC operator was most displeased. As he continued to air his sentiments, his diplomacy began to deteriorate until his conversation resembled nothing more than an outburst of venomous profanity. If you are going to spend a huge percentage of your life working, then it is only right to be passionate about what you do. He certainly appeared to love his job.

It had been a long night. It was early morning when we finally established a piquet and curled up in our sleeping bags. While watching the contact had been exciting, it was not the same as actually being on the ground with the men who were taking fire.

Our patrol was not in danger, but we did feel guilty that our mates were copping it and we couldn't be there with them. And while we did our part, it still felt hollow and we were left feeling more frustration than elation. Directing support fire from a distance does not stir any of the same emotions as active battle.

The squadron pulled back and we were tasked to observe the after-effects and the reactions of the enemy.

We had initially deployed with four days' rations, which had now been stretched to six. It looked likely that this would be extended by another 48 to 72 hours. *Great, another three days of dreaming about food*, we thought.

The next morning a British commando battalion, which was tasked to sweep through the villages, began to arrive. By mid-morning the Brits were firing artillery rounds into the mountains to our front. The guns would blaze away three times, which would be followed by 30 seconds of silence, followed by three deep *crump* noises on the adjacent ridgeline. It was surreal to watch. The rounds sailed over the top of our position and slammed into the rock with a deafening shriek of piercing metal.

It was a show of force, and it appeared to work. The squadron and commando elements formed up on the line of departure – the place where an assault or attack would begin from – and our patrol was once again consigned to watch from atop this fucked-out mountain. We sighed to ourselves. *How in the hell did we land such a frustrating task?*

We weren't men who liked to watch – we were participators. Sure, many Aussie men love to watch a game of cricket but that wasn't enough for men like us. Watching the Australian cricket team wreak havoc only ever inspired us to initiate our own game of backyard cricket, so we too could feel the elation of hitting the ball over the fence for six. We only watched enough to pick up a few of the finer points before having a go ourselves. As far as our patrol was concerned, the previous six days equated to a lifetime of watching. We wanted to play.

The reality of our situation was that there were more than enough players for this game. Although we were desperate to join in, who really cared about six men perched on top of the mountain? This, we agreed, must be what it feels like to be the twelfth man. It was pure agony watching the squadron move through the village, and we hoped the boys wouldn't hit too many sixes. What fine team players we were!

We saw a village elder approach the squadron commander, assuring him that there were no Taliban in the village. This didn't surprise any of us. What was he expected to say, with the mountain to the rear of his house being pounded by artillery shells and a commando battalion praying for some action in his face? To top it off, there was the best part of an SAS squadron 'loaded for bear' – heavily armed. Of course he was going to deny it.

The little porcelain cups of chai weren't too far behind. The villagers were keen to broker a deal. 'Don't attack our village and we will give you some token ammunition caches that we don't really want' – that was their philosophy. Well, it worked. Instead of advancing into contact, the men were chaperoned around the village by several very friendly long-bearded men, who only the night and days before had attempted to kill Australian soldiers. This was a confusing war at times.

The squadron and commando elements completed their search and, as agreed, took control of several weapon caches. It was now time to go. Well, so we thought – or hoped. Our patrol was ordered to remain for another two or three days on top of the mountain, and the only way of filling our bellies came via thoughts and dreams. Thinking about hot chips, a slice of pizza, even a shitty burger, just didn't hit the spot. Regardless, we remained in location and continued to observe the enemy villagers, who were probably well aware now that they were under observation. Accordingly, we sourced very little tangible information.

Finally, we received our command to head back down the mountain and join the squadron. It was great to catch up with the boys and to hear their experiences first-hand. The men of that isolated patrol had performed exceptionally well. Some handled the situation better than others, but all deserved to be proud of their efforts. These men would later be enveloped in a wave of controversy, very disappointingly, due to a dispute within the patrol. The men were courageous but there are many fogs to war.

≡

The end of our tour of Afghanistan arrived with an overwhelming sense of futility. How best could we think about our role there and what we'd achieved when it felt like such a drop in the ocean? Our trip was eventful, but what did it all mean? I had no time to reflect. Within three weeks I was out of the green machine and off again, this time to the United Arab Emirates for a three-month trial. My family held on for what was supposed to be one final trip away.

Then came Iraq.

PART FIVE

SECURITY TASK, HADITHA DAM, IRAQ

MARCH 2004

ONE

I accepted a short-term contract in Iraq while on a four-week break from a position as a special operations adviser in the United Arab Emirates, where I had moved with my family. It was some 18 months after my extended time in Afghanistan, and it would be reasonable to say that in the UAE I was feeling unfulfilled. It was essentially a training role and I missed the rush of operations. Iraq was immediately tempting – from the perspective of my sense of sanity and my professional satisfaction. The chance to be properly challenged and to perform to my limits in one of the most unforgiving environments in the world seemed too good to pass up.

Every morning in the UAE was the same and it reminded me of servicing vans in my father's workshop. I would try to gee myself up for another six hours in the office but each day it became increasingly difficult. Some people enjoy days of nothing – good for them – but there were weeks where we ran fewer than three hours of training because of our trainees' endless supply of creative excuses. So each week I had 32 hours to dream of being somewhere else.

At the end of each day I would walk in the front door, pulling at my hair and muttering, 'I can't do this shit any more.' And after another six months my wife couldn't stand it either and gave me the green light to go to Iraq for a seven-day contract to see if I liked it. The seven days expanded somewhat. My first task was a reconstruction project in the brutal Anbar province. It would be more than four long months before I was reunited with my family.

Like a hungry lion, Anbar never sleeps. The roaming, snarling, roaring and devouring insurgents there could not be caged or discouraged. From Fallujah to Ramadi, from Hit to Haditha, this area of Iraq had sharp teeth. Since the war began, many US soldiers have lost their lives in Anbar. The lion's appetite was never satisfied and with every new victim its confidence and hunger only increased.

Without the support of the local population for an international presence, the situation in Anbar was always going to degenerate into an endless bloodbath, with a contingent of security contractors and engineers stuck in the middle. During a midnight departure from Alasad Airbase, a US marine bailed us up, incredulous. 'What in the hell are you guys doing? No-one goes out into the jungle at night – not even us!' US tactics soon changed – trying to stay one step ahead of the roadside bombs became everyone's highest priority.

The environment was extreme and unpredictable. Every day became more dangerous and stressful than the next. One of my greatest challenges was to mould a group of security contractors (former soldiers from the United Kingdom, America, Australia, New Zealand and South Africa) into a well-drilled, formidable force. It took a while but we got there, courtesy of some exceptional former soldiers and hours upon hours of hard work.

Running the gauntlet in non-armoured vehicles while attempting to dodge roadside bombs on Highway Twelve, a 100-kilometre stretch of road leading to Haditha Dam, was by far the most dangerous work I had been involved in. And it wasn't just the external conditions that made life difficult. Private security contracting had one significant disadvantage when compared with being part of the official military machine – there were some individuals involved who were just not cut out for this line of work.

After all I had learnt about the importance of surrounding yourself with people you can quite literally trust with your life, the repercussions of this were painfully obvious. Leaving the Regiment for private enterprise had not been an easy decision to make, but it was the right one. But unfortunately, some of the cowboys in Iraq were a cause for concern. Where was their sense of pride in their work? Where was their determination to be the best they could be? I knew I was a bit demented in that department, but as I faced some of the greatest threats of my career, I found some of their attitudes deeply disturbing.

Why had I left the Regiment that I loved so much? How had I wound up in Iraq as a security contractor rather than in service, working with soldiers I respected and could trust? It was a decision that had come about in two stages.

It's the nature of the job that your tide of emotion is always high and hard to keep in check. After many deployments in countries as diverse as Afghanistan and East Timor, I chose to leave the Regiment in December 2002 in order to spend more time with my family. My youngest daughter, Sian, was 17 months old and I had spent only 10 weeks in her life. It was time to make some changes.

Moving to the United Arab Emirates seemed like a way to continue the work I enjoyed in a context where I could spend plenty of time with my family. But my banal occupation drove me insane. Although getting back into the SAS was an option, I wanted to remain in control of my life. This was even more important for my wife. We knew that in the private sector we had an element of control. When we decided that enough was enough, I could resign on the spot. I could also choose where I wanted to work, for how long and on what task. Iraq, Afghanistan, Indonesia,

Africa . . . there were, and still are, many opportunities for guys with my skill-set.

As it panned out, I went to Iraq for the challenge of trying to operate in one of the most hostile operational theatres in the world. It wasn't about the money, as I am not motivated by dollars. I'm driven to perform outside my comfort zone. I love to be tested, and running operations in Iraq was a difficult challenge. I wanted to prove to myself that I had the stomach for such an environment, even though I was there of my own accord.

I'm fortunate to have probably the most understanding wife in the world. My goals and challenges, and my obsessive drive to conquer them, must be an incredible hardship for her to endure. However, when things become too crazy she does pull me back into line. This was why, when I accepted a position in Iraq, Colleen didn't push me to spend a designated amount of time at home each year. Instead, she opted for a maximum number of days in the country. Her advice was simple, but showed how deeply she knows and understands me: 'Okay, you miss the rush of operations. Please go and get it out of your system. I know you'll give it everything you have. I'll be able to cope for 12 months. It's just 365 days. Whether you do long or short trips is up to you.'

How could coming home to a more normal life, where my family was not dreading 'that' phone call, require any thought at all? Having my children look me in the eye and beg to be able to come with me during the heart-wrenching goodbyes at the airport was soul-destroying. I would approach the departure terminal and, with one final look over my shoulder, witness a horrible scene – three children with outstretched arms and tear-filled eyes. A stronger man would have got back in the car and resigned on the spot, but an addict just takes a deep breath before turning his back and disappearing into the terminal.

And it had become an addiction: I struggled to let it go. I would return to my family after a deployment and attempt to lessen its grip, but the serpent of adrenaline coiled tighter and tighter around me. As good as the drug was, deep down I knew I had to find my rushes closer to home.

TWO

From our current standpoint in history one could argue that the Iraq War was not only illegal and unjust, but a crime against humanity. From a military perspective, however, the initial invasion of Iraq was a tremendous success. The Iraqi forces were rapidly subdued and coalition casualties were low. The United States was demonstrating its unequalled capability to concurrently project and sustain its forces in several theatres of conflict around the world. The US Secretary of Defense at the time, Donald Rumsfeld, must have been confident with the initial progress of the Iraq campaign, but he and his team of strategic planners did not envisage the turmoil that would ensue. Iraq is now a highly unstable nation and the sectarian violence within its borders may well erupt into mass genocide.

Iraq does, of course, have many historical precedents. Soldiers the world over have been deployed abroad on waves of nationalistic fervour in support of questionable causes. But regardless of the rights and wrongs, soldiers on all sides have to engage with the same level of intensity in a campaign based on lies and deception as in an operation of unquestionable morals and principles.

Unless one's country is being invaded, a soldier's loyalty is, first and foremost, to his mates. A patriotic duty to one's country is commendable, and everyone is aware of the larger picture, but this is not what holds soldiers together during battle. This could be the one aspect of war that Hollywood gets right, despite its excessive glorification of battle. Even Forrest Gump was aware of it! In the reality of war, it is the camaraderie and not wanting to let your mates down that motivates a soldier to fight. To be regarded by your mates as a soldier who is 'suspect' under fire would be a heavy burden to carry. Soldiers may, at times, be political pawns, but as far as they are concerned they are a team: not necessarily a team that always agrees wholeheartedly with their government, but a family of brothers who look after one another – no matter what is asked of them.

Iraq was and is a country desperately in need of help, particularly in the rebuilding of its shattered infrastructure. In past conflicts, military personnel were primarily responsible for reconstruction or rebuilding projects, but this was a tremendous drain on military assets. Troops known as 'static security' remained at a fixed location and could not be utilised for mobile tasks. If a power station needed to be rebuilt then military engineers would be employed, supported and protected by combat units, which would severely hamper efforts to carry out offensive or security operations.

This still occurs, especially for the security of military bases and airfields, but the majority of reconstruction in Iraq is now carried out by private companies that source their own security personnel. These security contractors are a vital component of the fledgling rebuilding process. Their presence allows a greater proportion of military assets to be utilised in the war's offensive effort.

World politics aside, handing the reconstruction efforts over to civilians creates a lot of problems, not least the arming of thousands of private security contractors to protect civilian engineers. The number of security contractors employed in Iraq reached a peak of approximately 20,000 during 2004. This was the second-largest force in the country, behind America's troop contribution.

And therein lay the problem. Some contractors hailed from special forces or highly competent infantry backgrounds. Unfortunately, and quite worryingly, there were thousands who did not. Although security companies rigorously vetted their employees, there was such an incredible demand for armed security personnel that thousands of men who did not have sufficient experience to perform such hazardous work made their way to Iraq. These guys were now 'armed and dangerous'. Some were mentally unstable, grossly overweight, poorly skilled or all of the above. The vast majority of these men were weeded out as the industry began to scale back and become more competitive. In 2004, however, it was mostly a matter of making do with the men you had, but there was no love lost when many of these guys could no longer find employment. Iraq was not the place to send poorly trained former soldiers to be babysat.

One guy I came across claimed to be a former soldier but was eventually identified as never having fired a weapon before. He had actually made it into Iraq but was found wanting during the first live-fire range practice. An ape would have looked more comfortable holding a weapon than this guy.

A trained soldier grasps a weapon by the pistol grip and has his trigger finger extended along the outside of the trigger guard, unless he is about to fire the weapon. The other hand gently supports the weapon in a balanced position. What this pretender was doing looked very wrong. He held the weapon well away from his body, like he had been told it carried an infectious disease. Instead of grasping the rifle by the pistol grip, he actually strangled the upper receiver at the top of the weapon, making it near-on impossible to fire. The other hand clenched the tip of the barrel near the flash suppressor. This isn't the most effective way to become an accomplished marksman, but may be a good way to lose a finger.

When it came time to firing the weapon, he didn't even place the rifle in his shoulder and take aim. He was laughable. He fired from the hip, violently pulling on the trigger rather than applying a gentle squeeze. In truth, it was far from a jovial matter. When this man was confronted about his lack of skills, he laughingly stated: 'Yeah – I lied on the CV and managed to get into Iraq. You can't blame a guy for trying.'

Another man I heard about told the operations staff that he didn't want to deploy to Baghdad as it was too dangerous. This guy made it clear that he would prefer to stay down south where things were more peaceful. For reasons that still elude me, he wasn't thrown straight on the next plane home but was instead sent straight to Baghdad.

At the time, our Baghdad teams were required to deploy anywhere from Mosul in the north to Musayyib, a volatile area 56 kilometres south of Baghdad. My gut instinct told me that this soldier's lack of fortitude was a bad sign, but the decision wasn't mine. I decided that perhaps he deserved the benefit of the doubt. That was until we spent some time on the range. We were rehearsing vehicle contact scenarios, where a consultant has to exit his vehicle, take a firing position and shoot several targets. We would often number the targets from 1 to 20 and randomly call out three numbers. The contractors had to engage the targets in this order, to prepare them for a crowd environment where target selection and recognition is critical.

During the dry practice scenarios, safety catches remain fixed and no-one is to fire their weapon. On three occasions this suspect soldier pointed his weapon directly at my chest when he exited the car. He had no awareness of safety. I counselled him before we advanced onto the live-fire practice, and I positioned myself directly behind him so I could control him if he got a little wayward with his weapon.

I failed. This guy exited the car and disengaged his safety catch before he had established a firing position. He then fired a three-round burst from the hip. The first round entered the engine bay above the wheel and the next two bullets penetrated the bonnet. Mr Incompetent was quickly unloaded and removed from the range.

On the return drive from Baghdad to Kuwait, he lay down on the back seat and went to sleep. When he was asked to concentrate, for safety's sake, all he had to offer was, 'Fuck that, I'm over this shit.' This pretender then had the nerve to argue with Kuwaiti Ops that he should remain employed on the tasks down south. When I was asked for a third explanation as to why this guy should be sacked, I exploded and resigned. After the dust had settled the questionable consultant was sent home and we carried on with business.

During another range practice, one consultant was having some difficulty hitting an A4-size target at a range of 25 metres. As the consultant was in the prone position – lying down – and the weapon had a bipod, just how the operator could miss the paper with every one of 30 rounds perplexed me. *Surely the weapon must have a bent foresight*, I thought.

I asked my mate Joe, an exceptional marksman, to have a try. He picked up the weapon, moved back to 40 metres, loaded a fresh 30-round magazine and, while standing up, calmly put 30 holes in the target. We attempted to coach the troubled individual but soon realised that there was little point. He was so frightened of firing the weapon that he was snatching the trigger with such intensity that his rounds would miss the target by more than a metre. Considering the short range, and that no-one was actually shooting back, this was quite a cause for concern. He was a lovely guy, but in Iraq, what does lovely mean? He was a liability, so he had to go.

Sadly, the list of those unsuited to the work was a long one. There were those who were incompetent behind the wheel. During a complex ambush scenario at Haditha Dam some months later, I briefed the guys to look after the cars and take it easy when reversing. Due to the remote location of our project, we could not afford to damage any vehicles. They were our lifeline. A US marine major whom I was friendly with was watching the training. On the very next scenario, one of the consultants, while reversing his vehicle out of the ambush area, became confused about which way to turn the steering wheel. Then he tried to depress the brake but accidentally hit the accelerator. Another consultant, who had exited his vehicle and taken up a firing position, saw this wayward Pajero thundering towards him, so he quickly jumped back into his vehicle just seconds before the other car slammed into the door.

I turned to the marine. 'So what do you think?' I joked. 'Do you like the way we do business?'

He laughed. 'Lucky you told that penis to take it easy. Imagine what he would be capable of if you put him under a bit of pressure.'

The highly competent former soldiers who were scattered throughout the security companies despised these pretenders. So why did men who didn't have to be in Iraq make the decision to go there? For many, it was the pull of the almighty dollar. For others, it was the excitement and challenge of performing in the most dangerous environment on earth – to be part of the campaign. Others missed the camaraderie associated with their time in the military, and relished the opportunity to work with old friends and likeminded people. Some were even there to express their disagreement with the war, following what they saw as a moral obligation to assist in the reconstruction effort. For others still, it was all they knew or all they wanted to do. They were being paid well, so were willing to run the gauntlet until either they were blown apart or the work dried up. In a place of such dangers and challenges, it was an additional source of anxiety I could have done without.

THREE

One vital piece of Iraqi infrastructure that had been flagged as a major reconstruction project was Haditha Dam, a hydroelectric facility that provided approximately 15 per cent of the nation's electricity. The turbines had been neglected for many years and were functioning at less than half their capacity. The US Corps of Engineers contracted a civilian engineer team to assess what would be required to return output to original specifications. Haditha is located in the north-western province of Anbar, which was deeply embedded in the 'Sunni triangle' – a hotbed of insurgent activity. Two four-man private security teams were formed and given the task of reconnoitring the dam site before moving to the Iraq–Jordan border to pick up seven 'clients', engineers whom they would escort back to the facility to carry out the assessment phase of the project.

The man who allocated the operational tasking was a British former SAS squadron sergeant-major. Jim was a man of unquestionable integrity, loyalty and steely determination. His ability to multitask could be compared to that of a mother of sextuplets. He possessed the work ethic of a thousand soldier ants, was scrupulously honest and, aged in his mid-forties, was as fit as men 20 years his junior. He was a great company man and a compassionate leader who cared about his men. We were good friends and had previously worked together in the UAE. I knew him well and was aware that he hated weak fucks. But besides fellow weak fucks, who didn't! He was my kind of man.

I was chosen to lead the task. I'd been in Iraq for about two weeks, even though technically I was still employed in the UAE. The months before the deployment of the reconstruction team had seen a steady increase in the number and intensity of incidents around the Haditha area. Reviewing the period revealed a rollcall of conflicts and tragedies. On 19 February 2004, several coordinated groups of masked attackers driving white pick-ups simultaneously attacked the Haditha and Haqlaniyah police stations. Several Iraqi police officers were killed. A US armoured response was deployed to assist, and in the ensuing firefight one American soldier was shot in the neck and another received shrapnel wounds. Nine insurgents were killed.

Five days earlier, on 14 February, a US armoured patrol had entered the village of Barwanah to investigate reports of a possible improvised explosive device (IED). The patrol was hit with a barrage of rocket-propelled grenades (RPGs) and small-arms fire from approximately 12 enemy combatants, who subsequently attempted to assault the armoured tanks. The Americans fired approximately 10,000 rounds during the contact. Another three days before that, an IED composed of two 155-millimetre artillery shells was located on Highway Twelve near the Haditha Dam turnoff. One and a half kilometres of communications wire was traced back to a firing point. The list of recent skirmishes stretched back to late January and beyond. The road to Haditha Dam was well and truly a hotspot.

I knew that this job was going to be challenging, as well as dangerous. The trip would see us pass by the north of Fallujah, a city that was in dire need of some anger-management classes. That hotbed of insurgency would later live up to its bad reputation. The two reconnaissance teams were formed just 48 hours before the trip. Of the eight team members, there were only two guys who were actually looking forward to the journey (me and my team 2iC, Pottie). This wasn't surprising. Another consultant, who had previously travelled to Jordan while employed with a different security company, had been asked to delay his leave to join our operation, as his experience on this pioneering trip would have proved invaluable. His reply hadn't instilled anyone with hope: 'No thanks. That's a suicide trip you're going on. That's a one-way ticket.'

It was true that the journey had the potential to be extremely hazardous, but such exaggerated comments were damaging. The consultant insisted that it wasn't possible to purchase fuel between Baghdad and Jordan, and that a Toyota Landcruiser would need two tanks to make it to the border. A round trip would require four tanks, he said, and the team couldn't carry enough fuel. His paranoid predictions of doom and gloom weren't to be trusted, but their negative effect on the group was undeniable.

Our 'motivational speaker' consultant later bumped into members of the team and asked what project they were on. When they answered, 'The Haditha Dam task,' he just shook his head and repeated his mantra: 'Oh, the one-way trip.' His comments were insidious and encouraged a negativity that had to be contained.

I wondered what this guy was doing in Iraq and stabbed him with my eyes whenever I heard his pathetic voice. But for now, I had to ascertain the dangers we faced. I had little confidence in two members of my team. I would have replaced them in a second but, given the limited choice at the time, this was as good as it got. The other four-man team appeared decent but had no previous history together, so a lack of trust intensified their apprehension. Not an altogether promising start to a new project.

I spoke to both teams the day before we left and told them not to dwell on the negative aspects of what might happen. We had to be positive, so I asked them to identify reasons the trip would be a success. Of course, there were a lot of questions left unanswered, but this was half the challenge.

Another problem was that our team had no intelligence of the Haditha area. Unfortunately, the company that had employed us was yet to gain military contacts willing to divulge such information. Our task was unquestionably dangerous, and even though we knew there was a military base at Alasad Airbase, it wasn't clear whether we would be granted access without US Department of Defense badges.

Issues that in 'normal' life would be trivial took on mammoth importance. In Haditha, how and where would we source fuel? Where would we be fed and accommodated? Were there military assets at the dam? These were the basics, and in this hostile location there were follow-on issues to be considered. What if we arrived at the dam and were met by a few hundred irate insurgents? Instead of accommodation and a warm meal, the team might be given orange jumpsuits before becoming international TV stars, notorious for being separated from their heads. It wasn't an overly rosy picture. Apart from anything else, orange is just not my colour.

We had no idea what we were in for, but both Pottie and I were confident that we could make the task a success. If nothing else, we had each developed a strong trust in the other's ability. If everything went to shit, at least we could rely on one another!

We also faced a worrying shortage of equipment. An 11- or 12-hour drive to the dam meant going through some extremely remote locations. This was not like travelling a major highway in Australia and only having to watch out for rogue trucks crossing over the white line. In Iraq we were constantly on the lookout for potential enemy or roadside bombs, and we had only the most basic mapping at our disposal. Ironically, we were being guided by a tourist map in one of the most inhospitable places in the world. It was seriously inadequate.

In the early days of private security operations in Iraq, there were a lot of shortfalls. Lack of ammunition became the bane of our existence. Each man was issued with three 30-round magazines. I knew only two of my magazines were serviceable. My previous training and experiences in the military guided my thoughts and reactions, and in times of relative 'quiet', images of our team in contact and imagined future operations flitted through my mind. I wasn't torturing myself with doubts – it was an essential part of establishing team protocol. No planning for a job is ever complete without some imaginative run-throughs beforehand.

In some of my imagined scenarios I'd fire the first magazine very quickly to reclaim the initiative, which would leave me with just one magazine before I'd have to reload. In an SAS patrol each man carries a minimum of 10 magazines and has weapons that are at least likely to work. Our weapons had been purchased on the black market. Although the AK-47 is a reliable rifle, there was always the chance that a round would jam in the chamber, reducing it to some sort of medieval club.

Well, it was the promise of a challenge that had brought me to Iraq, and it was a challenge I had received. There was no point complaining. Every other team and security company was in the same situation. It was just a matter of trying to make things work with what you had. The management team was aware that this was a shit sandwich, so to speak, but they were doing a fantastic job with the limited assets they had at their disposal and would have given more if they'd had it.

The private industry is, of course, primarily focused on money. There is always a clash between the managers on the ground and the suits back in their air-conditioned offices in New York or London. One group cares about the men, their level of training and how they are equipped. The other cares about the bottom line – profits. 'How much money are we going to make out of this? Who cares that the men are deploying with substandard equipment – that's why we pay extortionate insurance costs.'

In all probability the office-dwellers didn't think like this, but as we hit the roads day in, day out during those early days in Iraq, few of the men were able to resist seeing it that way. Our operational director, a part-owner of the company we were working with and a former legend of 22 SAS, managed to achieve a balance. By all accounts he was one hell of a soldier in his day and, although he was surly most of the time, he fought tooth and nail for his guys on the ground. He also subjected himself to the same dangers as the men working for him. He was a man's man, a hard-hitting, angry, former regimental sergeant-major who had been decorated in battle. Every security company needed men like this to keep the suits in check. He always backed our decisions and provided support, and the boys on the ground were always grateful.

Our two teams were employed on other tasks until the Haditha Dam contract had been signed and a lot of money had been paid. Once it was approved, it was all systems go, and we had one evening to prepare for the task. The vibe was one of urgency as we packed vehicles and tested equipment. I had received my final team member earlier that day, so we carried out vehicle contact drills until after midnight. Quite a contrast from operations in the SAS. The following morning we were issued with Thuraya satellite communication sets. These would be our lifeline and the only means of emergency communication with the operations room in the event of an incident. Considering the lack of preparation time, we were as ready as we could be.

FOUR

Come sunrise, it was a relief to get going and begin the first phase, a six-hour drive to Baghdad. We departed in four soft-skinned – non-armoured – Mitsubishi Pajeros with two men in each vehicle. From a security, military or even civilian perspective, driving in non-armoured vehicles meant that we were seriously compromised right from the outset. Armoured vehicles would be rapidly sourced over the following months when the insurgent activity and accompanying loss of Western lives escalated.

Perhaps the deaths of two security consultants in Mosul not long after we began our task prompted this requirement. One of these men was part of our security team. Who would have thought, as we drove to Baghdad that day, that this sprightly Irishman and father of a four-year-old son had less than six weeks to live?

The contact involved at least three attacking vehicles, two of which had taken up front and rear blocking positions. The third insurgent vehicle engaged from the side. The security team's rear vehicle provided protection, which enabled its lead vehicle to mount the gutter and ram its way to safety, thus saving the client's life. The two security contractors in the rear vehicle died in the ambush. The US military was involved in four separate contacts in Mosul that day. If there is any positive to come out of a good man being killed, it is the fact that he did not suffer – he was shot 82 times. This man was a diligent operator who was skilfully able to sense danger. He was not one to switch off and lose concentration and was incessantly on the lookout for potential triggers. It was this mindset that identified the ambush and contributed to a client and two security contractors being spared on that fateful day.

The last words this man said to me before jumping in a vehicle and departing on leave were: 'Hey, matey, take it easy and don't forget to tell Shaibah Ops that you want me back in your team when I come back. You guys take care, as I gotta get home to see my wee man and take him to the zoo.'

=

The intense situation we would be working in for the next few months was exacerbated initially by the fact that only one member of our team had previously been to Baghdad, and he was barely an asset. He actually had no idea how to get to the fabled 'Green Zone' – the designated secure area in central Baghdad. He was not even able to pinpoint its location on a map! So dire were our circumstances that I virtually had to interrogate him to get the information I needed: that the Green Zone was 'somewhere near a bridge' that crossed the Tigris River. In an increasingly uncomfortable situation, this was mildly encouraging. Trawling around Baghdad looking lost was likely to draw untoward attention to our under-armed, under-protected team.

Despite the odds being against us, I was able to source a precise grid to the entrance of the Green Zone at Skania, which was a US logistics base on the primary north–south highway. Route Tampa was a six-lane sealed highway with a very, very uncomfortable potholed unsealed section of approximately 170 kilometres in the middle. It would take another 12 months or so before the two sections of sealed highway were joined. For those forced to use it, this couldn't come soon enough. Travelling this section once was one time too many.

The south of Iraq is dry, barren and relatively benign in comparison to the more fertile and restive centre. While travelling its tempestuous surface, our vehicles maintained a spacing of no less than 50 metres. The large military convoys that rattled past us at regular intervals stirred up considerable debris, and the choking dust sometimes reduced visibility to five metres. Our convoy felt its way though the orange powder while trying to dodge the heavy shadows of the intimidating US military tonnage. It was like travelling on a highway at night with your headlights off, only to be surprised by a bull appearing in your path the second you turned them back on. There was no shortage of near misses as the US military trucks and vehicles passed within feet of our darting Pajeros. Being crushed by a truck laden with a couple of tanks would have been a poor start to our trip.

Our first stop was a US refuelling station known as 'Cedar'. All civilian traffic had been redirected and only military and Department of Defense cardholders were able to gain access. The break offered a chance to refuel, stretch our legs, relieve our aching bladders and relax. Most guys were always topped up with water, as a contact in such a remote area could have resulted in a very thirsty couple of hours, but this was a double-edged strategy. With too much, you'd find yourself rocking to and fro, your knees clenched tight, as your body armour pressed perfectly against your bladder. Each bump required a conscious effort to relax the detrusor muscle to stop from pissing your pants.

The area between Cedar and our next destination, Skania, was an unpopular section of unsealed road. When we finally alighted to refuel and revive ourselves, I felt like a cartoon character that had been squashed between clashing cymbals. Although the vehicles were now stationary, the jolting and shuddering in our bodies was like stepping onto dry land after weeks at sea.

Once we regained our equilibrium, we restocked the vehicles with US rations and bottled water. They now looked like a set of family wagons heading off for a week of camping. But it was time for the team to get down to business and make the final push to Baghdad. The fraught drive was worlds away from setting up camp and throwing a few snags on a barbecue back in Oz. The mood of the guys became deadly serious. There was no jovial or relaxed talk. We were sharply attentive to this highly dangerous environment and the task at hand. I'd estimated that the trip from Skania to Baghdad would take 90 minutes. We emerged from an arid landscape into fields of healthy date palms, and 'By the Rivers of Babylon' immediately sprang to mind. Unfortunately, such a haunting, spiritual melody didn't quite fit our vision of post-war Iraq.

The locals were coolly indifferent. Nobody was friendly and the vibe became increasingly eerie. There were no smiling children or casual waves. Here, in central Iraq, we were offered piercing stares and looks of contempt. This was disconcerting and another blow to team morale. With the overthrow of Saddam Hussein, this Sunni-dominated area was in turmoil, having lost their stranglehold on power.

It was obvious that we were disliked. The Sunnis didn't care who was here for the war and who was here for reconstruction – as far as they were concerned, we were all invaders of their country. It was a strange feeling, as we felt no hatred or animosity for them. We disliked the insurgents, but only because they were trying to end our lives. A suicidebombing or roadside ambush could occur at any time, and our team was acutely aware that we would have to be fast and reactive. These were the politics of survival.

Travelling the roads was a lucky dip, and we knew that all the training in the world might not be enough to keep us safe. The best and the worst operators would be equally shredded by a roadside bomb. Adding to this stress was the fact that I was unsure which roads were blocked off and which areas were the most hazardous to pass through. Although we were driving blind, I was determined to take the most direct and fastest-flowing route to the Green Zone.

We turned off Route Tampa onto Route Irish (the road that led towards the airport) and were immediately confronted by heavy traffic. Baghdad had a population of more than 5 million people and, since the war, had no decent system of traffic control. I instructed the team to close up as we attempted to weave our way through the maze of vehicles without pissing off the locals. It was a simple enough directive. The aim was to minimise any unwanted attention, so there was to be no erratic driving or honking of the horn.

We scanned our surrounds feverishly – roadside stalls, vehicles to the left, right, front and rear, overpasses, off-ramps, oncoming traffic – it was controlled mayhem. Needless to say, driving around Baghdad is exhilarating. Some of the men were excited and some were nervous. Either way, we all had racing hearts. Things were going well and we maintained our momentum. There were no traffic lights and everyone on the crowded roads believed they had the right of way, so the larger or most damaged vehicles generally penetrated the wall of traffic most efficiently. It was obvious that we were Western-looking and armed. So although we were unwelcome, we were generally granted a little space. We took what we could.

Navigation, even with an out-of-date tourist map, was relatively easy and we approached the entrance to the heavily fortified Green Zone within 20 minutes of entering Baghdad. Once access was granted we moved directly to the KBR refuelling station. Our security company had a presence inside the Green Zone but, unlike the military, our team could not expect a lot of support. It had been stressed to us that we were on a separate project and were not entitled to use assets provided by another client. Where was the sense of teamwork? We weren't even given accommodation within the Green Zone and were directed to move to the Palestine Hotel, across the river.

After our vehicles were secured in the hotel's car park, we took all essential items inside. The eight of us, with loaded weapons slung over our shoulders and arms heavily burdened with equipment, were expecting looks of complete horror from the hotel personnel. Were weapons allowed inside a hotel? But this was Baghdad. We attracted very little attention as we were issued with keys to rooms on an upper floor.

That evening I sent off a situation report back to the Kuwaiti Ops and, more importantly, ordered room service. The food was actually pretty good. Most guys ordered a soup that was far less bland than anticipated, which was accompanied by a thin steak with oily chips and a salad topped with goat cheese. We had to make the most of it – who knew what we'd be eating tomorrow? There was every chance that for morning tea we'd be chewing on little pieces of lead.

FIVE

The first issue the next morning was navigation and the lack of suitable mapping. I was aware that we needed to head west, so I was looking for the major east–west arterial road that would link back up to Highway One, the road leading to the Jordan border. Many roads couldn't be accessed but, after some initially chaotic driving, we found a major road that led past the notorious Abu Ghraib prison.

This was not before the driver of our second vehicle, a medic who was beginning to fall apart from the stress, ran straight into the rear of our lead vehicle. There was only minimal damage but I was concerned. If this man could not remain calm in traffic, how would he cope with the stress of a significant ambush? I had planned to get rid of our panicky medic at the very first opportunity, but for now he'd have to remain behind the wheel. Ridiculously, former special forces operators who were qualified in advanced trauma and life-saving techniques could not be utilised to fill the medical role because, due to insurance issues, this position could only be filled by former Medical Corps personnel.

From an operational perspective, some of our medics

were unsuitable for private security operations. Others, however, were outstanding not only in their field of expertise but as team members. But this medic was a weak link in a chain that was looking stressed enough already. The only other option was to make him the vehicle gunner, but he would most definitely not have had the presence of mind to make a snap decision regarding whether to fire or not. His vacant eyes made me think of a kangaroo staring into a spotlight. He was clearly overwhelmed and incapable of doing the job. To be fair, he was a nice enough guy who was just out of his depth in this environment. But he was supposed to add value to the team's capability, not detract from it. All we could do was encourage him and get him through this stage of the operation.

Our map had a scale of 1:500,000, so it was near-on impossible to determine which highway we were travelling on. It was also measured in degrees and minutes so I used my navigational training to work out the appropriate eastings and northings down to a one-mile increment, and that made things a lot easier. There was no doubt that we'd link up with Highway One, but the million-dollar question was whether we would enter the highway at Fallujah or further south. As much as I tried to block them out, the paranoid comments of the man who had refused to go on this trip still resonated: 'If you fuck up and drive into Fallujah, then you're dead.'

I ordered the vehicle to stop on an overpass so I could work out our precise location. It was pretty obvious where we were. A sign informed us that the ominous city ahead was Fallujah. You could almost hear the anger bouncing between the city's 55,000 dwellings. We turned right onto Highway One and remained almost silent while we skirted around the city. If it had been a horror movie there would have been lightning cracking over the top of the bustling metropolis. Instead the day was clear and bright, but it was still far from reassuring. Each breath of the insurgent stronghold exhaled an anti-Western sentiment. We could not have been less welcome.

=

Several months later, while picking up supplies at the Jordanian border, I met a former special forces soldier who was running an escort task from Jordan to Baghdad. I asked him what he was looking after and he just pointed to half a dozen trucks loaded with 30 bright and shiny police cars. I didn't mean to laugh. He had a dozen Western security consultants and another dozen Kurdish soldiers to protect the convoy. He was extremely apprehensive about driving past Fallujah with such a prized booty. I would have been too.

He asked if we would travel in a convoy with him and I offered my help, with qualifications. 'Sure, but we turn onto Highway Twelve just before Ramadi and won't be departing before 10:00 hours.' I had my own plans to enter the dangerous village of Hit during the hottest part of the afternoon. Insurgents may be dedicated but they were less likely to be lying in the dirt waiting to blow our convoy to hell and back when the temperature was in excess of 50 degrees Celsius.

Unfortunately, the consultant was edgy and impatient. He left before 07:00 and, not surprisingly, their convoy was ambushed. Sadly, half their Kurdish soldiers perished.

=

There was no respite from the rising tension as we approached Ramadi. Navigation was now a piece of cake as the GPS was set on degrees (lat long) and I could rapidly identify our position on the map within a quarter of a mile. We were about 25 kilometres from the turnoff to Highway Twelve, the primary road leading to Haditha Dam. The map showed two major roads and I chose to take the better-defined, which ran towards Alasad Airbase.

About a kilometre out from the turnoff, we slowed a little, maintaining 50 to 70 metres between vehicles. The primary turnoff was easily identifiable and our convoy entered the off-ramp that looped beneath Highway One. I briefed the team to maintain spacing but not to separate, ensuring our vehicles could constantly support one another.

Highway Twelve was a sealed two-lane road that ran parallel to the Euphrates River. At times it was right beside the river, at others the river would be about eight kilometres east. The highway wound through many small villages, and the Alasad turnoff was approximately 60 kilometres further north.

This road would prove to be one of the most dangerous that we encountered in Iraq. It wasn't long before we saw large craters on the verge from roadside bombs. The ordinance that appeared most popular were the South African-made 155-millimetre artillery pieces. If sited correctly they could quite easily throw a seven-tonne military truck on its roof. A vehicle would be peppered with large shards of jagged steel and the exploding gases would likely throw a car off the road in a ball of flames.

Our non-armoured Pajeros had no chance if hit by

such a force. The 100 litres of petrol secured in the rear would join the party nicely. We were all horrified when we noticed seven craters in one 30-metre stretch of road. Even the most incompetent insurgent couldn't fuck that up. If the medic or anyone else in the team wasn't nervous before, then they were now. What would it feel like to be ripped apart by a roadside bomb? Would your body be turned into an instant tea-strainer or would your limbs be scattered in every direction? Well, the answer is a bit of both.

The terrain quickly turned mountainous – a magnificent ambush area and perfect for killing or maiming. That we could be on the receiving end of an ambush only heightened our alertness. When we were about three kilometres from the Alasad turnoff I notified the team, and again when we were only 300 metres shy. We reduced speed but maintained vehicle spacing. This area was far from friendly.

A reminder of the area's perils came six weeks later. I was approached by a nervous man at Alasad Airbase. He was in charge of a four-man security team and was tasked to escort an engineer who was assessing the powerlines in the area. He was deeply concerned for the safety of his team, and I agreed with him. After the initial assessment phase of the Haditha project was complete, I never deployed fewer than five vehicles and 11 consultants on operational road moves. When I informed him of this, he just shook his head and said that his employer was 'taking the piss' and trying to complete the assessment on the cheap. He had to get going and, with fear etched across his face, asked for my Thuraya contact details. We exchanged numbers and I told him to get in touch if anything went wrong.

Two weeks later, he and his driver were ripped from their vehicle by a mob of raging insurgents who were heading off to join the battle in Fallujah. The US military briefed me on the incident but would not go into detail about his injuries. Apparently they were too horrific. He was in the lead vehicle and was approaching a village at speed when they were confronted by a hostile crowd numbering in their hundreds. The vehicle screeched to a halt just 30 metres from the crowd, and the driver attempted a three-point turn. In his panic, however, he drove into a ditch.

The crowd gained confidence and set upon the vehicle. The driver had his weapon torn from his arms but managed to successfully flee with dozens of men hot on his tail. The man I'd met was not so lucky. He was literally ripped apart, dismembered by the ferocious mob. Around the same time, another team of four security contractors was ambushed in Fallujah. The charred remains of their dismembered torsos were a vivid reminder of the consequences of an insurgent attack.

I had briefed my team that, in the event of an incident, it was one in, all in. If an angry mob attempted to stop the lead vehicle, then the Pajero would become a 1.5-tonne weapon and so would the trailing vehicles. This would surely put fear into any would-be attacker. We decided that if today were going to be our final day in this world, then as many of those responsible would also be read their last rights via a bit of two-way AK-47 action.

Needless to say, the drive was extremely tense. Pottie was travelling with the team medic and was able to reassure him to some degree. My 2iC was a South African former special forces soldier and a great guy to have on board. He was intelligent, well-skilled and always ready to respond. He enjoyed this experience but would later spend many months at home recovering after being injured by a roadside bomb.

As we approached the turnoff for Alasad Airbase, the cars closed up slightly to make the necessary left-hand turn. Once our rear vehicle had signalled its completion of the turn, we slowed our pace, as any approach to a military base, especially during times of war, must always be undertaken with extreme caution. Vehicles packed full of explosives were regularly detonated at military checkpoints, and the last thing we wanted was to be filled with large-calibre American bullets because of an overzealous approach.

We slowed down well within sight of the checkpoint and displayed an A4-sized Union Jack. We hoped that by being identified as British-sponsored personnel we would be given the thumbs-up from the American guard. Luck was on our side. A British project manager for another security company was waiting at the gate for his colleagues to return, and he was able to organise access for our team. His assistance, particularly after the stress of the drive, was warmly appreciated.

What a great guy he turned out to be. He was a big-picture man, a real team player with no interest in playing politics or making life difficult for other security companies. We were all doing the same job. He told us that if he could be of help, then all we had to do was ask. He quickly led us to the refuelling station and then invited us to the mess. We were famished after a day of heightened tension.

The Brit and I established an excellent rapport, but the

relationship was relatively one-sided. He provided additional mapping and gave us a security brief of the area. We exchanged emergency contact numbers, and all that I could do to show my extreme gratitude was to ask if there was anything I could offer in return. As it turned out, he was a little light on for ammunition. We weren't in a much better position, but I handed over a meagre 400 rounds. It was all we could spare.

During this brief respite, we learned that a company of US soldiers had secured Haditha Dam, just 40 kilometres north of Alasad Airbase. This was welcome news. Just before we departed, the security manager offered one final piece of advice: 'Take care out there, mate. The road between here and Haditha is horrendous. I've never seen anything like it. Keep off the verge and try to stick to the middle of the road. If you get hit, call me and I'll organise for some assistance.'

Fully aware that every minute that we now spent breathing was not only precious but also depended on luck and skill, our convoy re-entered Highway Twelve. We passed by the village of Al-Baghdadi, a densely populated area, and received many surprised looks from the locals. They may well have been thinking thoughts of hate, or thoughts of disbelief that we dared trespass, but disregarding their toxic stares, we continued on our way.

As we went on, the number of roadside holes became more numerous. Silence filled our vehicles as our eyes strained for signs of the dreaded roadside bomb. It was obvious that the insurgents were very active in this area. Whoever was planting these roadside bombs was highly motivated, as digging this many holes would send even a plumber's labourer into early retirement.

My right hand held my rifle, the barrel resting against the dash. My left hand cupped the radio fist mic and also pinned my map to my thigh. There was no time to daydream. We assessed the road for anything out of the ordinary. A dead dog, a plastic bag, a fresh mound of dirt. We scanned the high ground for insurgents, assessing parked cars, oncoming cars, merging cars. My eyes constantly flicked from the road ahead to my side mirror (to keep an eye on vehicle spacing) to my GPS to my map. Our senses were heightened, heart rates elevated, and our hands were moist. It was intense. We knew we were alive, but we were also aware that could change quickly.

I ordered a right turn at the first western entrance road to the dam. Our vehicles crested a small knoll and there it was – Haditha Dam. Although we were still two kilometres shy of the facility, we were struck with awe for this engineering marvel that spanned almost seven kilometres. Lake Qadisiyah radiated a brilliant blue, a striking contrast to the orange desert that bordered it. The magnificent body of water was easily restrained by the enormous concrete arms that cradled, with unflinching confidence, the icy run-off from Turkey. This father of engineering power was never going to allow his progeny to fall. But equal support was provided by mother earth. Her body pushed up against that of her husband, her arms intertwined with his. Together, their strength would embrace and protect their children indefinitely, until they were summoned by the mighty Euphrates to release the millions of litres that were their offspring.

While awestruck by the dam's majestic charm, we didn't forget to close up as we approached the western checkpoint. The welcome wasn't quite what I'd hoped for, as we were aggressively waved away by the guards.

I left my weapon in the car and, with the trusty Union Jack in hand, slowly approached the sentry on foot with my arms held in what I hoped was a non-threatening, surrender position. The breeze was like an icy dagger cutting through the air, making my eyes and nose water. Approaching a military checkpoint looking like you have spent the entire day crying was sure to instil respect! Needless to say, I left my sunglasses on.

I was made to halt five metres from the checkpoint by an AK-47 pointing at my chest. These were not Americans – they were Azerbaijani soldiers, none of whom spoke any English. I was signalled to wait while the radio operator frantically chattered into the handset. You didn't have to be able to speak Azerbaijani to realise that they were informing their operations room of our presence. We sat patiently, and within 10 minutes a more accommodating figure dressed in US military fatigues approached the checkpoint.

We were soon granted access and directed to the operations room. When we arrived, I told the team to relax and have something to eat while Pottie and I went to meet the commander of the area, an American major. I informed him that the US Corps of Engineers had contracted an American engineering team to carry out an assessment of the turbines. Before I'd even requested any support, the major offered us accommodation and food. He also provided some mapping and an initial threat assessment of the area. What a man! Things were going so well that I seriously thought about asking for a couple of armoured vehicles complete with 50-calibre machine guns, but that might have stretched our still-developing friendship. With a departing handshake, the major ordered one of his men to provide our team with a tour of the facility – on the proviso that we would meet later in the day to discuss whether any further assistance would be required.

This, we learnt, was a common trait in the US military. They would often go out of their way to lend support, even if we were not American. They appeared to have a soft spot for Australians. While they might have difficulties in pinpointing where Australia was located on a map of the world, and some even had no idea what language we spoke, they certainly knew who Crocodile Dundee and Steve Irwin were. For us, that was enough.

I became good friends with several of these guys and have kept in touch. A couple recently travelled to Oz to visit. One thing always remains consistent: Americans are incapable of saying 'G'day, mate' without it sounding like a takeoff of a dated Paul Hogan advertisement. They also have a tendency to add a mysterious 'I' to the word and linger on this letter like a tenor grappling with a falsetto. Even when they give it their all and say the phrase with total conviction, to us it still sounds so very, very wrong. Australians cringe to hear a phrase that is usually so friendly mocked or bludgeoned, even innocently.

Another common gaffe these guys often committed was to ask if I was from New Zealand. The only possible response was to tell them how much I liked their country, Canada. That was normally enough to do the trick. Allegiance to your nation is a big issue. Jim, the British former SAS soldier whom I worked alongside for several years, is equally appalled when asked if he's an Aussie. I've been asked at times where I reside in the UK. Jim is now highly proficient in the use of profanity, and me, well, I don't mind Freddie Flintoff, Newcastle brown ale or bacon and egg rolls. We all have to give a little from time to time.

But no-one calls an Aussie a Kiwi and gets away with it. You have to draw the line somewhere.

=

The hydroelectric facility was enormous and the internal stairwells led into a maze of underground chambers and voids. There was an overwhelming and pungent smell of methane throughout. Nauseating as it was, we continued lugging our equipment to the living quarters that had been allocated to us, which were on the seventh floor. As we wandered the facility, the Iraqi nationals working there stared at us coolly, seemingly offended by our presence. It was obvious that our clients would require a 24/7 escort when travelling around this facility.

There were two wings, East and West, with 10 levels above ground. The Americans occupied the East Wing while the Local National Dam Management team and Azerbaijani soldiers occupied the West. There was evidence of significant struggles as numerous doors had been forced, and on every level we saw internal bullet strikes and scored surfaces, possibly from distraction grenades. We later heard that a US Ranger unit had initially secured the facility in an encounter where they were met by relatively low resistance. The Iraqi military had then attempted to retake the plant, which resulted in over 400 being killed. The majority of these men were from local militia units, so the hate-filled eyes that constantly swept over us were hardly surprising.

The lower levels were dark, noisy and cold. Oil-stained walkways and exposed live electrical wires were an occupational health and safety nightmare. In Iraq OH&S concerns must have seemed trivial: there were plenty of more gruesome ways to lose one's life. Perhaps accidental electrocution would have been one of the better options.

SIX

I established communications with Kuwaiti Ops and was informed that the clients would be arriving at the Jordan–Iraq border first thing the next morning. You've got to love those little surprises. The task had been brought forward by 24 hours, so our tour of the facility would have to be put on hold.

The team moved to our vehicles while I exchanged emergency numbers with the US operations room. The major was concerned that we were travelling the roads in non-armoured vehicles and without the support of heavy weapons. One of his first questions was, 'What are you armed with?'

He was astounded to hear my reply: 'AK-47s with three rusty magazines.'

The major did say that if we gave him notice, he might be able to arrange some 'top cover' – a couple of gunships – to escort our vehicles past Alasad Airbase. While the gesture was much appreciated, for now we were on our own. We didn't have the luxury of time on our hands. It was 14:00 hours and we were uncertain how long the trip to Jordan would take. At least we would soon know whether or not we would be able to purchase fuel along Highway One. Things had gone exceedingly well and we were hoping that this next leg would prove no different. As it turned out, we would complete the final 150 kilometres in darkness.

We set off once again, after confirming our orders and enacting the possible scenarios and outcomes of the trip. It didn't take long before we were reminded about the perils of Highway Twelve. This time around, the numerous holes lining the verge were not a surprise.

A common insurgent tactic was to plant new bombs in old holes. Of course! Why not? Most of the work had already been done, so it was just a matter of lowering the shell in before connecting the initiation device and throwing a bit of debris over the top. Sometimes insurgents attempt to limit their time of exposure and connect the initiation set first. Occasional reports of two, three or four men found blown to shreds around the area of an IED usually indicated that it had been detonated during installation. There was no sympathy from us – as far as we were concerned, it was a shame it didn't happen more often.

These insurgents wouldn't have had a chance to reflect on where they went wrong. A 155-millimetre shell bursting within such close proximity would vaporise anyone within a metre or two, and if you were further away then the expanding gases would send a percussive wave that was so violent that one's eyes, eardrums, lungs and internal organs would rupture. Then there are the large pieces of razor-sharp shrapnel that cut through the air with a sickening shriek. These pieces of steel would mercilessly tear into flesh and dismember with such brutal force that arms, legs or heads were often ripped from their foundations.

There is nothing romantic about a well-placed roadside bomb.

≡

During the second phase of the project, I received a Thuraya text message saying that the boys had been targetted by a roadside bomb. On the primary road between Jordan and Baghdad, four 155-millimetre shells were dug into the verge around the vicinity of Ar Rutbah. The bombs were placed five metres apart and detonated in between the first and second vehicles. All four vehicles received fragmentation strikes and several had windows shattered.

But luck was on their side: due to the vehicles maintaining a 70-metre spacing, none of the guys were injured. Poor placement of the bombs was another saving grace, as the negative camber of the bank redirected much of the blast away from the road and into the guardrail.

As soon as I received the message, I assembled all the remaining security contractors and briefed them on what had just occurred. I believe that when something goes wrong there's a possibility of things spiralling out of control. It was imperative that the guys remained calm, drove at a sensible speed and maintained spacing. There's no joy in surviving a roadside bomb only to be blown to shreds two kilometres down the road as you rejoice in your good fortune. In Iraq, this has happened many times.

I ordered the security teams at the dam to equip themselves and we waited in our vehicles until the mobile teams returned. This became standard operating procedure. It would minimise the time that guys would be vulnerable if stranded on the road following an attack.

After the teams returned we immediately debriefed the incident. It emerged that, while refuelling at a service station, the guys had been somewhat aggressive in posture. Rather than trying to blend in, they'd dominated the area. Secondly, all the vehicles had been positioned in the left lane. We changed this formation immediately. I was relieved that everyone was okay, and when we were tasked to return to Jordan the following day to pick up equipment, I re-adopted my usual position in the lead vehicle. Luckily the guys had the presence of mind to record the precise location of the incident, which was something the team leader had seen me do several days before, when the rear of our convoy had been shot at by two black BMWs.

I intended to investigate the bombing site, so I ordered all the vehicles to adopt a defensive perimeter 200 metres before it. My vehicle then continued for an additional 200 metres past the area and propped while I ran back in with a camera to record evidence of the attack. I was aware that insurgents sometimes placed new bombs in old holes, so I took a little extra care and crawled in on my stomach. I captured several images and collected half a dozen large pieces of jagged metal, which we used to identify the type of ordinance used. The expanding gases had distorted the guardrail and debris was spread over hundreds of metres. I couldn't believe that no-one had been killed. Diligent vehicle spacing was the main reason these guys survived. The following evening, after another seven hours on the roads, I gave the guys the pieces of ordinance that I had collected. Looking at their faces as they ran their fingers across the razor-sharp pieces of metal, I realised that everyone was now fully aware just how treacherous our job could be.

Sadly, one of the men who survived this incident was later killed by a roadside bomb, on the road between Shaibah and Baghdad in November 2006. Rich was 36 years old and the proud father of a young daughter. He will be remembered for his love of the England rugby team, his strong work ethic, humorous personality and, above all else, his ginger hair. He also beat me in a competition in the gym at Haditha Dam. Damn it, Rich, you selfish bastard! You didn't even give me the opportunity to reclaim the title. Wear the victory with pride, Big Red. You well and truly earned it. You are missed.

≡

Our convoy continued south, past the Alasad turnoff, past the restive town of Hit and towards Highway One. A hundred kilometres passed without incident, and although the main highway still had the potential to be extremely dangerous, the team relaxed somewhat after leaving the crater-lined, narrow confines of Highway Twelve. We had been tasked to locate potential refuelling stations and safe houses along the highway that led to the Jordanian border.

I don't believe there is such a thing as a 'safe house' in Iraq. Insurgents had heavily penetrated the Iraqi police and security forces, so to rely on them was unwise. A smiling face could not be trusted; a person's true feelings were usually reflected elsewhere. It is easy to turn up the corners of one's mouth and show a few teeth, but the eyes rarely lie. Only a true professional can master this trick. The eyes are like the back cover of a novel – within seconds you have a very good idea of what the story is about. In close protection tasks, security teams are encouraged to wear sunglasses to prevent giving away information in this way. Even a man who is soft at heart can appear stone-cold behind an impenetrable pair of *Terminator*-like shades.

After another 90 kilometres our convoy passed what looked like a refuelling station on the southern side of the road. We recorded the information for confirmation at a later date. This area of Iraq appeared almost uninhabited. At this stage of the trip, that was fine by us. We wondered why an insurgent would waste a tank of petrol and travel all the way out here just to blow someone up. To us, it didn't make sense. That said, we would later survive days where up to six suicide-bombers rammed their explosive-laden vehicles into military and civilian security convoys on an eight-kilometre stretch of road between the Green Zone and Baghdad International Airport (BIAP). On days like that, the road would be littered with flesh and burnt-out vehicles. We heard a blast, saw the plume of smoke and eyed the charred remains of US soldiers. Sense or not, this was reality and part of daily life in Iraq.

≡

With significant population centres towards the Jordanian border, we had to pay particularly close attention to overpasses and parked vehicles. With the exception of a few overpasses that had been destroyed as a consequence of the initial air war, the six-lane carriageway was in pristine condition. We maintained a speed of 140 kmh, which was safe enough in winter. Such speeds would not be recommended or allowed in summer, as the roads become so hot that they begin to melt, which resulted in high-speed tyre blowouts.

These were quite common. One time, during the peak of summer, I was travelling along the scorching road from Baghdad to the southern Shaibah Log Base as the temperature climbed above 50 degrees Celsius. The lead driver, Si, was an exceptional talent behind the wheel. He was nicknamed 'Fox' and was a dynamic young man with a wicked sense of humour. Fox was fiercely intelligent and his willingness to learn was inspirational. He was an Englishman, but I couldn't hold that against him! He didn't hail from a special forces background but he could and should have. It was no accident that I worked with Si in Iraq, Indonesia and Afghanistan. He was a brilliant operator. Wherever I went, I made sure that Mr Morale wasn't far behind. Si and his team leader, Joe, were two of the best guys I worked with in Iraq.

Si, Joe and I travelled many kilometres together around Iraq. I trusted them to stand with me, whether it was the harshness of the environment or its people that was trying to take our lives. Si was a skilled driver, which was lucky as seatbelts were rarely worn in non-armoured vehicles. We didn't need the extra encumbrances when trying to return fire in a contact. Armoured vehicles allow you more time to react, as small-arms fire is not a major concern – and so seatbelts are strongly advised. A head slamming into an armoured window can be lethal. The sickening crack of exploding bone is the most likely outcome.

I was the convoy commander in the lead vehicle. As we drove, I noticed a slight shudder radiating through the floor and steering wheel of the vehicle. Perhaps I did learn something from my time as a motor mechanic all those years ago. I glanced over at the speedometer and asked Si to knock it back from 135 kmh to no more than 115 kmh, because 'a front-tyre blowout at this speed would be the end of us'. Si and Joe laughed, but Si did back off the accelerator.

Within seconds, however, there was an almighty *bang*. Our vehicle veered to the right and then spun 180 degrees while still travelling in excess of 100 kmh. Si recalls locking eyes with the driver of the second vehicle, who was now doing his best to dodge this spinning silver blur in front of him.

The rear vehicles were under the impression that we were now in contact because a tyre had been shot out, but in reality the tyre had burst because of the excessive road surface temperature. The remaining vehicles continued past the suspected kill zone while our vehicle kept sliding (now sideways) towards a guardrail. Every member of the team thought it was only a matter of time before the exposed rim that was now sparking along the bitumen would grip and throw our vehicle into a murderous roll.

Si kept his foot off the brake and the vehicle somehow settled on its three remaining tyres. Joe and I congratulated him for preventing a roll-over, which probably allowed us to keep on living. The boys immediately secured the area and we carried out a rapid tyre change drill. The teams were expected to be able to change a non-armoured vehicle's tyre in no more than four minutes. We had to set the standard so, with the adrenaline still pumping, it was easily achieved.

=

Si and Joe typified the best of the mateship and camaraderie of service. Joe, in particular, was a huge source of inspiration and a true friend. He was a warrior, probably the only truly fearless man I have ever served with.

Joe was a former Rhodesian SAS soldier and Selous Scout. One evening Joe, I and two marine officers, Sean and Jon (who had just returned from the Battle of Fallujah), sat down and shared our past experiences. We bonded and will always remain friends. After Joe spoke about some of the things he had done and seen ... well, everyone else remained pretty quiet after that.

The three of us were in awe of this man. He was a legend, a warrior, a gangster. He could be so creative, funny and warm, but everyone had confidence that, should our situation become dire, he would become a fearless killing machine. His marksmanship was outstanding. I first noticed this when we were conducting live-fire range practices from moving vehicles. Most of the guys had no idea when it came to shooting on the move from the front passenger seat of a vehicle, but Joe was the exception. He lined up his weapon and squeezed off the rounds perfectly, with either hand – it didn't matter, he could fire with both. He was that extraordinary mixture of elegance and brute force, if the occasion called for it.

In many ways, Joe reminded me of Kane. What a team the two of them would have made. Without hesitation I would consider these two men to be the toughest human beings I've met.

Even after I had returned home, we kept in touch – one of those bonds that you know will be lifelong. While writing this book I received an email from Joe, who was still working in Iraq. I had already written the paragraph above, trying to capture his spirit, when this message came through. It felt like my memories had conjured him up. He wrote:

> [I] have just returned from leave in the UK and am chuffed to be back. I enjoy my leave breaks but after about two weeks I need to come back here ... My eldest daughter has a room for me because she doesn't want her son growing up not knowing his granddad – he's almost nineteen months old now. I spoil him rotten when I'm back there. I'm still based in Baghdad ... My spare time is used training and painting. I'm painting in acrylics and oils, and it looks promising. As for training, I have a chin-up bar outside my room and do 200 per session per day. None of these protein-munching bloated youngsters here can outdo the 'old man', as they call me. There's a real good bunch here ...
>
> You're right, in a way, civi life is so different! That's why I love it here – semi-military with mates around. I'm staying here until I know in my heart that it's time to leave for good ...

Joe was killed by a roadside bomb – an explosively formed penetrator – in Baghdad in April 2007, just three days after he sent me this message.

I mourned his passing like no other and, upon hearing news of his death, went for a vicious run to clear my head. I could not have run any harder and, when I was finished, I felt physically spent and psychically raw. I delivered the contents of my stomach to the mountain. I had not shed a tear for many, many years but for Joe I made an exception. I don't know if he would have been proud or disgusted that his passing had such a profound effect on me. I tried to capture the spirit of this man in a poem.

Sonnet for Joe
A fearless being of strength, heart and soul.
A man of raw contrast like fire and rain.
A warrior of war who humbled all.
Your poignant passing is tainted with pain.
You have silenced hundreds in battles past,
Yet you espouse satirical humour,
And unlike human life, your art will last,
A legacy of your aesthetic hours.
Your stories as a scout remain untold,
Except for the privileged trusted few,
But soon all will read of those years of bold,
A testimony of a legend true.
A roadside bomb may have ripped you away,
But this sonnet for you is here to stay.

SEVEN

Back on Highway One, our convoy continued west for another 170 kilometres before we came to a bustling petrol station with several shops and a domed mosque nearby. We decided that we would try our luck and see if we could source petrol. Now we knew how Mad Max felt – driving through the desert while low on fuel. The area looked like a scene from the movie *From Dusk Till Dawn*. This was the Iraqi version of the Titty Twister, but where was Salma Hayek when you needed her?

Our vehicles were refuelled two at a time. The service station attendants refused to make eye contact, speak or liaise with us at all. It was as if they were scared of possible repercussions. But they wanted our US dollars and we needed the fuel, so our vehicles were filled while an uncomfortable silence hung in the air. Our team remained alert and courteous but offered nothing more. To act overfriendly might have been misconstrued as a sign of weakness. With our vehicles topped up, we resumed our journey without the added anxiety associated with running out of fuel.

According to my map, the next area of interest was the town of Ar Rutbah, 250 kilometres further west.

This town would later become a major cause of concern as several private security details would be violently ambushed along this stretch of highway. In one instance, the insurgents wiped out an entire convoy of 12 trucks loaded with accommodation trailers. They first targetted the two security vehicles, and once this had been achieved, they spent the next 20 kilometres systematically destroying all the others. No-one was spared. Twenty kilometres is a long way to drive an under-powered truck while being subjected to a merciless and brutal attack. The burnt-out carnage remained on the road for several weeks and was a stark reminder of the deteriorating situation. It was strange to see an accommodation hut freakishly positioned in the right-hand lane. Numerous bullet-holes and some slight damage from the relocation bore silent testimony to the attack, but otherwise it was pretty much intact. It was a surreal sight. I wondered if anyone had decided to move in.

We passed Ar Rutbah as the last rays of light sank beneath the western desert. Our four vehicles pressed on through the night, cutting through the dark like the penetrating stare of an owl. We were being transformed from diurnal creatures into creatures of the night. Who would adapt best to nocturnal operations? Who would become the hunter and who would be relegated to prey?

An icy gale battered our vehicles, as if we were being pushed around the highway by a remorseless bully. At last we came to a fork in the road: Syria or Jordan. All that remained between us and Jordan was 80 kilometres of desolate highway. Our vehicles devoured the kilometres of nothingness quickly, until we came across hundreds of sleeping trucks that were waiting for daylight and their safe passage out of Iraq.

After weaving our way through the maze of tonnage, we passed through the first checkpoint without any trouble. We continued to the final checkpoint and positioned our vehicles in an orange-gravelled open area adjacent to the crossing-point to Jordan. It had been a long, anxious drive. I established a two-man security piquet while the rest of the team tried to snatch some sleep. But no-one could. Our vehicles became ice boxes as a deathly chill whipped, hissed and clawed at the vents and windows. When the sun finally rose, it too had a frozen heart, offering a sting to our eyes but little warmth.

We tried to freshen up before our clients arrived by splashing icy water on our faces and slicking back our hair. At the meeting, I issued a detailed brief to the clients that included not only the security situation in Iraq, but an insight as to what to expect on the roads and the set-up at the dam. Finally, and most importantly, I briefed the clients on what to do if an incident occurred. Our seven American clients were then allocated vehicles before our team magicians got to work.

Our clients had been informed to pack light, but I would hate to see what their idea of heavy was. Every vehicle was so jammed full of bags and equipment that there was no way whatsoever to see out the back. The last vehicle was the only exception – it was vital that the rear gunner was able to fire accurately if required. The clients were predominantly large men, but there was no whining about the lack of legroom. Their minds were occupied by far more pressing issues.

EIGHT

I informed the leader of the construction project that a lack of conversation in the vehicle should not be construed as anything personal. There would be plenty of time to get to know each other later within the safe confines of Haditha Dam. Now was work time, which for our guys meant total concentration, with little or no non-operational talk. We retraced our steps along Highway One and refuelled at the Titty Twister. Our overladen vehicles continued for several hours in relative silence until my command crackled through the speakers:

'The turnoff for Highway Twelve is two kilometres east. Maintain spacing and close up only when overtaking. In the event of a disabled vehicle, all remaining vehicles are to continue through the incident area before propping and providing fire support. Clients and drivers are to remain in the vehicles. Over.'

'Vehicle four – roger your last,' was the standard reply. It was not required that every vehicle confirmed receipt of the message, as that would mean excessive radio chatter. If the lead vehicle provided information then only the last vehicle was required to respond. In a large convoy of seven or more vehicles, then vehicles three or four might be briefed to repeat the transmission to ensure the signal was passed through the entire convoy. After all, a seven-vehicle convoy could easily be spread out over more than 1500 metres.

The team member who was later killed in the Mosul incident had renamed Highway Twelve 'Ambush Alley'. Our clients had been briefed on the possible dangers of Highway Twelve, but nothing could have prepared them for the IED holes that lined the road. I announced the numerous craters during the journey, with the clients hanging on my every word. They quickly fell silent, apparently suffering from a sensory and information overload. I'm sure they were feeling pretty uncomfortable that armoured vehicles had not been sourced for this project. Their requirements would have changed, now that they had experienced the realities. But in the end, it all comes down to dollars.

It wasn't just the vehicles and equipment, or the lack thereof, responsible for my increasing sense of concern. Two members of my team were just not measuring up. The medic was beginning to fall apart from the stress, while my driver lacked skills and integrity. What a combo. Hopefully I could get rid of them before it was too late.

On a positive note, Pottie, my team 2iC, was proving himself to be solid. It would achieve nothing now to dwell on the shortfalls. We were deeply embedded inside the Sunni triangle and, unlike before, we now had seven men who had employed us to keep them alive. The weak links would have to be axed at a later date.

Another area of concern was what to do with our clients in the event that our vehicles were disabled and we had to break contact on foot. Most of these guys were reasonably fit, but there were one or two who were perhaps only one good meal away from a heart attack. I decided to employ a rearguard action where two or three contractors would attempt to delay any follow-up forces while the remainder of the team escorted the clients to a defendable location. If we received casualties, then it would be a matter of staying put and fighting it out. When travelling with clients, there was very little room to manoeuvre.

Our convoy reached Alasad Airbase in the early hours of the afternoon and, once again, our priority was to source fuel. We then re-entered the lion's den for the final, potentially violent, 40 kilometres of the journey. Even those clients who had initially put on a brave face couldn't hide their astonishment when they viewed this stretch of road. The two clients in my vehicle were tall men, but they lowered themselves nicely onto the back seat. They weren't accustomed to wearing heavy body armour or Kevlar helmets for five or six hours but there were no complaints. We also advised them to wear safety-glasses, as a window being shot out at speed would result in tiny shards of glass being propelled into their faces.

Being blinded in a contact would be terrifying. Not knowing where the enemy was, and having to put your complete trust in a stranger, would no doubt stir more than a little anxiety. I turned to see how our clients were faring, and the looks on their faces painted a picture of pure fear. Their mouths were open and their body armour appeared to be rising and falling rapidly with their laboured breathing underneath. One of the men was holding the upper sides of his armoured vest in a death grip. The tendons and veins on the rear of his hands were extended and his knuckles radiated white. I'm sure their hands were sweating – mine were. I had to continuously wipe them on my pants to prevent the sweat from making my weapon slippery.

The engineers were brave men. They weren't just scared; they were, in many cases, petrified. We security contractors could at least be partly reassured by the weapons in our hands. If all was lost we had our rifles to defend ourselves with. The rifles also offered one other possible solution in the most desperate of situations. Some of the men had discussed this explicitly, and it had a terrible but persuasive logic to it. Using a bullet on yourself would only ever be an absolute final resort, but Iraq was a place where last resorts were never far from your mind.

Images of one's head being hacked off and buzzed around the world via the internet was just not an option. A family would eventually find a way to cope with a loved one being killed in Iraq. But they would never recover from witnessing, or even knowing about, a barbaric beheading. This would haunt a man's family forever.

I had discussed this sort of thing with Colleen: 'If I'm missing, then your nightmare is over and it's time to move on. I assure you that there's no possibility that you'll be exposed to a video of me chained up in an Iraqi dungeon and begging for my life. I'll make sure of it. My soul will be long departed from my body before you are even notified that something is wrong.'

Never
I will not be taken captive
and they will never steal my pride.

I will fight like a rabid dog,
until all my mates are gone.

I will then attempt to flee on foot and try to make it home,
unless my legs are taken from me,
then stay and fight I will.

Rest assured I'll keep on firing,
no doubt ending many lives.

But my final bullet saves my dignity,
I'm signing off goodnight.

―

Two months later, the Haditha Dam manager (an Iraqi national) approached the reconstruction project manager and delivered some startling information that resurrected our thoughts of capture. He had been informed that the insurgents from Haditha, which had a population of 90,000, would 'attempt to kill the security guards who drive the Pajeros and capture the American engineers'.

He stressed that this threat was very real, as the insurgents had informants working at the Haditha facility. These informants were providing information to their comrades about our team's composition, weapons and equipment, and movements.

The project manager immediately informed me. Naturally, as the leader of the security contingent, I was not overly enthused by their plan. Due to the quality and reliability of the source, I passed the information to Kuwaiti Ops and requested that all road travel cease for a 48-hour period. The request was approved.

Being captured was playing on the minds of the engineers, but it was also deep in the thoughts of some of the security contractors. Some weren't able to control their fear and requested to be removed from the project. A man would have to be beside himself to ask to be sent home before the end of his six-week rotation. Getting out of Iraq might preserve your sanity but to achieve it, other men's lives would face further risk due to an additional road move.

But confessing your inability to continue is crucial. Once a man succumbs to fear, he is only able to think about his own self-preservation. He thus becomes a liability. His sentiments are infectious and it is better to remove him immediately from the project, so that a single dose of fear doesn't become a pandemic. We read such thoughts on the faces of our engineer clients, but also on the faces of some of our consultants, who were employed to protect them.

We remained vigilant on the drive back to the dam, and fortunately our overladen vehicles made the return journey without incident. Once more we were stopped at the Azerbaijani checkpoint, and I approached the guards on foot. Ten minutes later an American soldier granted us access. At least they were consistent.

=

After parking our vehicles, the entire team launched into a vigorous calf-burning workout as we unloaded them. Down seven flights of stairs, up seven flights of stairs, down seven, up seven. Breathe in a bit of methane gas and then walk up and down some more stairs. Up, down, breathe in methane, up down, gotta love the methane. Up, down and more stinking methane.

Even for someone who likes training, this was punishing. Added to this joy was the fact that several flights were in total darkness due to blown bulbs. Attempting to weave your way down a visionless stairwell with arms loaded high with stores was about as much fun as it sounds. Especially when you think the steps are finished and you stride out confidently expecting your right foot to settle at the same level as your left!

The evening was filled with briefs and admin duties. Just the thought of setting up stretchers made me want to drift off to sleep. Initially, we slept well but the evenings were frightfully cold – perhaps not quite a Siberian winter, but the chilling shadows that swept through the corridors via the broken windows and doors that were left ajar patrolled the stairwells like icy ghosts. The wintry wind that lashed the outdoor shower block was equally intimidating.

The clients were an intelligent bunch of men and impressively task-oriented. There were several among them who greatly believed in what they were doing and took a lot of pride in the fact that they were helping in the reconstruction effort. One man worth special mention was Glen, an incredibly kind-hearted soul. He was a former US marine aged in his mid-fifties. His love for his wife and children was impressive: he was a selfless man who put others first at every step of his life. This must have been a tiresome journey for him. By the end of the project he was in a dire need of some rest. His wife sent a letter and Glen shared a small section with the project:

> Life is not about arriving at the finish line looking well preserved or kept. It is about feeling and looking completely

worn out while a deep satisfaction radiates from your tired soul. There should be no regrets, nothing but a calm glow of fulfilment as one peers into one's partner's eyes and whispers, 'Why, thank you, that was one hell of a ride.'

We remained at the dam for five days and, with the initial assessment complete, it was time to go. Most of the stretchers were buckled by the combination of bodies that were a little too heavy and stretchers that were a little too cheap. No-one likes a shoddy night's sleep. God help the insurgents: with our aching backs and impatience with freezing wind-whipped showers in the dark, taking us on would have been like trying to take a bone from a hungry dog. 'We can return when the weather warms up a little,' laughed one of the clients. I didn't have the heart to point out the problem with this philosophy, but Haditha had nothing in between. Icy winds would be replaced by searing gales and dust. The transition, like two cars colliding, was abrupt. There was no balmy spring making life easier in between.

We thanked the US major and his operations staff before setting off. The journey along Highway Twelve passed without incident, and so did the client drop-off at Jordan. I was advised to depart for Baghdad only if I was certain I could make it back before last light. I knew we were going to be cutting it fine, but thought that the chances of being hit by a roadside bomb late in the afternoon were considerably less than first thing in the morning. We went for it.

NINE

We were just outside Fallujah, gearing ourselves up for the run into Baghdad, when Kuwaiti Ops called. Apparently, one of the clients had left a bottle of sample water in our vehicle and it was essential they get it back. It looked certain that we would be turning around and driving another four hours back to Jordan. As I cursed my luck and began to plan the return trip, my driver nervously spoke up. In halting terms he informed me that he had thrown the bottle marked 'HD sample water' in the bin at Alasad Airbase.

This was the same individual who later broke our only funnel for refuelling and, rather than confessing, threw it into a bin and kept quiet as we spent 20 minutes looking for it. It was the final straw. His track record was poor. I'd had to take him aside and tell him to refrain from eating in front of the clients unless he first organised something for them to eat. I'd often return to the vehicle and find him munching away on a packet of chocolate biscuits. This was easily fixed: I would take the packet and pass it to the clients in the back, telling them to eat the lot. Then there was his constant moaning about how much his back hurt. On one occasion he asked one of the clients to roll up a jumper and place it behind his back for him. Other times he refused to drive because he was too tired.

I had to make a decision: should we go back to the dam to organise a replacement sample or not? My driver, not as apologetic as you might hope, had a typically surly response: 'I'm not going to be killed for a bottle of sample water.'

My reply was immediate and unequivocal. 'You don't have to. I'm fucking you off as soon as we get back to Baghdad. Drive on.'

We made Baghdad and returned to the Palestine Hotel to await instructions. Before long Kuwaiti Ops made contact. They informed me that the next phase would require just one team, my team, to head back to Jordan to pick up a client and return to Haditha Dam. Fabulous. The second team would return to southern Iraq. Heading back to Ambush Alley with just four operators, two of whom were struggling, bordered on insane. They were orders, but it didn't take a genius to see that they were irresponsible, inadequate and left us incredibly exposed.

One of the men who was due to take leave identified the shortfall and approached me that evening. 'Hey Keithy, your driver sucks, man. I'll put back my leave and go with ya if you want to piss him off.' His only stipulation was that he wanted to be in the lead car with me.

I was impressed by his attitude. Volunteering to put himself in harm's way meant he had to be a little crazy. In other words, he was my kind of guy. I requested permission for the lion to replace the mouse. Kuwaiti Ops approved the request and the unwilling driver was sent home.

At least now we had some decent mapping. We headed back past Fallujah and picked up our client, Glen, from

Jordan the following morning. We then moved back to the dam to retrieve the bottle of sample water. It was ironic that the goose whose actions had led to the repeat trip was not actually here. Glen asked where he was and I was completely honest, admitting that he was not up to the task so was moved on. My candour cemented a strong bond between us.

Glen was a former US marine so immediately understood the implications of a contractor being so far below the required standard. A feeble excuse would have been an insult to his intelligence. Glen was also not surprised when the driver of the second vehicle was given his marching orders. His erratic driving had nearly killed both himself and Pottie when he panicked and forced a truck off the road. He was unable to maintain spacing and his vehicle had become isolated. He then attempted to close the gap and narrowly avoided a head-on collision. To be totally honest, he did nothing to prevent the incident – the driver of the truck took the evasive action and prevented a couple of fatalities.

≡

I was involved in a similar situation in Afghanistan 18 months later when Si and I travelled from Kabul to Kandahar on a security assessment task. We had spent many hours training our interpreter, Sonny, as a driver. Considering he was behind the wheel of a beat-up Toyota Corolla, and the fact that if we were ambushed, both Si and I could immediately return fire, we thought it was a sound option. I was proved wrong.

The road from Kabul to Kandahar takes six hours by car and passes through some highly dangerous and remote locations. Due to budget constraints, we had no funds for additional security, so we decided on a low-profile approach. We draped local dress over our upper bodies and even removed our sunglasses whenever we approached a built-up area.

Not long after entering Zabul province, two four-wheel drives – filled with approximately 14 armed men – forced our vehicle off the road. In an instant, Si and I disengaged our safety catches and took aim. I exited the Corolla and came face to face with three Afghani men, two of whom had wild and frightened eyes. Their safety catches were still applied so I knew I had the initiative.

I took a gamble and flashed my US Department of Defense badge and yelled at Sonny to tell them that we were on a reconstruction project. He said nothing and remained frozen at the wheel. The tension was palpable. The situation became increasingly hostile and, after several more prompts, Sonny spoke; the men lowered their weapons.

They were border guards and said that the area was far too dangerous to be travelling around with so few security personnel. Although I would never task another security consultant to do what we were doing, it was a risk we were willing to take – once. Our excitement did not end there.

Sonny was rattled by the incident and, upon reflection, Si or I should have taken the wheel. But we didn't. About an hour from Kandahar, on a two-lane stretch of road, Sonny attempted to overtake a slow-moving bus. I could see another bus approaching but, before I could tell him to wait, Sonny pulled back in behind the bus and slowed down.

Good decision, I thought.

Then without warning, Sonny accelerated and pulled out into the oncoming traffic. Despite my yelling at him to stop, we were soon level with the bus and were now looking at death. The oncoming bus was now less than 20 metres away when the driver yanked on the wheel.

The oncoming driver's eyes must have looked similar to mine. Very fucking large and round.

Si and I braced for impact, and I think I recall hearing someone yell, 'Fuck you, Sonny!' It was probably me. But Sonny was capable of more.

He slammed on the brakes and lost control. We were now veering sideways and were sandwiched between two buses. Somehow we exited unscathed, to the sounds of blasting horns and screeching tyres. If Sonny wasn't spinning before, he now resembled an egg that had been thrown in the blender. He remained this way for the next 24 hours. Relieved to be alive, I immediately told Sonny to pull over and thanked him for the near-death experience. It was exciting, but his days of driving were well and truly over.

===

Back at the dam, having found the elusive sample water, we departed for Jordan the following morning. The US Ops room expressed concern for our four-man team. They believed that driving two non-armoured vehicles around this part of Iraq was courting danger.

I agreed.

The great rapport that we had established meant that the US advice was like a friend's. They were right, but there wasn't a lot we could do about it. I asked if the major could organise an air escort for the next morning, as we would have to depart before the roads were cleared. He said it was probably too late to organise but he would see what he could do.

The following morning we departed just before first light. We had travelled no more than 10 kilometres when two rotary-wing gunships straddled the road from high above.

'Are they for us?' Pottie asked.

'I think so,' I replied.

This was more like it. The choppers surged ahead and cleared the numerous *wadis* and suspect areas ahead of us. In one particular area the two birds hovered above a creek crossing and waited for our vehicles to make it to the other side safely. This air cover was maintained until we passed the village of Hit. The pilots then gave a very clear thumbs-up before heading back to Alasad Airbase. That US major was one hell of a man.

Once again we made the five-and-a-half-hour trip to Jordan without incident. Then we returned to Baghdad while also attempting to validate additional fuel stops. By this stage we were running close to empty and, despite the threat of danger, we had little choice but to source fuel at a service station that was several miles west of Fallujah. It wasn't a safe area to enter, much less make a stop in, but we didn't have a choice. Sometimes, even in the face of a daunting threat, you just have to go for it.

Watching Reyne, my three-year-old son, run and launch himself into an Olympic swimming pool can be somewhat unsettling. What begins with utter conviction and confidence very quickly turns into a fevered thrashing until he reaches the steps.

I vividly recall one day at the pool before he was able to swim. I was distracted for a minute as I helped his elder siblings fit their goggles. I turned back and noticed that Little Mr Impatient (surely not a genetic thing!) had disappeared into the water. As a wave of angst drained the colour from my face, I ran to the poolside, cursing my poor parenting. There he was, at a depth of more than two metres, calmly sitting on the bottom.

Retrieving him from his watery perch, I expected either tears, sobs or, at the very least, a spluttery cough. Instead, I was given a cheesy grin before he asked if he could do it again. This is the same child who observed other children at swimming lessons get overwhelmed by fear and anxiety, screaming like a crew of chainsaws stuck on full throttle. When the swimming teacher threatened to throw the cryers into the middle of the pool, Reyne, looking excited, put up his hand and asked if he could have a go too.

It is these attributes that worry his mother, Colleen. Not his exuberance for life, but his fearless nature coupled with his drive to do exciting things. Such traits seem guaranteed to lead him on a similar journey to mine. Although many people comment that Reyne is like me in this, the thing that I find most disconcerting is that he is far more gutsy and radical than I was at his age. Does this mean that later in life he'll require more intense rushes than even his dad?

I've never had the luxury of being able to do by halves anything that excites me. Trying to maintain a balance has always proved to be a challenge, and one that I am yet to conquer. It may be a challenge that is beyond me. Any skills I have, any achievements I make, have rarely been through natural ability. It has always been my demented level of drive that has made things possible. I try to achieve a balance, try to put less of me into fewer pursuits, but as soon as I have a spare five minutes I begin looking for something else to throw myself at. At times I hate this side of my personality and admire those who are able to cruise while enjoying their surrounds. To smell the roses would be divine.

Where does this asphyxiating level of drive and determination come from? Is it ingrained at birth, an indelible gift from my genes? Or is it learnt? I believe that these qualities are so deeply etched that they must always have been there. This mindset was certainly suited to an all-consuming lifestyle in the SAS, but since leaving some years ago, nothing I do or achieve is ever enough. Nothing scratches that itch.

Prior to my first patrol signals course, we were provided with Morse code training sets to assist in our preparation. After learning the alphabet and numbering system, I began to crank up the cadence on my beep-dashing machine. We were expected to have a thorough understanding of the characters on day one of the course to allow us to quickly attain a standard of five words per minute. In the week leading up to the course I could comfortably take Morse code at 14 words per minute while watching television. The skill came naturally to me, but it was the hours of commitment that made it possible.

And my obsessiveness was even worse if I didn't succeed at something I had set my mind to. God forbid I fucked up – my level of determination and self-reflection would spiral out of control. Before being a fully-qualified patrol medic (I had one week to go of a six-week intensive course), my patrol commander asked if I would like to place an intravenous line into one of the patrol members for practice prior to test week. We were severely dehydrated, so there was no shortage of volunteers (victims) to choose from.

The man I chose had never been given fluid before. I was also told that the Corps medics usually had difficulty extracting blood from him, as the veins in his arms were deeply embedded. In training, 20- or 18-gauge cannulas were usually preferred, as they are significantly smaller and easier to slide into a vein. Not knowing that he was nervous of needles, I decided to use a 16-gauge cannula in order to really test myself.

After preparing my intravenous bag and placing a tourniquet around his upper right arm, I was concerned that I was unable to locate a decent vein. I made a selection on the back of his arm before showing him the 16-gauge cannula. My comment didn't display a great bedside manner: 'Look at the size of this freaking thing. It looks more like something you'd stick into a horse than a person!'

I lined up the cannula at 45 degrees and inserted the needle into the back of his arm. The vein I was going for rolled and I missed. Without a word I removed the cannula and placed an alcohol swab over the site. Things then became interesting.

My victim passed out and began to make choking sounds! My initial reaction was horror. *Great, not only have I missed the IV, but I have killed one of my mates!*

My patrol commander, an outstanding man with years of experience, asked me what I was going to do. I informed him that I would simply maintain a patent airway and monitor his vital signs. I then laughed and said, 'I think he just passed out.'

We elevated his lower extremities to increase the blood flow to his major organs and brain, and within 30 seconds he had rejoined us. To my huge relief, he sat up; I apologised for missing his vein, then he passed out again. It was the choking sound that followed that grabbed my attention. Once more I maintained a patent airway and recorded his pulse. In his dehydrated state, his pulse had dropped to 28 beats per minute. Basically, his body had gone into shock.

After he came to, I administered small sips of water and offered him some chocolate to suck on. The colour soon returned to his face.

I reflected on my efforts, and once we returned to base I asked for a word with my patrol commander. I basically fell on my sword and told him that missing a vein in a non-trauma situation was inexcusable and that it would not happen again.

The commander dismissed my concerns out of hand. 'Everyone misses a vein from time to time. I'm more concerned that he fainted,' he said.

That evening after I arrived home, I grabbed a cannula and began to practise by inserting the needle into pieces of fruit. I must have jabbed a banana and orange 300 times over the following days. I passed my medical testing but the real test would come two weeks later, when my patrol commander asked me to administer IVs to the entire patrol.

After three successful IVs I turned to my former patient. He looked just as concerned as I was. He didn't want to faint, and I didn't want to be the cause of it. I took my time, located a vein on the front of his arm and slid the needle into him – albeit without the horse-needle smart-arsery. I received flashback – blood flow into the rear of the cannula – so I slid the plastic cannula inside his vein. I was in.

≡

Similarly, the first time I fired a pistol on my close-quarter-battle (CQB) course, I was far from impressive. After firing 10 rounds at the A4 piece of paper from a range of four metres, I was mortified that there were only two holes in the 16-centimetre circle, and three bullets had missed the target altogether.

My team leader, who came to have a look at the training, glanced over my shoulder and whispered, 'Would you like a shotgun?'

That afternoon I stood in front of the mirror in my room and practised my CQB stance-and-draw sequence. If I mastered the basics, then surely my shooting just had to improve. The same man who offered me the shotgun, Buzz, entered my room and asked me to join him in the gym.

This would normally be an invitation I would never have turned down, but this time I did. 'Are you serious? You saw my freaking shooting today. I was all over the place. I'm going to spend an hour or two working on my stance and pistol draw.'

Obviously wanting a training partner, he immediately reassured me: 'Mate, it's the first time you've fired a pistol. Trust me, you'll get heaps of practice.'

I would not be persuaded and stayed in my room, working on my footwork.

Two days later we were given our first validation shoot from a range of five metres. My first four bullets landed in the bullseye. No-one was more surprised than me when I passed.

Once again, Buzz peered over my shoulder: 'Hmmm . . . how in the fuck did you manage that? Must have been a fluke!'

By persevering when I was under par, I'd made myself well above par. I was not the most accurate shot on the course or in the troop, but I was able to compete with the guys who were.

Many years later, as a contractor in Iraq, I was running some pistol training and I placed a target approximately 45 metres away. I withdrew a Glock 17 and fired one round. Joe, a former Selous Scout and a poetic shot with a rifle, approached the target and said, 'Hey, Fenno, you missed.'

I'd half-expected to miss – after all, the target I was going for was an A4 piece of paper with a black circle in the middle of it. I hadn't fired a pistol for some time, so from that range I didn't expect to hit the paper.

Joe laughed. 'I mean, you missed the black dot in the middle. Only by a couple of centimetres. Where in the fuck did you learn to shoot like that?'

Impressing a man of Joe's incredible background gave me a kick, but with that shot I was just lucky. Obsessiveness and determination get you a long way, but nothing quite beats just being arsey.

TEN

The windswept station appeared devoid of life. Pieces of debris and dust flicked across the ground like a scene from a western. I positioned our two vehicles 100 metres from the bowsers before moving in on foot. Pottie remained with the vehicles, ready to provide fire support. He was always ready to lend a hand.

The station looked deserted but we needed fuel so I had to try. I stuck my head into a room where there were about a dozen Iraqi men watching television. They were startled yet venomously excited to see a lone Westerner. They looked back and forth at each other as if to see who would make a move on the idiot who dared to enter their domain.

I sensed the danger and immediately flicked my safety catch onto fire. The distinctive sound of an AK-47 being made ready is something these guys would have heard many times before. I was signalling that, despite the fact that I was severely outnumbered, any conflict wouldn't be a one-sided affair.

I told the men in the room that I needed fuel, but they just snarled and shook their heads. One man began hitting his fist against his chest. Half-expecting to see froth at the corners of his mouth, I nodded my head in return and told them to start up their generator. After a grudging pause they did, with obvious reluctance but also with a tinge of curiosity.

Seven men followed me out the front while the others disappeared out the back. Pottie had already positioned himself at the bowsers. I told him to get ready, as things could soon turn nasty. He ran his eye over the men surrounding me and said in a level voice that they would need more than seven to get the job done.

His bravado was appreciated, but I made sure to tell him there were at least five more Iraqis out the back. Their faces occasionally peered around a brick wall. I briefed our drivers to bring their vehicles into the station one at a time and, as soon as they were refuelled, to quickly back out the way they had come.

The Iraqi men again pounded on their chests, chanting 'Ali Baba' and claiming themselves to be thieves. They began yelling out to other friends in front of a shop some 200 metres away. Pottie and I weren't intimidated. Sure, they would have loved to steal our vehicles and our lives, but if they were truly confident, they would have just done it. Several men pressed their faces against the windows of our cars in order to have a good look inside. Things were swiftly getting out of hand. I maintained my distance while also keeping my weapon fixed on a thickset man who appeared to be the natural leader of the group.

Our team medic again proved that he was totally unsuitable for this line of work. After refuelling, he failed to follow my simple instructions. Instead of immediately reversing his vehicle, he parked adjacent to the building. This was a highly compromised position, and he could easily have been shot by anyone inside. Several men approached his vehicle and he just turned away from them, visibly shaking with fear. They were now aware of our weak link.

I got on the radio and told him to drive his vehicle out of the station. He appeared to struggle even with these basic commands. I tried to remain calm and approached the medic, firmly directing him where to go. Finally, he obeyed.

With both vehicles topped up, I paid for the fuel while Pottie covered the transaction. We then covered each other back to our vehicles. The men in the service station began yelling and whistling to their friends up at the shop as we departed. *Too late, fellas*, I thought, as we gathered momentum and thundered along the highway.

It appeared that we had caught these men off-guard. They obviously weren't confident that they could overpower our team without sustaining casualties. As we drove, I made a note that this station was only to be used to source fuel in an absolute emergency.

≡

Near the intersection that led into Fallujah, Pottie called me over the radio: 'There are three suspect black BMWs closing in on our vehicle, over.' I peered over my shoulder and observed the vehicles buzzing around the rear of Pottie's car like a swarm of killer bees.

Immediately I ordered a 'heavy rear drill', where both of our team vehicles were positioned side-by-side while Pottie and I took up firing positions and aimed our rifles at the aggressive-looking occupants. The suspect cars soon faded away, and after a kilometre we reverted to our normal formation.

Unfortunately, it wasn't long before they tried it on again. The first encounter could well have been a rehearsal for an attack. We had no chance of outrunning these highly engineered machines, so we fell back into the heavy rear drill and were a little more aggressive. Once again the suspect vehicles retreated. I told Pottie that the next time they approached we'd slow down and signal the BMWs to pass. It would be easier to control the situation from the rear.

Almost on cue, they appeared again. We slowed to 60 kmh and signalled to them to pass. Each vehicle was loaded with six men, who all looked to be in their twenties and thirties. They faced us with strong stares as they slowly passed. I locked eyes with a man who was seated in the back of the lead car. His eyes, filled with hate, searched for complacency, a weakness he could exploit. He and his companions would certainly have seen that our rifles were pulled firmly into our shoulders, our safety catches were disengaged and our muzzles were pointed directly at them.

If these men were going to attack, then they would have to make it quick; once it started, I planned to take out the immediate threat, followed by the driver. If I could shoot the driver in the head then his foot would fall flat against the accelerator, causing the vehicle to lurch forward and probably to veer sharply to the left or right. If this wasn't corrected in a second then they would be off the road and upside down. But there were 18 of them and just four of us. There's no place for arrogance in our line of work. If given the opportunity, these guys would be merciless.

My eyes told this man that any act of aggression would

most likely result in him and several of his friends being killed. My years in the Regiment, and the tens of thousands of rounds I had fired over that time, gave me the confidence that I could outclass these guys. You know if you have the drop on someone. They know it too. It would be a tall order to slay our entire team without suffering casualties. After several kilometres of high-stakes chicken, they finally pulled off the road and headed back towards Fallujah.

Other security contractors were not so successful; four men would be slain in Fallujah shortly after this event.

≡

That evening we returned to the Palestine Hotel and were informed that, with the assessment phase of the project now complete, the following morning we were to return to Shaibah Log Camp in the south of Iraq. This six-hour drive, however, proved a little more interesting.

On the morning of departure we learned that Route Tampa, the primary road leading south, was closed indefinitely. The insurgents had detonated a vehicle bomb and destroyed a major bridge, sending tonnes of concrete and metal into the water. This was frustrating, as not only was the alternate route through Al Khut considered more dangerous, but I didn't have suitable mapping of southeastern Baghdad. I had a tourist map of central Baghdad, and then it was back to my trusty 1:500,000 country map. A picture of my arse would have been just as useful.

We located the highway leading to Al Khut and some 20 kilometres later came to a prominent roundabout. One of the roads led south, the other headed due east. Neither road appeared more prominent than the other, so considering Al Khut was in the south, we took the southern road. Big mistake.

After several kilometres the road narrowed and led through a series of highly populated villages. We continued through another roundabout before passing a mosque where at least 40 men were assembled. As we drove past the crowd, they appeared to become excited and several men began to run towards the mosque. Perhaps they knew something that we didn't know.

The road we were travelling on soon came to a dead end. *Fuck*, I thought. They were excited because they knew that we'd have to come back. We'd effectively ambushed ourselves.

Every second became vital. We headed back along the road and saw dozens of men throwing 44-gallon drums and large blocks of concrete onto the road. We had been blocked in. I ordered the vehicles to stop and reverse.

On the other side of the median strip was another lane that was still clear. The medic in Pottie's car began to panic as he struggled to reverse his vehicle, all the while calling out, 'We're gonna die, we're gonna die.' My driver performed well and we made it to the mosque just as several pieces of concrete landed on the road. The crowd went wild and several men ran their fingers across their throats as we accelerated past.

My heart was pounding. I knew I'd fucked up. It had been my call on which road to take, and that had left us in this incredibly vulnerable position. But I also knew that now was not the time to reflect – it was the time to set things right.

As my vehicle entered the roundabout, a van halted

immediately in front of us, causing us to screech to a halt. I removed my safety catch and placed my finger on the trigger. Although my heart was still thumping inside my chest, my rifle felt steady. I attempted to control my breathing. The rear door of the van was thrust open and I was expecting armed men to appear.

I began to take up the slack in my trigger when a young man jumped out of the van and slammed the door shut. He looked at me briefly before darting out of the way as the van moved on. Some men from the mosque were running towards the roundabout now, but we didn't hang around to see what they wanted. It was time to go.

The medic was really starting to lose it as we drove on, but Pottie, as always, remained a rock. 'Hey, Keith,' he said, 'I thought it was about time we found some action.'

I laughed and, in the lightened mood, ordered my driver to slow down and take it easy. Provided we didn't do anything silly, like run off the side of the road, we'd probably get away. As we drove past local villagers, those who recognised us as Western looked as shocked as our poor medic. But before they could react, we were gone.

Luckily, I had ruled my country map into one-mile increments so I was able to work out roughly where we were. I also realised that there was a dirt track some 17 kilometres further south that led back onto the Al Khut Highway. I informed the guys of my intentions and reminded them that when something went wrong it was essential to remain calm, or our problems could intensify rapidly. I maintained a constant visual to confirm our precise location, and I estimated that it would take 20 minutes to make it back. I then located a series of powerlines ahead that led back to the highway and breathed a sigh of relief when I realised the track was open.

As we continued south, our bodies and minds were able to relax a little. It was still dangerous, but in comparison to where we had been it seemed relatively benign. We eventually reached Shaibah Log Camp and then continued on to Kuwait. I sacked the medic and was asked if I'd consider running the reconstruction phase of the project. I would be responsible for 23 security contractors, 12 Gurkha guards and 10 clients. Why not?

ELEVEN

During the first Battle of Fallujah, thousands of US troops were required to cordon off the city. Hundreds left Haditha Dam and only 37 remained. Many outposts were also abandoned, which meant there were no troops north of Haditha or between Highway Twelve and the Jordanian border. In other words, a void of several hundred kilometres.

The reduced number of military personnel and the increased threat made several of our clients extremely anxious. But things were to get even worse. We received intelligence that insurgents in Haditha planned to attack and overrun the dam. In the months leading up to the Battle of Fallujah, around the Haditha area US soldiers were targetted by roadside bombs and ambushes at least three times a day. There were times when our medics lent support and treated US casualties. But now it seemed like the insurgents were intent on getting close and personal.

One hundred and fifty Azerbaijani soldiers were responsible for securing the outer perimeter of the dam. I had inspected several of their defensive positions and, although they looked okay from afar, I had little confidence that they would be able to stave off a well-planned and coordinated attack. I didn't need to look far to reach this conclusion: their most vulnerable defensive position was secured only by a 50-calibre machine gun.

That sounds okay, but the reality was that there was dead ground leading to within 50 metres of this gun and it only had a 10-round belt loaded. The remaining ammunition was stored in sealed boxes that were secured in plastic sleeves. The two soldiers who manned the gun would have no chance of sorting that out at night if they came under attack.

With an attack looking more likely each day, I informed Kuwaiti Ops that an attempt to flee could prove disastrous. I decided that we would hold firm and secure the seventh floor of the West Wing. The 37 US marines would secure the seventh floor of the East Wing. The Azerbaijani soldiers would secure the outer perimeter. In the event that either side was overrun, we would break contact to the other side.

We spent three days rehearsing for the attack. Our aim was to secure the stairwells and corridors by creating choke points where the insurgents would be unable to utilise their greater numbers. We felt ready. Then we received intelligence that they were on their way – 1500 to 2000 of them.

I was confident we could hold our position and, to my relief, so were the guys. After countless hours of rehearsals, I couldn't help but be a little curious, even keen, to see if all our hard work would pay dividends. Most of our clients were fairly calm. I kept Kuwaiti Ops and our clients' security manager in Washington abreast of the situation.

The insurgents were moving ever closer. Eight kilometres away, six kilometres away. When they'd made it to within five kilometres of the dam, a couple of US gunships came to the party. With this, our approaching visitors decided to call it a day and that was that.

One of our clients, a really lovely guy, had reached the limit of what he could endure and wanted out. To move him I had to risk the lives of 11 security contractors, but fear is infectious, so we got him out fast.

We reached Jordan just before last light and moved to a small abandoned military outpost. We had not seen a single military vehicle since leaving Haditha Dam. This unnerved our client even more, and he began to break down, saying, 'This nightmare is never going to end.'

I told him that he was now at the border and at first light he would be taken across. We had 11 guys to secure the outpost and he would sleep next to me. But he was so paralysed by fear that he could no longer see reason and became entirely consumed with his own survival.

After escorting him safely into Jordan, we remained at the border until 10:00 hours so we could make the most dangerous part of our return trip in the hottest part of the day. Luck was on our side.

We were 18 kilometres away from Haditha Dam when we saw, at the side of the road, a seven-tonne US military truck that had been blown up. The US convoy, the only one that day, had been hit at 13:00 hours by an IED, and this attack had been followed by an ambush. Thirty insurgents had occupied the high ground with rifles and machine guns. They had attacked the marines, who'd responded with heavy-calibre weapons and automatic grenade-launchers. Unlike us, the marines were equipped with armoured vehicles. If we'd been an hour earlier, it's likely that at least one of our five vehicles would have been incinerated by the blast. Thirty insurgents pouring lead into our remaining cars would have been interesting. Who knows how it would have turned out?

Towards the latter stages of the project, on yet another road move, I was in the lead vehicle when my driver pulled out to overtake a truck and noticed a utility coming the opposite way. Unlike Sonny, this guy pulled back in behind the truck but the young Iraqi man driving the utility panicked and drove onto the verge. He then overcorrected, and the next thing I heard was, 'Victa 1, this is Victa 5 – the utility vehicle just ran off the road and flipped several times.'

I felt compelled to return, so after ordering our guys to secure the road and cordon off the area, Joe and I went back to assess the situation. What I witnessed made me feel sick.

The utility was upside down and looked like a pancake. The roof was flattened level to the bonnet, and the wheels were still spinning fast. Half a dozen Iraqi men helped us turn the vehicle over.

We kicked the door open and saw immediately that the front seats had collapsed. There was a motionless body wrapped in rags – but he was looking at me. *What the fuck*? I thought.

Not only was this guy still alive, but he started to move his arms and legs. I checked his neck before pulling him from the vehicle. He began to walk. Several Iraqi men cheered him on, and with this we left.

The situation on the roads had become almost untenable. We still hadn't suffered a single casualty but the US marines were being hit daily. I decided to minimise all road travel, so from now on our clients would be flown out of country from Alasad Airbase.

Because of the dangers of road travel, at the completion of the project Kuwaiti Ops were hesitant about us driving out of the area in non-armoured vehicles. To fly all of the security consultants, Gurkha guards, vehicles and equipment out of country was not impossible, but it would cost hundreds of thousands of dollars.

I spent days studying the US intelligence reports and concluded that it was feasible to drive out, providing it was well planned. After delivering our demobilisation orders, I asked if anyone had any questions or problems.

One man raised his hand. 'We will get hit, 100 per cent.'

I asked him whether, if we had to drive, he agreed with my plans.

'Absolutely,' he replied. 'But it's not enough. They have to fly us out.' This man, a well-respected soldier who had fought in the Angolan wars, was unrelenting in his position. 'Keith, I have been rained on enough in my life. I want you to fly me out.'

I thought about his comments and looked into his broken eyes. I was aware that I'd have to risk the lives of 11 men to get him to the airfield, but he was no longer an asset to the project. He had to go.

We escorted him to Alasad Airbase the following morning. When we arrived he took his pistol out of his holster and nearly shot himself in the foot. He was shaking as I took the weapon from him, and his parting words were, 'I'm fucking losing it.'

I began to prepare for the demobilisation drive. I had two options – to head back down Highway Twelve and try to hit Fallujah at 04:50, which was the time of the first call to prayer, or to travel in a north-easterly direction towards Bayji. At the time, the area around Fallujah was out of control. The problem with the latter option, however, was that the dusty stretch of road was regularly set with anti-tank mines.

The road was sealed, but insurgents had been known to dig holes in the asphalt, set an anti-tank mine, cover it with sand and splash some black paint over the top. To a car travelling at speed, the change in road surface would be almost impossible to identify. I knew of one young platoon commander who had noticed a piece of rubber on the track that hadn't been there the day before. He decided to check it out. Beneath the rubber he found two mines, with a third buried in the side of the bank at window-height and linked to the others by a piece of detonating cord. If a vehicle had hit the mines, no-one inside would have survived.

So my options were: roadside bombs and insurgents, or roadside bombs and anti-tank mines. After a lot of thought, I chose the bombs and mines. I offered to drive the lead car by myself but Joe and Si would have none of that. Joe said, 'If we hit a mine, then we take the hit together.' I was relieved; it's at times like this that you really get to know a person.

I delayed our departure until 07:30 so we would have the best possible chance to identify any disturbance in the surface of the road. Our convoy of thirteen vehicles headed north-east. By now I did not have to remind the guys to maintain vehicle spacing.

After 10 kilometres we saw several large craters in the road. We passed a sign reading DANGER! BEWARE OF MINES. 'No shit,' said Joe. I knew that an American truckdriver had been killed along the road the previous week and I wondered if this was where it had happened.

Our eyes remained glued to the road as Si kept our speed below 60 kmh. We came to another series of craters and Si managed to steer the passenger side directly through one of the holes. I grimaced, half-expecting our vehicle to leap into the air in a dance of flames.

Joe looked at Si and said, 'If you ever do that again, I am going to belt you up.'

I laughed but was a little more diplomatic with my words. 'If you have to run into a hole, then at least have the decency to do it on your side, not mine.'

Si laughed. 'Sorry, fellas – I was just making sure the hole was clear for the boys behind.'

We made it to Bayji, refuelled at a US base and headed for Baghdad. By this time, driving around in non-armoured cars was an exception to the rule and definitely not cool. Most security companies had spent many millions of dollars on armoured fleets. But we'd been told that a fleet of armoured vehicles was waiting for us in Kuwait, a further nine hours south, so we had no choice.

Sixty minutes later, we entered the outskirts of Baghdad. Our rear vehicle reported seeing a carload of men who were running their fingers across their throats. These jokers obviously thought our guys were in armoured cars and couldn't open fire. As much as our boys would have liked to flick some lead in their direction, they just maintained their composure and refrained.

Finally we arrived at the Green Zone and the guys were congratulated on their efforts. They had operated in one of the most volatile regions of Iraq in non-armoured cars without sustaining a single casualty. We had travelled those roads for five and a half months and the threat from Iraqi insurgents had only ever increased. But the intensity of living on the edge for such an extended period of time had taken its toll, not only on the clients but also on the operators.

TWELVE

Following the Haditha Dam task, our security teams were redeployed to Baghdad and employed on a countrywide engineering assessment and maintenance project. At the height of this project, Jim, as the project manager, and I, as the operations manager, coordinated 120 security personnel who were employed to protect 50 engineers, as they travelled to and from 18 sites between Mosul and Basra. Operations in Iraq brought many difficulties and obstacles, but the locals' perceptions about our presence always affected me the most powerfully.

In Iraq we were constantly on guard – tense, anticipating, expecting. We simply didn't know whom we could trust. Although we were a part of the reconstruction effort, not the war, many Iraqis who opposed the Coalition occupation didn't care to make that distinction. As far as they were concerned, we were foreign, we carried weapons and that was more than enough reason to want us dead.

Even our Iraqi staff, employed in the kitchen, laundry, or fuel and rations supplies, didn't smile. There was complete lack of warmth. We wondered, how deeply did they hate us? Or was it that they were afraid to be seen acting friendly to a Westerner? Would their lives be cut short because of their connection to us? Many Iraqis who were found with foreign identification cards were killed. They lived with a constant threat of being tortured, beheaded or shot. And since rockets and mortars were being fired into the International Zone (as the Green Zone was now called), Iraqis who worked with us were subject to the same dangers as those who chose to be combatants. They also had to venture out of the fortified safety zones each evening when they returned to their homes.

Sometimes the hatred for us was clearly about more than fear. Strangers on the side of the road ran their fingers along their necks in a cutting motion and tried to lock eyes with us. These overt displays of enmity were easy to deal with. An operator could just mouth the words 'Fuck you' right back at him, and hold a venomous stare to show that he wouldn't be intimidated. The insurgents were well aware that a weapon pointed at them from behind an armoured window was no threat at all. It was a win–win situation for the insurgents. They could display their hatred openly and detonate a roadside bomb whenever they felt like it.

Harder to deal with than this immediate, prejudiced hatred was the anger and disdain from people who knew someone killed as a result of the invasion. One particularly shocking and tragic event still lives deep inside my mind.

The threat levels along Route Irish, the road that led to Baghdad International Airport (BIAP), were extreme. I deployed with our security teams largely because I felt guilty sending the guys onto the roads during times of heightened risk. It was just easier to go with them. If there was an incident, it would be the designated team leader's show. I would simply help with the fighting and, at the very first opportunity, send off a contact report requesting assistance if needed. If there were numerous teams and it was a complex task, the team leaders would run their teams and I would oversee everything on the ground. The drills worked well and all the team leaders and 2iCs were outstanding. There wasn't a lot to worry about.

On one particular day I deployed in the lead vehicle as a gunner. We were returning from the BIAP and the traffic on Route Irish was at a standstill. There had already been six suicide carbombs on Route Irish, and there had obviously been another incident now. We always ensured our vehicles never remained stationary for an extended period of time, but a few minutes was acceptable until the team leader ascertained what was going on ahead. The convoy was ordered to maintain spacing and allow room to manoeuvre, should we be attacked.

We saw a US military convoy 100 metres ahead, so we decided to remain in place. Several jittery vehicles from another security company attempted to edge past our convoy but after several forceful hand-gestures, and the fact that the traffic ahead was at a standstill, they had little option but to stop. Our guys then repositioned their vehicles to prevent these clowns from interfering with the integrity of our convoy.

Slowly the vehicles ahead began to inch forward. Our eyes strained in every direction to identify any possible threat. Being static on the roads is an extremely vulnerable time. Everyone begins to wonder if the delay is part of a ploy to channel vehicles into an ambush or roadside bomb.

As our cars meandered along the road, I caught sight of an old white sedan with a shattered rear window and a bullet-riddled windscreen. I could see an Iraqi woman trying to stand up while shaking uncontrollably. She had exited the car from the passenger side and held her arms in a surrender position as she tried to straighten her frame.

She was in complete shock. I noticed that her glasses, although still on her face, were cracked and bent. Her hair had been parted by a large-calibre bullet that glanced her head but did not penetrate her skull. Blood was streaming down her face and her open hands were also bright red. She looked like she had seen a ghost. Her eyes were wide open, as if her eyelids were held apart by matchsticks. The area of her face that was not red with blood was white, a ghostly white that made her appear almost transparent. Her lips were blue and she had droplets of blood in the corners of her mouth, but it was her violent shaking that had the greatest effect on me.

I glanced forward and saw a US patrol parked on the side of the road. It was clear that they had opened fire on the vehicle, no doubt believing it to contain a suicide-bomber. The young soldiers stood there just staring at the woman with mouths wide open. No-one was giving directions or orders – they, too, looked like they had seen a ghost, one likely to revisit them for many years to come, I thought. The man who most likely had opened fire was being consoled, and a fresh-faced officer was trying to make sense of the situation.

As we drove past, I looked beyond the shaking woman and into the vehicle. There was a man in the driver's seat with a seatbelt holding him upright. His head was tilted back and firmly planted against the rear headrest, which was plastered in blood. So was the rear seat and ceiling.

I locked on to the man, searching for signs of life, but he no longer had a face. His head had been transformed into the shape of a funnel, hollowed out and featureless. Where his eyes, nose or mouth would have been was a gaping, sickly, red depression.

This, coupled with the state of the distraught woman, most likely his wife, was sickening and was taking its toll on the young soldiers, who were trying to comprehend the mess they had created. The young officer walked towards the woman, his weapon down by his side, defeated.

Losing mates in combat must have been hard enough for these young men, who in many cases were more like boys. Making a tragic mistake where you take away an innocent life would be a far greater burden to carry. The image would grow heavy and, over time, would drag a soldier down in shame. These men would require counselling if they were to lay the incident to rest. Their faces told me this.

How could they make such a mistake? The answer is distressingly simple. Many soldiers in Iraq are national guardsmen who have only a basic level of training but have been called upon to serve in a time of need. Most are young and lack combat experience. They are anxious, poorly prepared and working in the most hostile country in the world. Those who remain in Iraq on combat operations for more than a couple of months have most likely faced the trauma of losing a close friend, which only exacerbates their anxiety and fear.

The more suicide-bombers there are who target US military vehicles, the twitchier the young soldiers become. A car that fails to heed warnings to slow down or back off could well be facing an inexperienced and nervous soldier, not a man who has spent many years making decisions based on sound judgement. It is a deadly cycle that gains momentum: the greater the number and success of suicide-bombers, the more anxious the US soldiers become, and the greater the number of Iraqi civilians who are killed by poor decision-making. The greater the number of Iraqis who oppose the US presence, the more the attacks increase, the more civilians are slain, and the more the Iraqis hate America. It is brutal and unrelenting.

≡

There have been hundreds of suicide attacks in Iraq. It is an extremely successful tactic, as the target vehicle and all those inside are generally incinerated in a second. Anyone who has spent much time in Iraq has seen the devastation and knows men who have been killed by this means.

One vehicle packed with 1000 pounds of explosives rammed into the side of a B6 armoured car and detonated in a ball of thunderous flame. The car was thrown 25 metres into the air and landed on its roof. All five occupants were immediately killed, their bodies impossible to recognise. There was no chance of survival. The bodies of the three clients were welded together on the rear seat by the immense heat of the blast. The security contractors in the front suffered a similar fate, their bodies melted in an instant. The ghastly faces of victims often have their mouths wide open, as if screaming at the top of their lungs in pain before they die.

My closest call with a suicide-bomber took place alongside a hard-hitting operator nicknamed 'Heater'. This guy, a former Australian SAS soldier, epitomised the stereotype of Mr Cool and was just the sort of man you'd want by your side if things got nasty. For someone so talented he was also surprisingly humble. He was an intelligent man who didn't say a lot, but when he opened his mouth everyone listened. I would regularly ask his opinion about operational matters.

He was so overqualified for the work he was doing it was almost comical. He had no desire for responsibility and wanted to be where the action was. He should have been a team leader but refused. I had no problem with this, as he was the best rear gunner in the company, a highly dangerous and important position. His decision-making was second to none, the perfect person to secure the rear of a convoy.

Heater was well aware that I was frustrated as the operations manager. I had been quietly spoken to on several occasions for constantly deploying with the teams. On one particular day of heightened threat, I was envious that the guys were deploying and I vented to Heater.

His comments were blunt and to the point: 'You're the ops manager, aren't you? So what's the problem? Fuck those cowards who never want to leave the office. It's your call. Just jump in the rear vehicle with me.'

He made it sound all too easy. He was right – as long as the ops room was manned and the rapid-reaction force briefed, what did it matter if I got out and about as often as I wanted? So I'd cop a bit of shit about it – who really cared? At least if something went wrong I'd be on the ground with the boys.

The teams deployed to a power plant in Baghdad and the journey was relatively straightforward. The company we worked for had a comprehensive intelligence cell which, when we requested it, provided an analysis of all the main arterial roads around Baghdad. We asked for information on the types and timings of all attacks that occurred. Suicide-bombers, complex attacks, small-arms attacks and IEDs. The data was collated from all recorded events over the previous 30 days. Using these statistics, it was possible to reduce the threat to us considerably.

The major concern was a 'vehicle-borne improvised explosive device' (VBIED). We had armoured vehicles now, so a burst of AK-47 fire wasn't an issue. The statistics highlighted windows of opportunity where threat levels could be minimised. High-threat times were also identified. For example, 90 per cent of VBIEDs were detonated between 07:00 and 10:00 each day. Just by travelling outside these times, the teams were less likely to confront a VBIED.

In six months of travelling all over the country, from Mosul down to Basra, we were fortunate not to suffer a single casualty. We were lucky, but you also make your own luck. No unnecessary road moves were ever permitted. The contractors wouldn't be expected to make several trips to the BIAP for client pickups. They would depart during a low-threat period and remain at the airport all day, only returning during another period of lesser threat. Avoiding being incinerated is all about the law of averages. It is imperative to minimise road travel and, if possible, to combine several taskings into one. Heater and I monopolised the rear vehicle, and it was a buzz working with such a quality individual.

The return trip from the power station had been uneventful, and we began to relax as the convoy closed up and waited to pass through the military checkpoint. There were two queues. One was for military vehicles or Department of Defense contractors, and the other for all local traffic. We were static in traffic, 50 metres shy of the checkpoint, when I noticed a white, old-model vehicle move from the civilian to the military lane. This was strange. The vehicle had just one Middle Eastern occupant, a man who stopped his vehicle no more than 30 metres behind us. He stared in our direction with both hands grasping the steering wheel.

It was an old banged-up vehicle that looked heavy – it could have been worn suspension or a load of bombs. The driver looked tense. Why was he in the military lane? Something inside me clicked and a shiver passed over my body. This vehicle fitted the stereotype of a suicide-bomber.

Immediately, I placed an open hand out to the man to inform him to stay where he was. Heater and I both took aim at him. The convoy was informed that a suspect vehicle was stopped behind us in the military lane.

Heater and I waited in nervous anticipation. Was this a suicide-bomber? Why was he just sitting there and staring at us so intensely? Was he trying to decide whether we were a target worthy of his death? We were three security contractors. We didn't look like a diplomatic convoy, but he wouldn't care. We kept our weapons trained on his chest and he just stared back, still gripping the steering wheel with both hands. It was intense.

We were even more endangered because we were in a retro-armoured vehicle, which is a cheap alternative and offers minimal protection only. If this car exploded at a distance of 30 metres, what would the shock wave do to us? Would our eardrums and lungs burst? Would we have time to duck our heads before large chunks of metal sailed over the metal plate that covered our rear seat?

We didn't have enough information to open fire but would have to make up our minds immediately if things changed. We were expecting his vehicle to surge forward as he depressed the accelerator pedal all the way to the floor. Was he going to do it? I also realised that momentum, even if he was killed quickly, would carry his vehicle many metres closer to us. We couldn't move forward. If we tried to force our way into the checkpoint, we'd be filled with bullets, courtesy of the US military. They were nervous enough without us making their job even more difficult. We just had to sit it out.

Safety catches had been disengaged for some time now. It was up to him. If he accelerated aggressively towards us, he was going to be killed. But what if he remained calm and gently rolled our way? Was he capable of such controlled deceit in the moments before he vaporised himself? I told Heater I would give him one final warning before shooting out his left front tyre. After that, if he still continued, my next round would be into his chest.

The man then started to smile, then appeared to break into laughter. He threw his car into reverse and backed up about 50 metres, began to make a right-hand turn and then briefly stopped. He looked at us one last time before driving off.

What were his intentions? Was he a bomber who got cold feet? Was he carrying out a rehearsal in order to see how close he could get to the checkpoint before being challenged? We will never know.

The horrific waste of suicide-bombing as a strategy really hit home. After all, who really cares if three security contractors are killed, other than their families? The bomber would have blown himself into thousands of pieces for no real gain. The futility of it all. Why would someone want to end their own life to achieve something so small? We weren't a trophy worth giving up one's life for. Maybe that's why he drove away.

I reflected long and hard on the differences between myself and the suicide-bomber. If I were him, rather than blow myself up once, I'd try to kill as many soldiers as possible for as long as possible. Killing two or three men who weren't in the military, and sacrificing my own life in the process, just wouldn't be a worthwhile task. This man and hundreds just like him had a different outlook. They were quite happy to do it. I have tried to understand why, and although I am aware of several differing motivations — from belief in a cause to familial financial reward — I guess, just like suicide, unless one has thought about it, how can one pass judgement?

≡

If I'm completely honest with myself, the real reason that I was there with Heater, and the reason that I deployed so often with the teams, was a basic desire for excitement. I didn't want to miss out. In that respect, I hadn't changed much since my first deployment years before.

But with experience and responsibility had come a new set of motivating factors. Most powerful was my sense of guilt. I wanted to keep my mates alive. I'd encouraged many of my friends to join this project, and I was responsible for sending them out each day. If I was concerned about a threat to the team, I would deploy with them. So, too, would the project manager, Jim.

In my attempts to get so involved in the task, in minimising their risk to exposure, I almost drove myself crazy. I don't know if it worked or if we were just lucky, but it made me tired. So tired. I had very little or no fear for what might happen to me – my wife wouldn't have been overjoyed to hear this – but I knew I did not want to confront a friend's wife and try to explain that her husband had been killed because I made a poor decision.

When we discussed it, Heater reassured me that we were all here of our own accord. 'The guys are as well prepared as they are ever going to be,' he said. 'It wouldn't be because of you.'

The men trained hard, the rapid-reaction force was always on standby when a team was mobile, and the ops team put an enormous amount of thought into the tasking, but I'm still relieved I don't have to live with the thought that I had killed a friend.

=

In Iraq, I saw devastation and tremendous loss of life, tragedies and horrors that occurred for no better reason than the human tendency towards war. But my experience after Iraq, when human destruction was not the cause of the suffering, affected me even more powerfully.

PART SIX

BANDA ACEH

JANUARY 2005

ONE

A man and his two sons posed for a photo. Their despondency cut deep into the lens. It was such a potent sense of grief that for a moment I froze, camera in hand, rendered inoperable by the tide of emotion that radiated from the subjects. *Click.* The photo was taken, the image captured, the misery recorded for history.

I paused again, not wanting to share this distressing image with the father. He would take no joy out of seeing his sons' vacant stares. The boys weren't looking into the lens but gazed in the direction of where their house once stood. Their mouths and noses were covered with white surgical masks to prevent them from smelling the stench of death that hung thick in the air. Their mother and sisters were gone, buried under the rubble of their home in front of them.

It would have been impossible for the man to lift the slabs of rubble on his own. He knew where his family were but was helpless and could only stare at the site and mourn. The boys were well dressed and stood hand in hand, while their father had his hands on their shoulders. One of the boys had a graze on his left leg. Their father's bloodshot, sleepless eyes were swollen and tired. His face was an agonising image of sorrow, but he was carrying on. He had to continue to live, for his two boys depended on him.

≡

On 26 December 2004, I was at home in Australia, packing my bags and wishing for the day to end before I returned to Iraq. The day before departure was never pleasant. I usually spent it reflecting on all the things that I should have done and would attempt to do the next time I returned home. I'd begin to distance myself from my wife, and my children would struggle to understand why Dad had suddenly become so tense and serious. Although I was still physically present, in reality I was no longer at home.

Running operations in Iraq was stressful. A poor tactical decision from me could very well result in the death of a close friend or colleague. Therefore, I always began analysing intelligence reports 48 hours before I returned so I could have a smooth transition.

I sat at my computer, trying mentally to put myself back in Iraq. As I worked, news of an earthquake and tsunami flashed across my computer screen. The early reports did nothing to prepare me for the scale of the catastrophe. Images from Thailand and Sri Lanka dominated the broadcasts. The footage showed a swollen horizon and waves washing into the lower levels of tourist resorts. People were initially surprised and intrigued but this soon turned to fear as the water levels began to rise.

There were no early pictures from Banda Aceh, as the region's infrastructure had been totally wiped out. An entire Indonesian army battalion had been annihilated, including several hundred police officers who were accommodated in the same barracks. While the earthquake created terror, the tsunami consumed everything in its path. The Western world was oblivious to the extent of this brutality and it would be many days before the horrifying depth of the devastation was known.

I boarded the flight to Iraq thinking that several thousand people had been killed across Asia. I landed in Baghdad to news that the death toll was estimated to be in excess of 100,000. I took this knowledge in and spared a thought for those lost, but I was more concerned about getting back into the swing of things in Iraq.

As with so much private contracting work, I swung between thriving in my work as a security operations manager and finding it deeply frustrating, wondering what I was even doing there. One afternoon in early January the operations director of the company I worked for came to see me. He wanted to know how good my Indonesian was. In the context, it was a strange question.

'It used to be pretty solid,' I replied, 'and it wouldn't take me too long to pick it back up.'

The director, John, asked if I would like to lead the security element of a humanitarian assistance mission into Banda Aceh. I didn't realise it at the time, but agreeing to coordinate this task would open a door to one of the most fulfilling experiences of my life, one which would change the way I thought about my vocation forever.

My knowledge of the situation in Banda Aceh was limited, but I quickly familiarised myself. An earthquake measuring between 9.1 and 9.3 on the Richter scale, the second-largest earthquake in recorded history, had devastated the north-west Sumatran coast. The quake had struck at 07:58:53 local time on 26 December 2004. Within 30 minutes a tsunami had crashed into Banda Aceh, consuming everything in its path. The wave was driven by a power unprecedented in recent history. Its legacy was widespread death and destruction.

Imagine you are standing 100 metres in front of a 30-metre dam wall. The space between you and the dam is littered with vehicles, debris, trees, sheets of corrugated iron, bricks, stones and the various other detritus that is part of an overcrowded Indonesian city. You stand there and watch as some greater being lifts the dam wall into the sky in one swift motion. You hear the sickening roar of water that explodes towards you with the force of an atomic blast. Heavily laden trucks are picked up like toys and hurled towards you. As you are hit by the force of the wave your body is crushed before your mind even has a chance to identify that this is real. This is the death that hundreds of thousands faced in Banda Aceh.

After my lengthy stint in Iraq, I was no stranger to loss of life on a large scale, but the situation in Banda was unlike anything I had faced before. To date, in almost five years of fighting in Iraq there have been over 4000 US military personnel killed. Estimates of the number of Iraqi fatalities vary, but according to the Iraq Health Ministry survey, around 400,000 Iraqis have been killed (as of June 2006). These are devastating figures representing an unthinkable loss of life.

Over 230,000 people were killed in Banda Aceh – not in years, months, weeks or even days, but in minutes. The wall of water that struck Banda Aceh was so fierce, so violent, so destructive that everything within 800 metres of the coast was entirely laid to ruin. Areas up to 1.5 kilometres into the city merged with the ocean, and the deadly torrent of brown death continued for two kilometres inland in some places. At the mercy of Mother Nature, hundreds of thousands of people met an untimely, swift and violent death.

Initially, Heater and I were deployed to Banda Aceh to protect a team of engineers whose task was to establish two mobile water-treatment units. These units were capable of turning 1200 litres of brown sludge into potable water every minute. This was a humanitarian assistance mission and our role was to ensure the engineering task was a success. We were facilitators. Our knowledge of Indonesian customs, our ability to converse in the local dialect and our contacts with the Australian military would allow these engineers to do their jobs.

Before we arrived, Jerry, the project manager, had flown to Banda Aceh and spent an uncomfortable night dodging mosquitoes and heavy rain. In the morning he decided that the task could not go ahead. There was no accommodation, it was difficult to source vehicles, the military weren't helping with flights and no-one seemed to speak English. I was desperate to change Jerry's mind and knew that we could achieve all these things within 24 hours.

Heater and I arrived in Medan and I asked Jerry to watch Heater at work. He had spent a lot of time working in Indonesia and was an exceptional linguist, and within minutes he had arranged vehicles and supplies. But Jerry was still not convinced. I quickly sourced a flight for Heater on a military aircraft to Banda Aceh, and in less than 12 hours he had secured a three-storey villa for a base, three vehicles with drivers, cooks and people to wash the team's clothing. As far as we were concerned, there was no reason for this task to be cancelled.

We knew how to get things done. When we were told that there were no flights available, we walked to the rear of the terminal, spoke with the air movements officer — sometimes paying a bribe — and we got our flight. Corruption works both ways. When we needed a forklift, we went straight to the Indonesian general in charge of the reconstruction effort and started a conversation in Bahasa. Once we had established this connection we asked for a forklift; to our delight, he said yes. The boys in Medan were kept busy arranging trucks to transport the units into Banda and strengthening military contacts. The Australian army later came to the party and sprayed not only our villa but also the street that we were living in with a substance to rid the area of mosquitoes.

The list of things to do was endless and I have never seen a team of men so determined. Their hearts and souls were in this task, and being part of such a worthwhile task would change the direction of my life.

TWO

Banda Aceh had been the scene of a separatist struggle since the mid-1970s. The Free Aceh Movement (*Gerakan Aceh Merdeka*, GAM) violently opposed Indonesian rule, resulting in a resistance campaign that resembled East Timor's. But Banda Aceh was pretty much off the Western radar until the Boxing Day tsunami crashed into its coastline.

Following the tsunami, a ceasefire was agreed upon, but the engineers who were deploying with two large desalination units opted to take security. Several of the engineers and security contractors had previously worked together in Iraq and had established a tight bond and a high level of trust. Although the threat in Banda bore almost no resemblance to Iraq, the company that employed the engineers decided to send in a six-man security detachment to ensure the safety of their employees. I had been chosen to lead the task as, along with my SAS background, I was a competent Indonesian linguist, having completed a six-month intensive language course during my time in the Regiment.

Although I'd been sceptical about leaving the troop for six months, the experience had been brilliant. The course comprised eight hours' instruction per day, with a teacher for every four students. We were also expected to study privately for a minimum of three hours a day. Of course, I gave it a fair bit more than that. How obsessive can you get? Weekends were an excellent chance to catch up on the comprehensive word lists that we had been given during the week. We were often given over 50 new words to memorise each day. There were many skills to master — speaking, listening, reading, writing and translation. Our study schedules had to include all of the above if we were to maximise our efficiency.

Families once again had to be understanding. Some wives must have breathed a sigh of relief when their husbands told them that they weren't deploying anywhere for six months, but many weren't prepared for a study schedule that bordered on demented.

But my language skills served me well in Banda. Logistically, being able to speak the lingo allowed us to get the job done, but it also meant we had a huge emotional involvement. Speaking to the locals, interpreting their broken voices and hearing of their tragic loss, touched me deeply.

Death surrounded these people, and it has been said by many a soldier that once you have smelt death you will never forget it. So true. The stench of death is unique, so strong and so repulsive that it remains seared inside one's memory. That distinctive stench was in no small part responsible for the depth of horror I faced when I arrived on the island of Sumatra. Never in my life had I experienced such a feeling of dread as when we stood atop the rubble that had become the tombstone of Banda Aceh. But I had smelt this odour before.

On the morning following the tsunami, the day before I arrived back in Baghdad, a 107-millimetre rocket had landed just outside our compound, no more than 40 metres from my accommodation hut. This was a close call, and a rocket landing amongst crowded accommodation huts could easily have claimed many lives. On another occasion, while seated at my desk in the operations room, I heard a tremendous blast. I immediately donned body armour and went outside to investigate. Eight Nepalese guards had been killed when a rocket struck their mess tent some 200 metres from the ops room.

It was not uncommon for a bullet to sail through a hut's tin ceiling and embed itself in the floor. Nor was it unheard of for a piece of metal from an RPG burst to land on one of the huts in a clatter, as if pebbles had been thrown onto the roof. Rockets and mortars were fired into the International Zone regularly. This one, on 27 December 2004, had claimed a life.

The rocket had slammed into the earth no more than a metre from an Iraqi man who was employed as a security guard on the front gate of the adjacent compound. We acknowledged these guys whenever we entered or departed our compound. The dead man was unlucky but wouldn't have felt a thing. He had left the relative safety of his guard box and ventured into the open, perhaps to relieve himself. The rocket had sailed over the outer perimeter wall and detonated next to him with a tremendous roar.

Several pieces of metal and rocks penetrated the tops of our accommodation trailers. The guard was not riddled with holes but blown in half. His torso was completely severed, his twisted limbs flung in one direction and his mangled upper body in another. Several security contractors ventured out and made the grisly discovery. They placed a blanket over the guard's remains before informing his colleagues. 'It would have been quick,' they consoled themselves.

I have often wondered if there's any awareness when death comes so instantaneously. Does the mind have time to think, 'Oh shit, there go my legs, and here goes my body. How freaking unlucky was I to be right beside that 107-millimetre rocket?' I doubt it – the blow would have knocked him senseless immediately, like someone being king-hit in a fight. You'd feel nothing.

In my more morbid, reflective moments, I can't help but think it has to be better than dying of cancer or being shot in the stomach, where it takes a couple of hours of agonising misery before you finally say goodnight. This man was alive and then he was dead – there was nothing in between.

The following morning, having arrived and heard the news, I joined some members of the team to investigate the site of the explosion. A large crater, over a metre in diameter, clearly identified the rocket's point of impact and the very place the man had ceased to breathe. The earth that was previously hidden a metre below the surface, safely tucked away from the violent Iraqi sun, was now scattered across the surface with all its differing colours. Next to the murderous hole, a large dark stain marked the soil. The blood on the ground was dry and crusted, and this, coupled with the scattered shards of bones and pieces of flesh, was a stark reminder to us of the fragility of our existence. Although I didn't know the guard personally, I felt hollow and numb.

But well before we reached the site, we were steeling ourselves. From a considerable distance away came the sickening smell of death, filling the air with a grotesque and unmistakable flavour of sadness. I had only smelt this foul aroma once before, when as a child I stumbled across a cat that had been struck by a train on the railway tracks behind our home. John, a friend who lived up the road, helped me dispose of the body. We thought the incinerator can, still alight with cardboard boxes, was as good a place as any to dump the mangled body.

With sticks we managed to pick up the maggot-riddled remains, cringing with every step towards the fire – there were no more than 20 steps before we could get rid of the thing. We flicked the body onto the fire and thought we had done a good thing. Alas, within seconds the vilest smell we had ever experienced wafted out of the drum and into our nostrils. The stench continued over the fence, and the grey deathly smoke enveloped the street like a ghastly blanket of fog. It was so putrid that we fled the funeral pyre, fearing that we had done something very, very wrong.

We ran through the gate, around the front, onto the road and finally several houses up the street with our T-shirts pulled over our faces. We stopped and were astounded to find that the smell had overtaken us. A slight westerly breeze had spread the odour without lessening its rankness. We began to dry-retch. It was my first introduction to the trademark stench of death and decay. Its true horror is difficult to revisit and capture in words. It is a memory that should only be suppressed.

=

In Banda Aceh, the waft of dead, decaying bodies seeped out of the ruins. Tens of thousands of corpses lay beneath the surface, entombed in a muddy grave of twisted metal and debris. The situation was exacerbated by the stifling humidity. The thick, wet air embraced the scent, which hovered and wrapped itself around us. There was no escape for the victims in Banda Aceh, or for us as we tried to make order from all the chaos.

Yellow trucks packed with human remains ferried the dead to mass graves on the outskirts of the city centre. Thousands were dropped into body bags. Thousands were not. Decaying limbs and faceless skulls were piled high in the rear of the trucks, a most unenviable task. The drivers appeared to complete their task with impassivity, as if they were unloading a trailer of soil. The scale of the tragedy numbs one's senses to the point where carrying on with living seems possible again.

The Acehnese are some of the most resilient people I've met. Perhaps this is because of the hardships so many of them have faced since birth. Whatever it is, they should be proud of the fortitude that enables them to wake up, breathe and get on with life. Many thousands of lives were lost in the tsunami, but many stories of survival also emerged. Horrific and heartbreaking as their tales were, the local people were intent on sharing their loss. It may well have been their way of dealing with the tragedy.

One young man, who was inspecting our water-treatment units, approached me with a surprisingly cheery disposition that only partly masked the grief and horror visible in his eyes. A contrast of extremes. I greeted him in Bahasa and he immediately warmed. We chatted and he was appreciative that we had arrived to lend support. As we talked, he told me of his personal tragedy. The tsunami had taken away everything from him except his life and his memories. His mother, father and sister were all missing, yet he was still able to muster a smile as he talked about the previous three harrowing weeks while he searched for their remains.

I asked where he thought his family were, and he replied, 'Probably somewhere out to sea. Thousands of people were swept into the ocean when the waters receded.'

I was confused about how he could abandon his search, but after seeing several of the recovered bodies I understood. They no longer appeared human and identification would be impossible. The humid conditions had stripped the bodies bare in less than a month. There was no skin, very little hair and no internal organs. The humidity and parasites had dissolved them with the same efficiency that a scorching sun melts ice. The skulls had nothing more than tufts of hair remaining and the mangled skeletons contained tendons and sinews but very little else.

The young man, aged in his mid-twenties, had no other family, yet he was not as distraught as I would have been. I was surprised. How did he remain so strong? How could he inspect the water-treatment units that we were bringing into the country with such diligence? How was he able to live? He was friendly and warm but his great sadness was still apparent. He suppressed these feelings and continued to function. '*Maaf, sedih sekali,*' – 'Sorry, very sad,' – was all I could muster as my right hand gently patted the area of my chest above my heart. I didn't know what else to say.

He just grabbed my hand, looked deep into my eyes and replied, '*Terima kasih teman saya. Saya senang sekali anda sekalian datang di sini untuk membantu orang Indonesia,*' – 'Thank you, my friend. I am very happy that you all are here to help the Indonesian people.'

His situation was unthinkable but, in Banda at that time, heartbreakingly common – to lose everyone and everything that you love in one cruel stroke. I admired him enormously, trying to imagine if I could have shown his strength. I'd never wish to experience his loss, but if presented with a similar situation, I would like to emulate this man's deep dignity and strength. He was indeed a warrior from within.

The bodies were transported and piled into a series of trenches near the airport. There was very little time for emotion or sensitivity in this dismal task. Squashed on top of each other, the corpses were rolled off the trucks and into the mass grave. There was a real chance that an outbreak of disease could increase the hardship, so the expedited disposal of the bodies was not a task of sentiment. It was a real and very human necessity.

Sitting back in my own home in New South Wales, writing my recollections of operations past, I listen to the sounds of 'normal' domestic life ringing out from the other room. The rewards back here are considerable, but as I retell old stories and relive the incidents that still haunt my dreams, I feel the ache of loss.

When the most remarkable and powerful friendships you will ever have in your life become severed by distance – both in geography and lifestyle – it feels like the death of a friend. And this separation is not a gradual loss. At one moment we are laughing and taking the piss out of each other, and then we part ways.

Back in civilian life you miss those who would challenge you in the gym or on a cross-country run. My email inbox is bloated and my phone continually beeps with messages from my former life, but it's not the same. These snippets from my past are valued but they don't fill the void of separation. For some strange reason, those who know me seem to think that I have made the transition to life as a home dad and university student with ease. They are so very mistaken. My past won't let me go that easily.

The day after I received word of Joe's passing, the phone was ringing hot. This time it was Drewy, hilariously funny, totally irreverent, everyone's mate, but also the guy who keeps the lines of communication open between us all. But Drewy was uncharacteristically sombre. He informed me that three of the boys, three Australian SAS soldiers, had just been killed in a Victorian car accident. I knew them well and, just like Drewy, had shared a laugh with them all. They had recently been involved in challenging and dangerous operations, so to survive those and be killed in a car accident seemed a tremendous waste.

For some peculiar reason, the painful news didn't drag me deeper. I was already feeling so low after Joe's death that the additional loss did not seem to compound the pain I felt. It wasn't possible to feel any lower. I felt sick, but I could not fall any deeper. I'd already shed a tear, for fuck's sake, and I wasn't going to do it again. The three of them were warriors, passionate soldiers who were loved by those who knew them. It was impossible to have a dull party with those guys around. They lived, worked and played hard. Such a combination rarely allows one to grow old.

Kane was away working and he sent a message that helped to strengthen my soul.

At times we may drift from our true selves but at heart we are warriors. Sadly, many warriors die. It's what we do for a life that separates us from those who never know the honour or companionship associated with that price. Men like Joe are not forgotten, and he could not have asked for a better brother than you.

Kane called me a couple of weeks after sending this message, but his voice resonated with despondency. Not being one to hold back, he simply blurted out two words: 'Jezza's dead.'

Now it was my turn to lend support. Jerry was Kane's closest mate in Melbourne, a fiercely loyal and passionate man. Kane's words that 'sadly, many warriors die' were indeed prophetic. Jerry, a man who was rather fond of a fist-fight, died in an altercation in which he was looking the other way and still had his hands in his pockets. He was cheated by a cheap shot and died in Kane's arms after hitting his head on the pavement.

The year 2007 was rapidly proving to be pretty average, and funerals were beginning to top my list of social engagements. It also resurrected feelings of nostalgia, as I struggled to come to terms with leaving behind a major part of my life.

THREE

A dead face stares up into the sky from its bed of mud and debris. Two hands appear to hold one another, like a mother embracing a newly born child. One is significantly larger than the other, but the hands can no longer feel. They are frozen, stalled at 8:46, the time the clock ceased to function and was swept off the wall of a kitchen, living room or hallway in a building that, most likely, no longer exists.

Were the family who lived in this home killed at the same moment that the clock stopped telling the time? Were the hands that hammered the nail into the wall and mounted the clock still alive, or were they buried in the mud below? If a set of hands stayed with the clock, would that mean that the person would be still alive? The clock is damaged but not crushed or entirely destroyed. The pattern of swirls surrounding the face has been scratched and chipped, and the glass is shattered. Only a small section remains, in the lower-left portion of the white face. Only the numbers from 9 to 4 are visible; the remainder are covered in a thin film of mud, hidden from the world and no longer the centrepiece of a proud home, hanging for all to see.

An orange thong sits on the dark-brown mud. It is from a left foot. The colour of the sole would be unidentifiable except for a small cut on the inside and the strap that has been torn and now lies lifeless over the rear of the sole. Is the person who was wearing this item still breathing? The distinctive plug has been ripped out of the centre, while everything around the thong has been flattened and covered in six feet of mud. Where is the person who walked on this sole as the wall of water approached them?

Distressing pictures of missing persons were plastered all over the windows of the airport in Banda Aceh. I asked a man if it would be offensive to photograph these images, and he replied that it was fine. 'It is important that the world sees the devastation that has happened here,' he told me.

The man was a well-educated individual who was in Jakarta on business when the tsunami struck. He was a wealthy man from an affluent neighbourhood in close proximity to the coast. His entire family and extended family were gone, all 18 of them. There was nobody left. The street where he once lived had been swallowed by the raging torrent. He wore dark glasses and a smart suit. He was calm but looked terribly alone. Here was a man who lost his residence, all of his possessions, his entire family and most of his friends, yet he was able to talk to me and, above all else, was grateful for our presence. He didn't seem to be wallowing in self-pity and wasn't bitter about the cards he had been dealt. I didn't know what to say or do but just listened to his heartrending story. It was a privilege to speak with such a strong man. I was in awe.

The first photo I captured was of three children. A good-looking six-year-old boy with a cheeky grin is on the left, his left arm draped over the shoulder of his younger sister. Their two-year-old brother stands on the other side in a bright-yellow shirt. The children are well dressed and look happy. There is a circle around the boys' faces. They are missing.

Being a father with three children of similar ages to those in the picture immediately took my thoughts back home. I missed my children and wanted to hold them so very badly at that moment. I wanted to protect them and ensure they were safe. I don't believe there would be anything more devastating than to lose one's child. Tens of thousands of children were killed in Banda Aceh. One class of schoolchildren numbered 43 on the morning before the disaster. Only six turned up for class four weeks later.

The second photo was one I have since studied in depth, trying to make sense of the associations. A total of seven people are shown as missing. A husband has put the picture of his wife and children on one side, and perhaps his sister and nephews on another. The man's wife is 24 years old and her face is one of quiet elegance. Their 11-month-old son is pictured below with a full head of hair and large smile. Another woman, aged 22, is next to the child.

The second page displays a beautiful woman with a smile that is so sincere and so warm that you feel you could open up and talk to her about anything. She is aged 35. Her eldest son, who is 10, is on her right. Her eight- and six-year-old sons are below. Three women and four children wiped from a family. They had been missing for a month. Their bodies would never be identified.

The next photo must have been taken during a family get-together or celebration. There are eight family members sporting large smiles with hands draped over one another's shoulders. They are all brightly dressed and the youngest child, no more than two years of age, is sitting in the lap of his father. The toddler is contentedly comfortable and is leaning against the man's chest. Both look relaxed and happy. It is a picture of love.

The six remaining figures are a mother and five more children, three girls and two boys. The family looks tight-knit, where everyone enjoys each other's company. The mother is kneeling above her children and has her arm proudly touching the shoulders of two of them. There is much love, and the familial bond evident in this photo is a stark reminder of what our lives should be about. Life in these photos is not about the size of a television, the weight of a gold chain or the brand of car. The people in these photos exude a sense of contentment and yet, in contrast to our Western materialism, they have much less. In heart and soul, however, they are prosperous. They love and are loved in return. As I gaze into the photo, I hope there were no lone surviving children in this family. They deserve to rest in peace as one.

The final photo I took is no less distressing. A mother, at the left of the picture, has her head and body covered in a white shawl while she holds a fan in front of her chest. A branch with three large, brilliant-red jalapenos, a much-loved delicacy in Indonesia, is painted on the front of the fan. The woman is 33 years of age and 155 centimetres tall. The details of her age and height add depth to the image. She had lived.

Her son is pictured to her right, clothed in a blue-collared shirt and jeans. The boy, four-and-a-half years old, is wearing a red cap backwards. Next to him is a photo of his seven-month-old sister lying peacefully asleep. She has a magnificent head of black spiky hair, and a look of complete and utter calm as her little chubby arms hang down by the side of her body. Their father, who placed this photo here, went to work with a wife and two children. By nine o'clock that morning they had all been stolen from him. His legacy will be a constant rerun of 'What ifs'. He may learn to live but he will never get over the grief.

These people are far from alone in their grief. There are thousands of parents who have lost their children and, likewise, thousands of children who have lost their parents. The orphanage near the airport overflows with the lost and homeless.

News reports stating that 'an estimated 200,000 people have been killed by the Boxing Day tsunami' take the human loss and emotion out of this disaster. They distance the event for those in the West. A statement of bald facts belies the loss and devastation evoked by these photos, by the sight of survivors digging in the mud and rubble for their loved ones, by the smell of death that hung in the air in the days and weeks following the tsunami.

And yet, despite all the hardship and grief that confronted us, several of the engineers we were protecting began to complain about the uncomfortable living conditions. 'It's hot, I don't like the food, there are too many mosquitoes, we are working too hard for such a humid environment, sleeping on a stretcher hurts my back ...' The complaints indicated that these men had started to become numb to the grief that surrounded us, and to our purpose of being in Banda.

Thank goodness the project manager, Jerry, was a man of great fortitude and compassion. He was aware that his company had sent him to the site of the disaster not as an act of compassion but as a money-spinning, publicity-driven exercise. The donation of $14 million worth of water-treatment equipment was hardly an act of philanthropy. They came to Banda Aceh not to help anyone but in the hope of making money.

Jerry, despite working for one of the largest corporations in the world, was a man with integrity who also knew how to get the job done. He believed in this task and so did we. He was a natural leader and, while he did not hail from a military background, his relentless work ethic, his desire to lead by example and his ability to motivate others would have seen him held in high regard in any military unit.

Jerry also sensed that his team was weakening and that morale needed boosting. He and I concocted a plan of motivation designed to shock the engineers out of their self-centred complacency. These men were benefitting from this disaster in the form of huge remuneration – we all were – but their hearts remained immune to the hardship around them. If they were to grow from this, they had to be shown the value of humility and humanity.

From my military background I knew there was a fine line between what we should and should not expose the civilian engineers to. To show too little might have resulted in the men not being motivated enough to put up with the conditions, but to show too much could well see them overly traumatised.

As for the security contractors, well, they performed like Trojans and applied themselves wholeheartedly to the task. One character, Harps, was a former SAS soldier and mate I had known for years. He had an enormous appetite for hard work and, during our time in Baghdad, was the most efficient team leader in getting his team up to speed. Harps was also an abrasive individual who hated incompetence. I generally found this side to his persona rather amusing. He definitely didn't have a problem with self-confidence. In fact, I think he still believes he is the hardest man to have come out of the Regiment. Harps, KVA and the other security contractors set the standard and led by example. This mindset aided our efforts to inspire the team of engineers.

FOUR

'Guys, what you will witness will affect you. If it doesn't, then you have no soul. You must be made aware that tens of thousands of children have lost their parents, many thousands of parents have lost their children, entire families have been wiped out. We know it's hot and the mosquitoes are annoying, but you guys are being paid a lot of money to be here and you are here to provide the survivors in Banda Aceh with clean drinking water. You are here to help sustain life. When things get hard, we want you to think about some of the things that you are about to see and use it for motivation. This is one task in your life that you can be proud of. Let's go!'

Our first stop was a bridge that was about a kilometre from the coast. Its river was now some 20 feet below, but there was evidence that the torrent had once covered the bridge entirely. The railings were buckled or torn away and a 44-gallon drum had somehow been wedged underneath one of the railings. The force must have been devastating. Vessels lay 12 feet from the water on the banks, their hulls destroyed.

The banks of the river were littered with six feet of

debris. Corrugated iron, palings, shredded boats and housing materials had all been mashed together. And, worst of all, woven into the carnage were thousands of bodies. The stench was overwhelming. Bodies were being exhumed from the wreckage while we were there, but the engineers were only able to watch from a distance.

Several of us were granted permission to inspect human remains. It was shocking. One body bag I saw contained three skulls and a thighbone attached to a crushed pelvis. The first skull was small. The front teeth were gone and only the front of the skull remained, with a flap of hair attached. The top and rear of the skull were missing. My chest hurt as I realised that it once belonged to a child.

The second skull was also missing several teeth but was otherwise pretty much intact. Deep fractures ran through the bone. The third piece had the remnants of a skull but no facial bones. If the force of the tsunami completely flattened vehicles, like an empty can of cola being squashed underfoot, it is little wonder that these skulls suffered a similarly violent end. This comprehension compounded the shock of the visual we were confronted with as we moved throughout this torn and devastated land.

We moved on to the city centre. It was a peculiar guided tour, but the engineers really had to feel the pain of this lost city. The streets were covered in mud. Ground-floor shops were littered with debris and only the obvious corpses had been removed. The drains must have been choked with bodies. The putrid smell told us this. Shopkeepers were trying to clean up their businesses and keep despondency at bay.

I spoke with a woman who was staring into the alley next to her home. She was wearing a brightly coloured orange dress that hung just below her knees. There were several muddy stains on the front of her dress and her thongs were stuck in the sickly mud beneath her feet. She was limp, shattered, empty. As we talked she revealed her loss. She had been on the first floor when the wave roared down the street. Her husband and children were in the shop below — they perished.

When our clients heard this woman's tragedy, one man cried and the others all had tears welling in their eyes. Her grief and loss made the city and their place in it real. It was gradually dawning on them that while human life is fragile and frail, it is also something to cherish while you can.

We returned to our vehicles and I glanced across the street at a woman who held a broom in her hands. Like many others affected by the tragedy, her eyes stared vacantly at the mess she was confronted with. How could a mere broom sweep this ocean of mud from the sidewalk? Perhaps her sweeping action was an instinctive part of her survival, a way to deal with the devastation that surrounded her. We remained silent, wrestling with these shocking images and smells. We felt empty.

Later we saw footage of the tsunami. It was a bright, warm morning and Banda was a bustling hive of activity. People, cars and motor-scooters jammed the streets. One scooter had an entire family of five balancing on it. There was dust, fumes and commotion. Although the city had been damaged by the earthquake, on the surface all appeared normal. The footage was taken from the first floor of a building.

The cameraman was leaning out a window when a series of screams caught his attention. He panned to the middle of the street as a one-foot wall of water swept down the road. Panic set in immediately as people on scooters attempted to force their way through the crowd. Many people simply stopped and stared at the watery onslaught. Their incomprehension of what confronted them is almost palpable. This was a violent torrent of muddy water. It was rushing down their streets and consuming everything in its path.

The street came alive even more, but now the movement was not of normal day-to-day living. It was a city filled with screams and fleeing bodies. The wall of water, no less than 12 feet high now, poured and bounced down the road. Such was its ferocity that everything in its path was sucked to the bottom and pounded by the debris it had already swept up.

Eerily, the screams ceased. All that could be heard was the water's malevolent roar. One woman managed to scale the side of a building and was pulled onto a first-floor balcony. A vehicle washed by, upside-down and less than two feet below her. She had managed to survive but the anguish on her face and the rising hysteria enveloping her body indicated that she had left a loved one below. Those at ground level weren't swept away in the torrent. They were crushed, battered and dead in an instant.

FIVE

The images that flashed around the Western world of the tsunami in Thailand were a far cry from the reality of Banda Aceh. Banda was too graphic for general viewing. After watching the water flow through the Thai resorts, I pictured myself there. I'm a reasonably strong swimmer and I assumed I would probably have survived. However, after watching the images of the tsunami ripping its way through the streets of Banda, I realised I was wrong. Not even an Olympic swimmer would have had a chance. Living to see another day post-tsunami had nothing to do with fitness, strength or intelligence. If you were caught in its path, then you were going to die.

Viewing this footage has made me reflect deeply. I, too, live near the ocean. What would I have done to improve my chances of survival in such a situation? What if I'd been with my wife and children? Perhaps this is a part of soldiering. When you're out on patrol such thoughts arise constantly. Survival can be enhanced by planning. As you move you look for areas of cover. Areas that might provide protection should you suddenly be contacted by the enemy. All good soldiers hold at the back of their mind an awareness of physical safety and ways out: *If I was shot at right now from that direction, I would go there . . .*

I've walked along the beach and wondered which houses would have escaped the rage of a tsunami and which would have drowned. I've thought about trying to throw my children onto a balcony or the branch of a large pine tree. Would they have had the strength to hold on without me being there to encourage them? I've dreamt that I threw my youngest son onto a balcony; I am preparing to throw my youngest daughter when the wall of water arrives. I have my wife held in between my thighs while I cling to the railing with two arms. She is holding our six-year-old daughter. I manage to release one arm, grab my daughter by her arm and fling her onto the balcony.

The dream, or rather nightmare, never ends in the same way. Sometimes I drop my wife, sometimes we both fall. Once I didn't throw my youngest daughter high enough and she fell into the torrent below, and I jumped in after her. Another time I saw my son balancing on a roof – he looks over the side and topples into the mess.

I guess that's the definition of trauma, the inevitable by-product of witnessing such things. What I have seen and experienced has touched me. I have been with my family in the park and thought to myself, *If a wall of water came right now, what would I do?* How do you choose which of your children to save first? The wall of water that hammered the coast of Indonesia was as high as a fully grown coconut tree.

It is not only the wave. The ocean behind is at the same height and provides an endless supply of power. There would be no escape. I have wondered if my son at pre-school would survive. Would the wall of water envelop the school? I know my daughters would be okay, as their school is perched on the side of a hill. My wife tells me how, where she works, they like to watch the enormous freighters that glide into the harbour. Her office is on the first floor. Would a wall of water wash the building away? These are thoughts that now enter my mind.

As we drove the vehicles closer to the Acehnese coastline, we were confronted by even more poignant sights. The closer we got to the sea, the more enormous the levels of destruction and loss. The area within 500 to 800 metres of the ocean was reminiscent of the devastation in France during the First World War. This area of Banda took me swiftly back to two photos I'd seen of the village of Pozières. The first, a black-and-white image, was taken in 1914. There is a wide Roman road that dissects the village and on either side are quaintlooking terrace homes, all connected. I read about a beautiful orchard and tranquil fields of red poppies. This gorgeous village was destroyed by war.

Pozières was pounded into a ghastly quagmire of rubble, muddy holes, trenches and sickly bodies. A ghostly photo taken in 1916 doesn't remotely resemble the picture taken two years before. There are no human-made structures standing, and only the ghosts of shattered tree stumps prevent the landscape from being completely flat and lifeless.

In Pozières, proportionally more officers were killed than enlisted men. Banda Aceh was similar. The most affluent suburbs were closest to the coast. The most highly educated, wealthy and prominent figures within the community were the first to go. Another sombre parallel must have been the stench of death – it was everywhere.

Tens of thousands of rotting corpses below the surface, meshed with rubble and painted with mud.

Western Banda and Pozières had one common characteristic – there was nothing left.

Our clients were left with one remaining image before being taken back to the accommodation. A middle-aged woman walked towards us along a track that had been partially cleared of debris. Her son was slightly ahead of her, rolling slowly upon a black scooter with blue handlebars and an orange and yellow seat. They greeted us and shook our hands. The woman was wearing fawn pants, a white long-sleeved shirt with embroidered sleeves, and a white head scarf. She had been searching the rubble with her son. I asked about her family and she simply pointed towards where her house had once stood.

'My family are under the rubble,' she said with a heavy sigh and broken voice.

I asked if I could take a picture of her next to her son and she smiled. She has a loving face that has been changed by grief and loss. Her son's eyes look pained. They have lost much but they still have each other.

Wearing a set of dark sunglasses to hide my misty eyes, I related her tragic story to the clients, who looked upon this woman with admiration and sorrow. They had seen enough, so we moved to our vehicles and returned to the villa. Again we remained silent. Deep in thought, each man reflected upon what he had witnessed.

How trivial are some of the little things that we worry about in life, and in contrast, how very strong and resilient were many of the people we had crossed paths with that day. One of the engineers began to cry. He called his family at home, sobbing. He needed to speak with someone he loved. We all did. The entire team of engineers was humbled, and never again did we hear a single complaint from them. They worked themselves into the ground, believing in the strength of a beautiful people. Life was moving on, and we had work to do.

I am sitting at home working on this book when an email comes through: the offer of a deployment to Afghanistan. Three months' work. Leaving almost immediately. I sit and look at the screen for a while. It sounds like a decent gig. I know a couple of the guys who will be there at the same time. My heart picks up a bit of speed just at the thought of getting out there amongst it. I'm never going to lose that feeling in the pit of my gut – that hunger to be on patrol again, pushing myself to my limits. The recollections I've been working on, the stories I've been writing and rewriting, living and reliving, are what make me who I am.

I have taken many things from my time as a soldier. I've learnt a lot about myself. And each different deployment, each individual patrol I was involved with, each operation I oversaw, galvanised in me a strong sense of wonder at my fellow human beings. Banda, despite its human and geographical trauma, offered a space that nurtured a fractured humanity. From my work there, I know that it is a land that will eventually find peace through the compassion and belief of its people. And even in the less peaceful places I have visited, the extraordinary men I've fought alongside have demonstrated the capacity for strength, for healing and growth in the dark corners of the world.

Kane and Mick have left the Regiment too, and although we live in separate parts of Australia they often send an email or text, particularly when they know I'm struggling to deal with my new home-dad, bathroom-scrubbing, vacuum-pushing, dishes-stacking, clothes-washing, essay-writing lifestyle. A recent email from Kane was typical of the friendship that survives our changing lives:

> Bro, stay tough and true – makes one feel alive. I'll come up next week – let's just surf and hang out.

And from Mick:

> Hi mate,
> How're Col and the kids? I'm going to buy a ski and a paddleboard. Let's train up and do the Coolangatta Gold in two years from now.

I now rise early most mornings and grab a few waves before the day begins. It provides a strange mixture of calmness and adrenaline, and is a nice reminder of the rewards of home. I previously never had the time to pursue outside interests. This has been good for me.

Of course, there are still times when I lie awake at night wrestling with some of my past experiences. I just accept that these are a part of the way human minds process complex and dangerous situations. Now the question I must face is how to put my knowledge, my training and my energy into use here at home.

But the offer of work in Afghanistan is a good opportunity.

It's a chance to not only get back into the fray, but visit some of my Afghani friends – Baktiar, Maroof, Noor, Gulgan, Sonny, the guards and the ladies, whom I haven't seen for almost two years. But I'm not sure. My life is now much more than just the sum of different rushes of adrenaline. I need to talk to Colleen about it. Weigh up my study and work commitments. Go over logistics with my publisher. Take my kids to the beach. It's a decision I'll need to make quickly, but it can wait a few hours longer. This won't be the last offer. It can wait until I've worked out what is best for me and my family.

I turn off my computer and walk outside to see what life has in store for me today.

ABBREVIATIONS

AO	area of operations
BIAP	Baghdad International Airport
CHOGM	Commonwealth Heads of Government Meeting
CQB	close-quarter battle
CT	'can't talk'
DoD	Department of Defense (USA)
EA	emergency action (assault)
FAC	forward air controller
FOB	forward operating base
GAM	*Gerakan Aceh Merdeka* (Free Aceh Movement)
IED	improvised explosive device
IET	Infantry Employment Training
NVGs	night-vision goggles
OP	observation post
PSD	private security detail
RAP	regimental aid post
RIB	robust inflatable boat
RMO	regimental medical officer
RPG	rocket-propelled grenade
RRF	rapid-reaction force

RSM	regimental sergeant-major
RV	rendezvous
SAS	Special Air Service
SSM	squadron sergeant-major
2iC	second-in-command
tacsat	tactical satellite
VBIED	vehicle-borne improvised explosive device
VM	vehicle-mounted

ACKNOWLEDGEMENTS

To my lovely wife, Colleen, whose altruistic approach to life granted me years of freedom to chase the adrenaline-charged lifestyle I craved. For this gift of love, I express heartfelt gratitude – it is to you I owe the most. And to our three wonderful children, Tahlie, Sian and Reyne. I love being your dad.

To my wonderful parents, Bob and Shirley. Apart from the time I kicked the garage, filled the crutch of dad's pyjamas with itching powder or held that party when I was 16, I wouldn't change a thing from my childhood. I truly appreciate your endless love and encouragement.

I would also like to extend my warmest thanks to Robyn Morris for giving me the confidence to write and for her literary support. And thank you to Mary Cunnane, Nikki Christer, Julian Welch and Michael 'Jack Black' Williams for making it all happen.

Finally, to the boys! My hard-hitting brothers, who challenge, inspire and motivate me. I won't mention your names; you know who you are.

WARRIOR TRAINING

CONTENTS

	Prologue	v
1	Craving a Change of Life	1
2	The SAS: All or Nothing	17
3	Week One: Exposing What Lies Beneath	29
4	Week Two: Operating Alone	63
5	Week Three: Lucky Dip	75
6	Acceptance via Performance	93
7	RTI Training: A Test of Self-belief	111
8	POW Camp: Ostracising Those Who Resist	143
9	Hospitals and Africa: Humanitarian Operations	159
10	Physical Training	197
11	Dealing with Transition	225
	Epilogue	257
	Acknowledgements	265

For my grandparents, Gerard and Mary.
And my parents, Bob and Shirley.

PROLOGUE

Not all SAS soldiers enjoy parachuting. While jammed in the back of a 22-seater bus on our way to RAAF Base Pearce for jump training, I noticed that one of the guys was white-faced, his hands gripping the seat in front of him in the same way that children sink their fingers into their parents' arms while on a rollercoaster for the first time. He looked like he was about to vomit.

'Hey, mate,' I said. 'You feeling crook?'

'I hate this shit,' he answered, relaxing his grip and pushing his head into the seat.

'What, driving to Pearce?'

He laughed. 'Nah, parachuting, smartarse. This shit freaks me out.'

I sat confused for a moment, trying to comprehend why someone who hated parachuting would put himself through the rigours of life as an SAS soldier. 'What about abseiling, climbing, diving – do you get off on any of them?'

'Get off?' he said. 'Definitely not. I get off on sex.'

'Fair enough – but then why are you in the Regiment?'

All SAS soldiers must overcome their fears.

'Because I wanted to test myself, to prove I could cut it.'

This guy – a quiet, unassuming man – was a solid performer. He went on to scare the shit out of himself for another six years before deciding enough was enough. It requires a strong mind to continually embrace fear rather than run the other way. In my view, the toughest men in the Regiment weren't those who enjoyed what was thrown their way, but those who were uncomfortable and yet managed to keep their fears in check.

In battle soldiers will experience a range of feelings, from fear to exhilaration, depending on the intensity of the engagement. So what separates the men who hold their nerve from those who don't? I believe that training and mental preparation are vital to performing well under adverse conditions. When things go wrong, you cannot simply succumb to your natural survival instincts; you have to make decisions based on sound judgement.

My aim in this book is to inspire readers to believe in themselves and to reflect upon how they deal with adversity. Regardless of whether you're a doctor in Afghanistan, a student in Great Britain, a miner in Australia or a tour guide in Tanzania, self-belief and thorough preparation are critical to success.

By the time most people reach old age – if they manage to hang around that long – they will have experienced the best and worst of life, from love and the thrill of achieving their dreams, to failure, heartache and death. They are wise, for they have lived.

Many soldiers also gain a wide range of experiences, from forging life-long friendships and overcoming exciting and challenging tasks, to dealing with immense hardship and staring down death. This is particularly so for special-forces soldiers due to the rigor of their training and operational deployments. But rather than absorbing these golden highs and brutal lows over an entire lifetime, a soldier might experience them in a few weeks, months or years.

Men and women often return from war different people. Some struggle with what they have seen, while others are able to rationalise their experiences, contextualise events and use the lessons they have learnt to propel them through life. Many SAS soldiers fall into this latter category, which is a tribute to their self-belief, determination and mental strength, and to the incredible training they receive. But what happens to these soldiers when they leave the Regiment? This book offers an insight into the training and mindset of SAS soldiers, and how we negotiate the transition between two vastly different lives.

≡

Ever since I was young, I have been intrigued by high-performing individuals and teams, especially those who excel in challenging or adverse conditions. How do they do it? What makes them tick?

Since the formation of the Australian Special Air Service Regiment in 1957, fewer than 1500 soldiers have earned the right to wear the highly coveted 'sandy beret'. Even during difficult times – after the devastating loss of 15 SAS soldiers in Townsville in 1996, for example, when two Blackhawk helicopters collided during counter-terrorism training – the Regiment won't lower its impeccable standards just to fill positions. Only those who show potential and pass the rigorous selection process are accepted.

SAS soldiers must not only display exceptional levels of physical fitness and endurance, they must also be team-oriented, able to think clearly during high-stress situations, and capable of processing a large amount of information in a relatively short period of time. Applicants don't have to be Olympic athletes and brain surgeons, but they must possess a particular mindset that enables them to prepare themselves physically and mentally for the challenges they will endure on SAS operational deployments. I love this about the Regiment – irrespective of how thin the ranks become, its standards never waver.

It wasn't until I left the SAS in December 2002 and spent several years as a private contractor running operations in Iraq and Afghanistan that I truly appreciated the extraordinary quality of the men who make it into the SAS. The Regiment, like any organisation, has an internal pecking order. Soldiers are continuously assessed, rated and counselled by their superiors; this guarantees that each soldier is aware of his own strengths and weaknesses. The men are also assessed informally by their peers. Due to the challenging nature of SAS training and operations, every man becomes highly conscious of his own ability, and of the ability of the men around him. There is nowhere to hide.

Every SAS squadron has its 'jets' (those who are a cut above), its 'average Joes' (the majority), and its poorer performers (those who hover around the minimum standard required). But after 30 months contracting in Iraq and Afghanistan, where I attempted to mould a contingent of men from contrasting military backgrounds and nationalities into a formidable security force, I realised that *all* SAS soldiers – even those who are performing at the lower end of their experience levels – are exceptional.

=

Following the publication of *Warrior Brothers* in 2008, I received many messages of support from former and current soldiers, and from non-military people, including one email from a man who had been contemplating suicide. He was inspired by the actions of some of my friends and changed his mind. I received another note from an 83-year-old woman who had lived through decades of angst after her husband had returned from World War II a different man. He has since passed away, but she found something in *Warrior Brothers* that gave her a sense of why he was the way he was.

I never expected an elderly woman – besides my Nan – to read my book, let alone to take the time to drop me a line. Her letter moved me but, to be honest, it was not for that reason that I'd written *Warrior Brothers*. For me, writing was cathartic; it allowed me to document my thoughts and to interrogate my inner self. Initially, I had no intention of letting others read the material; I just wanted to get it out of my system. In some respects, my computer's hard drive had a more honest account of who I was than most of my family and friends did.

As my email inbox began to swell with hundreds of messages, I was humbled – blown away, really – that others were drawing strength and inspiration from some of the people and experiences I had written about. I hope this book offers more of the same.

1

CRAVING A CHANGE OF LIFE

As a young man growing up I had no idea that Australia had a special-forces unit called the Special Air Service Regiment. Then I read an article about an SAS team being involved in an incident in Somalia, which gave a vague description of what the SAS was and what its soldiers did. If I was to pinpoint the exact moment that I decided to strive for the SAS, then that would be it. The actions of the hard-hitting guys at the centre of that incident inspired me.

I had been restless for a couple of years. I was 19, and although I had contemplated leaving my trade as a motor mechanic before I was fully qualified, my father had encouraged me to persevere.

'Look, mate,' he'd said, 'I know you want a job that's exciting, but if you hang around for two years and

At 17, my job as an apprentice motor mechanic didn't do it for me.

get your ticket, then I'm sure you'll get your chance.'

He was right. Sitting in the military recruitment office and watching a video of soldiers parachuting was all the motivation I needed to join the army.

When I met the recruiting officer, I did my best to act cool and not sound desperate. But I couldn't help asking: 'If I join the army, do I get to parachute?'

'Providing you meet the medical and physical requirements, there's a very good chance,' he replied, as a slight, sardonic smirk worked its way to the corner of his mouth.

I tried not to grin, thinking I had just nailed the scam of the century. *Who gets paid to jump out of planes?*

The recruiting officer had a cloth parachute badge on his right shoulder, the mark of one who was qualified. I bet that he, too, was trying to remain straight-faced: he knew very well that real military parachuting was vastly different from the recruiting videos he had just shown me. The videos were filled with images of soldiers jumping out the back of planes and gliding through the sky under canopy. But they never showed footage of anyone landing.

I asked the recruiting officer another question: 'Are there decent gyms in the army?'

He smiled the sort of smile that said: *You fuckwit — of course there are decent gyms in the army.* But his answer was a little more diplomatic. 'The army has some of the best training establishments in the country.'

So I get to parachute and train in the gym, I thought. *Where do I sign up?*

I filled out the appropriate paperwork, enrolled at TAFE to further my education, and waited. I must have called the recruiting office half a dozen times to check on my application. And then it came – an official-looking letter announcing my test dates.

So in October 1993 I travelled to Sydney for my medical, psychological and aptitude testing. If I was found suitable then I would be interviewed later that afternoon. I passed the initial tests with no problems. One of the first questions I was asked during my interview was: 'If you were sent to war, could you kill a person?'

I was so pumped to have made the interview stage that I'm surprised I didn't say something like: 'If you let me in the army then I'm happy to kill as many people as you want.' But in reality my thoughts then were much the same as they are now. 'It would not be something that I would enjoy,' I said, 'but if I was confronted by a situation where I was required to take a life in order to save mine or another, then I would.'

My application was approved, and a few months later – on 25 January 1994 – I joined the Australian Army.

Saying goodbye to my parents. I joined the army at the age of 20.

≡

Our induction ceremony was held in Sydney before we were herded onto buses and driven to 1RTB – the 1st Recruit Training Battalion at Kapooka, Wagga Wagga. During the ceremony one enthusiastic guy told me that he had been in the Army Reserve, and that I should let him know if I needed a hand. Apparently polishing boots and brass was 'a piece of piss'. Within three days of our arrival at Kapooka, this same guy walked into my room and said: 'Fennell, you have to help me escape! I can't take this shit anymore. I gotta get out of here – I'm goin' crazy!'

He was an intense little bastard with a red face and wiry physique, but he was also a little crazy – in a likeable and humorous way. The next night – wearing just a pair of grandpa-type underpants – he came into my room asking for change so he could grab a Coke from the machine downstairs. Lights out was at 2200 hours; anyone caught out of bed after this time was going to have their face yelled off and possibly be subjected to some bullshit punishment like scrubbing bathroom tiles with a toothbrush. Besides that, the Coke machine was at the bottom of 'God's stairs', an internal stairwell that was only to be used by our instructors.

I couldn't fathom why anyone would want to run the gauntlet for a can of Coke, but I got out of bed, unlocked my cupboard and pulled a two-dollar coin out of my wallet.

'Thanks, man – I owe you one,' he said as he scurried down the hall.

The next thing I heard was his can of Coke slamming into the bottom tray of the machine. Anyone within 100 metres would have heard it. *Surely he'll get busted on the way back to his room*, I laughed to myself. A minute later he strolled into my room with a large smile on his face, drawing on his can of Coke like he was a gangster sucking on a Cuban.

'Hey, Fennell, want a sip?'

I visualised his sweaty lips on the can, held back a dry-retch and refused the offer. 'No thanks, mate. You have it.'

'I'll put the change in your drawer.'

'Cool.'

Within five seconds of him leaving my room and re-entering his own, which was just across the hallway, an angry white light burst through the doorway.

'Which one of you fucks was out of bed?'

Neither I nor my room-mate answered.

The angry prick – the duty corporal – turned on the light. 'Were you out of bed?'

'No, sir,' I replied.

'I'm a corporal, fuckwit.' He turned on my room-mate: 'Was it you?'

'No, Corporal.'

'I saw someone's shadow near the window. Who was it?'

I opted to play dumb. 'I don't know, Corporal.'

The duty corporal was aware that unless we admitted it, there wasn't a lot he could do. He turned off the light, shone his torch into the room opposite, then disappeared down the hallway.

The next morning, during a routine inspection while we were having breakfast, our section commander found the loose change in my drawer. I was yelled at for nearly 10 minutes and accused of promoting thievery. When quizzed as to how the money got there, I said I planned to use it for the pay phone when we were allowed to call home.

'Call home? I'll tell you when you can call home, fuck-wit. Do you understand?'

'Yes, Corporal.'

'Next time you'll be charged with insecurity. Get out of my sight, shit-stain.'

I marched up the hallway and straight into the room of the guy who put the change in my drawer.

'Hey, Fennell, what'd he say?'

'He asked me why the money was in my drawer and I told them you put it there. You have to go to the office.'

'Man, you're shittin' me?'

'Yeah, I am.' I left his room laughing.

The only things I enjoyed about basic training were the physical training, our four-day furlough and the couple of nights we had on the piss. Getting yelled at didn't really do it for me, but some of the one-liners were amusing. While marching back from the range, my section commander yelled: 'Hey, Barrington, close your fucking hand when you march or I'll come over there and stick my dick in it!' Even in the Regiment, soldiers on selection are sometimes surprised by the odd witty remark. On one course, the trainees were lined up waiting for their turn in the shower when one of the senior instructors – a guy with an ability to remain completely deadpan – bellowed: 'Trainee 66, you've got a great arse. What do you feed that thing – cock?'

I can honestly say that I entered the army with one aim in mind: to join the SAS as quickly as possible. The physical training we did at Kapooka was only mildly challenging, as most of the pack marches and runs had to allow for the soldiers at the bottom of the group. We were constantly reminded that the army was about teamwork – a section is only as fast as its slowest man.

Negotiating obstacles during basic training.

At times I found this frustrating, as the physical standard of some guys was so far below what I expected that it was painful. When someone puts in, regardless of what level they are at, then no probs. But when someone dives on the ground like they've just been shot after a casual 500-metre run, then I tend to question their commitment to the team. I longed to be part of a hard-hitting group of men who all wanted to go the extra mile. I'd seen *Chariots of Fire*. If we had to run, then that's how I wanted it to be.

At Kapooka I met a few like-minded people, so each evening we would supplement our training with sets of chin-ups, push-ups and sit-ups. As for our section commanders giving us grief, well, there appeared to be some sort of code – they left us alone while we were training. During one of our evening sessions, one man, Dalton – a blond-haired guy with a sharp sense of humour – passed a comment that gave me confidence.

'Hey, Fennell, I reckon you're going to make it into the SAS.'

I finished the push-ups I was doing, then faced him and raised an eyebrow, thinking he was taking the piss.

'I'm serious ... you're focused, man. There has to be guys who get in, and I think you'll be one of 'em.'

≡

Our platoon was expected to be sent to the infantry training centre in Singleton, but as it was already at full capacity we were sent straight to Brisbane, along with another nine or 10 platoons – some 300 soldiers in all. Although the training program there was comparable, I did feel a little ripped-off. We arrived at Enoggera, in Brisbane, in the early afternoon; unlike at Kapooka, where we'd been met by half a dozen screaming instructors, our opening address was almost civil. Later that day we were taken for a run around the area and introduced to Enoggera Hill. The weather was humid, the road steep. I have no doubt that Townsville's Castle Hill and Enoggera Hill in Brisbane are two of the most challenging short runs around.

Over the next three months we were trained as infanteers. The physical training (PT) – a blend of circuits,

Obstacle course, basic training.

runs and battle training – was brilliant. My favourite session was the obstacle course: a series of walls, river crossings, traverse ropes and towers. Towards the end of our infantry training, Rog – a stocky and confident soldier – and I applied for the SAS selection course. We both passed the physical, aptitude and psychological testing and were fortunate to be given the chance to attempt the course the following year. Most infantry soldiers are required to spend a couple of years in the Battalion.

We had no idea what we were in for – the challenge was daunting. If we were to listen to all the negative comments about how impossible it was to make it into the SAS, then we would have failed the course before it even began. At the completion of infantry training, I was presented with an award for 'best at physical training', which definitely enhanced my confidence.

I tried to imagine what sort of man made it into the SAS. How much fitter or stronger could they be? Physically,

Rog and I were in the best shape of our lives. We just had to believe in ourselves. I had never met an SAS soldier or knew anyone who had passed the selection course, but I was certain that even SAS soldiers were human.

Our platoon spent most of the next five months on field training exercises near Quilpe, a hot, dry area 1000 kilometres west of Brisbane. One late afternoon our section was allocated a defensive position along the bank of a river. I was lying near a log and kept myself amused by taking aim at a couple of sheep that were grazing on the opposite bank. There didn't appear to be a lot to eat.

I had a sick sense that someone or something was looking at me. My right ribs were flush against a large hole in the log. I shuffled back a little and peered inside. I was initially intrigued by a pair of beady dark eyes less than 20 centimetres from mine. I thought they belonged to a mouse. Then the creature stuck out its tongue and slithered towards me.

Instantly I lost all composure. 'Aahh!' I shouted as I rolled out of the way, my left hand coming up to protect my neck. The snake followed me, positioned itself atop the log and flared its neck. It was a healthy specimen with a girth the size of my lower arm.

Locky, a bushy who was a natural with a rifle, also leapt out of the way. 'Hey, Keithy, when you get back to Brisbane go and get yourself a lottery ticket. That's a king brown. If it had nailed ya' on the face or neck out here then it would have been all over.'

I didn't say anything but just stood there holding my neck.

Locky looked at my face and laughed.

'I thought it was a mouse so I didn't bother moving,' I said.

'You fuckin' idiot,' said Locky, laughing harder.

≡

In October 1994 our platoon was sent to Brunei for a month of jungle training. Vietnam movies like *Platoon* give an accurate impression of the sounds, insects and weather of jungle operations, but I was still surprised, after just a five-day patrol, by how taxing that environment can be.

The humidity underneath the canopy is stifling. With no breeze, the air remains thick and dense. I have seen guys hyperventilate and panic during arduous physical activity. They complain of not being able to breathe; they gasp, with large frightened eyes, like a smoker who suffers from emphysema. Everyone is soaked from head to toe by his own perspiration. If a patrol is to last for five days, then you generally remain wet for five days.

Jungle training camp, Brunei.

When your skin stays wet in a humid environment, the onset of 'prickly heat' or heat rash is inevitable. The pores of your skin become clogged, meaning the skin struggles to breathe. As the sweat glands release fluid, the moisture is trapped beneath the skin, creating a profound stinging sensation and a red rash.

The first time I experienced prickly heat was while eating a canteen of steaming noodles in the Bruneian jungle. I was nearing the end of my meal when, as a result of the hot food inside my stomach, I began to sweat. I stopped eating – which in itself is significant! – and pulled up my shirt, as I was certain I was being mauled by insects. After one of the boys checked my back and gave me the all clear, I resumed eating. As the hot noodles slid down my oesophagus into my stomach, my body began to perspire again.

What in the hell is going on? I thought. I felt as though my skin was bursting underneath the surface. Upon further inspection, a mate noticed I had a red rash all over my ribs and back.

'You've got heat rash,' said another. 'It sucks – I get it all the time.' He then pulled out a couple of alcohol swabs and scrubbed my back. Instant relief!

When operating in the jungle, depending on the tactical situation, you should always attempt to go to bed dry. As a minimum, we learnt to replace our socks or our feet would soon rot. Having said that, soldiers will generally only carry one spare set of clothing, and monsoonal rain is pretty difficult to hide from. Within three days, most of our clothing and sleeping equipment would be damp. Then it's just a matter of sucking it up and enjoying the experience for what it is – a chance to bond with nature.

One time, while lying in an ambush and being belted by rain on a training exercise, the guy to my left side looked at me and smiled.

'That's better,' he whispered.

'Did you just do a piss?' I asked, a disturbed look on my face.

'Yeah, I was freezing. Now I'm warm.'

Some men are able to hold it together and some aren't. While on patrol, our platoon was instructed to halt while the section commanders conferred with the platoon commander. I was the section 2IC and sat on the track with everyone else. My section commander was annoyed with this and thought I should know better. Unable to control his frustration, on his way back through the men he launched a boot into my right kidney. I was caught unaware and winded. My face filled with blood, my eyes flashed. It was a struggle, but I dumped my pack and began to stand up. He had apologised before I was on my feet, so my angry red face and I sat back down.

≡

By December of 1994 I was nearing the end of a promotion course – subject two for corporal – and was looking forward to getting home for a few weeks. In my quest to be different, I left a message on my girlfriend's answering machine. I rambled on with some banal account of what we'd been up to before casually asking her to marry me. I didn't find out her answer for 10 days. My anxious wait ended with the completion of the field phase of the course. Colleen said yes.

Our final parade was held at the 8/9 RAR boozer. I didn't bother having a beer. The remainder of our platoon had been granted leave a week before. Three of us – including Bradd, a mate who would later make it into the Regiment and narrowly avoid being turned into a tea strainer by the Taliban – decided to drive from Brisbane to Sydney as soon as we knocked off. We left in a convoy: three shitty cars with three impatient drivers. We hadn't had a decent night's sleep for nearly 10 days. The sensible thing to have done would have been to tackle the drive the following morning after a full night's sleep. Instead, driven by impatience and a strong desire for sex, we rolled out of Enoggera at 1600 that afternoon.

Nine hours later I woke up to the sound of tyres on gravel and a honking horn. My car had left the road, and I was lucky to avoid some large trees. I had fallen asleep, and chances were it would happen again. Bradd had seen my car drift then leave the road, so he'd slammed his hand on the horn.

I got out of my car and approached the white lights behind me, embarrassed and half-grinning.

'I just saved your life, dickhead,' said Bradd, smiling.

'Yeah, that was close. I'm going to get my head down for a few hours,' I said.

'Yeah, I felt myself go a couple of times too,' said Bradd. 'What time do you wanna get going?'

'About five . . . or whenever we wake up,' I said.

We made it home and I got engaged. For me, life carried on.

≡

I enjoyed my time in the Battalion, but I was never content. Training for the SAS selection course dominated my thoughts the way a writer dreams of getting published. My desire to be an SAS soldier was all-consuming.

2

THE SAS: ALL OR NOTHING

There are those in life who whine about missed opportunities. 'I could have made the Olympic swim team ... I've always wanted to trek through Nepal ... I could have been a doctor ... I wish I'd spent more time with my kids when they were young ... I should have tried out for the SAS ...'

Some people prefer to pull others down, to make excuses about why others have achieved – rather than addressing the real reasons for why they themselves did not. Surely those who spend hours worrying about what others are doing would be a little more content if they kept life simple and concentrated on themselves. Then there are people who call others lucky: 'She's lucky, he's lucky, they're lucky ... I'm so unlucky.'

I believe people generally create their own luck – it's called hard work.

While I was training for the SAS selection course, I was chastised by one man who had recently been posted to the 6th Battalion as a section commander. He'd previously been a member of a reconnaissance platoon in one of the

Townsville infantry battalions and had a grandiose opinion of himself. When he heard I was panelled for selection even though I had only been in the army for 10 months, he became irritated.

'Hey, private – I hear you're doing the Cadre Course,' he began.

'Yes,' I said.

'Yes, *Corporal*,' he replied with a sly grin on his face, looking to his left and right to make sure others were taking notice.

I bit my tongue and played the game. 'Yes, Corporal.' There was no doubt about it. *You're a tool*, I thought.

'How much fuckin' nav ya' done?' he asked, referring to navigation.

'I completed subject two for corporal, which enabled me to square my nav away, Corporal.'

'Huh, I heard about that fuckin' course. The Cadre is nearly all nav. It takes a soldier three or four years to get the skills. Without solid nav, you won't have a chance.'

I found out afterwards that this guy had previously attempted selection. He made it to the end of the first week. I made a mental note of our conversation and used it on selection for motivation when things got tough.

≡

The army was beginning to look like an all or nothing option, at least in the short term. If I failed the SAS selection course, then I was to be discharged from full time service. I joined the Ready Reserve scheme, a one-year commitment, due to missing the regular enlistment by a few weeks. I was not prepared to wait another 12 months

On exercises in south-east Queensland with the 6th Battalion.

and was told during enlistment that I would be able to transfer to the regular army at the completion of my 12-month obligation. The training was the same so I signed on. What we weren't told was that the politicians were determined to make the scheme a success. For this to happen, soldiers were required to return for 35 days of continuation training each year. Obviously, if soldiers were absorbed into the regular army, this would not be possible. It was decided that soldiers who had completed promotion or specialist courses were of value to the scheme so would not be offered regular positions. You gotta love performance punishment. At the end of the year, seven soldiers from our company were offered the opportunity to join the regular army. My platoon sergeant, Howie, knew I would be pissed so called me into his office.

'Hey, Fennell, the army, just like life, isn't always fair. What can we do about it? Nothin'. You want regs?'

'Yes, Sergeant,' I replied.

'Then all you gotta do is pass the selection course. If you don't get injured you'll go alright. You're fit enough. Don't worry about how long you've been in the army. Those SAS flogbags will teach ya' everything you need to know.'

I liked Howie. Behind his fiery sergeant persona, was a man who cared about his guys.

'I was a sergeant by 26 and now I'm a fat bastard who gets to sort out admin bullshit for guys like you.'

His honesty made me laugh.

'You'd get bored in the battalion. Why stuff around, you know what ya' want. Now piss off and go run up the mountain or do whatever bullshit you need to do to make sure you get in.'

I thanked Howie for his advice and left his office feeling pumped. I was getting married so it would have been nice to have had the security of a fulltime job if I failed the course, but the uncertainty made me more determined.

≡

After our engagement party, Col and I returned to Canberra, where she was employed at a local radio station. While she was at work, I would train, preparing myself for the SAS selection course. After a few days, a couple of mates, Arny and Rog, came down to visit. Rog, who looked a little like Tom Cruise – when Tom Cruise was still cool – was also with us when Col selected her engagement ring. She has never been intimidated by the relationships I have with my mates. In a sense, my brothers are her brothers.

Rog and I were both attempting selection, so we donned packs and tackled some of the mountains around Canberra. I had marvelled at the steepness of the terrain many times and often aspired to take them on. Although the area was private property, I couldn't resist the temptation to scale a steep mountain. For me, walking somewhere for the first time, taking in the angles, colours, vegetation and terrain, is far more exhilarating than a ride on a rollercoaster. I get to choose the speed of ascent and how hard I make my heart beat. It's a time when money and possessions mean nothing, like taking off on a wave, when the immediacy of living the moment means complete and utter freedom.

The immediacy of living the moment.

If I succeeded and was accepted into the SAS, then Col and I would be moving to Perth. In Canberra, Col's boss and close friend Jacqueline was less than thrilled at the prospect of Colleen being taken away. She thought SAS soldiers were psychopaths, so from the day I met her she referred to me as 'Killer'.

'So, Killer, tell me — what are you going to do if you don't make it into the SAS?'

I felt like I was being interrogated by my girlfriend's father. I had no idea what else I wanted to do. My sole employment ambition was to join the SAS. Nothing else turned me on. Being unemployed and clueless about where I was heading was not the answer Colleen's over-protective friend wanted to hear. So I said: 'I'd go to uni and get a degree.'

'Really... What will you study?'

God, who is this woman? I thought. 'Mathematics. I'll be a maths teacher,' I said with little conviction. I had as much desire to be a maths teacher as I did to return to my trade as a motor mechanic — none.

'A maths teacher? Where will you live?'

A long way from you. 'Brisbane, perhaps back in Wollongong,' I said, realising the importance of getting Col's friend and boss onside.

'What about Canberra?' she asked.

Not as long as you're still there. 'We haven't discussed where we'd live,' I said.

Colleen wasn't concerned in the slightest and let Jac know that she would definitely be moving to Perth. 'He'll get in,' she said, as she poured chocolate syrup over her favourite meal — pancakes and ice cream.

I appreciated Col's belief in me, but although I knew I would never voluntarily remove myself from the course, I planned to approach the course just one day at a time. Colleen maintained this unflinching confidence in my ability throughout my years in the Regiment, never allowing the thought that I could be killed. This wasn't the case during my time running operations in Iraq and Afghanistan as a contractor, however. Waking up in the middle of the night drenched in perspiration as I wrestled with tactical options did catch her attention when I was at home.

Despite keeping Col well-informed – and this helped – it wasn't until she read *Warrior Brothers* and gained access to some of my most private thoughts that she fully realised the fragility of the soldier's lifestyle.

≡

I returned to the Battalion in Brisbane on 4 January 1995. The SAS selection course was 11 weeks away. Three days later we deployed up north for our final six-week training exercise. Although it was difficult to find the time for extra training sessions when we were out bush, Rog and I were issued double rations. Instead of eating one disgusting can of ham and egg each day, we were able to chow down on two. This would have to be my least favourite meal in the military. Purely out of interest, I have eaten dog food before – both the tinned and biscuit varieties. The biscuits are alright, but tinned dog food is very, very average. Still, I would probably consider ham and egg to be even viler.

Due to exercise constraints, we were afforded very little time to train. A couple of 3.2-kilometre webbing runs, augmented with push-up and sit-up circuits, were as good as it got. But that all changed as soon as we returned to Brisbane. Where possible, we followed the SAS's three-month training program, pounding the roads and tracks around Enoggera. But it didn't take long for our feet to fall apart. We tried everything, from wearing a thin second pair of socks, to regular soakings with Condy's crystals and spraying our feet with methylated spirits diluted with water. We'd already missed several weeks of training so, rather than allowing our feet time to heal, we taped them up and kept going.

On one stifling morning Rog and I each loaded two concrete blocks and a 20-litre jerry can into our packs before scrambling up the mountain. I didn't know which part of my body hurt most – my feet, legs, back and shoulders, or my lungs, which were rising and falling at an alarming rate. The only motivation we got was from each other. If I wanted to take my pack off, sit down and take time out, I could. I knew I didn't have to be there and that the pain was self-inflicted, my own doing. In the back of my mind was a niggling little voice, which reminded me that although I was putting in the effort, there was no guarantee I would pass the course. But I decided that if the program said that I was to wear a pack and punish myself for three hours, then that's what I would do.

My preparation for selection wasn't ideal – I suffered damaged ankle ligaments, was on crutches for a while, had infected feet and faced the possibility of a medical discharge. I had a choice. I could look for excuses, justify them to myself and then perhaps try again the following year. (I knew of a sniper from the Battalion who had trained for selection four times, and each time he had pulled out the week before departure. He never did make it onto the course.) Or I could give it a go.

Life very rarely turns out the way we think it should. Those who wait for everything to line up perfectly before tackling their dreams are often the same people who arrive at the penultimate years of their life frustrated about what might have been. I decided that I would never live this way.

So I had a dodgy ankle – big deal. The army had shitloads of strapping tape.

≡

To pass the SAS selection course, you need to be self-motivated, disciplined and capable of setting mid- to long-term goals, and you have to have an ability to follow through when things become challenging. Those who are successful are not supermen. They just know what they want and are prepared to put in a great deal of effort to make it happen. Anyone who attains the top of their chosen field shares these attributes.

We are all motivated to achieve different things in life. I am drawn to new challenges and excitement. I am competitive by nature, but I don't gauge my success by comparing myself to others. Thinking about what someone else earns, owns, is doing or has done is negative. It makes you dissatisfied, destroys your self-esteem and prevents you from reaching your potential. Irrespective of what others around me are doing, I set my own goals and try to be relentless in my quest to achieve them.

I've also tried never to be discouraged by negative comments; instead, I often use them for motivation. When someone says 'You haven't been in the army long enough to pass the SAS selection course' or 'You should finish your degree before you write a book', they enhance my desire to achieve. The motivation is already there, but I'm constantly searching for ways to make it stronger — whatever it takes to give me the edge I need.

Each year hundreds of applicants apply for the SAS selection course. The screening process, designed to weed out those who are unsuitable, begins nine months before the course. Applicants must pass the special-forces barrier test in order to prove they are physically capable of beginning the training. If a soldier fails to attain the minimum physical requirements, he will not be accepted onto the course because it's unlikely he will be able to complete the arduous three-month training program.

The next test assessed aptitude; it was the same test that applicants complete when they apply for the Australian Defence Force. SAS soldiers must be able to think clearly under stress and be able to absorb information quickly. Soldiers are graded on their ability to answer questions quantitatively and qualitatively. There is also a detailed section on problem-solving. The test isn't designed to be completed — there are too many questions. An applicant either displays the minimum aptitude required or doesn't.

The next test was a 300-question psychological examination. 'When you're standing in a room, do you feel like people are staring at you from dark corners?' Who in his right mind would say yes to that? Rationally, it was relatively easy to work out what you were supposed to answer. There were many questions like this, framed in different ways. The assessors were looking for consistency and I took a reserved approach when answering the questions.

During my interview, I was questioned about one answer I'd given.

'Private Fennell, in your psychological examination you answered that you didn't know if you had a higher tolerance to pain than most other people. Please explain the reasoning behind your answer.'

'From a young age, I have always pushed myself physically,' I said. 'But it's impossible for me to ascertain if my pain threshold is superior to others', as I don't know what other people are feeling. The only serious accident I've had was a broken arm when I was young. I don't recall how I handled that situation.'

'But if we were to ask you whether you thought you could push yourself further than most people, which is something that is required of an SAS soldier, then what would you say?'

I grinned and realised that they were basically telling me the answer they needed to hear.

'From what I have seen when I'm training with my peers in the Battalion,' I said, 'I think I do have an ability to extend myself further than others.'

'Thank you,' the assessor said.

And thank you, I thought.

3

WEEK ONE: EXPOSING WHAT LIES BENEATH

Only those who show potential are accepted into the SAS selection course. The number of applicants varies from year to year. One course might begin with 80 men, another with double this number. On our course there were 150 starters.

The first nine days of selection are designed to shock the participants and wear them down. The soldiers must pass many physical tests. If a soldier fails to make the minimum cut-off time on a run, he might be allowed one re-test. If he fails this, he's generally removed from the course. The first week is also when the most trainees drop out. It is not uncommon for 75 per cent of the course to be gone by day eight. On some courses the drop-out rate is even higher.

During the second week, the soldiers are assessed on their individual navigational skills and their ability to work independently – operating alone. With no one to provide motivation, only the most highly disciplined and self-motivated soldiers are capable of passing this phase of the course.

There is also a roping component that is designed to

test those who suffer from a fear of heights. You don't need to enjoy yourself in order to move onto the final phase of the course, but you must complete all the activities to prove you are capable of operating outside of your comfort zone.

The last four or five days are the most exacting. Those who remain are divided into teams and sent from one gruelling activity to another. The men are subjected to enormous physical activity and at the same time are deprived of food and sleep. When soldiers are running on empty, who of them remains team-focused and who looks out just for themselves? Men who sneak into the bush to sleep, who volunteer themselves for the less arduous tasks or who fail to contribute to the team are soon identified as non-team-players and usually fail the course. The SAS requires high-performing personnel who can remain team-oriented regardless of what is going on around them.

It's impossible to determine how many soldiers will be left at the end. On some courses, up to 20 per cent of the applicants might complete the course, while on others there will be fewer than five per cent. I know of one course where just one officer and four soldiers remained. On average, only five per cent of soldiers who apply and 10 per cent of soldiers who attend the course make it into the SAS.

The directing staff (DS) who assess the trainees are predominantly senior SAS soldiers who hold the rank of sergeant or above. The DS carry notebooks and continuously scribble down whatever they observe, whether it's positive or negative. At the end of each day the DS get together and discuss the performance of the trainees.

The trainees are assessed on their physical fitness and

endurance, integrity, self-discipline, motivation, ability to work with others, acceptance of responsibility, leadership potential, stress management and work ethic. All comments by the DS are recorded in a trainee's personal file.

At the end of the course, the DS will meet and discuss the attributes of each trainee. The documentary evidence that was collected throughout the course will be closely scrutinised and a decision will be made about whether a trainee shows potential – that is, whether they are suitable for further training and assessment. It's not uncommon for the DS to disagree about soldiers' potential; when this occurs, it's the senior instructor (SI) who makes the final decision.

≡

Rog and I headed to Amberley Airfield on 21 March 1995. It was a sultry, cloudy afternoon. The following morning, with no expectations and oversized lunch boxes, we boarded a C130 transport aircraft. First stop Sydney, second stop Melbourne, third stop Adelaide, fourth stop RAAF Base Pearce, Western Australia.

Even the C130 was foreign to me – I had never flown in one before. At RAAF Base Richmond, in Sydney, dozens of soldiers from the 3rd and 5/7 Battalions boarded the aircraft. There were a few tense faces, but as a group they appeared far more relaxed than I

Packed and ready for SAS selection.

felt. These guys were all regular soldiers. I looked them up and down, searching for strengths and any obvious signs of weakness. I wondered who would be there at the end. How fit were these guys? How many years had they been in the army?

Rog and I were both 21 years old. Most of these men appeared to be several years our senior. I noticed that there were officers, corporals, lance corporals and privates in the group — in fact, there were more soldiers with rank than without.

I remember three soldiers in particular from that flight. One had an adolescent face. He appeared to be only 18 or 19, was of slender build and probably weighed no more than 70 kilograms. I was surprised when I found out Craig was 21. He was there at the end.

Another guy, Mick, had dark skin and looked exceptionally fit. He had strong, large-veined arms and a thick neck. He wore dark sunglasses and had a peculiar grin. He too was there at the end.

I also noticed an olive-skinned man who seemed about 25 years of age. He looked fit and wiry. Brian was a full corporal and would go on to pass the course too.

I had to force myself to eat during the flight. I tried to sleep, both by dropping my head onto my knees and by pushing it back against the netting, but I couldn't. My body was anticipating something violent when the plane finally touched down. Sleep was never going to happen.

We landed at RAAF Base Pearce some 13 hours after departing Amberley. It was early in the evening and the sun was still up. I wondered what we'd be asked to do first. My imagination and pulse were running wild. Trying to second-guess what was coming created additional angst. I knew if I was to be there at the end I would have to settle down and back myself. There would probably be confusion and mayhem, perhaps a lot of yelling, but I decided I would react to whatever instructions were thrown my way and to nothing else. I wasn't going to be crippled by the nervous energy that had silenced the plane.

The rear ramp was lowered and hot air rushed into the aircraft. I felt nervous but in control. I saw a couple of SAS soldiers dressed in military fatigues standing on the tarmac behind the aircraft, their eyes focused on the C130. I knew they were SAS soldiers because they wore the trademark sandy beret. I had never seen an SAS soldier in the flesh before.

A confident man with a deep voice walked onto the aircraft. He was around six feet tall, of medium build and aged in his forties. Although I have a clear image of this man in my mind, including his expressionless face and confronting stare, I can't recall the precise words he spoke.

I'm very much a visual person. I'm often able to recall detailed information, mainly numbers and images, from my past. It's not always a good thing – my mind is cluttered with lots of useless information. Abstract things seem to be etched most deeply, such as the names of three Russian gymnasts from the 1988 Seoul Olympics – Dmitry Bilozerchev, Valeri Liukin and Vladimir Artemov. I saw their names on the bottom of the television screen in white bold writing, thought they were a little weird and have never forgotten them. Although this level of recall has been a useful skill, there are also ghastly images rolling around in my head that remain too clear. I wish this wasn't the case but I'm resigned to the fact that these memories will never fade, not even a little.

Upon exiting the aircraft at RAAF Base Pearce, we retrieved our equipment, were marched off the runway to a sparsely vegetated area and told to line up. We were facing the setting sun. As we stood at ease – our feet shoulder-width apart and our hands crossed behind our backs – the wing sergeant major (WSM) introduced himself and mentioned the names and positions of a couple of other people. We were told to remember these names.

He then had a question for us: 'Can anybody tell me the role of the SAS?'

There was no way I was going to open my mouth. But there were a number of soldiers who were keen to be recognised.

'Reconnaissance,' said one man.

'Yes, strategic reconnaissance. What else?' said the WSM.

'Counter-terrorism,' said another.

'What else?'

'Gather intelligence.'

And then came an answer that took us all by surprise.

'Kill people.'

'What was that?' said the WSM.

'Kill people,' said the man, even louder than before.

Even if someone truly believed such a thing, who in their right mind would say something so ridiculous? I thought to myself.

The WSM didn't miss a beat. 'Kill people, you think? Well, the last person I killed was someone who tried out for selection and didn't drink enough water.'

The WSM called out our names, and in groups of 12 we were ordered to grab our kits and jump on the trucks.

Once we were in, the rear canopy was tied down, leaving us sweating in the dark. The drivers drove fast, revving their vehicles hard. I looked at the other shadowy figures seated around me. Some heads were down, others flicked nervously to and fro, but no one said a word.

The truck stopped, the rear canopy was unlaced and we were told to get out. I saw a dozen soldiers swimming in a murky 25-metre pool, and dozens more lined up, waiting for their turn. We were told to remove our boots and everything from our pockets. My right ankle was heavily strapped with my foot locked at right-angles to my lower leg. I had wrongly presumed we would be doing a hell-march when we arrived in WA. I removed the strapping tape, revealing a tender, swollen joint.

We were required to swim 300 metres while dressed in military fatigues. The first 100 metres had to be freestyle, and after that any stroke was permissible. I recognised a regular army corporal from another Enoggera-based infantry battalion. He had a powerful build, was aged in his late twenties, and was the first in his squad to complete the swim.

This guy and I had crossed paths at least half a dozen times while training in Brisbane. On two occasions, while we were both weighed down with heavy packs, we walked past each other from opposite directions. It's obvious when someone is training for selection. I said: 'Good morning, Corporal,' but received no reply. I described the man to my platoon sergeant and he immediately knew who I was enquiring about.

'That's Jay,' he said. 'He's a real tough bastard, a jet' — army slang for a high-performing soldier. 'He'll piss it in.'

The next time I saw Jay he was shuffling down the mountain while I was stomping up. When we were no more than a metre apart, I looked him in the eye and said, 'G'day, Corporal.'

This time he sneered and shook his head, as if disgusted that a soldier with less than 12 months' experience in the army had the gall to attempt selection, or even to speak to him. *Arrogant prick*, I thought. I have never rated people who look down on others. It doesn't matter what you own, how many degrees you have, where you live, what you do for a job or what position you hold – if you're a wanker, your cock is all you've got, and all you're ever going to be.

Jay stood at the end of the pool, removed his shirt and waited for the second phase of the test: a 25-metre swim underwater while wearing camouflage pants. Once again Jay was first, breaking the surface looking composed and confident. At least half the guys in his squad failed this test.

Then it was my turn. I was then a pretty average swimmer, capable of swimming a kilometre in approximately 19 or 20 minutes. Swimming freestyle while dressed in military fatigues is especially tough, as you cannot glide. I was no Grant Hackett but had no trouble completing the first swim. I exited the pool behind two others and waited for the remainder of our squad to finish. Our next test was the 25-metre underwater swim.

I was surprised by how many guys were failing this test. I dived into the water knowing that if I was to fail, they would be pulling me from the water unconscious. I would not break the surface before I touched the opposite wall, no matter how much it hurt. I'd drink the pool dry and crawl along the bottom if I had to. I was excited and swam quickly, burning up lots of oxygen. The cam pants were a hindrance, and so too was the filthy water, which made it impossible to gauge the end. More than half of our squad failed the test, possibly because their nervous energy robbed them of oxygen. I was pleased to have passed.

We changed into dry fatigues and once again boarded the trucks. The stuffy darkness was less intimidating than before. Forty-five minutes later we arrived at Bindoon training area. I had no idea where we were. We were placed in squads and introduced to our directing staff (DS). I was in Eight Squad. Our DS, a fair man who had no intention of being a prick just for the sake of it, told us to ensure we thoroughly cleaned our eating utensils after each meal.

'Most of you guys have worked hard to get here. Don't let yourselves down with poor hygiene. If you get sick, even for a day, then you won't be able to cope with what's expected. If I find food or filth on anyone's KFS' – he meant our knife, fork and spoon – 'then you'll owe me 50 push-ups. Got it?'

'Yes, sir,' we replied.

We then assembled in the mess tent and were addressed by the senior instructor (SI), a captain who was in charge of the course.

'Men, welcome to the 1/95 SASR selection course. You are all going to be challenged, so I would like to offer you some words of encouragement.'

I leaned forward, keen to embrace any advice on offer.

'But none comes to mind,' the SI said, turning his back and walking away.

Talk about an anticlimax. It was a remarkable comment that took me completely by surprise.

We were sent to bed at 2300 hours. Our accommodation comprised lines of hootchies – two ground sheets joined together, draped over a piece of rope and staked at the corners. We slept on stretcher beds. There were two men to a hootchie and 12 to 16 men in each squad.

At midnight we were woken for a fire drill. We were also informed that day one had just begun. Yesterday, which in reality was just a couple of minutes ago, was just an admin day.

On Thursday 23 March 1995, I scribbled in my diary: 'Worst night sleep ever.' Quite a surprising comment, considering I wasn't cold or in threat of losing my life. Fear of the unknown well surpasses reality. I checked my watch and it was 0400 hours. I decided to get up early and have a shave. *This could save me some time later*, I thought.

=

When I reflect on other experiences I've had – especially midnight road moves I trialled in Anbar province, Iraq, when I was running the security component of a reconstruction project – I can see I learnt to deal with stressful situations quite differently.

After being heavily scrutinised by the suits in London about my decision to hit the roads at night without any night-fighting capability (weapon lasers and night-vision goggles), I knew I would come under fire from above if we were hit and lives or assets were lost. But I knew that the US marines with whom we were collocated were being mauled three times a day on the roads around Haditha

Dam. I was aware that command and control, as well as trying to vector in support assets, would be far more difficult during the hours of darkness, but in order to dodge the insurgent bombs, it was a risk I was willing to take.

Lying on a warm asphalt surface at Alasad Airbase while waiting for the most suitable departure time – 0100 hours – I had no trouble dropping off to sleep. Sure, I was anxious, but over the years I had learnt to control my thoughts in order to be able to sleep when required. I knew that the return trip to Jordan, taking 10 or 11 hours, would be mentally demanding, so a couple of hours sleep were vital if I was to remain focused. We never did get hit at night.

≡

At 0545, my clean-shaven face was tucked deep in my sleeping bag when a song from the movie *Pulp Fiction* – 'Stuck In the Middle With You' – screamed out of a large set of speakers that were positioned on the fringe of our hootchies. This incited mayhem; some guys ran off to the bathrooms to shave, others frantically threw on their military fatigues, others yelled questions – 'What's the dress? What do we wear?' – while a few men just stood up and waited.

The words 'PT kit ... dress is PT kit' were passed down the lines. PT kit comprised joggers, black shorts and a white T-shirt with your surname written on the front and back. We were split into two groups and told that we would be doing a BFA – a basic fitness assessment. The BFA was the standard fitness test for the Australian military. Group one would complete the five-kilometre run (at own pace), while group two – my group – would perform a push-up/sit-up test.

For this test, each soldier was required to do 60 push-ups to a cadence – no more, no less. I felt pretty confident. I knew I was capable of pumping out double that number in a two-minute period if required. Up to a dozen soldiers were told to stop because of poor technique. During the sit-up test, the corporal physical training instructor (PTI) berated a man who struggled to do 20 sit-ups. The required standard was 100.

'Jellyneck, did you do any preparation at all for this course?'

'Yes, sir.'

'Bullshit! What are you doing here? You can't even do 20 sit-ups. Did you follow the three-month training program?'

'Umm, yes, sir. Parts of it.'

'Parts of it! If you didn't follow the program, and it is obvious you didn't, then you have no chance of passing this course. And you've probably taken the position of someone who really wanted to be here. Do you think you should continue?'

'Yes, sir.'

'If I were you I would seriously consider my volunteer status. You're a disgrace.'

The PTI was not an abusive man, just passionate. I would later get to know him very well. Kane (my training partner in the Regiment) and I had many hardcore training sessions with this guy. He was a freak with a ridiculous set of arms. And they weren't bloated, unpractical, body-builder arms that clag out after one set of chin-ups. These guns could pump out five sets of 20 as a warm-up. Weighing in at 90 kilograms, he was a tremendous athlete. A testament to this was his ability to win the first *Gladiator* television series. At work he ran a mean circuit, but our troop generally ran our own training.

After completing the sit-up test, we moved to the start line for the five-kilometre run. Guys from the first group had been streaming in for five minutes, then, to my surprise, Jay the corporal — the guy I'd seen in training — crossed the line in a time of over 22 minutes. Hunched over and sucking in the big ones, he no longer looked confident and composed. I'm not sure if his time was good enough to pass, but that was the last I saw of him. The next day, I noticed his bed space was empty. The jet, the tough bastard, the man who would piss it in, was out of there.

I completed the run in a time of 18 minutes and eight seconds. There were a few gazelles who kicked my arse, but I was content with my time.

After breakfast we were lined up in squads on a gravel parade ground. We were ordered to lay out our ground sheets and remove everything from our packs, webbing and echelon bags. We were also required to remove all our clothing except our underwear and hats. The air was hot and dry. I felt anxious; sweat trickled down my ribs and the soles of my feet stuck to my groundsheet. A member of the directing staff read out a list of items, one at a time, that we were instructed to hold in the air. Anyone who was missing an item had their name recorded for failing to assimilate simple instructions. They were punished later.

The DS then inspected our packs, webbing and the pockets of all our clothing to ensure we didn't have anything that wasn't on the list. If soldiers declared the items then there would be no problem. If guys were hiding things – such as food or specialist equipment – and it was found, then they would be removed from the course due to a lack of integrity. I had spent considerable time waterproofing all my equipment. The DS removed each item from its snap-lock bag with care and precision. They methodically inspected the seams of my clothing, looked for hidden compartments in my pack and thumbed their way over every inch of my belt. They displayed no emotion.

In the afternoon, two physical training instructors smashed us with a weights circuit. I enjoyed it – I was being paid to do what I loved: hard training. Our efforts were heavily scrutinised by up to 10 directing staff. We were expected to hold nothing back. For me, the most painful exercise was the tyre shoulder press. By the end of the session, most guys struggled to raise their hands above their heads, me included.

The following morning we were told to dress in military fatigues, grab our rifles and weigh our webbing – it had to weigh a minimum of eight kilograms. There was a lot of yelling and guys were running everywhere. In squads, we were marched down a track and informed that we were doing a webbing run test. The required dress was boots, cams, webbing and rifle. To pass the test, we had to complete the 3.2-kilometre course in less than 16 minutes. We were not permitted to wear a watch.

Whatever your fitness level, a webbing run is one of the most painful and difficult physical tests in the military.

The added weight sees your legs heavy with lactic acid after the first 200 metres, and your heart rate will soon be operating at its maximum beats per minute. Just like running up a steep sandhill, there is no cruise mode, even for guys who can complete the run in 12 or 13 minutes. It is a grind that burns your lungs, calves and thighs from start to finish. We weren't informed of our times, simply given a pass or fail. I finished sixth. The 20 soldiers who failed the run were given one more chance. Those who failed a second time were removed from the course.

This type of fitness – battle fitness – is critical for SAS soldiers. If SAS soldiers are in heavy contact against a numerically superior force, then they must be able to break contact while heavily laden with equipment. The stress upon their bodies – and minds – will be extreme. It's vastly different from throwing on a set of joggers and running fast. A strong will is required to embrace the pain and to continue pushing when your legs are begging to be able to walk. Those who choose to walk are those who fail.

I'd pushed hard on the run so I struggled through breakfast. I was a bit nauseated and forcing the food down only exacerbated the feeling. We then completed a navigation exercise before lunch. In the heat of the afternoon, we boarded trucks and departed. I was certain we'd be doing the airfield run, a punishing session with a huge reputation. But this wasn't the case.

We assembled in a hangar and were briefed. 'Okay, men, yesterday you completed the BFA – the basic fitness assessment. There is nothing special about that – everyone in the military has to do it. You'll now complete the special-forces BFA. I'm sure you'll find it a little more challenging.'

The first test was 60 push-ups. *Easy enough*, I thought. I was wrong. The cadence was agonisingly slow: just one push-up every four or five seconds. Guys who broke form were told to stand up. There were many. After 50 push-ups in three and a half minutes, my thighs began to spasm. This pissed me off. I made it to 60.

The second test was maximum chin-ups.

'When I say "adopt the position",' the PTI said, 'the front row of men will grab the bar – overgrasp or undergrasp – and hang at full extension. On the command "go" you will complete one set of maximum chin-ups. Are there any questions?'

Wisely, no one answered.

'Adopt the position.'

On this command, one man, whose thick arms were covered in tattoos, jumped on to the bar and began a frenzy of chin-ups. The directing staff repeatedly yelled at him to stop but he didn't seem to notice. He had completed 13 or 14 before he stopped. The others were made to hang at full extension while the eager man was counselled.

'You failed to assimilate simple instruction. None of those chin-ups will count.' This was followed by silence, then: 'Go!'

The man managed another 10. He was credited with six because of poor technique.

I was in the fifth line to begin and chose undergrasp. I completed 20 but was credited with just 16. I was not happy with this. After the course, I trained up and set myself a minimum standard of 25. A few years later, Kane, Mick and I were invited for a session with the Regimental

PTI. We managed 126 in five sets, with a five-minute break in between each set, but this was as good as it got. Clawing your way up the side of an oil rig in the middle of a Bass Strait winter can be dangerous. For an SAS diver, chin-ups are like insurance – you pay up front and collect during times of need.

The next challenge was 100 unsupported sit-ups, then we were taken outside and briefed on another test, a 2.6-kilometre run. We were wearing PT kit and carrying our rifles. We would only be informed whether we had passed or failed the run at the finish line. The course, a hot gravel track, ascended a series of ridges. I finished in the top eight with a time of nine minutes and 54 seconds. Three-quarters of the course failed to make the cut-off time of 10 minutes and 30 seconds. The heat was unbearable. I felt sick.

Surely that's it, I thought. But this was SAS selection, so of course there was more to come.

We were told to start running up the track to a parked truck. The first 20 guys were to jump in the back, and everyone else was to keep on running. We had no idea how far we'd be expected to run. I was the 23rd or 24th guy to the truck, and my heart rate was through the roof. I had missed the cut so I kept running. Those who made it to the truck were soon yelled at and told to get out and get going too.

We ascended false crest after false crest. I longed for the finish line. I tried to anticipate how far, realistically, we would be made to run. I was thinking 20 kilometres. There were a couple of drink stations but the white plastic cup of water at each one was barely enough to moisten my parched throat. I knew I was overheating, and my head began to ache.

The red, gravelly track continued on and up. My legs felt weary and my brain like a fried egg. We ran for 11 kilometres, all the way back to camp. When I arrived, guys were guzzling from 20-litre jerry cans. I had a turn but only managed two or three gulps before I thought I was going to vomit. My legs and hands were shaking; I was definitely suffering from heat exhaustion.

We showered and readied ourselves for dinner. There was no down time. Everything was rushed, every moment was hectic. At the completion of the third day we had lost almost half the course. At least 60 or 70 guys were gone. Some had suffered injuries and some were asked to leave, but most left because they'd had enough.

I couldn't eat that evening. I dry-retched after putting a single piece of chicken in my mouth. The lasagne fared no better. So I filled my stomach with fluid and hoped my headache would fade soon. I went to bed feeling like shit. But I had made it to the end of day three. *Just 17 or 18 days to go*, I thought.

Day four began with a 90-minute PT session. In groups of five we were given a large truck tyre to guide around the gravel tracks of Bindoon. Our team decided to have two guys pushing from behind, a guy to the left and right to steer, and one off to the side resting.

On a flat road it worked pretty well. Going uphill was hard work but the tyre was easy to control. Downhill was another story. Up to eight hands would be pressed down on the rubber as the tyre gained momentum, in a feeble attempt to slow it down. Most guys lost a fair portion of skin off their palms. Rogue tyres sometimes broke free, only slowing down when they collected the group in front.

There was no shortage of prying eyes watching our every move. The DS constantly pulled notebooks out of their trouser pockets and scribbled away. I tried to take no notice. I placed my efforts and attention solely on the task we were completing. *If I do this right*, I thought, *everything else should take care of itself.* Trying to second-guess what someone thinks of your efforts is a waste of energy. And the thought of kissing someone's arse, especially in the SAS, never entered my mind.

$=$

In the Regiment I socialised with guys I liked, regardless of their rank or position. Trooper, corporal, sergeant, warrant officer or 'Rupert' (an officer) – what did it matter?

I remember chatting to Todd (a good mate) and Buzz (our team commander) at a function at the Gratwick Club – the SAS watering hole at Campbell Barracks. A drunken sergeant approached us and said: 'When you guys are finished kissing your team commander's arse, I'd like to have a chat to him.'

His comment incensed me, almost to the point where I thought about landing one on the prick's chin. Todd was an angry bastard at the best of times, and I could see he was thinking something similar. We'd only been in the troop for 12 months, but as far as we were concerned, we were free to talk to whomever we liked. Buzz was a sergeant, but so what? He was also a mate.

Buzz saw our faces change. As a good leader does, he

took care of it. 'Hey, these boys are fucking solid and I'm chatting to them. The Gratto's their pub, not ours.'

Thankfully, there wasn't much of that sort of attitude in the Regiment. The only pecking order that most guys cared about was performance.

Am I anti-authoritarian? I don't think so. I just don't believe that rank or social standing gives you the right to speak down to others. Condescending language is the language of the inept – bigoted souls with something to prove.

≡

The guys of Eight Squad were team players. From the outset we all had a strong sense of camaraderie. Many squads had already folded because of withdrawals, resulting in the merging of two or more groups. Our squad, with only a couple of withdrawals, remained intact.

After breakfast on day four we were driven to Julimar. The trucks stopped and let us off, we threw on our packs and webbing, then the trucks drove on again. It was hot and the sun was burning into the shoulders of our camouflaged shirts.

'Follow me,' ordered the SI, taking off down the track.

The pace was hectic. After 15 minutes the lead group of a dozen soldiers was told to stop and join the back of the line. Twice I worked my way to the front, only to be sent to the back. I then decided to stay in the middle. The pace remained fast, and some soldiers struggled to keep up.

After 45 minutes I removed a water bottle from my webbing to take a drink, but my ankle rolled on the side of a large tree root. I had not re-strapped it after the pool swim, which was a decision I would come to rue.

Fuck, I thought. The pain was pretty intense. Someone helped me to my feet and I kept walking. For five minutes I felt nauseated and my ankle throbbed, lacking stability.

Ten minutes later I rolled it again. *That's that*, I thought. *Only made it to bloody day four.* I tried to stand up but my ankle couldn't bear my weight.

My DS – a fair man – approached me and asked what had happened. He could see the distress on my face. 'Look, mate,' he said. 'I reckon those trucks are only a couple of hundred metres up the road. Reckon you can make it?'

'Yes, sir,' I replied as I got to my feet.

Then the WSM arrived, and he was not so positive. 'Would you like to remove yourself from the course, trainee?'

'No, sir.'

'Then why were you sitting down?'

'I rolled my ankle, sir.'

He didn't believe me. 'I think you should re-evaluate your volunteer status.'

'No, sir, I will never remove myself from the course. I damaged my ankle prior to selection and got rid of my crutches three days before the course.' I had no reason to lie. All he had to do was check my medical documents.

The WSM called a medic over.

'He's done a decent job on this,' the medic said. 'It's already bruised.'

'If you strap it it'll be okay,' I said.

'Your ankle's gonna swell – strapping tape might inhibit your circulation,' said the medic.

'His ankle's already swollen. Strap it up and see how it goes,' said the WSM.

The medic used the best part of an entire roll to secure my ankle. It was now impossible for it to roll. I rejoined my squad, which was just a couple of hundred metres up the track.

That afternoon we were sent in pairs on a navigational exercise. My partner was a signaller named Cassidy, an intelligent and genuine guy. I was disappointed that he wasn't there at the end of the course. We returned to our squad base location, as ordered, after last light.

'How's your ankle?' enquired my DS.

'No problem,' I said.

'Of course there's no problem, but how is it?'

'Fine, sir.'

'Look after it tomorrow. That goes for all of you,' he added to the group. 'Air out your feet. You all know you've got your 20-clicker –' our 20-kilometre pack march – 'coming up. If you don't make the cut-off time then you've got Buckley's of passing the retest. You've really only got one shot.'

Our DS had a different approach from the others. He was keen to offer encouragement if he thought you deserved it. That evening our squad members got to know each other a little better. Our DS kept the conversation going with a few questions, but he left most of the talking to the guys.

The next morning, with a second list of checkpoints to navigate to, Cassidy and I headed off. We pushed hard through the morning, which meant we could take a bit of time in the middle of the day to dry out our sleeping equipment. Throughout the afternoon we managed our speed to ensure we reached the rendezvous on time. We had made it to the end of day five.

Although we'd been told that day one of the course only began the day after we arrived, it was really a ploy to unsettle us. After the long flight, the angst of expectation, the swim test and then being woken up at midnight after barely an hour's sleep, the guys were feeling shattered. To then be told that day one had only just began was like sprinting over the finish line of a marathon and then being told you still had two kilometres to go. But the SAS wants men who aren't discouraged by extended finish lines.

As you near the end of a deployment, most soldiers are excited to get home and see their families. At first you might be told: 'The deployment will be six months, and then you'll all be home for Christmas.' But with two weeks to go, things change. Instead of hiding next to the chimney to scare Santa on Christmas Eve, you are hanging out in Afghanistan or Iraq because your deployment has been extended by three months.

You then have a choice: you can be a sook, or you can put it behind you and crack on with business. In my experience, SAS (and army) wives are some of the toughest women around. My wife had more than a decade of extended finish lines. Sure, she was often disappointed, but not once did she give me any grief about it. If

Colleen abseiling.

something is out of your control, then worrying about it is pointless.

≡

Day six, Monday 27 March 1995, was a big day. We were woken earlier than normal. The usual nervous mayhem of not knowing what's going on buzzed through our hootchies like a swarm of bees on adrenaline.

'Dress is cams, webbing and packs,' someone yelled. 'Weigh your packs – we're doing the 20-clicker.'

I ran to the scales to weigh my gear. We were told that our packs must weigh a minimum of 20 kilograms and our webbing at least eight kilograms. But we weren't permitted to remove weight if we were over. My pack and webbing weighed 26.5 kilograms and 9.5 kilograms. With my rifle, I'd be running with 40 kilos.

We marched to the start line and assembled in squads, which were dispatched at 60-second intervals. One by one the groups departed. Some men walked, some ran, most shuffled. Eight Squad would be the second-last to leave, seven minutes behind the first group. The seven minutes would be deducted from our times at the end.

I had no intention of doing this test again. A couple of guys in our squad had talked about doing it together. *No way*, I thought. This was an individual test. With the exception of any hills and drinks breaks, my plan was to shuffle the entire way.

Finally, it was our turn to leave. My heart was already beating hard when we lined up. We were told to go, and go I did. I was determined to pass this test the first time. For the first couple of minutes my legs felt heavy, but I soon settled into a rhythm. I was the first from Eight Squad to reach the trailing members of Seven Squad.

'Hey, take it easy, mate – you'll burn out,' someone yelled.

I felt pretty good so didn't take any notice. I ran for 20 minutes, before slowing down to take a few sips of water. Trying to hold your breath and drink when your body is craving oxygen is always a struggle. I occasionally got it wrong, coughing and spluttering as water was sucked into my lungs. I continued running before I put my water bottle away.

After an hour I had passed at least half the starters. I knew Rog was in Two Squad and I was looking forward to saying g'day. Fifteen minutes later I recognised his stocky frame shuffling along the track some 200 metres down the hill. I increased my efforts, running almost as fast as I could, and pulled alongside him. He wasn't wearing a hat, and streams of sweat ran down his face and neck.

'Hey, mate, I've been trying to catch you for the last 75 minutes,' I said. 'How're you feeling?'

'Yeah, okay. What about you?' he said.

'Same. Feet are burning, though.'

'Tell me about it.'

'I'm gonna get going,' I said. 'Smash it, mate!'

'Grab me a beer when you get there,' said Rog with a smile on his face.

I picked up the pace and didn't stop running until I came to a steeper section of track. Halfway up, two guys shuffled past me. *What the fuck?* I thought I was going hard. Except for the SI, who wasn't carrying a pack, these were the only guys to pass me. I must admit, it did piss me off.

I saw several DS at a drinks station halfway up the hill to my front. There was also a man with a video camera. I filled up my water bottles and followed the track to the right. I knew there were at least four guys in front of me.

The track wound its way up the mountain. I stopped shuffling and walked fast. The sound of approaching footsteps behind me took me by surprise. *I don't believe it – not someone else overtaking me*, I thought. I glanced over my shoulder and started running when I saw it was the SI.

'Are you coming first, trainee Fennell?'

He knows my name – surely that can't be good. So much for being the grey man. 'No, sir. I'm the first member of Eight Squad, but I know of at least four others in front.'

'Why do you want to be an SAS soldier?'

'I love soldiering and I want to take it to the highest level, sir.'

'What will you do if you don't pass the course?'

'I'm not considering that option, sir.'

'That's a bold statement.'

'No, sir. If I fail the course then I will be discharged from full-time service.'

'Why's that?'

I then explained the ready reserve.

'Well, don't worry about that. The regular army can keep the fodder. We're after thinking soldiers,' he said, smiling.

The SI didn't say a lot, but his body language and comments appeared positive. I reached the top of the hill. 'Excuse me, sir,' I said, 'I'm going to double-time.'

'Don't let me hold you back,' he said.

I started running. Twenty metres later the SI ran past me

and soon disappeared. *Bastard,* I thought. My feet felt like they were on fire. I kept on running.

I looked at my watch and thought that the end would have to be close. I reached another water station and, this time, the DS recorded my name. *This was strange,* I thought.

A kilometre later, a DS approached me and asked, 'Trainee, how far do you think you have to go?'

'I'm not sure – it could be another five kilometres,' I said.

'Five kilometres?' he said, surprised. 'How's your time and space?'

'I believe the last water station was approximately 20 kilometres, sir. By my estimates, I should have already finished.'

The DS smiled and nodded his head. 'Fair enough.'

Around the corner was the finish line, and I was eighth to cross. We had to provide our trainee and squad numbers.

'Trainee 67, Eight Squad,' I said.

The sergeant PTI, a short, balding man with an athletic build and dark hairy legs, looked up from his time sheet and said, 'Eight Squad? Well done. That's an excellent time. Go and dump your pack over there and get yourself a drink.'

I removed my boots and socks to inspect my feet. Apart from a large blood blister underneath my right big toe, my feet were fine. My ankle, still heavily strapped, felt like it was being strangled. I made a slight cut in the strapping, which did relieve the pressure.

A medic came to inspect my feet. 'I can drain that blood blister for you and pump it full of antiseptic to help dry it out, if you like?'

'Yes please,' I said.

He drained the blister, filled a five-millilitre syringe with a yellowish fluid and smiled. 'I forgot to tell you – this shit really stings.'

I did my best to show no emotion, but my big toe was totally freaking out. My diary entry that night said it all: 'Ouch, ouch, ouch, instant fucking burn.'

I threw on a fresh set of socks, stretched my legs and tried to eat a cold bacon and egg sandwich. I was stoked to have passed the test.

That afternoon, we were tested on our basic signalling, medical and weapon skills. Test one: set up an ANPR 77 radio and use correct ratel (radio telecommunications) procedures. Test two: treat an array of medical conditions, from heat illness and leg fractures to snake bites. Test three: basic weapon handling.

Three hours later, the corporal PTI with the massive guns smashed the hell out of us with metal pipes. He didn't bash us with them – it was a weights session – but I probably would have preferred it to the 90-minute flogging our shoulders and arms received.

At midnight we received a lesson on Morse code. *Alpha – dit-dah; Bravo – dah-dit-dit-dit; Charlie – dah-dit-dah-dit . . .*

I woke early the next morning. My first thought was: *Made it to day seven.* It was now Tuesday 28 March. My legs, hips, lower back and shoulders were as stiff as they'd ever been. I no longer tried to anticipate how many days there were to go. Thinking too far ahead was dangerous. When things became more challenging, I even broke my day up into two-hourly blocks. *Made it to 1000 hours; midday; 1400 hours . . .*

The day began with another physical test – a 15-kilometre hell run. Once again, our dress was cams, webbing (eight kilograms), boots and rifle. It was less than 24 hours since we'd completed the 20-kilometre pack run, and most guys were heavily fatigued.

After two kilometres my legs loosened up and I maintained a steady cadence. At approximately 10 kilometres, while running up a sharp gradient, I noticed a sniper from the 3rd Battalion ahead. Battalion snipers are some of the most highly respected soldiers. I increased my pace and caught him up. We were at a similar physical standard; we'd consistently finished near each other on the previous physical tests.

'Hey, mate, how're your legs?' he asked.

'Pretty fatigued,' I replied.

'Let's smash it to the top of this hill,' he said.

'Yeah, let's do it.'

Halfway up, he said: 'Keep going, mate; I'm gonna walk for a bit.'

I felt okay so I continued on. I finished in fourth place in a time of 97 minutes and six seconds. My legs were shattered. We'd been allowed 100 minutes to complete the run, and more than half the course had failed.

As soon as I had finished, I felt my legs begin to tighten. I pulled out a water bottle, took small sips and stretched. I saw Rog come in. His legs were also starting to cramp, so we helped each other stretch, offering words of encouragement. I stood up, spun around and noticed the SI standing directly behind me. Wearing a dark set of sunglasses and a blank face, he'd been listening to our conversation. It was slightly unnerving – this time he gave away nothing.

We were then ordered to line up and were told we would be running the 15 kilometres back to Bindoon training camp. *Holy shit*, I thought. My legs were hammered.

A couple of guys remained seated. They'd had enough and voluntarily removed themselves from the course. The rest of us began the march. Five hundred metres down the road there were several trucks. We were told to get on and were driven back to camp.

=

The first week of the course was designed to wear us down, to remove our protective shells and expose the quality of the flesh beneath, to weed out the majority of those who were unsuitable. After just those seven days, there were 80 or 90 empty stretchers at base camp. Seeing this enhanced my self-belief. The intense physical testing ensures that applicants are at the minimum physical standard required, but it also deliberately wears them out, so that their performance in the more challenging phases of the course will reveal their true persona – what lies beneath the surface.

After breakfast, it was time for more mind games. The SI assembled the course and told everyone that he had lost his compass and that we had to help him find it. We were also told to bring our packs and webbing. The SI's pack did not cut into his shoulders the same way that ours did. Nor was he hunched over, which suggested to me that his pack was filled with perhaps just a bulky sleeping bag and a pillow. Holding a map upside down, he began walking down the road. He was a tall man with long legs – this guy could stomp hard.

The pace was frantic, and within 20 minutes soldiers were strung out over hundreds of metres. The SI told our lead group of eight or nine soldiers to keep going, and to stop in the shade some 200 metres up the track. For the first time on the course, he also offered some words of encouragement. 'Well done, men. I'll be back in a few minutes.'

As soon as the SI left us, one soldier — a guy who was struggling to keep pace — vented: 'Fucking slow it down, guys...' His whining antics continued all the way to the shade.

The SI returned a few minutes later and it was on again. I was up the front and on his left side. I struggled to match his stride and so had to continuously break into a shuffle to keep pace. It was a hot day and the dry air stripped our mouths and throats of moisture. Fifteen minutes later the SI once again stopped our lead group. To say I was relieved was an understatement.

He stormed off and when he came back, his voice was terse. 'As you can see,' he said, 'I have split the course into three groups: those who are serious, those who are undecided, and those who are wasting our time. Group one, you will march with me. We've cut away the crap, now keep up.'

Never have I tried to walk so fast. We had been marching for about six kilometres when the SI glanced at the guys to his left and right and arrogantly increased the pace. This continued for another two kilometres.

I was locked in a mental battle with the SI, although he didn't know it. *I bet you've got a pillow in your pack, you fucker. I'd like to see how you'd go with a bit of weight in there.* I was determined to break him, just once, but that was never going to happen. Whenever I angled in front a little he stepped it out. *Bastard!*

I then began to fight my own mind. One part of me was pissed off that I'd gone to the front, because now the SI would notice if I fell back. But each time I thought about dropping back, my pride gave me a kick up the arse. Physically, however, I was on the limit. I knew I could only continue that pace for another minute or two.

Fortunately, the SI slowed down. 'Well done, men. Have a seat in the shade.'

Upon reflection, it was probably silly to flog myself like that. There were still two weeks to go. But thoughts of self-preservation never entered my mind. In hindsight, I've often wondered whether I should have approached that first week differently – whether I ought to have saved myself a little. But my answer remains an emphatic no. I was determined to give an honest account of myself.

I was naive for thinking that, just because the SI had said 'well done', the march was over. A tough-looking man, an SAS sergeant with a solid build and gruff voice, told our group to line up on the track. 'Can you guys run?' he asked.

So the nightmare continued. *A damn tag team*, I thought. The sergeant left the track, so we fell into single file behind him and ran through the bush. I was second or third in line. I was initially apprehensive that I would roll my ankle, but as my thighs became charged with lactic acid, my worries disappeared as quickly as the fluid from my body. It was stifling, and the speed ridiculous. Once again, my legs screamed at my mind to slow down. My mind's reply: *Suck it up, you freaking pussies.*

We ran for 800 metres. The sergeant was also surprisingly positive. 'Well done,' he said. 'Drop your packs and take a seat. The trucks will be here soon.'

My legs were dead. With shaking hands, I removed a bottle from my webbing, unscrewed the cap and sucked it dry. My hands soon settled down. *What's next?*

4

WEEK TWO: OPERATING ALONE

At midday on day seven we began a solo 36-hour navigational exercise. On the way to my fifth checkpoint, after about six hours of hard going, I was soaked in perspiration and was walking like my testicles were the size of soccer balls. I dropped my trousers and saw that my groin and inner thighs were weeping, chafed raw. We weren't permitted to wear bike pants or skins underneath our fatigues, as all applicants had to be assessed under identical conditions.

I didn't have time to stop so, without taking off my pack and webbing, I pulled a clasp knife out of my pocket and sliced my soggy underwear down the sides. Watery blood trickled down my inner thighs. 'Man, you'd never get sex looking like that,' I said aloud. I threw my underwear into a magazine pouch, pulled up my pants, fastened my belt and kept walking. That night I smothered my groin in army foot powder. It did relieve the stinging sensation.

The following morning I dug a hole, buried my underwear and continued on. In the early hours of the afternoon

I reached the final rendezvous, my ninth checkpoint. There were eight or nine guys who arrived before me. The first couple were experienced soldiers, members of the 1st Battalion.

A couple of hours later the WSM briefed the remaining course applicants. 'We're sending you all out again because you failed to complete enough checkpoints by night. You'll all be given the grid coordinates at your drop-off locations.'

In groups of up to a dozen soldiers, we were squashed into the back of a 'sixby' – a six-wheel Land Rover – and driven to our individual start locations. Each time the vehicle stopped, a soldier was told to get off and given an eight-figure grid reference. My trainee number was the third to be called out.

The man responsible for providing the grid coordinates was my original DS. 'Prepare to copy your grid.'

I grabbed a notebook out of my pocket and told him I was ready. He then read out the coordinates.

'What's your bearing?'

I told him.

He nodded his head. 'Good. Look, mate, you're doing really well. Keep it up.'

I calculated that I would be traversing some thick and undulating terrain, and that the distance to my first checkpoint was 5.3 kilometres. Navigation by night or by day uses exactly the same principles, but it's easy to wander off your bearing during the transition from light to dark. The tree you line up in your compass can quickly disappear in the shadows.

After 45 minutes I had travelled 2.8 kilometres. I sat down, had something to eat and – following the advice I had received – waited for darkness to devour the landscape. Twenty minutes later I resumed my final 2.5 kilometres. I hit the ground several times, tripping over logs and rocks; once I slid down a gully. I had a small torch on a lanyard around my neck, but it stopped working after the gully incident so I used the light on my watch to illuminate my map and pace counter. My destination was a creek junction. According to my map, the vegetation was going to be dense. It was.

With 50 metres to go, I peered deep into the darkness, searching for a glow stick or any sign of light. I knew one of the DS would be at the checkpoint. I saw nothing – just shadows with contrasting degrees of blackness. Eighty metres later I had still not found my checkpoint. The ground rose sharply to my right, so after consulting my map I turned left and pushed deeper towards the creek. *It's gotta be close*, I thought. *Trust your compass and paces.*

I lost my balance and fell again. As I got to my knees, I noticed a flicker of light. But when I stood up it was gone. I leant forward and there it was – a faint glow further up the creek. As I closed in, the glow became brighter – it was a checkpoint.

When I got there I half-expected to be told I was at the wrong one. I was given another eight-figure grid reference, before being told to move 100 metres into the bush and lie up for the night. I was permitted to leave at first light.

The following morning I headed off for my eleventh and final checkpoint. When I reached the target – the junction of two tracks – I called in my coordinates and was informed to wait in place. A vehicle would be dispatched to pick me up.

Over the radio I heard that half a dozen trainees had become 'geographically embarrassed' – a fancy term for being lost. One was told to move in a northerly direction until he reached the main road. During the night, this guy had lost his map. He was a Battalion sniper; he completed the course but was not accepted.

While waiting for the truck to arrive, I checked my notebook and calculated how far I had travelled during the two navigational exercises. The total was 43 kilometres.

=

Later that afternoon – day nine – we had our last 90-minute session with the PTIs. It was one to remember. We were divided into teams and given another truck tyre to push around. *Great*, I thought. *More skin shredded from my palms. Oh well, I don't have the energy to masturbate, so what does it matter?*

The second phase of the session comprised a circuit of chin-ups, push-ups and sit-ups. The finale was 10 minutes of gruelling abdominals. We pushed through the burn, hit that numb feeling and kept on going. Then the muscles ceased contracting. When this happened, we were ordered to rest with another set of chin-ups.

Friday 31 March was a roping day and, according to my diary, was a 'great day'. After the previous nine days, our bodies welcomed the lower intensity. But for some soldiers, climbing a 10-storey tower and completing a 60-metre traverse – sliding along a rope suspended between two towers – was utter anguish. If this freaked them out, then I'm sure the next exercises – a forward rappel, then a 10-storey building climb and emergency stop – were enough to push them over the edge.

You don't have to be a base-jumping adrenaline addict to be an SAS soldier. But you must be able to overcome your fears in order to get the job done. The applicants who didn't complete these activities were removed from the course.

That evening, the 50 of us who remained were jammed into the back of a couple of seven-tonne trucks and driven to Lancelin, a coastal military training area 127 kilometres north of Perth.

≡

Besides being a team player, SAS soldiers are selected on their ability to work independently – to operate alone. Accordingly, the next phase of the course was a four-day individual navigation exercise. Each soldier was required to complete as many checkpoints and travel as many kilometres as he could.

We weren't told when the activity would finish or how many kilometres we were expected to cover – it was a test of personal discipline and self-belief. How hard will guys push themselves when there is no one around to make them? We were given guidelines, one of which was that there was to be no walking on tracks. If a soldier was caught moving along a track, he'd immediately be removed from the course for a lack of moral integrity. The WSM was so clear about this that I was almost too shit-scared even to cross over a track, let alone parallel one.

In one sense, I was relieved to have made it this far and looked forward to spending four days alone. I planned to rest for 10 minutes each hour and break for 30 minutes during the hottest part of the day. I would walk until it got dark and then push on for another 30 to 45 minutes. How hard I pushed was up to me – I was responsible for shaping my own destiny.

It was a bit like rocking up to your office job and finding a note on your desk informing you that everyone else – including your boss – has been granted leave for the immediate future. You, however, are to begin working your way through 20 large boxes of paperwork, each box the equivalent of a week's normal work. You're not permitted to go home and you should sleep on the floor. It's summer, the air-conditioning has been turned off and your office is infested with thousands of flies. There's enough food to last you five days – nothing too exciting, of course. You'll be hungry, but you won't die from a lack of sustenance. When you choose to eat and sleep is up to you. And finally, there are to be no Google searches, no email and no phone calls – just you, your 20 boxes of paperwork and a few thousands flies. Oh, and there are a couple of snakes somewhere in the office – but don't be concerned. Although dugites are poisonous, they're not aggressive and should keep to themselves.

After four days alone, with no end in sight, how hard would you continue to push? On the SAS selection course, three boxes of paperwork would be deemed a solid effort, two and a half a fair effort, two boxes adequate and one box – the equivalent to a week's work in four days – a fail. Pack your bags, you're going back to the Battalion.

For safety, each man carried a radio and was required to send a daily message to confirm his location. Apart from the DS at the checkpoints, we were alone. In four days I saw only one other trainee; he was traversing a ridge over a kilometre away.

My first leg was 10.8 kilometres. When I was about halfway there, I stumbled into a small clearing and found two large green garbage bins. I lifted one of the lids and found it was brimming with marijuana. I called it in.

'Say again, trainee 67?'

'This is trainee 67. I have just found two bins filled with marijuana at grid reference –'

'Wait, wait out,' was the reply.

I then heard an older voice, a voice with greater authority. I confirmed my previous message and was ordered to remain where I was; they would send a vehicle to collect it. Ninety minutes later a six-wheel long-range patrol vehicle came into view. I showed them the pot, they put it in their vehicle and I continued on. I lost an hour and a half; it would probably have been quicker to sit down and smoke the lot.

On the way to checkpoint two, 16.8 kilometres away, I miscalculated how much water I would need to carry. Essentially, I was being a little softcock and tried to carry eight litres, rather than the 10 I should have. I then lost two litres when one of my bladders burst. As a consequence, I spent a very thirsty couple of hours crossing the sand dunes. The heat was extreme. While walking across the dunes, I thought: *If I screw up my navigation and can't locate the checkpoint, I could be in a bit of trouble here.* I was dizzy but still coherent. My tongue felt swollen, and the rear of my throat was as dry as the sand beneath my boots. I would never make this mistake again.

I've seen senior soldiers in the Regiment do this while

deployed on operations. When men are carrying up to 65 kilograms, the thought of leaving a water bottle or two empty can be tempting. Once it affected the operational security of our patrol. Anyone who has experienced extreme thirst – that painful sensation that dominates your every thought and makes you scared because you realise your body is starting to shut down – is reluctant to ever go there again. Fortunately, I had learnt my lesson early. The first thing I did when I reached the checkpoint was fill up my water bottles – all of them, all eight litres.

Negotiating the prickly saltbush and dealing with the flies tested my mental toughness. I wrote the following in my diary:

Had at least 200 flies on pack, body and face. Sun was intense; sweating, flies were attracted to fluid: nose, lips, corners of eyes and bleeding hands – disgusting bastards were relentless in their quest to feed. I reached the green terrain [most extreme vegetation] *and movement was once again slow. Backs of hands were bleeding, shins and thighs red-raw from tearing through saltbush. Nearly went mental from flies. Wanted to scream but instead decided to sit down and kill flies for 20 minutes. Kept going, pushing through saltbush was extremely painful. Mental state severely tested.*

≡

If there was one guy who was jetting our course, from what I observed and heard from others, it was a particular soldier from the 1st Battalion. He was aged in his late twenties and had blitzed the previous navigational exercises.

My good mate Evo later told me that while he was having a break on our first nav exercise, he saw the guy charging through the bush.

'It was almost intimidating,' Evo told me. 'This guy was a machine. When I saw how hard he was going, I realised I had better lift my game so I packed up my things and got going. Seeing him motivated me to go harder.'

This guy's peers spoke of him as though he were a legend; he probably already was in the Battalion, where he'd been deployed to Somalia. He seemed like a good bloke – intelligent, personable and tough.

On our second day alone in the bush in Lancelin, I stopped to have something to eat and checked my radio to hear what was going on. I heard a deep, familiar voice – it belonged to the jet from the 1st Battalion. He was asking to be removed from the course. I couldn't believe it and turned up the volume.

Unlike others who had withdrawn, this man was asked numerous times whether he had thought about his decision. He was also asked if he was aware of the consequences, to which he replied: 'Yes, sir.'

Generally, anyone who requests to be removed from the course is never permitted to try again. In saying this, however, I'm aware of a couple of exceptions. If a soldier is relatively young then he might be given a second chance due to his lack of maturity or mental toughness. At 20, one is definitely not a boy, but might still be a little underdone in regards to being a bona fide man. Everyone is different and, depending on what they've experienced in life, some young men are mature beyond their years.

In Western society, life today is a little easier compared

to what previous generations lived through. My great-grandfather soldiered through both World Wars. His son, a teenage infanteer, fought at Tobruk, El Alamein, Kokoda and Borneo. My father left school and started full-time employment at 14. I'd had no intention of following in his footsteps, but I was 15 when I left school. For most people, though, those days are long gone.

A soldier aged in his late twenties who voluntarily removes himself from the course, whether or not he has personal issues clouding his mind, will not be afforded another chance. His dream will remain unfulfilled.

Some people are incapable of working alone. They require support, feedback, positive encouragement and camaraderie. The SAS requires team-oriented people who can also go it alone.

A few soldiers thrive on working independently. Skip, a fit man who won both the cross-country and triathlon races in the Regiment, gave me his thoughts on the solo navigation exercise at Lancelin in 1995. 'Mate, it was the best part of the course,' he said. 'Four days on your own with no one giving you shit – it was great!'

Skip was posted to the sniper troop, a job that requires plenty of patience and an ability to operate in the smallest of teams – two men. Skip's a solid operator and, despite having been dealt a few extra challenges in life, he's one of the mentally strongest and most balanced soldiers I've known. He's a tremendous asset to the Regiment.

I also enjoyed being left alone, but I definitely wouldn't go so far as to say stomping around Lancelin while being mauled by flies was great.

Comfortable operating alone: Skip in Afghanistan.

On Tuesday 4 April, I arrived at my final checkpoint. I had completed approximately 68 kilometres. Some of the more experienced soldiers who really pushed themselves walked in excess of 80, while others completed less than 50.

I listened to a couple of guys from the 1st battalion explain how initially they'd tried to force their way through the dense three- to four-metre scrub. I was intrigued, because I'd spent the best part of four days burrowing through the shit. They'd done it once before using the ridgelines to skirt around the most inhospitable terrain. Other soldiers had used well-worn animal tracks. I was paranoid about using tracks and was conscious of my limitations, so I'd kept it simple and stuck to bearings and paces. Unlike some, I hadn't got lost – a couple of guys ended up outside the training area – but I had expended far more energy than I should have.

I could no longer feel the soles of my feet, and the tops of my shoulders were no better. I dug my nails into the skin on one shoulder but felt nothing. This numbness would remain for the next 10 or 12 weeks. My shins, knees, thighs and the backs of my hands were covered in hundreds of tiny thorns. I spent weeks squeezing little pieces of Lancelin out of my inflamed, tender skin.

I had no idea what to expect during the final five or six days of the course. This might in fact have been a good thing, because my naivety kept me sheltered. I would soon be in the ugliest place I had ever seen.

5

WEEK THREE: LUCKY DIP

Wednesday 5 April – day 15 – was another roping day. We received fresh rations for both lunch and dinner, a welcome change from the ration packs that only ever filled half the void.

That evening we were placed in squads of nine or 10 soldiers. At 2200, we commenced 'lucky dip', the final phase of the selection course. The next four and a half days would be the most physically demanding of my life.

A cool change swept across the landscape, and with it came rain. The DS could not have hoped for a more perfect end to the course. At 2230 our squad was placed in an ambush. After two and a half hours lying on our stomachs – the prone position – we were told to maintain a 50 per cent watch. Working in pairs, we could take turns sleeping but were not permitted to use sleeping bags.

I couldn't sleep. I had lost a lot of weight and shivered incessantly. In my diary I wrote: 'Coldest night ever'. I have since had many nights that have proven far more uncomfortable but, at the time, this night was my benchmark.

At 0445 we left the ambush location and patrolled to a

designated rendezvous (RV). It was a relief to get moving. Our packs, webbing and rifles kept us company, but we were also provided with a few other bits and pieces to drag along. First there were two trunks filled with sandbags, four metal poles and two lengths of rope. We lashed the poles to the trunks and headed towards our second RV, six kilometres away. Eight of us carried the two boxes while one guy walked ahead and navigated. A couple of men rotated through the navigational responsibilities; the rest struggled with the boxes.

The second activity was a four-kilometre stretcher carry, followed by a five-kilometre pack march. Our patrol was tasked to carry two 'casualties' – human-shaped dummies – to safety. An 80-kilogram man would have been a decent challenge, but these larger-than-life creatures were made from sandbags. While trying to raise the first stretcher, two of the squad members lost their balance, and the stretcher wedged into the back of one man's neck. He was then assigned light duties and instructed to walk ahead and navigate.

We tried again, our lower backs straining under the excessive weight. After considerable stuffing around, we were on our way. But we had walked less than 20 metres when the first stretcher went down. The DS then made a call for our patrol to ditch one of the stretchers. That was great, but it still didn't lighten our load. After another below-average effort, the DS removed a couple of sandbags.

'You guys are a joke. Seeing as this patrol has no heart, we'll remove the heart and lungs from your casualty; we might as well keep you all the same.'

Next they removed two sandbags from the centre of the

casualty. A little later they removed half of both of his legs. If my back wasn't about to snap, I would probably have found this overestimation of our combined ability a little amusing.

Our evening meal was identical to both breakfast and lunch. *Where's their imagination?* I thought. We were given nothing. That evening we were tasked to make a shelter large enough to accommodate our entire patrol. We had to continue working until the DS decided it was suitable.

We set about making a lean-to. By midnight our enthusiasm had begun to wane. It was obvious that this task was designed to keep us awake. Most of us had also had very little sleep, if any, the previous night. The DS hid in the bush and observed our actions. Who would continue to work, and who would walk into the darkness and lie down when they think no one is watching? My eyes were heavy. I felt delirious as I dragged my groundsheet covered with leaves to the shelter. I scattered them on top then went back to collect some more.

At 0130 we were ordered to establish a piquet and go to sleep. We were to be up by 0500, so each man had a 25-minute piquet to enjoy. I remember being woken for my turn. I sat up, glanced at my watch and spent the next 20 minutes fighting sleep. Surprisingly, at 0240 I felt awake and began to think about food. I drank some water, which helped to quieten my noisy stomach.

At 0245 I woke the next guy, got back into my sleeping bag, pulled my head deep inside and drifted off. With each change of shift I woke, checked my watch and became frustrated that I was awake. I heard others snoring – I craved some of that.

It was now 7 April – day 17. I couldn't believe I'd made it this far. But we still had three or four very long days to go. Breakfast was delicious – more of nothing. I didn't care, as the lack of sleep and food had left me feeling nauseated.

We struggled off to our next activity. *What a surprise*, I thought, *more stores to carry*. This time we were given four logs, two tyres, a box holding an engine, and several pieces of rope. We made a trailer that didn't roll. Every few metres, the wheels would flop to the sides and the trailer would grind to a halt. We persisted with this design throughout the morning.

At one point we heard the crack of a rifle shot. We took cover and waited. The noise had come from another patrol; one of the soldiers had accidentally fired his weapon – an unlawful discharge (UD). The offender had his rifle slung on his back, but the safety catch had disengaged on another piece of equipment. Some time later, when handling his weapon, his finger found the trigger – *bang!* This soldier completed the course but was not accepted.

He came back the following year, and the year after that. Anyone who trains for and completes three SAS selection courses is committed. He made it into the Regiment and has proven to be an outstanding soldier. Everyone fucks up or comes up short every now and then. I didn't have long to wait before it would be my turn.

We eventually decided to disassemble the trailer and carry the stores. I noticed that the sun was high. *On a normal day, it would nearly be lunchtime*, I thought. I began to see black spots, and my vision blurred and then narrowed. I stumbled a couple of times but kept going.

'Have you been drinking enough water?' asked the supervising DS.

'Yes, sir,' I replied. No sooner had those words escaped my mouth than the black spots returned. I stumbled again.

The DS stopped the activity and made me sit down on a log. The others were ordered to continue.

'How much water have you consumed today?' he asked me.

'At least two litres, sir,' I replied. Then I dropped the water bottle I was holding – my hand was shaking uncontrollably. *What the hell is going on?* The DS told the others to wait and called one of the patrol members over. Thommo, who was performing well, was ordered to set up his radio and call in a medivac.

'I'm alright, sir,' I said and then my body seemed to shit itself – not literally, but my vision blurred and my extremities began to spasm. I was a mess.

An ambulance arrived and I was told to get in. I tried to argue but was told to shut up. I was taken back to camp and examined by a couple of medics. A hardarse DS, whom I had run beside on one of the pack marches, came over to see what was going on.

'What's up?'

'I'm fine, sir,' I said. 'Just got dizzy and fell over.'

The medics pricked my thumb and assessed my blood sugar level.

'It's three times below the minimum range,' said the medic. He looked a little like Keanu Reeves, just bigger and fitter.

'Yeah, he's hypoglycaemic,' said a sergeant medic. 'At this stage of the course, most of them would be. But he's pretty lean. Give him a shot of glycogen and get him back out there.'

'Righto,' said Keanu.

I would later be in the same troop as Keanu. At the time he was working as a medic on the selection course to gain experience.

'How ya' doing, mate?' he said to me. 'When your blood sugar levels get that low the body just shuts down. I'll give you a shot of glycogen and you'll be on your way. Happy?'

'Yes, Corporal,' I said. I was relieved to not be thrown off the course.

My body had gone into glycogen debt, similar to what a marathon runner experiences when they 'hit the wall'. The body stores approximately 2000 kilocalories of glycogen. Endurance athletes – marathon runners, triathletes, cyclists and cross-country skiers – can delay the phenomenon by 'carbo-loading' the day before. We had not been afforded such a luxury.

I'd begun the course weighing in at 79 or 80 kilograms. Due to my age and the way I trained, I had a high metabolism and a low percentage of body fat. At the end of selection, I weighed in at 66 kilograms – a drop of 13 kilograms in less than three weeks. I don't know how he managed it, but there was a guy who began the course at 65 kilograms and hobbled off at the end looking like he had been released from a prisoner-of-war camp. Men aged in their mid to late twenties, especially those who had a slightly higher percentage of body fat, fared far better during the latter stages of the course. They may have found the first week taxing, but after that they maintained superior levels of endurance.

I had never felt like a weak prick before and I hated it. After the course I was told to get in the gym and work on my endurance levels. I didn't have to be told twice, and by the time I completed the post-selection reinforcement cycle, I had achieved a better balance between strength and fitness. I never wanted to feel physically vulnerable again.

=

After being issued the glycogen injection, I was monitored for 60 minutes before being returned to my patrol. The men were seated in pairs, resting. Our next task was to pull and push a trailer filled with equipment up a dirt track, over a crest and beyond.

That evening our patrol was directed to move to a track/creek junction and RV with an agent. We would receive further directions upon arrival.

The agent, an SAS soldier, spoke with a ridiculous accent. It was hard to take him seriously, but when he said: 'Move to the hotbox and share the food amongst yourselves,' he could have been speaking Swahili and we would have understood. We removed the lid and shone a torch inside. Our first meal in two days was fish heads and rice soup. Those who could not bring themselves to eat it would not have the energy to complete the course. There wasn't a lot, but we divided what was on offer and devoured the lot.

The eighth of April, my birthday, was a day of dreams. The previous evening's meal had excited my stomach. I wanted more but had to be content to taste only my thoughts. I didn't think about sex, only food. *Chips and gravy, a slice of pizza . . . I'd even settle for a piece of bread smothered in margarine*, I thought.

Throughout the morning we had to carry a four-metre inflatable boat along a track. Those with previous roping experience, like the commandos, who had completed climbing and roping courses, were invaluable when it came to tying down the equipment. I knew a few basic knots – a round-turn-two-and-a-half-hitch and a reef knot – but as the saying goes, 'if you don't know knots, tie lots'.

I was placed in charge of our next activity. The Regimental Sergeant Major (RSM) delivered my instructions with a calm, no-nonsense demeanour. This man, aged in his forties, had finished the Regimental cross-country race that year in the top five. And he was always in the gym with a few of his mates, lifting big weights and screaming for just one more rep. His chunky forearms commanded respect. Like a key in a lock, he was a good fit for the position of RSM.

With the assistance of a commando reservist who was particularly adept at tying a 'truckie's knot', we fastened a rope to two trees on opposite banks of a deep creek. Then, using karabiners, we attached the boat to the rope and pulled it, laden with all of our packs, across the creek without allowing it to touch the ground. Our patrol, aided by a fallen tree, then traversed the gully. We completed the task with two minutes to spare.

We continued to another RV and were met by the man with the absurd accent from the night before. Once again, his accent annoyed me, but the last time we'd met he had given us food. This time he gave us two armoured personnel carrier (APC) tracks to carry. We rigged a single track to a pole. Four men carried each track, leaving one man spare to navigate. The same guy who had navigated several times previously volunteered himself again. This had become something of a habit – a frustrating one.

Traversing uneven ground made it difficult for us to spread the weight squarely. The taller men's spines were often ground into their pelvises as the shorties walked on their toes in an attempt to carry their share.

As my birthday drew to a close, I felt like shit but was pleased to have made it to the end of another day. There was no cake, or any food at all, for that matter. Day 18 was dead.

According to one of the DS who we spoke with after the course, on day 19 we were supposed to have been given a ration pack. But they forgot, so we filled our stomachs with water. Besides faecal matter, there is very little that I would not have eaten at this point. We were, literally, starving.

Once again, we were afforded little sleep. The following morning, we were given 13 jerry cans filled with water to carry between nine people. We each squeezed a jerry into our packs and then took turns carrying the remaining four. After a couple of hundred metres I felt like my forearms were going to explode. We soon changed tactics and slid a stick through the handle so we could carry one of the spares between two men. The DS in charge of this activity appeared genuinely concerned about the wellbeing of our patrol. After one short rest, I fell over while trying to stand up. *Not again*, I thought. The DS told me to take my jerry can out of my pack. I refused.

'Look, sir, if I can't carry my own pack then I shouldn't be here.'

'Alright, but if you fall over again I'm getting you out of here so the doc can have a look at you.'

I was certain that if this happened I would be forcibly removed from the course.

I tried to stay focused, counting my steps as I walked. Two other men fell over. I didn't want to sit down during rest stops, because trying to stand up was a greater effort than plodding along. We reached a dam. The DS told us to sit down and wait. He then walked off. The weather was changing and rain looked imminent.

At the edge of the dam was another pile of stores: 44-gallon drums, poles and more rope. We had to get ourselves, our personal equipment and the stores to the other side. Essentially, we were required to make a raft. The raft wasn't pretty but it held together.

We ferried half the guys and half the stores across to the other side. We swam beside or behind the raft, using our legs for propulsion. Two of us were tasked to swim the raft back to pick up the others. The water was freezing. I was probably in the water for 40 or 50 minutes, and I knew I had to change out of my wet clothes at the first available opportunity.

Still carrying our packs loaded with a single jerry can each, we walked for another 2.5 kilometres. With each step the water squelched from our boots. At our next rest stop I put on a clean and dry set of fatigues. I've usually got pretty solid legs, but as I dropped my pants I was shocked by the white sticks that appeared – they seemed half the size they had once been. I could easily cup my hands around my upper thigh and overlap my thumbs completely.

Our next task was to winch a three-tonne vehicle onto the road using a series of pulleys. After we achieved this we were told to push it. One of the guys had injured his leg so he was ordered to steer. The remainder of the team pushed the vehicle for just over two kilometres. On one small rise, the vehicle stopped and began rolling backwards. We chocked the wheels with stones and then rolled the vehicle to and fro as we painstakingly ascended the positive gradient. The DS assisted us to push the vehicle over the crest, and we continued down the hill. It began to drizzle. We were physically shattered.

A cold snap arrived, and with it came heavy rain. The chill bit deep into our wet bodies. I tried to stop shivering as it made my muscles ache. In the early evening we met up with another patrol before being left to our own devices. In pairs, we joined our hootchies together and got into our damp sleeping bags. *Fuck me . . . this is ridiculous*, I thought.

We were soon told to dismantle our hootchies and move to a designated ambush position. Half the remaining patrols were placed in the same ambush. Throughout the night it rained, sometimes hard, sometimes soft, but it was always wet and always cold. At that point I didn't care if I was accepted into the SAS. I was spent. My body was struggling to regulate its temperature. My hunger was gone, replaced by shivering nausea.

In the early hours of 10 April 1995, I heard two voices, then some shooting. The ambush was sprung. Our patrol, as per our orders, assembled at the rear of the ambush location and departed. Over the next hour, the dark sky dissolved to grey and the rain stopped.

For the entire course I had taken each day as it came. I'd tried not to anticipate what lay ahead. But I was no longer able to do that. I pictured the instruction handbook we'd been given before we started the selection course. The dates written on the front page were 23 March to 10 April. It was now 10 April. Was this just another mind game, or would it indeed be over soon? In four and a half days we'd been given one meal – fish-head soup. We needed sustenance. If this was to be the last day, what time would it end? There might still be 17 or 18 hours to go.

We walked up a hill to a hangar and saw other groups of dishevelled men sitting inside it. Then I saw Rog's face. He too had lost a lot of weight, perhaps more than me.

'It's over, mate,' he said. 'We did it. We finished the fucking thing.'

Our feeble hands embraced in a solid shake. I dumped my pack and sat on the floor.

'You want a brew?' Rog asked.

'What – are we allowed?'

'Yeah, look over there.'

I sat down and removed my boot to inspect my foot and ankle. The strapping tape was cutting deep into my instep. It took me 10 minutes to tear it off, revealing a deep wound on top of my foot. The stench made me grimace. The skin on my foot was an ugly white and mushy, like a corpse pulled from the water. I looked up and saw the SI, the man who had orchestrated the three weeks of pain we'd endured, watching me. His face remained deadpan. Then he walked away.

You don't have to accept me, I thought, *but I've finished your course and I gave it everything I had. Neither you nor anyone else can ever take that away from me.*

Then came breakfast. Neatly arranged on several folding tables were a dozen loaves of bread, buns, boxes of cereal, and milk. No hot food or anything too rich, as our stomachs wouldn't have handled it. I grabbed a hot cross bun and half-filled my cups canteen – my metal mug – with cocoa flakes and milk. I took a bite from the bun and dry-retched. I didn't even give myself a chance to swallow the brine before I took another bite and forced it down. It stuck in my oesophagus, then I began to hiccup. I drank some milk, which relieved the congestion, and I switched to cereal. Halfway through that, I finished the bun. I had eaten very little yet my stomach felt full and tight.

One soldier pulled up his shirt and said: 'Hey, check this out. I've got abs! I've never had abs before – they're usually covered with padding.'

I laughed to myself. *I've dropped so much weight that the ridges in my stomach are probably my backbone.*

We were permitted to shower, so I retrieved my toiletries and a towel from my echelon bag, threw on a pair of thongs and walked to the shower block. The place was abuzz with dirty, gaunt faces and bodies that carried the same weeping red sores, a legacy of one's pack or webbing rubbing through the skin.

Some guys were taking the piss out of each other, shocked by the change in their mates' faces and physiques. I set my shaving gear up on the sink and wiped the misty mirror. I hadn't seen my reflection for a couple of weeks. My eyes were sunken and dark, my cheeks dissolved flat. I was surprised just how tiny my head had become. It was as if my face had fallen off.

The sinews in my neck were more pronounced, and my clavicles were exposed like a shirtless coathanger. I could clearly see where my sternum connected to my rib cage. All this in less than three weeks.

Yet what we had endured was nothing in comparison to generations past. Millions of men and women – both allies and adversaries – suffered for years in POW camps. Of the 91,000 members of the German Sixth Army who surrendered at Stalingrad in World War II, only 5000 made it home. The majority perished in Soviet labour camps from disease and malnutrition.

≡

Having a crack at the SAS selection course was good for me. Sure, my aim was to become an SAS soldier, but being pushed beyond my limits taught me a lot about myself. As a person I had grown considerably, and over the next 12 months there would be much more to come.

I'd learnt many lessons, the most important being that if I wanted something badly enough, then I should trust myself and go for it. Life is full of pessimists, people who say something can't be done. And even if they're right and you fail – so what? Those who embrace their dreams and come up short have not truly failed. Failure belongs to those who didn't have the courage to step over the starting line.

≡

About thirty men remained, a mix of soldiers and officers. We boarded a coach and drove to Campbell Barracks, Swanbourne – the home of the Australian Special Air Service Regiment. I dozed most of the way, but the winged dagger on the front gates grabbed my attention.

Our first task was to clean our rifles. The quartermaster was stringent – he wanted them handed in spotless.

I think we were given hotboxes for lunch, to control how much food we were eating. Our eyes were definitely larger than our shrunken stomachs. Going too hard too quickly could make us sick. For the rest of that afternoon we cleaned and returned our personal stores. There was a lot of sitting around.

While this was taking place, the DS were discussing the performance of each trainee in detail. Our test results, our leadership potential, our ability to work independently and as a member of a team, our capacity to absorb information, our personality, work ethic, integrity, discipline, physical fitness and endurance – all aspects were scrutinised by the panel.

As the hours passed our sense of anticipation grew. Everyone who remained had finished the selection course, but who would actually be selected?

Later that afternoon we were advised that the mess opened at 1700. Our next timing was 0730 the following morning, so our time until then was our own. We were escorted to the transit accommodation and issued rooms, four men to each one.

I went for a walk and found a payphone outside the Regimental Aid Post (RAP). I called Colleen and left a short message on her answering machine. I then called my parents and spoke with my mother. She was aware that I was doing some type of selection course, but she didn't really know anything much about the SAS. We were close and spoke often, sometimes for hours, but I had never explained the course in great detail, just in case I failed. I told her I was pleased to have finished, and that if they didn't accept me I would try again the following year. Ma wished me luck and said she had a feeling I'd be accepted. Mother's intuition – if anyone knew what sort of person I was, it was her.

There were several guys waiting to use the phone so we didn't speak for long. Besides, it was nearly dinnertime and I wanted to see how much food I could squash into my stomach. Although I was full within five minutes, I kept eating for at least 30. My stomach ached and I found it difficult to breathe. I lay on my bed shirtless, my pants undone and my legs splayed, in an attempt to minimise any pressure on my stomach.

Rog stuck his head in my room. 'Hey, mate, a few of the guys are going to Fremantle to grab a beer and a steak. You coming?'

I felt like I was in labour and four weeks overdue. 'Nah, mate, I'm gonna chill out and lie here for a while.'

'Cool, brother, I'll see you tomorrow.'

Grab a steak? Are they freaking serious? I thought. *Just breathing hurts.* As it turned out, the guys didn't have the energy to party and were all in bed by 2300 that night.

I had a restless night's sleep and woke up hungry. I went to the mess and had a couple of bowls of chocolate cocoa flakes. I had just completed the most challenging course in the Australian military, yet when given the opportunity to eat, I chose a children's breakfast cereal ahead of pancakes, bacon, eggs and toast.

Just walking around still left me light-headed. I couldn't feel the soles of my feet at all, and after breakfast I spent 15 minutes squeezing thorns out of my shins, knees and thighs. The hours crawled by. We cleaned vehicles and anything else the quartermaster could think of. In the early afternoon, while we were seated on the grass outside the quartermaster's store, the SI made an announcement.

'The following men are to follow me inside. Everyone else is to remain in place.'

The SI disappeared with about eight men, a combination of soldiers and officers. When he returned we were told that those who remained had been found suitable for further training. There were no congratulations – just a warning that anyone who failed to perform during the next phase of the training would also be sent back to their units.

Colleen was right – we would be moving to Perth.

6

ACCEPTANCE VIA PERFORMANCE

I had passed the course and was accepted into the SAS. I was fortunate – not everyone in life realises what they want to do for a job and then sees it come to fruition. I had set a mid-term goal and had dedicated myself wholeheartedly to making it happen. Injury, age, endurance and negative comments were some of the obstacles I was confronted with, but from the outset I had known what I wanted and my motivation had not wavered.

Whenever I set myself big challenges, the first thing I do is ask: why am I doing this? What is my motivation? Without a strong and true desire, you'll struggle to push through adversity.

I wanted to work with the best soldiers in the Australian military, and I wanted to be deployed on the most challenging tasks. I craved an exciting occupation where I would be tested. Soldiers don't join the SAS for money or because it sounds cool. The men are passionate about soldiering and strive to take it to the highest level. Desire spawns motivation, and motivation creates opportunity. You don't need to venture far for that – motivation comes from within.

=

The day after the selection course ended, we were granted four days' leave. The only proviso was that we must not do any physical training. For once in my life, going for a run or to the gym was the furthest thing from my mind. We were given some learning booklets to study at our own pace, but besides that our time was our own.

I was the only soldier from the 6th Battalion to pass the course, so initially I wasn't part of any clique. The guys from the other battalions, especially the 1st, 2nd and 3rd Battalions, were already tight.

Still feeling fatigued, I decided to walk to the beach to check out the ocean. I love the water and usually feel a sense of calm when in its presence. It was a cold, wintry day, and a strong southerly wind was sweeping up the coast. Campbell Barracks backs onto the Indian Ocean, a pristine and much sought-after location in the heart of Perth's 'golden triangle'. From the back gate of the barracks I followed an obvious sand track to a sentry tower that overlooked the beach. I climbed the tower, and while I was there an effeminate Asian man joined me. I thought this was a little weird, so I left.

I tucked myself into the northern side of a sand dune and watched the choppy waves slap against the sand while I drifted in and out of sleep. Fifteen minutes later, I opened my eyes and saw a man walking across the beach in front of me. He was staring at me intently. After a while he retraced his footsteps, walked around the sand dune I was sheltering behind and positioned himself 10 metres behind me. I immediately sat up and my body prepared itself for battle.

Surely this fucker isn't going to try and mug me, I thought. *Does he seriously want to have a go?*

I casually glanced over my right shoulder and eyeballed the man. With a furrowed brow, I turned my head back, stared at the sand in front of me and tried to work out if what I had just seen was real. *Did he just have his cock in his hand?* I looked at the man again, and this time there was no mistake – he was stroking his erect penis while staring at me.

'What in the hell are you doing?' I yelled.

The man, aged in his mid to late thirties, didn't say a word but tried to bend his cock back into his tracksuit pants. I stood up. He began to panic, trying to decide whether he should run or remain where he was.

I shouted: 'Are you fucking serious?' and kicked some sand towards him. Before me was a man who was uncomfortable with confrontation. He rolled onto his side and crumpled onto the sand.

I had no intention of taking it any further. I stormed up the beach and didn't look back. I told a few of the guys what had happened, and for a short time I was nicknamed 'Dune Boy'. It was then I learnt that Swanbourne Beach was a hangout for gay men. I should have realised that when the other guy had joined me in the sentry tower.

My issue was not that the man was homosexual – people's sexual preference has never bothered me. He has as much control over choosing his sexuality as I do: none. But I found his actions confronting as they caught me off guard. It was the same as if a heterosexual male had been tossing off while looking at a woman on a beach.

In fact, the first guy I told was homosexual. He had also passed the selection course and would become a close mate of mine. When he saw my reaction, he told me much later, his initial thoughts were: *Great, Fenno's homophobic. There's no way I'll ever be able to be honest with this guy.*

He was wrong. I found out about his sexual preference two years before he came out publicly, and I kept it a close secret. I always considered him to be an exceptional soldier and often commented to my wife that he was one of the most grounded and mentally secure soldiers I knew.

Some people have a perception – created by the aggressive nature of SAS training and operations – that all SAS soldiers are Alpha males. But it's only partly true. Most of the guys are complex individuals, and are far more open-minded about things that fall outside the 'norms of society' than most people expect. When bullets are slamming into the earth around you – when things become a little crazy – there are no thoughts or concerns about anyone's sexuality. Why should there be? All you give a fuck about is whether the guy next to you is competent, and whether he'll stay by your side if the situation becomes dire.

My first days in the Regiment were definitely interesting. But there was much more to come.

=

The next night, the majority of the soldiers on our reinforcement cycle went to the Swanbourne Hotel for a few drinks. A couple of men tried to position themselves above others – an alcohol-induced, self-proclaimed order of seniority. Considering I had only joined the military the previous year, they felt they had to let me know that I was a 'jube' – a new guy – and so relegated to the bottom of their pecking order. I was advised to keep my mouth shut and learn. I wasn't the only guy who was spoken to that night. Initially, there was a dominant group within our cycle. It's easy to govern as a pack, especially when you're targeting lone guys who are yet to establish themselves.

An officer also chimed in, having a crack at me for being a 'Ready Reserve' soldier. 'I heard you were a Ready Red Rooster,' he said at the top of his voice. He repeated this several times, laughing out loud and then he began to crow.

I just nodded my head and smiled. I looked at the man and thought: *You look more like a goose than a rooster*. I remained reserved and eventually returned to the barracks. It's not a long walk – 1.2 kilometres at most – along a road lined with pine trees. But it was long enough for me to reflect on what was said.

At first I tried to recall if I had said something to antagonise these guys. *Was I being a smartarse?* But then I wondered to myself why guys like them waited so long before attempting selection. If they were so good, why did it take them so many years to make it into the Regiment? Was it a lack of confidence? Did they need to wait for a dozen of their mates to do it with them? Sure, some of them had big reputations in the Battalion, but we weren't in the Battalion anymore. We would all have a steep learning curve, but mine would be a little steeper.

I'd made it into the SAS but I felt like an outsider. The last time I felt this way was 18 years earlier, at pre-school. I still remember a red-headed girl and three boys banishing me from the tree-house because I was wearing a

Photo time at pre-school, aged four.

belt. For weeks the group followed me around and hounded me off every piece of equipment in the playground. I began to hate Tuesdays — pre-school day — so I conned Ma into letting me stay at home. As a four-year-old I was shy and lacked confidence, but this was no longer the case.

Sitting on my bed, I mulled over a couple of options: I could confront those responsible and have it out, or I could double my efforts and earn their respect via performance. I was already highly motivated, but their comments did inspire me to work a little harder.

The next day, while the others recovered from their hangovers, I spent hours working with a piece of rope, practising my knots. Our first course was a four-day roping course.

I also began to familiarise myself with Morse code. We would later be expected to send and receive Morse at 10 words per minute. After memorising the characters, I began to practise on my Morse trainer — a device that beeped random characters, both letters and numbers. There were dials to control the sound and speed.

I'd wake up early, throw on a set of headphones and practise while the others slept. This continued throughout the day. Whenever I had a few spare minutes, I'd turn on my Morse trainer and scribble the characters into a large notebook. When it was full, I bought another.

Before our signals course even began, I could comfortably watch television and receive Morse at over 14 words per minute. I was tested at the end of the first week of the course and was the first to qualify.

During our survival training we were given a lesson on lock-picking. That evening, with Chris, a diligent, intelligent soldier who had a keen interest in demolitions, I purchased some hacksaw blades and we set about crafting our own set of lock picks. Each evening while watching television, I would work my way through a dozen padlocks. When I became bored with this I used to break into Todd's room, or wander outside and pick the ignition lock of a mate's Toyota 4Runner.

After our reinforcement training, I returned home and went to visit my father at his workshop. His front door is stitched with deadlocks, sliding bolts and padlocks. I pulled a lock pick and torsion bar out of my wallet and began raking the pins.

Dad scoffed and said: 'You'll never get through those.'

Five minutes later I opened the door and shot my father a grin.

'Jesus,' he said. 'I'll have to get another couple of padlocks.'

I laughed, relocked the door and tried again. My next attempt was quicker.

The men who had a go at me at the beginning of the reinforcement cycle were, in fact, excellent soldiers and decent guys. They'd been drinking that night and shot their mouths off. There probably isn't a person alive who, under the influence of alcohol, hasn't done this – me included. But I was young and took their comments to heart. I have always possessed an extreme desire to perform, their comments only made me more obsessive.

By the time we reached our dive course, two months into the reinforcement cycle, we were aware not only of how we were performing, but also of how everyone else stacked up. Past reputations now meant nothing. Those who worked hard did well. Those who didn't, or who perhaps were not suited to special operations, struggled or were moved on. Strong friendships were forged, and by the end of our reinforcement cycle many of us were inseparable.

I would later work with one of these guys for years, both in the Regiment and when contracting in Iraq and Afghanistan. I've always admired his toughness and the satirical, almost cavalier manner in which he negotiates dangerous situations. Ten years after our selection course he still remembered what he'd said.

'Mate,' he told me, 'I know I've said it before, but I just want to apologise for giving you shit at the Swanny that night. Bloody hell – of all the guys to have a crack at!'

I laughed. 'Yeah, don't worry about it. We were young and you were full of piss.'

'No excuse. I was a prick. It's always bothered me, mate, and I just wanted to let you know.'

'You do know you did me a favour? You guys inspired me to go harder.'

'Bullshit! You would have gone hard anyway.'

This guy later sent me an inspiring email after reading

Warrior Brothers. He didn't have to, but he took the time to craft something special. I realised then that we can all be hypercritical beasts at times, but those who grow the most are those who reflect with the deepest honesty.

≡

SAS soldiers are selected for their ability to think clearly during high-stress situations. This sometimes means suppressing your natural survival instincts. The comprehensive training SAS soldiers receive, coupled with mental preparation — mentally rehearsing the sequence of actions that are to be carried out — allows them to make the right decision in a timely manner. This training once saved my life.

We were on a parachute training exercise. As we all fitted our parachutes — pulling down on the leg straps, wiggling our hips and making grunting noises — an outsider would have thought we were engaged in some kind of torturous bonding ritual. You then have to bend over and heave on your shoulder straps. As you attempt to stand up it feels like your neck and genitals have been squashed into your stomach.

If a rogue testicle isn't tucked away properly, it is now that a man will pay the price: the straps will tear into his groin without remorse. It's easy to tell if a man has been a little careless when packing himself away, because a leg strap biting into a testicle is not something a man can hide. His face will contort, and a web of veins in his face and neck will pulse to the surface. This is usually followed by a squeal that would embarrass a kitten as he bends over again, his fingers frantically trying to free himself. SAS soldiers are a passionate lot; besides laughing, they may well come to their mate's aid and further tighten his shoulder straps.

Standing semi-hunched while waiting for parachute safety checks is as much fun as walking barefoot across a lawn full of bindies. I ogled the safety supervisor who was methodically working his way down the line, wondering why he was taking so long. I then noticed that he too was squashed into a parachute harness, and that his face had taken on the same hue as an overripe tomato.

He arrived – grinning – and began tugging at my equipment. 'Hey, Fenno, your static line looks dodgy. I'd use another parachute if I was you.'

'You freefall pussies are such pessimists,' I replied. 'It's only 1000 feet and we're landing in water – we probably don't even need a parachute.'

We were conducting an 'over the horizon' night jump, and the wind was gusting at 20 to 25 knots, the maximum allowable speed when jumping into water. Although we were jumping 'roundies', with a 50-kilogram pack hanging off the front of our harnesses, we had no fears about breaking a leg or shortening our spines, since we were only jumping into water.

Our Squadron Sergeant Major bellowed at us: 'Zulu One, winds are on limits but we'll make the decision whether or not you jump once we're over the drop zone. Move to the aircraft!'

We grabbed our packs and waddled out the hangar door towards the C130 aircraft, relieved that we would soon be in the water and able to take a piss. Once aboard, no one switches off. We fitted our seatbelts and silently recited the order in which things will take place. *The sooner we exit this claustrophobic, gut-wrenching machine, the better*, I thought.

'Six minutes,' the safety supervisor shouted, and we repeated his call down the line.

We stood up, hung our packs off the front of our harnesses, and then attached our parachute static lines to the cable overhead. The faint red glow illuminating the cabin was soon interrupted by another safety supervisor, who moved down the line with a flashlight, blinding the boys as he carried out his final safety checks. All joviality was now gone, and the men had moved into their own private worlds of deep concentration. The safety supervisor remained professional and offered little more than a wink and reassuring slap on the shoulder to confirm that my checks were complete.

With the rear ramp down, the three-minute call was silenced as the wind lashed the rear of the aircraft. The 30-second call saw us shuffle into position, bunched tight, adrenaline coursing through our bodies. All the men were wearing their fins – flippers – to negate any additional hassle when we hit the water. The only possible drawback, besides catching the wind as we exit the aircraft and being flipped upside down, would be a slightly delayed departure. We were to follow our two Zodiacs – four-metre black boats powered by twin 25-horsepower engines – out of the aircraft, and for every additional second we wait before jumping, we can expect a 100-metre swim. A four-second delay equates to a good 400 metres. We waited, staring at the red light and willing it to turn green.

The green light kickstarted our hearts and our boats punched into the night, their large parachutes springing

104 **WARRIOR TRAINING**

Parachuting into Singapore Harbour.

to life. We attempted to drive hard off the ramp, but with the hindrance of our fins we could only dribble out the back like penguins, falling head first and off balance. My fins caught the wind and I flipped over onto my back. My sweaty hands remained white-knuckled across my reserve chute, ready to deploy it should it be required.

My chute opened with a violent jolt. *My testicles may well be squashed*, I thought, *but there's no time to ponder such trivialities.* It was time to unlock my toggles and steer towards the boats, which themselves would soon be in the water. Fixated on the closest craft, I willed myself across the black sky. Thirty feet above the water, I undid my chest-snap – the clip that secured the top of my harness – and unclipped my left capewell – a metal tab – to expose the small wire ring that, when pulled, would collapse one side of my parachute.

I assessed my speed and noticed that I was flying backwards. The water reflected just enough light to show me that I was going to land hard. I began to breathe quickly, trying to time my last breath before I made contact. The black water was flying under my feet like a treadmill on full speed.

I slammed into the water, and the gentle sound of the wind was overwhelmed by the gushing waves that filled my ears. I exhaled through my nose and mouth as I tugged at my left capewell, attempting to collapse the parachute, but the fucker would not release – it had seized up, perhaps because of one too many saltwater jumps. The wind gusted hard and I was dragged underwater, the parachute now acting as a kite.

My pack was still attached to my stomach, as I hadn't bothered to lower the line – it was just another thing to get tangled in the water. My heart was sprinting and my lungs were begging for air. With a greater level of commitment and using both hands, I wrenched on my capewell again, but still it refused to release.

I was caught in an ugly place. My instincts were to claw at the surface and attempt to get my head above water, but my training – a voice that was beginning to fade – told me to settle the fuck down and to try my other capewell. I reached to my right shoulder to locate the coin-like tab at the apex, but the cold water was inhibiting my dexterity. I felt like a beetle trapped on its back.

My body was pulled taut as the wind screamed again. To conserve my energy, I had to resist the urge to kick and thrash my way towards the surface. Finally, I located my right capewell, released the tab, put my thumb through the ring and pulled hard. *If only masturbation was this exciting.* I was still underwater, but my speed appeared finally to be slowing. My head broke the surface, I gasped for air and my chute collapsed into the water.

After half a dozen salt-watery coughs, I removed my leg snaps, pack, belly band and lowering line. I pushed myself up onto my pack and did a quick 360, expecting to see a safety craft so I could offload my parachute and get going. But as I rose and fell across the swells, all I could see was dark, choppy water. There was no sign of the red Cyalume glowsticks that should be illuminating the boats.

Although I was supposed to hand the apex of my parachute to a safety craft, I had no intention of wrestling with it in the dark. The harness, which I was holding in my left hand, would have to do. I removed a green Cyalume from my right wetsuit sleeve, cracked it and waved it above my head. I did another 360-degree turn but met with only cold, eerie darkness. I was 20 nautical miles off the West Australian coast, and unpleasant thoughts of what might be lurking beneath me briefly entered my mind, but there was little point worrying about the outcome of what would have been a brief and one-sided encounter.

After another 20 minutes passed, I saw the glow of a safety craft some 200 metres away. Again I waved the Cyalume above my head, before placing it in my mouth so I could kick more firmly to keep my head above water. I held onto my pack with my right hand, only letting go every now and then to wave the Cyalume towards the safety craft. My parachute had submerged completely, and remaining afloat required a sustained effort. I was no longer bobbing above the swells but was dragged through them by my heavy parachute.

After 35 minutes in the water I was struggling to stay afloat. I considered ditching my parachute but decided that drowning would probably be less embarrassing. *I'll reassess after 45 minutes*, I thought. Finally, after about 40 minutes, a safety craft meandered over. I passed my parachute harness to the bowman.

'Hey, mate,' he said. 'Both your boats are upside down – the closest one is probably 300 metres that way. If you have trouble finding it just give us a wave. We've still got one more guy to account for.'

I selected a star on the horizon as a point of reference and set off, relieved to be free of my parachute. I reached the boat 10 minutes later. It had been flipped upside down and its engines were full of water. As we worked on the engines in the dark – removing the spark plugs and pulling the engines over – the heavy seas and sickly waft of fuel saw all of us share the contents of our stomachs with the ocean. Twenty minutes later we were ready to go.

'Hey, guys,' yelled a man from the safety craft. 'The wind's picked up, so the exercise has been cancelled.'

Damn! Those fucking freefallers miss out again, I thought. I pictured them taking their parachutes off and laughing as they got back on the bus. Although I knew we still had a two-hour kidney-thumping transit to go, it was nights like this that attracted me to the Regiment.

While being dragged backwards underwater, my instinct had been to thrash around in order to get my head above water. But because of the severity of the wind gusts, this would have been futile. Remaining flexible does not mean cuffing it when things go wrong. If you have a plan, then it's more efficient to modify that plan than to formulate a new solution from scratch. My training, not my instincts, helped me to make the right decisions under testing conditions.

The men who passed the selection, roping, patrol and basic parachute courses returned to their units for four weeks, where each was to organise his removal and collect his belongings. I went back to Brisbane but was sent straight out to the bush, to play enemy for the new platoons that were completing their infantry employment training (IET).

My first task was to move to the junction of a road and a creek, wait for it to get dark and then ambush an infantry section. A couple of hours after last light, my colleague and I saw a distant glow through the vegetation. When the glow began to flicker and move, it became obvious it was a torch.

'You reckon those guys are looking for this junction?' asked my colleague.

'Yeah, probably,' I replied.

'Why would they be walking through the bush with a torch?'

'Don't know ... maybe they're lost,' I said.

We didn't have to wait long to find out. Out of the dark screamed a voice: 'Enemy ... enemy ... where are you?'

I recognised the voice immediately. It belonged to the tool who had questioned my navigational experience a couple of months earlier. We remained quiet.

'Is this guy for real? He's walking around with a torch?' said my colleague.

I moved onto the road and watched the torchlight disappear into the bush some 150 metres away, amid his fading screams of desperation: 'Enemy ... enemy ...'

We decided to remain in our ambush location. Ten minutes later we heard footsteps running up the track. They stopped 50 metres shy of our position and the familiar yells continued: 'Enemy . . . enemy . . . is anyone there?'

We remained quiet and the footsteps scurried away. Fifteen minutes later he was back. The lone man stopped across from our position, bent over and sucked in some large breaths. I thought about initiating the ambush and brassing him up. 'Enemy!' he screamed again.

'We're over here,' I replied.

'Thank fuck for that! Man, that's tiger country. We hit the wrong junction,' said the man, shining his torch in our direction.

How much nav ya' done? I thought, as the man's torch beam found my smiling face. I could tell he remembered our previous conversation, so what more was there to say? We ambushed his section and that was that.

7

RTI TRAINING: A TEST OF SELF-BELIEF

Resistance-to-interrogation training – more commonly known to soldiers as 'RTI' or 'getting bagged' – is a profound test of one's mental strength and self-belief.

Our troop had spent several days on a field training exercise. Our mission: to rescue the crew of a downed helicopter. With this completed, we boarded a couple of army trucks to be extracted. Although we were aware that RTI training was looming, the exact dates remained a secret so as to maximise the 'shock of capture'. When all the new guys were guided onto the same truck, we knew something was going down.

As our transport pulled into a brightly-lit hangar, it was surrounded by dozens of men dressed in black and white military fatigues. I gave them a smoke grenade to suck on and 30 blank rounds, which I fired on full automatic before a man with a pornstar moustache approached the back of our truck and yelled: 'Time out, time out! Put down your weapons and play the game. You have been captured. This is RTI.'

Putting up a fight was pointless. We knew the RTI experience was a requirement that all SAS soldiers must endure. *Bring it on*, I thought.

The acronym 'RTI' sounds pleasant enough, rolling off the tongue a bit like NFI – no fucking idea – but for me those three letters, in that sequence, conjure up a range of memories, from aching knees and hypothermia to 'bend over and spread your buttocks'.

I knew RTI would last for 72 hours, the length of a long weekend. Most soldiers complete RTI during their reinforcement cycle – the first 12 months in the Regiment before being posted to an SAS sabre squadron – but in our case the training took place the following year, four months after we had joined a squadron.

The aim of RTI is to educate soldiers about what to expect and how to react should they ever be captured by an enemy. It also provides interrogators – selected personnel from the Royal Australian Intelligence Corps – with guinea pigs to practise on. I reckon it's reasonable to draw a parallel between interrogators and male gynaecologists; there are those who are professional and brilliant at what they do, and there are those who might more aptly be described as 'suspect individuals'.

For the training to be effective, a captive is firstly fatigued – worn down by sleep deprivation, a lack of sustenance and extreme physical activity. He'll also be stripped of his visual and aural senses – made to wear blacked-out goggles and earmuffs – to disorient him. The captives are then pitted individually against a well-drilled team of intelligence officers, whose sole aim, generally speaking, is to extract information.

During times of war, what a soldier says during his or her first 72 hours in captivity might well decide not only their own fate but also the fate of others who have eluded capture. Additionally, if he or she releases key information about a mission then they could easily jeopardise ongoing operations. Therefore, in accordance with the Geneva Convention, soldiers are instructed to provide only 'the big four' – name, rank, regimental number and date of birth – and 'nothing more'. Considering that it's obviously illegal to yank out teeth, sodomise a captive, remove digits or break bones during training, you could argue that RTI training is unrealistic; in the current climate, at least, our adversaries' preference has been for other, more violent interrogation techniques.

In reality, when soldiers are threatened with decapitation unless they read dodgy confessions, they'll instinctively say whatever is required to remain alive. Furthermore, with the release of the graphic images of Iraqi prisoners being mistreated in the Abu Ghraib prison, it's evident that even countries who are signatories to the convention have at times failed to adhere to its requirements. But irrespective of whether or not the 'big four' was realistic, I knew that, if name, rank, regimental number and date of birth was all the information we were permitted to give, then that's all the information these intelligence clowns were going to get from me.

Before going 'into the bag' I was, somewhat naively, looking forward to the experience. *Seventy-two hours*, I thought. *It's not like they're allowed to break my arms or have their way with me. How difficult can it be?*

'Hey, Fenno,' asked one of the boys. 'You reckon we'll get bagged on our next patrol?'

'Hope so,' I replied. 'I'm keen to see if it's as punishing as everyone makes out.'

'What – you *want* to do it?'

'Absolutely!'

'What the fuck for?'

'I'm curious – and I'm sick of listening to everyone who has done it gob off about how fucked it is. It's only 72 hours.'

≡

Seventy-two naked, humiliating, wintry hours gave me a far greater appreciation of time. Three days is a bloody long time when someone else is in control of your life. Besides motivating me to never allow myself to be captured, RTI taught me a lot about myself. During those days of isolation, being subjected to sleep deprivation and water-board treatment – being seated in a mud pool and blasted by a fire hydrant – interspersed with several interrogation sessions, I knew I had to back myself, regardless of what was going on around me.

Todd and I were the first two guys dragged from the truck. Standing at six foot three, Todd was a large and pretty aggressive young man. He was also one of the better soldiers in the troop. He probably wasn't a people person. In fact, Todd didn't like people very much, but he did like me and a few others. On Todd's buck's night, we dressed him up in a black lycra suit and a gimp mask. He was furious but we all thought it was hilarious. Towards the end of the night, Todd was walking down the main street of Subiaco with Stevie when they were bailed up by a couple of louts.

'Hey, check out the fucking faggot,' said one.

The big guy in the lycra suit responded by knocking him out.

I wondered how Todd, one of my best mates in the troop, would get along with our interrogators.

Within seconds our hands were cuffed behind our backs, blacked-out goggles were put over our faces and muffs were placed on our ears. I was then led away, pushed into a stress position and searched. I heard the muffled sounds of a dog – a German shepherd – close by, and I smelt its rancid breath. The dog began to bark and growl, its saliva slapping my right cheek. Then, perhaps getting a little too excited, it made a choking sound and its master whispered commands of restraint. This made me laugh.

Someone grabbed me by the hair, lifted up my left earmuff and said in a sinister tone: 'You will play the fucking game, arsehole.'

Considering my face reeked of dog saliva, I was less concerned about the profane language than I was about whether or not that foul-breathed dog was infested with worms. After some time – possibly an hour – I was led away, pushed into the back of a padded vehicle and driven around. The driver, who had a tendency to brake into corners, drove like my 82-year-old grandmother: fast and erratically. The vehicle stopped and I was grabbed by the hair, led across a gravel surface and into a building. Two guards escorted me down what seemed like a long hallway. We passed through several rooms and several doors. My head was pushed down, as if to create an impression that we were entering small rooms. Then we stopped, my earmuffs were removed and the guards walked away. For several minutes there was nothing. No shuffling of feet, no whispers, no sounds of breathing, nothing. I tried not to swallow and my ears were straining for sound. Then a voice came out of nowhere: 'You are a prisoner of war and are not permitted to escape. Do you understand?'

'I cannot answer that question,' I replied.

'We will now remove your handcuffs,' said the voice.

I was somewhat relieved about this. My fingers were numb and the plastic cuffs had cut deep into my wrists.

The voice, serious and stern, continued: 'Remove your shirt and place it on the floor behind you.'

I followed the instructions.

'Remove your boots, socks and trousers and place them on the floor behind you.'

Once again, I followed the commands.

'Remove your underwear and place your hands on your head.'

I bent over, slid my underwear down my legs and took half a step forward with my left leg as I eased my underwear behind me with my right foot. I remained slightly hunched, my hands atop my head. For what felt like hours, but in reality might have been only a couple of minutes, I stood there in total silence, tense, exposed and vulnerable. Then the silence was broken.

'You will now be searched. Do not resist.'

My body was searched in a methodical manner by someone wearing rubber gloves: my hair, ears, the inside of my mouth, my armpits, groin and the soles of my feet. I thought – I hoped – it was over.

Then came the finale: 'Bend over and spread your buttocks.'

The person wearing the rubber gloves took his – or maybe her – time. Bent over and with my hands pulling my arse cheeks apart, I wondered if the army was legally allowed to stick a finger into my anus? I then heard slapping sounds as the gloves were stretched and released several times. That snapping sound of rubber on skin made my sphincter contract. A hand briefly touched my right buttock. My sphincter contracted more. I waited, still wondering if this was permissible in training. I swallowed a mouthful of saliva, which somehow made me feel better.

I then thought: *Fuck it*, and I zoned out. I let my mind go blank and became a zombie who didn't care. The gloves stretched and snapped several more times but the sounds were not sharp like they had been. They were distant and beyond offence. I was asked to relax my sphincter, which I did. Only a small piece of my mind remained open. I was able to follow simple commands but my emotions were not affected.

'Stand up,' said the voice.

Time to return to reality, I thought, and I switched back on, relieved that no attempt was made to fondle my prostate. I also realised that our interrogators had limitations – they were indeed not permitted to finger my arse.

'We will now remove your goggles,' the voice said. 'You are to look straight ahead. Do you understand?

'I cannot answer that question,' I replied.

'Don't try to be a tough guy. Do you understand?'

'I cannot answer that question.'

'A simple "yes" is all that is required. Do you understand?'

Once again, my reply was: 'I cannot answer that question.' This little game reminded me of the yes/no game my father played with my sisters and me when we were growing up. I had learnt then that the key is to pause after each question. Each question must be analysed separately from the ones before it. You cannot control the number or speed of the questions that are being asked, but you can control the pace of your answers. Regardless of how many questions the exasperated interrogator threw my way, I would take my time and answer the first one only. The interrogator's friend – momentum – is the captive's foe.

When my goggles were removed, the pain at the back of my eyes was like an extreme ice-cream headache. My eyes had no time to adjust, thrust from darkness into the most intense white lights I had ever seen.

'Look at me,' boomed the voice.

This guy thinks he's the Wizard of Oz, I thought. The numerous sharp glows that stabbed my eyes made it impossible to put a face to the voice. Through the light I could vaguely make out a desk, perhaps with someone seated behind it.

'What's your name?' said the voice.

'Keith Fennell.'

'Your full name?'

Prick, I thought. 'Keith Gerard Fennell,' I said.

'Spell it.'

I did.

'What's your rank?'

'Private,' I replied.

'From the equipment you were carrying it is evident that you are an SAS soldier. Therefore your rank would be trooper. What's your rank?'

'Private.'

'I'm going to ask you this question again. If you fail to tell the truth then you will not be protected by the Geneva Convention. Do you understand?'

'I cannot answer that question.'

This continued for several minutes, and the interrogator became increasingly agitated.

'What's your regimental number, Trooper Fennell?'

'I cannot answer that question.' The interrogator was addressing me as Trooper Fennell rather than Private Fennell, so I decided that I would not answer his question. I had to keep every question simple.

'You are obliged – you must answer that question!' yelled the voice. 'What's your regimental number, Fennell?'

I began to rethink my decision to declare my rank as private rather than trooper. Technically they are the same, but I decided there and then to continue with private, regardless of the repercussions.

The bright lights were turned off and the burning sensation at the back of my eyes dissolved. Before me, illuminated now by the regular room lighting, sat a bespectacled, pot-bellied man aged in his mid-fifties, with grey hair and a greyer beard. The voice now had a face.

After that glimpse, I decided to zone out again, staring at the top of the interrogator's head with lifeless, unfocused eyes. This seemed to annoy him, as he eventually left the safe confines of his desk and stood right in front of me, staring directly into my face. I could only presume that he was staring into my eyes but I kept my vision blurred so that his face resembled a grey hairy ball.

The interrogator asked the same questions over and over again. Occasionally I returned to the present and thought about how much I would like to knee him in the groin, but as his rants intensified and his spit splattered my face, I returned to the surreal comfort of emptiness.

'What's your rank?' said the angry grey hairy ball.

'Private,' I replied.

'What's your rank?'

'Pr —'

'Liar,' he interjected. 'What's your rank?'

'Private.'

'Liar. Your rank is trooper. What's your fucking rank?'

'Private.'

'Take this idiot away and let him have a think about it,' said the grey hairy ball.

My vision and hearing were once again stolen from me as the guards refitted my goggles and muffs. I was led out of the room, across a gravelled surface that pained my soft feet and into another building. The night air of the Northam winter chilled my skin, and over the next few hours this cold would seep into my core.

The guards pushed me onto the floor, crossed my legs and placed my hands on my knees. I would spend the best part of 48 hours in this position, the only respite coming in the form of punishment or sessions with the interrogators. For hours I sat there with aching knees, my arse numbed by the wooden floor. Although the goggles had a foam seal, they were painfully tight. With each hour they cut deeper into my face, until the pain across my forehead was on a par with my aching knees. Whenever I attempted to transfer weight from one arse cheek to another, a guard would grab my shoulders and force me onto the ground. The same would happen if a hand slipped from my knee.

I began to taunt the guards, letting one hand slide off my knee and then slowly replacing it as their footsteps approached. I heard other people coughing and realised I was not alone. I continued to amuse myself by sliding a hand off my knee and then returning it. *Nothing too obvious – just a couple of times an hour,* I thought. On one occasion I lowered my hand immediately after hearing the guard's footsteps fade. I then heard a floorboard behind me creak. *Fuck,* I thought, as an aggressive hand grabbed my hand and slapped it onto my lower thigh. The man pushed his knee into my back, raised my left muff and whispered into my ear: 'Don't do it again, arsehole.'

At one point I was dragged outside and pushed into a muddy pool of water, no more than a foot deep. But the gravelly bottom ground into my arse, and small stones wedged between my cheeks as well as my toes. Someone removed my muffs and told me that I was being punished because I lied about my rank. I sat there shivering, when suddenly a heavy blast of water smashed against my body. Compared to the deathly night air, the water actually felt warm. After a moment it stopped and the night air bit into my skin, and then the water came again.

I lowered my head, zoning out. I thought of

Resistance-to-interrogation training was a test of self-belief.

nothing – not the pebbles against my arse, not the metallic taste of the water or the cold against my skin. Nothing.

After half a dozen repetitions of this I was dragged from the pool and put inside a large freezer. Hanging out in a freezer after some quality time under a fire hydrant redefined my perceptions of what it was to be cold. I tried to mentally remove myself from that space in a feeble attempt to escape the cold, but I could not. I then thought about my grandfather and great-grandfather, and what they must have endured during the World Wars. Unfortunately, though, their stories are as dead as they are. No letters, no diaries – only pictures, medals and a few blurry memories remain.

I barely knew my grandfather or his father and yet, when tucked into the foetal position inside a freezer,

My grandfather Jack Fennell (second from right), after capturing a piece of German armour in the Middle East during World War II.

I thought of them. We were related, and their experiences gave me strength. I had been cold before – I knew what it was like to shiver – but this was special. At first I remained hunched over, nauseated and shaking just a little. But as time dragged on, the deep contractions within my muscles intensified, to the point where my body began to relax and ceased to tremble – the onset of hypothermia.

The day before my grandfather Jack died, I gave him a small ceramic pig I made in art class. Although Ma thought my creation was a hippopotamus, I was proud of that pig. I wondered where it was now. Then I visualised my interrogators' faces and thought: *Fuck 'em. Anyone who thinks up sick shit like this doesn't deserve to be told anything.* I don't imagine I was thinking too straight at this time, but I do remember being pulled from the freezer, taken to a room and given a blanket. *Hot or cold – I wish these fuckers would make up their minds.*

I was kept there until my core temperature rose. We later learned that the Regimental Medical Officer (RMO) was keeping a close eye on all of us during this phase of the exercise.

When Stevie, a hard-hitting operator with more attitude than a high-class hooker, collapsed onto the floor shaking, he was immediately removed from the training and examined by the doc.

'Steve, are you alright, mate?'

'Yeah, I'm just bunging it on,' he'd said.

'What, there's nothing wrong?'

'Nah, nothing – I'm good to go.'

'Guards, he's okay. Take him away.'

Stevie managed to surprise our interrogators on more than one occasion. In the middle of one heated session, he raised his hand and informed his interrogators that he needed to take a piss. He was told to hold on to it. Mr Attitude no doubt remained expressionless as he let go and pissed all over himself.

'Hey – what are you doing? Stop that, you fucking filthy man!' screamed the interrogators. Stevie ignored the abuse and continued to piss.

'If you want to act like a dog then we'll treat you like one,' one of them said. They had lost their momentum, and so, in an attempt to regain the upper hand, one of them grabbed Stevie by the hair and rolled him in his own urine.

≡

I spent most of the next day seated cross-legged on a folded blanket. We were instructed to perform a range of activities, depending on the number of gongs we heard. This was both annoying and a relief, for my knees were aching constantly. I don't remember the sequence, but one gong might have meant stand up, two to jog on the spot, and three to sit back down. This annoying game continued for hours. The following evening I was taken once again to the mud pool, blasted by the fire hydrant and then chilled in the freezer. My next interrogation session, however, was a little different.

There were two interrogators, one male and one female. The man continued to question me about my rank, informing me that I was an idiot and too pathetic to be an SAS soldier.

'Look at you, standing there, your shoulders hunched. You look fucking pathetic. I thought you SAS guys were supposed to be something special. I thought you guys were supposed to be in good shape. Do you get back pain? Your posture is the worst I've ever seen.'

Then the woman chimed in: 'Are you cold, Trooper Fennell?'

Considering that I had recently been pulled from a freezer, I most definitely was cold, but I knew what she was getting at. She wasn't enquiring after my wellbeing; this session was obviously designed to humiliate the captive and shatter his self-esteem.

The man continued: 'You're a fucking disgrace. Stand up straight. Have a bit of pride in yourself.'

'And he's cold,' said the woman. 'Trooper Fennell, do you know why I *know* you're cold?'

I didn't reply.

'Trooper Fennell, answer me,' said the woman.

'I can't answer that question,' I replied.

'Look down. Go on, I want you to look at yourself,' said the woman, her face as cold and ugly as a rotting corpse. 'Do it!' she yelled.

I glanced down at my naked body, purely to keep the mongrel bitch at bay, but I didn't bother focusing on my penis or testicles. I had a good idea where my testicles were – probably somewhere in my stomach. This little session was doing wonders for my self-esteem. I decided to zone out and leave the interrogators for a while.

One soldier who had completed RTI training the previous year had reacted a little differently. This guy – unlike myself, of course – was a chronic masturbator. When the female interrogator made derogatory comments about his manhood, he began to touch himself. The woman left the room and he was given a mud bath.

I could still vaguely hear the interrogators yelling at me.

'You're a disgrace to the Australian army,' spat the man.

'You must be freezing, Trooper Fennell,' added Miss Sarcastic.

'Stand up straight. Take some pride in yourself, you sack of shit.'

'Don't be shy. Are you embarrassed?'

'Look at his posture. You've got the physique of a scrawny old man.'

'A scrawny, cold man,' said the woman.

Their comments continued – a flurry of lefts and rights that lacked any real punch. I visualised how hard I had pushed myself over the years. With my mind's eye I reread a Christmas card from my first martial arts instructor:

Keith,
I am so proud that you have achieved your goal.
A black belt is a clear indication that you can overcome any hurdle in your life. You have the spirit of the mind and body.
Chief Instructor,
Chopper Charlie

I remembered the countless hours my mates and I had spent on our knuckles doing push-ups, and how giving in to the pain and dropping to our knees was not an option, because to give up would have been to let Charlie down. I remembered the disappointment on Charlie's face when I told him that I was leaving to pursue another martial art.

He didn't try to talk me out of it; he just thanked me and said he hoped I found what I was looking for.

I recalled being belted from one side of the hall to the other by Instructor Paul as he passed on some of the finer points of wing chun kung-fu. He regularly took me for one-on-one training at the end of class, which was a privilege that must be earned. Then there was the time when Paul palmed one of my students – also one of my mates – a little too firmly in the chest, fracturing his sternum in three places.

I might have looked naked and vulnerable on the outside, but mentally I recalled Charlie's words: 'Power of the mind and body . . . power of the mind and body . . .'

I felt untouchable after that.

=

Later that evening I was moved into a hot room and made to do a physical training session with the other captives – my mates. Although I was blindfolded, I could hear the

A street march and demonstration shortly after achieving my first black belt.

others being abused, bastardisation at its best. At first we were made to do a combination of sit-ups and push-ups. After I had completed several sit-ups someone grabbed my knees and ripped my legs apart. We were already naked but this person obviously wanted to see more. This continued every three or four sit-ups. And while I was doing push-ups, what I expect were the same hands grabbed my hips and rammed my genitals into the ground in a fucking motion.

This degrading experience continued over and over again. It began to feel somewhat personal. I was certain that some sick prick was getting off on this, so when those dirty hands grabbed my knees for the umpteenth time I quickly raised my goggles, eyeballed the degenerate and whispered: 'I know who you fucking are,' before replacing my goggles and continuing with the exercises.

The weasel didn't say a word but his eyes were frozen with fear. I knew I had his measure. The degenerate left me alone, but others weren't so lucky.

The interrogators honed in on one individual and began a tirade of abuse. I knew the guy they were targeting. Their rants were raw, humiliating and personal. The man snapped, removed his goggles and threatened his captors. Our session concluded soon after that.

After another sleepless night and 32 to 36 hours in captivity, I was led outside and forced to kneel down. As the gravel pierced my knees, the sun kissed my back – a paradoxical moment of torment and pleasure. My hands were cuffed behind my back, and my head was lowered close to the ground. A guard removed my earmuffs and goggles, revealing a single piece of white bread on the ground before me.

'Eat,' he said.

I hadn't eaten anything since well before my capture, so I forced my face onto the stale piece of bread. Fearing it might be taken from me, I sucked the entire slice into my mouth and tried to chew. The little saliva I had was soon absorbed into the bread, which became a large dry ball. Swallowing was now impossible and I began to choke on the dry bread, dry-retching, with my hands still cuffed behind me.

'He's choking,' said one of the guards.

'Greedy fuck,' said another, removing my cuffs to allow me to dig the bread from my mouth. Hunched over half a dozen soggy bread balls, I devoured the slice like a dog, albeit in more manageable portions.

Later that morning I was questioned by two male interrogators. For 40 hours I had given them the big four and nothing more. Halfway through the session, one of the interrogators – the guy with the porno moustache – threw a tennis ball to me, which I instinctively caught with my right hand.

The two went into instant celebration, congratulating each other for making me crack. They appeared so excited that for a moment I thought they might try to fuck each other. When the euphoria settled down the man with the porno moustache said: 'You're right-handed. You've tried so hard to give nothing away, and now, just like that, we know you're right-handed.'

Not thinking straight, I responded: 'Yeah, well you could have worked that out by looking at my weapon.'

Damn it, I thought immediately after, realising that I'd taken their bait. But rather than allowing myself to become frustrated for making a mistake, I decided to move on and forget about it. I made certain that I answered the next question I was asked correctly. And the one after that, and the one after that. The guards were relentless.

'You fucked up and said yes. We've got it on camera!'

'We've got ya', you fucking screw-up!'

'You told us you were right-handed and you said yes! Now, what's your rank?'

'Private,' I replied.

'Come on, you've already fucked up. Just be honest. What's your rank?'

'Private.'

One of the interrogators pushed me down onto a chair. The other – the man with the porno moustache – continued: 'You're scared, aren't you? I can see your heart beating in your chest. Look down and take a look for yourself.'

I kept staring at the man's forehead, slightly cross-eyed so as to blur his face.

'Fucking look down, you fucking chicken shit!' exploded the man. He became enraged, yelling into my face from less than a foot away. He grabbed my arm and wrote *BROKEN* on it with a thick black marker pen. 'If this was real then I would have broken your arm, you lying fuck. What's your rank?'

'Private.'

'You fucking liar!' The man closed in again. 'What's your fucking rank, you –'

While he was in mid-sentence, I locked eyes with the man, angled my forehead towards his nose and slightly cocked my shoulder, as if I was about to smash him in the face.

His voice broke. 'You ... you chicken shit.' His eyes flickered and broke contact with mine, and his Adam's apple rose and fell as he swallowed a mouthful of nervous tension. He knew I'd heard his voice waver. He knew he'd been unable to maintain eye contact, and he knew I'd seen him swallow.

I rocked back on my chair, knowing that I had, without really trying, just scared the shit out of the man with the porno moustache.

'Guards!' he yelled. 'Get him out of here.'

≡

In my experience, it's the eyes – the type of stare and the size of the eyes – that reveal the most about a person. Large, vacant eyes might indicate that a person is overwhelmed or terrified. Their decision-making may be slow, poor or even non-existent. I have seen this numerous times in many different situations, from soldiers parachuting or coming under enemy fire for the first time, to soldiers conducting close-quarter battle training, where they are expected to make decisions rapidly in stressful situations. I have also seen it with children in the surf, or with elite sportspeople who are taken out of their comfort zones.

For me, however, the eyes that remain the most vivid – the eyes that I can visualise with perfect clarity, although it has been almost a decade since we locked stares – belong to the first man I killed in combat. He is now gone, but that intense stare of complete and utter panic will remain burned into my memory until my own eyes become dust.

Yes, the eyes can reveal many things about a person. Eyes of hatred cut like blades. Eyes of determination are sharp and focused. Eyes of sadness are narrow and moist, while eyes of love are soft and bright. The interrogator's eyes during that final RTI session were sheepish, jittery and distant.

Upon reflection, our interrogators were highly intelligent men. A couple of these guys should be nominated for an Oscar, such was their ability to hold character. But I'm certain there was at least one individual who got off on what they were doing. The person who continuously ripped my legs apart, grabbed my hips and rammed my genitals into the ground seemed a little too enthusiastic. He was either a brilliant actor who should be in Hollywood, or a filthy prick who was taking mental pictures for self-gratification.

≡

If I was to rate all my experiences, then the most uncomfortable to endure was, without doubt, extreme thirst. After that sits cold, then hunger. Next comes a lack of sleep or, in this case, sleep deprivation. Following the interrogation session with the man with the porno moustache, I was forced to sit with my legs crossed, my hands on my knees and my head straight for the next six to eight hours.

Including our time on patrol prior to being captured, we had not slept in 60 hours. Twenty-four hours without sleep is no more difficult than a big night out. After two days and two nights without sleep, things begin to get a little blurred. On the third day, after several adrenaline-inspired highs and lows, rigorous physical sessions and three or four interrogation sessions, you become somewhat delirious. We couldn't pop a pill or down a strong coffee. Sitting there unstimulated, fighting to remain awake for hours on end, is probably as punishing as counting from 1 to 1,000,000 and back again.

Dreaming about sex wasn't an option either. Sitting there naked and rocking to and fro with an erection would probably bring a bit more time in the freezer – no thanks.

I began to dream of sleep in the same way I occasionally used to dream of urination as a child. I remember fighting that lower ache and arguing with my subconscious mind. *Is the toilet before me bona fide, or is it just a façade? I'm not dreaming. I'm at school, standing in front of a toilet, dickie in hand, ready to let go. I've checked, double-checked.* I squeeze my penis. *This is real.*

The instant relief of letting go is soon replaced by panic as I wake up, mortified, pissing all over myself. Lying in soppy sheets and pyjamas as the sickly waft of piss penetrates the night air was like a shot of caffeine. I was no longer confused – I was without question very much awake!

=

I fought to remain conscious, my neck snapping back and forth, as sleep, like a drug, began to take control. As I began to hallucinate from lack of sleep, my mind drifted back to other times in my life. I remembered my other grandfather, Gerard, and how he used to challenge me when we went running, although he was almost 70 years old.

I recalled the look on my father's face when he told my ma that he found John, one of his closest mates, slumped over a machine and dead, electrocuted. I remembered walking along the railway tracks with my next-door neighbour and his dog. The high-pitched scream of a train's horn still evokes an image of my friend, hunched-over, pale-faced, his mouth open and screaming. The metallic chattering sounds of the train overpowered his voice. His dog panicked and was cut in half.

When you're in the bag, you have a lot of time to think. The memories that kept me company were not always pleasant or logical. They were generally the more emotional or dramatic experiences of my life. Now, at the age of 35, I have a far greater reservoir of experiences, but then, as a 22-year-old, I used my past to garner strength.

Our guards must have found this phase of the training rather amusing. First the head would tilt, and then the neck would relax, allowing the head to fall. I would wake up, disoriented, unsure of where I was. The pressure around my eyes and over my ears from the goggles and muffs became accentuated over the hours. My head felt like it was clamped into a vice, and my knees like they were squashed beneath a bus.

And then came sleep. The relief, the euphoria of falling asleep, allowed my body to relax. With my chin nestled against my chest, I pumped deep, slow breaths into the air. I was asleep. I was free. Life had never been so good.

Slap!

Huh, what was that? Where the fuck am I? I thought. My breathing intensified. My heart revved hard as I tried to remember where I was. I attempted to touch my stinging forehead, but my hands did not respond. *Where are my hands?* I could not feel them – they were numb. I pushed my head onto my shoulder in an attempt to remove the pressure from my cheekbones, and a needle of light pierced my blacked-out world.

This is RTI training. I must have fallen asleep. My head aches because I'm wearing goggles and earmuffs. My knees aren't smashed or broken. They're sore because they're twisted and crossed, like they were back at school. I heard fading footsteps. One of the guards must have slapped me. Fuckers.

My body relaxed and my heart slowed as the shot of adrenaline dissolved into my system. Once again I duelled with sleep. And once again my mind succumbed as I drifted from reality.

The guards probably waited a couple of minutes before stalking their prey again. With silent steps they approach the dozing man, taking extreme care so as not to wake him. Once alongside their victim, they might signal to the other guards that they're ready to attack. They might even rehearse the strike, teasing themselves – a bit of foreplay. Then, when they can't restrain themselves any longer, they slap the sleeping man in the forehead and watch as their victim snaps from the surreal to the real.

Over the course of the afternoon, the guards, who were probably just bored, kept themselves amused by increasing the intensity of the forehead slaps. I decided to look for some amusement too.

After sitting still for a while, I slowly lowered my head to my chest and took deep breaths, imitating sleep. Over my own muffled breaths, my ears hunted for sound. In my mind I pictured a guard creeping towards me. I was rather surprised when I heard a faint noise in front of me – a muffled laugh. My heart was beating hard as I thrust out both of my legs, my right heel connecting with something hard – possibly a shin. The guard made a startled noise and stumbled. I recrossed my legs and the footsteps drifted away.

My head continued to sway, tilt and fall as I plunged in and out of microsleeps. Hallucinations became as vivid as real life. A dull pain scrambled my mind.

A hand touched my shoulder, and another raised my earmuffs.

'Sleep,' said a voice, 'sleep.'

I'm dreaming, I thought. *I'll probably piss myself next.*

I was gently lowered to the floor. I had no idea if what I was experiencing was genuine. But the pain in my knees and lower back began to fade. *Perhaps this is real . . . they're letting us sleep*, I thought. I relaxed my mind and left the conscious world. I imagine the transition from one state to the next would have been no more than 10 seconds, probably less. Although my bed was a wooden floor, to this day I have never slept so deeply.

Fifteen minutes later my body was shaken violently and yanked to a seated position. *What the fuck is going on?* I thought, as I relaxed and fell back to the floor. Once again a pair of strong hands ripped me off the floor and slapped my hands against my knees. I was convinced that I'd been allowed to sleep because I had a broken arm, so I signalled towards my right arm before attempting to lie back down.

My earmuffs were lifted. 'Fucking sit up, arsehole, or you'll get a cold bath.'

Those words – 'arsehole' and 'cold bath' – helped with the orientation. I was now fully awake, as if snatched from the clouds and dropped onto a bed of broken glass. I felt nauseated from a combination of hunger, lack of sleep and a violent awakening. I would experience this abrupt wakening many more times over the years to come, from rockets zinging overhead in the middle of an Afghani night, to deafening explosions as bombs and rockets pounded Baghdad's International Zone. My instinctive reaction was always to grab my weapon; in Afghanistan it was a Para Minimi, and in Baghdad a Glock 17 pistol that I kept on a drawer next to my bed. But during RTI training we just had to sit there and play the game.

A guard pulled me up off the floor and I responded by falling back over. I had little sensation in my legs; the hours sitting cross-legged had restricted the circulation to my lower limbs. The guard, convinced I was messing with him, pulled me to my feet and tried to drag me across the room. Again my legs collapsed beneath me.

'Stand up!' yelled the guard as he pulled my arms high behind my back. I groaned as my shoulder joints found new levels of flexibility.

'Stand up!'

I leant back and made the guard support my weight. He struggled to keep me off the ground, his awkward hands fumbling over my body. The guard seemed uncomfortable, not knowing how to support a naked man. I remember finding this amusing. Another guard came to assist, grabbing a handful of hair and my elbow.

This was a welcome distraction from the deep burn that radiated throughout my lower limbs as a rush of blood gave them life. I hobbled – was dragged – across the wooden floor and down several steps to the familiar gravelled surface. The pebbles were sharp and the night was cold.

We walked for 164 paces. I remember because, for

whatever reason, I decided to count them. *100 plus the age of my grandfather when he died*, I thought. I was pushed to the ground. Lying there, my genitals squashed against the gravel, I heard the distinctive *whop whop whop* of a Huey helicopter. My handcuffs were removed as the *whops* became louder. I held my breath as the Huey landed close by, the rotor wash peppering my body with small stones and grit. I wondered where the guards were and hoped that they were copping it too. I guess they were nearby, as I was soon yanked to my feet and buckled into the Huey. The rotors increased in velocity and the Huey lifted into the air.

How fucking cold is it? I thought. The wind seemed to cut my skin like shards of ice. I sat hunched over, my head down and my arms pulled tight against my chest. I raised my goggles and noticed that I was on the starboard side of the helicopter. I looked to my right and saw a large man in a helmet seated beside me. He glanced in my direction, noticed I had raised my goggles and turned his head away. *He's not one of them*, I thought. *He's just the loadmaster.*

I turned my head to the left and saw three familiar shadowy figures squashed side by side. I reached over and tugged the hair of one. The startled man, still wearing goggles, raised his head and flicked it nervously from side to side. I laughed and did it again. I grabbed another one of the boys on the shoulder and gave a friendly squeeze. This man raised his goggles and spun around. It was dark but he was grinning, his white teeth reflecting the minimal light. He raised an earmuff and whispered something to the man whose hair I had pulled.

The loadmaster then decided enough was enough and signalled for us to replace our goggles. I obliged and returned to darkness. With my vision gone, there was little to focus on other than the cold.

≡

The next 24 hours of RTI training were to be less physically exacting than the first two days, but I found it an even greater test of my self-belief. During our first 48 hours in captivity, we were subjected to three or four alternate interrogation techniques. Some guys who divulged information were interrogated up to a dozen times. During my more vulnerable moments, I thought about my heritage, what type of person I was, things I had achieved and who I wanted to be. At times I did begin to doubt some decisions, especially my declaration of my rank as private rather than trooper, but I did not let this affect my self-esteem; despite the physical and emotional abuse, I still backed my decision.

In life, there are always going to be detractors – armchair critics, usually – who say something can't be done or who criticise those who push the boundaries. But as I see it, if you don't believe in yourself, how can you expect anyone else to?

Following our joyride, I was escorted across a gravel surface and told to stand still. The night air seemed to lack commitment in contrast to the wind chill we'd experienced in the back of the Huey. I was still naked and cold, but the shuffling sounds around me suggested that something was different.

Then a man spoke. 'Remove your goggles.'

I followed his instructions and saw that I'd been lined up with eight other soldiers from my troop. It also appeared that we were now in a mock prisoner-of-war (POW) camp. I briefly locked eyes with a couple of guys and observed that they looked just as dishevelled as I felt. I was shocked at their condition. We had only been in captivity for 48 hours, yet the men appeared to have aged considerably. Besides their haggard hair, the lack of sleep had left their faces lined and their eyes sunken and red. Our group ranged from 22 to 30 years of age. Fortunately I wasn't the youngest, so I was not required to take part in the first ridiculous exercise. Our troop commander was given a thick, black jacket – which looked very warm – and Evo, the youngest member of our troop, was told to pick off the fluff.

Evo is an intelligent man with great common sense. He is currently employed in Kabul but he lives in Brazil with his partner and young daughter. Growing up with three brothers and being educated in a boys' boarding school

Evo running Colleen through the Heckler & Koch MP5 on an SAS family day in Perth.

provided Evo with the edge he needed for military life. But as he readily admits, any outward display of affection does not come naturally.

Evo is a perfectionist. He's driven, works hard and is able to think clearly under pressure. Like Todd, he was well suited to close-quarter battle training, as his ability to think on his feet enabled him to make a decision quickly. The three of us would later be selected in the lead water-assault team on counter-terrorism duties. Evo was also calm underwater, a pleasure to work with when we had to dive in heavy seas, poor visibility or shark-infested waters.

During the first phase of RTI, Evo had assessed the time very accurately. Whenever he was outside, he would gauge the intensity of the sun; after 48 hours in captivity he was within a couple of hours of the correct time. Most guys had no idea.

Watching Evo pick the fluff off the Boss' coat was mildly entertaining. It was a peculiar task designed to establish an order of seniority. A few guys sniggered, but I remember feeling very much on-guard, so I adopted a vague persona and remained alert. During the next 24 hours our interrogators would attempt to divide our group, to fracture our team and create alienation. They would achieve their aim.

8

POW CAMP: OSTRACISING THOSE WHO RESIST

Feeling like an outsider, like you don't belong, is something most people experience in life. Children who are always last to be picked on a sporting team, immigrants from very different cultures, and those in same-sex relationships are some of the more extreme cases of those who experience alienation. A child who is bullied or ostracised over a lengthy time can become withdrawn, lose his or her confidence and suffer from low self-esteem. If someone is told something enough times, then they'll probably begin to believe it.

For 48 hours our interrogators verbally abused and degraded us. Most SAS soldiers are confident men with strong personalities, so the individual abuse we suffered had only a limited effect. But now, in the mock prisoner-of-war (POW) camp, where we were in a team environment, the interrogators attempted to divide our loyalty to the group by ostracising certain men.

My memory of the precise details of the camp commandant's opening address remains vague. The commandant was a 'grey man', more mediocre than impressive, and so his appearance largely eludes me. He had a full head of dark hair, perhaps greying a little on the sides, and a lean build. But I do remember his eyes – not their colour but the intensity of his stare. It was difficult to ascertain what the man was thinking. I had only noticed this a few times before.

The commandant introduced himself, informed us that we were prisoners of war and warned us that we must abide by the camp rules if we wished to be treated in accordance with the Geneva Convention. He also stressed that our interrogation sessions had concluded. He was very clear about this: 'Your interrogation is complete. You must now work together as a team. If you do not work together or if someone breaks the rules, then the group will be punished.'

Soldiers are selected for the SAS largely on their ability to work together during adverse conditions. When we heard that the commandant wanted us to work as a team, we naively believed that these next 24 hours would be relatively straight-forward.

But sneakily – or masterfully – the camp commandant had no intention of allowing us to work together. From the outset the interrogators' aim was to continue to gather information; and if any man resisted, he would be ostracised and made to feel like he wasn't contributing to the team – that he was letting his mates down. What better way was there to disrupt a committed team of men than to attack the very ideals on which they most prided themselves?

≡

We were soon ordered to line up and sign for a pair of pyjamas. I had no intention of signing anything, and I discussed this with Evo and Pete. The senior member of our group – an officer – was then chastised by the commandant for failing to control his men.

This was clever. If the guards could seed self-doubt in the mind of the boss about his own ability to lead, then he might lose sight of what the interrogators were trying to achieve. It was a successful ploy. The Boss ordered the rest of us to sign for our pyjamas. In the military you have to sign when issued equipment. This was, apparently, just routine.

I stood at the back of the line and when it was my turn, I picked up the pen in my non-dominant hand – my left – and scratched an X on the page. I then looked into the eyes of the man who was playing the enemy quartermaster and waited for his reaction. I saw him glance at my 'signature' before handing over a pair of oversized pyjamas. *Why didn't he say anything?*

Upon reflection, it should have been obvious to me why he ignored my protest. Our captors had already received a number of signatures, so to press for one more might alarm our group; they didn't want us to realise that they were still gathering information. Our captors wanted each man to relax, to drop his guard. After that, the information – polluted and toxic – should flow like the Ganges.

The intelligence officers were highly skilled, experts at manipulation. They had a plan, were well-drilled and were working together to achieve their aim. In contrast, we were prisoners who had not slept in three days and had to react to the commands of others. We were also not permitted to speak to one another. Whenever the guards saw someone speak, the entire group – except that individual – was punished. With no ability to communicate, we were unable to formulate a plan. And with no plan, we were isolated.

During the next 24 hours numerous scenarios were played out. At one point we met with a mock representative of the Red Cross. We were seated in a large room behind individual desks arranged in neat lines – it was like a schoolroom. The Red Cross rep flashed us some identification before beginning his performance. He was charismatic, funny and sincere. This man was so sympathetic to what we'd gone through that anyone would have thought he'd been there with us.

He said he would try to improve our living conditions and would see if he could get us something to eat. When he asked what we'd like, he was bombarded with wishful requests. I sat there and said nothing. It was pointless contributing to the conversation – there was no way this man was going to be able to source KFC or pizza, as the men were requesting.

The Red Cross rep asked general questions to the group, to see who would respond. He then targeted individuals, first those who were willing to talk and then those who were not. I scanned the room behind him, searching for cameras or anything unusual. He asked me how I was; I just raised my shoulders, as if to suggest I didn't know. He was clever. Sensing my resistance, he immediately targeted someone else. His aim was to establish rapport and trust. Pressing the wrong person for too long could have meant that the others might cotton on and also withdraw from the conversation.

When he left the room I tried to communicate my concern to my mates: I believed they were still gathering information. A man then burst into the room and demanded to know who had spoken. I said nothing, and so we were punished as a group.

We all looked ridiculous in our pyjamas. The waistband of my pants was more than double the size required. The elastic had been removed, so I was forced to tie the pants in a knot to stop them from falling down. The result: a baggy crotch and permanent wedgie.

While foreign music blared from some loudspeakers, we were ordered to construct a vegetable garden. I didn't have a problem with this. Scratching at the surface of the dry earth with inadequate gardening tools kept me warm. Some guys began to laugh, both at the hideous music and at the way their mates looked with their pyjamas tied around their stomachs like a group of belly-dancers. We were only permitted to speak to the prisoner whom our captors had placed in charge. He was to be addressed by his surname prefixed by the word 'brother'. Brother Fennell was never placed in charge.

Our captors allowed some joviality. When smartarse questions like: 'This music is good for our morale – is it possible to increase the volume?' were asked, our captors responded with witty comebacks that were sometimes hilarious. The more relaxed we were, the easier it would be for them to extract information.

We were then seated together on the floor in a small room, where we were addressed and engaged in conversation by another man. Although he looked different, I recognised him from one of my previous interrogation sessions. He was the man whose voice had broken when I eyeballed him. He asked us questions about the Sally Man – an iconic and much-loved figure in the Australian military who would turn up out bush and provide soldiers with biscuits and brews. Everyone loves the Sally Man. It was then that I was targeted a little more aggressively.

'So, Fennell, tell me about the Sally Man.'

I just grinned a dumbarse grin and looked at the floor.

'Fennell, what's wrong – don't you like the Sally Man?'

The man's accent was even more ridiculous than the ones I'd heard on selection. I just nodded my head.

'You do or you don't?'

Once again I just raised my shoulders.

'What we have here is someone who won't contribute to the team. Why won't you contribute, Fennell?'

I stared at the floor.

'Oh, we have a sulker?' said the man. 'Someone's not happy. Perhaps you find it stressful here? The others don't appear stressed.'

This was brilliant work by our captor. There were sniggers throughout the room. I was now being ostracised, beginning to be made to feel inferior to the rest of the group.

The man left the room and I finally spoke: 'Don't you guys see that these fuckers are still gathering information?'

'You feeling a little bit stressed, Keithy?' was one jeering reply. A couple of other guys laughed.

I could see what was happening and I found it deeply frustrating. For failing to contribute – that is, to provide information – I was being vilified as a non-team player, someone who was too uptight. With every mocking comment from our captors – many of which were genuinely droll – a couple of my peers had chimed in and taken the piss.

POW CAMP: OSTRACISING THOSE WHO RESIST 149

A man then entered the room and yelled at me for speaking. My mates were ordered outside and made to do push-ups on the dirt while I watched.

'You men are being punished because one of your own does not respect the camp rules. He spoke, knowing that if caught, you would all be punished. It is clear that this man is an individual who does not respect others.'

The leader of our group was then abused and stood down. I was placed in isolation.

Our captors unwittingly did me a favour, since the time alone allowed me to gather my thoughts without distraction. I reflected deeply. No one enjoys feeling like an outsider, and for an SAS soldier, being accused of being a non-team player is up there with being considered suspect under fire. As much as I wanted to join my mates and blend in with the group, I decided to follow my instincts and provide our captors with as little information as possible.

When I was released I rejoined the group back in the vegetable garden. The officer who had been deposed had a quiet word in my ear; he ordered me to 'play the game'.

'Can't you see what's going on, Boss?' I said, irritated that now I was being ordered to divulge information.

'The interrogation is over. We're in a POW camp and I'm ordering you to play the game.'

I turned to the other officer in the group and reiterated my thoughts. He seemed a little more receptive. I could see him thinking about it, nodding his head but continuing to stare at the ground.

Our captors, however, were diligent and were always on the lookout for anyone talking. They didn't want us to work together anymore. The group was punished again, and it was no surprise that I was made to watch.

We were then taken to the room with the desks and encouraged to sing. 'Music and song are good for morale,' we were told. It was like karaoke but without alcohol. I remained quiet and watched the show.

'Who's next?' said our captors. I rolled my eyes and waited for the obvious. 'What about you, Fennell? Would you like to contribute to the team?'

'Come on, Keithy,' said one of the boys.

I placed my head down on the table and waited for the mocking to begin. It never came, as one of the boys — perhaps wanting to be crowned karaoke king — sang a country song loudly and out of tune.

Next we were told that we were allowed to write a letter to our loved ones, to inform them that we were alive and well. *You can't be serious*, I thought. *This is ridiculous. Surely no one here would be stupid enough to write a letter and address it home.* I was wrong. Portions of these letters were later read out during our debriefing session. Now that was funny.

We were given a piece of white paper and several coloured pencils. I realised that to do nothing would have been to make a statement, thus further alienating myself from the group. So I took a pencil and sketched a large rectangle. I drew lines across the diagonals and then neatly coloured in each triangle with a different colour. The drawing had no significance or meaning.

We were handed an envelope and told to insert our letter, seal the envelope and address it. I wrote a fictitious street name and left it at that. Our captors collected the envelopes and told us that they would be posted. In fact, they took them to another room and analysed them for intelligence.

Evo had written: 'If a tree falls in the woods and no one sees or hears it fall, then does it really make a noise?' The interrogators thought he had lost his mind and were so concerned that they spoke with his patrol commander, who pissed himself laughing and said: 'I told him to write that as a message to me.'

≡

We were exhausted, almost delirious. We had only slept for about 15 minutes in nearly 84 hours. It is little wonder guys were singing and writing letters home.

In the afternoon we were allowed to sit on our beds but were not permitted to lie down or sleep. Our captors had made a few changes to our seniority, promoting troopers and demoting officers. Those in command were afforded additional privileges.

Pete, a mate of mine, approached me, slapped me on the shoulder and said: 'Well done, mate. You've been fucking staunch.'

Any self-doubt I had instantly disappeared. I had enormous respect for Pete. He was a hard man who could physically extend himself further than most. He gave 100 per cent in everything he did, whether it was soldiering, training or consuming alcohol. Even after a big night he was always in the lead group on a troop PT session.

Pete was passionate about soldiering – he was a natural warrior who always put others ahead of himself. Whenever a volunteer was needed for a shitty job, Pete would be the first to raise his hand. I know I disappointed him when I made the decision to leave the green machine. In fact, I could tell he was a little pissed off because we were good mates — I was one of his groomsmen — and I hadn't discussed it with him. Essentially, I hadn't wanted to be dissuaded by men who loved soldiering as much as I did.

If I had to pick a team of men to join me in war, it would be made up of men I know would remain by my side, whatever was going down. There is no doubt that Pete, for his loyalty alone, would be in that team.

Pete later told me that while he was being interrogated, he had started to believe the captors' abusive rhetoric. I had too, especially when they told me how pathetic I looked. They had told Pete that he might as well open up, as his mate Fennell had told them everything.

'You know, mate,' Pete told me, 'that's where they fucked up. I knew you wouldn't say shit. After that, nothing they said affected me.'

It would have been the same if they'd said something like that to me. Before we went into the bag, our patrol 2IC said to Pete and me: 'Just remember, guys, big four and nothing more, or you're a weak cunt.'

Pete and I shook hands and recited the words. I knew Pete would never break, not ever.

The Boss continued to get a hard time for failing to control his men. Once again he told me that our interrogation sessions were over, and once again he told me to play the game. I shook my head. We were both tired and had read the situation differently.

It was late afternoon, the final hour before the sun knocked off, when I was once again summoned outside.

I saw a man with a video camera filming one of the boys – our new leader – while he discussed the finer points of abseiling. The camera then turned on me.

'Now you will show us,' they demanded.

I was tired, and fed up with confrontation. It would have been far easier to just go along with their tiresome game, but I couldn't. I thought about what the Boss had said. I then thought about Pete's comments. He gave me strength.

Here we go, I thought. *Back in isolation*. I shook my head and spat: 'I don't have to and will not be filmed,' before attempting to walk off.

One of the guards stopped me, grabbing my face and aggressively forcing it towards the camera. Now I was beginning to get really pissed. I pushed the camera away and yelled again: 'I'm not doing it!'

I was ordered to return to the accommodation hut. We all were. Once inside, we were told to sleep. But I was furious – sleep would be impossible.

Twenty minutes later, one of our captors approached me and asked me to follow him outside.

'I told you, I'm not doing it,' I said.

'Follow me,' said the man.

Once we were outside, another intelligence officer introduced himself and told me the training was over. Naturally, I didn't believe him.

'Look, you were right,' he said. 'We were still gathering information. You guys haven't had any sleep for nearly four days, so congratulations, mate, you did well. Our aim was to create conflict and isolate those who continued to resist. It'll all come out in the debriefing session later. For now, I want you to calm down – don't try to escape. Just go back to your room and get your head down. You're gonna need it.'

I still couldn't trust him but I calmed down, returned to my bed and slept. *These guys are switched on*, I thought, as it had indeed crossed my mind to break out. Evo, Pete and I had even begun to discuss options.

Two hours later an SAS troop – our mates – raided the camp and we escaped. The next phase of our training – escape and invasion – would last for another 72 hours.

We were given our boots, a water bladder and one set of military fatigues. We found some hessian sacks, cut a hole for our head and secured them around our waists – an attempt to stave off the cold. We walked for most of that night, covering almost 20 kilometres, before trying to sleep under a large water pipe that runs between Northam and Perth. The cold earth sucked the heat from one side of our bodies while the ferocious wind stripped it from the other.

'Hey, Fenno, are you asleep?' asked my patrol 2IC.

'Hell no,' I replied.

'We couldn't hear you rolling around so thought you were either asleep or dead.'

I laughed.

'You cold?' he asked.

'Freezing . . . too cold to sleep,' I said.

'Pull it in with us, mate.'

The five of us huddled tight. I had never spooned with another male before, but right then I would have spooned with my old man if it had meant I was going to be a little warmer.

The next day we met an agent, who provided us with

shelter and food. We would lie up during the day and move at night. Over the next two days we followed the pipe towards Perth, covering a total distance of just over 50 kilometres.

≡

During our debrief, the intelligence officers informed us that each of the three troops in our squadron were vastly different. Mine was identified as the water troop, as we were slightly more aggressive and extroverted by nature. *This was true*, I thought as my mind returned to the morning we had to sing.

Next the intelligence officers discussed how they had attempted to create internal conflict within the group: 'When some soldiers continue to resist, it's likely that others will do the same. We attempt to ostracise these people and turn the group against them.' They mentioned my letter with the multicoloured rectangle and how they'd spent considerable time analysing it, before realising it was just an abstract, token contribution that gave nothing away. Initially they thought I had been subdued.

Finally, they told us how they had intentionally pressured those in leadership positions and attacked their ability to control the team; the aim was that the captured leaders would coerce their men to fall into line.

Strong leadership is vital, for without it a team will fragment into smaller and less effective groups. For example, Evo, Pete and I had all continued to resist, so we'd gravitated towards one another. We had even begun to discuss an escape.

This is why men who fail to display leadership potential are usually not accepted into the SAS. In my opinion, when working in small teams *everyone* must have the capacity to lead. A patrol 2IC must be able to assume control if his commander is killed or wounded. It is vital that the person filling this position is not just a sound administrator but a competent leader as well.

In the military, you're trained to follow orders, and if soldiers didn't respond to orders there would be anarchy. Just because a leader might make a decision you don't agree with doesn't give you the right to fly solo. Not everyone can lead, and not every decision a leader makes is going to be popular or even correct.

So when a poor command is issued, what is a soldier to do? I've learnt to choose my battles. If there is little at stake then I'll probably let it slide and save my energy for something more important. If it's important, your skills of persuasion come to the fore. Most people are open to advice, especially if it's for their own benefit and is delivered in a non-threatening, positive way.

The SAS isn't a 'Chinese parliament' – where everyone's opinion is worth an equal amount – but anyone in a patrol can and does contribute when a complex decision must be made. The strongest leaders I know are not driven by ego or intimidated by the abilities of others. They embrace the knowledge and ideas of those around them in order to establish the *best* course of action.

Often it's a commander who comes up with the right solution because of his superior experience, but sometimes it's the least experienced member of the team. He might bring something new, or have an ability to think outside the box. And of course there can be any number of hybrid solutions. When time permits, I believe this option offers the most diverse and rewarding results.

≡

During my time in the POW camp I made some mistakes. Rather than become frustrated when I was ordered to 'play the game', I should have been more discreet with my actions. The times when I made an obvious stand – my refusal to sing, to discuss the Sally Man or to allow myself to be filmed – ended with me being targeted and ostracised. Conversely, the times when I was more prudent in my refusal to engage – such as when I signed my name with an X, or when I drew the multicoloured box instead of writing a letter – enabled me to blend into the group without giving anything away.

Overall, it was a huge test of my self-belief. Having our captors, a superior and several colleagues challenge my actions, especially at a time when we were all deprived of sleep, did make me question my decisions. I took the time – when I was in isolation – to assess my thoughts. I had decided to back myself, and although I was concerned about being branded a non-team player, you should never follow a team if it's obvious they're headed in the wrong direction.

This is a message that I've tried to instil in my children: 'If you know something isn't right, then trust yourself and don't allow yourself to be pressured by anyone. To make a stand – to remain in control – requires far more courage than to jump aboard the popularity train to nowhere.'

9

HOSPITALS AND AFRICA: HUMANITARIAN OPERATIONS

While deployed to Indonesia on a special-operations training team in 1996, our troop — a conglomerate of soldiers from the water, freefall and mobility troops — took part in 'Binta', a task designed to win the hearts and minds of the local people, who had been providing us and the Kopassus — the Indonesian special forces — with fresh food.

An Indonesian commander organised a couple of favours for us to do in return. 'Tomorrow morning,' he said, 'everyone except the medics will be painting the mosque.'

I was a patrol medic so I grinned and tried not to laugh.

'Medics,' he continued, 'you are to meet at the clinic at 7 am with your medical packs. You'll be doing circumcisions.'

Did he just say circumcisions? I thought to myself. Most of the boys were still trying to come to terms with their job of painting a mosque, so no one really acknowledged the patrol medics' task. *Nah, he probably just made a mess of the translation.* I didn't give it another thought and continued to take the piss out of the painters.

The next morning, relieved to have dodged mosque-painting duties and under the guidance of a corps medic, three of us walked up the hill to the clinic, our med kits slung over our shoulders. We didn't know what we'd be doing and we didn't care. *Whatever it was, it had to be better than painting the mosque*, we thought. As we trudged along the heavily dewed track, I noticed a bunch of boys sitting outside the clinic – there were 17 in total. They were aged between about six and 14. The commander's previous words – 'doing circumcisions' – bounced between my ears like an echo.

'Did any of you guys hear the commander say we'd be doing circumcisions?' I asked.

'Yeah, but I thought he must have fucked up the translation.'

'Me too,' said another.

'They can't be serious,' I said.

For the village boys, the thought of being circumcised was terrifying: their pallid faces told us so. But for their parents and families, it was exciting, a time of celebration – an important initiation from boy to man.

A couple of Indonesian doctors were in charge of the operations and our job was to assist them. From the outset, their lack of hygiene and disregard for sterilisation posed a moral dilemma. The doctors weren't changing their gloves between operations, and their bloodied medical tools were used on one patient and then the next. We were horrified by the potential for cross-contamination. And apart from all that, in Australia many people – including medical practitioners – believed the operation itself was unnecessary and potentially harmful.

'Man, these guys are military doctors but they don't give a shite about hygiene,' I said. 'I'm all for gaining experience, but lopping off some poor kid's foreskin isn't what I had in mind.'

But we knew that, irrespective of what we thought or said, these boys were going to be circumcised. That was a given. We had a choice: we could refuse to take part and walk away, or we could employ our own stringent protocols of hygiene in an attempt to make the operations safer. We were all qualified to administer local anaesthetic and were competent in suturing – tying stitches. We unzipped our med packs, laid out our equipment and donned gloves.

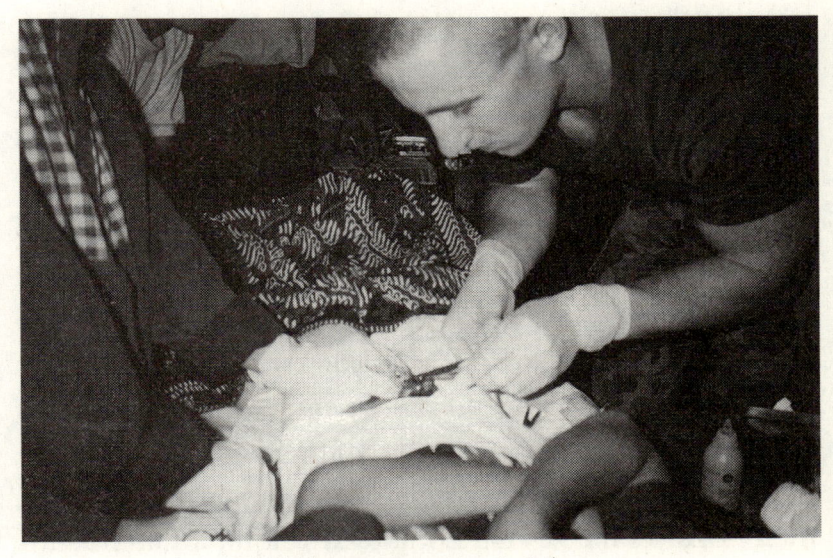

Moral dilemma: circumcisions in Indonesia.

While locking off the final suture on my first patient, I glanced at the boy's face to ensure he wasn't in any discomfort. I couldn't believe what I saw. The operation was not yet finished but a man who appeared to be the boy's grandfather had popped a cigarette into the corner of the child's mouth. I completed the stitch at the same time that a match sparked the cigarette to life. A coughing fit ensued.

'*Maaf pak, silakhan tunggu ya,*' I said – excuse me, sir, please wait.

The boy's grandfather just nodded his head in excitement.

I was more relieved than pleased with how the sutures looked. I'd taken my time. I wouldn't appreciate someone rushing stitches on my penis, and I'm sure this little guy would some day feel the same. I removed my gloves, shook the boy's hand and congratulated him for being very brave and strong. He smiled and I followed the doctor to the next bed.

As qualified SAS patrol medics, we were required to spend a couple of weeks each year attached to a hospital casualty ward to enhance our skills. We were permitted to give inoculations, to take blood, to establish IV (intravenous) access, to suture and dress wounds, and to assist with anything else that needed doing. Taking blood or establishing IV access in elderly people or children is far more difficult than it is in SAS soldiers. Most of the boys in the troop have veins like drainpipes, but if a soldier suffers from shock or blood loss, their veins soon contract. Locating a vein in a trauma situation is more like establishing a line in a young child.

When treating a casualty, SAS soldiers are advised to go for the median cubital vein – the large vein in the crook of the arm – but if access is unfeasible due to severe trauma or hypovolemic shock, they are trained to perform a venous cutdown – an emergency procedure where an incision is made in the ankle to gain access to the veins. Rehearsing on an old unconscious sheep in the hour before it is put down is one thing, but actually cutting into a mate's leg would take a lot of self-belief, especially if it had been many years since your initial training had taken place. The anatomy of a sheep's throat is comparable to a human's, so we were trained on them to perform other life-saving procedures, such as a cricothyroidotomy – making an incision in the front of the throat and inserting a small tube to bypass a restricted airway.

While working in Royal Perth Hospital, I was paired up with a sixth-year medical student. We were both under the guidance of a senior nurse.

'Which one of you would like to establish an intravenous line in the young girl in bed three?' the nurse asked us.

I looked at the soon-to-be doctor, indicating I was keen but I was happy if he wanted to give it a crack. He shot me back a look that said: *No thanks – I'm shitting myself.*

'I'll give it a go,' I said.

I established the IV. 'Nice work, Keith,' said the nurse.

Then it was the young doc's turn. An elderly lady also required a line. The doc swabbed the site and removed a 20-gauge cannula from its packet. He was having trouble locating a vein.

'Remember to tighten the tourniquet,' said the nurse.

He turned to me and said: 'Is it okay if you wait outside, because I get really nervous with someone watching me?'

I thought he was joking and laughed.

He secured the tourniquet around the woman's upper arm, wiped the site with an alcohol swab and lined up the cannula. Just before he punctured the skin he stopped again and asked the nurse and me to leave. I rolled my eyes and walked away.

'That really hurts,' I heard the elderly woman say.

I knew he had blown it – when you punch through the vein there is an instant dull ache. I had experienced this countless times in training while one of my mates attempted to persuade an assessor that they were in the vein. Some would even go so far as to turn on the IV and squeeze the bag, forcing fluid underneath my skin. I'd try to smile and would say: 'Yeah, good job, you're in, mate.' But in reality, what I really wanted to say was: 'You dick! My arm's killing me and I'll be left with a haematoma the size of a golf ball!'

While conducting his medical requalification training in the Regiment, one mate pierced my arm with an 18-gauge cannula. Over the years my arms had been stabbed many dozens of times, but never had I experienced such a sharp and intense pain. I knew he had fucked it up, but even the nurse who was assessing him was initially confused by the brilliant flashback of blood that had shot into the cannula. As he argued with the nurse, telling her that he was in the vein, I had to turn away because the pain was contorting my face.

'I don't think you're in,' said the nurse. 'How does it feel, Keith? Do you feel any discomfort?'

Discomfort . . . If this idiot doesn't stop arguing then I might have to punch him in the face, I thought. 'Yep, feels pretty good to me,' I said as I grimaced from the pain.

'I'm in,' he said as he attached the line and turned on the IV. But rather than clear fluid flowing into my body, bright-red blood shot up the line and began to fill the bag. 'See, look at the flashback,' he said in a pissed-off tone.

'Remove the IV,' said the nurse. 'You've cannulated his artery.'

He looked at me and I nodded with a clenched jaw and large eyes.

'Jesus, sorry, man.' He removed the cannula but didn't apply any pressure to the puncture and a stream of blood pulsed through the air, painting the grass at least 10 metres away.

'Put pressure on it!' yelled the nurse.

'Man, when it's my turn to jab you I'm gonna stick the thing in your eye,' I said, laughing.

He tried again on my other arm. This time he was successful.

At the hospital another time, a young woman – a model – arrived. She'd been involved in a minor vehicle accident and required a couple of sutures in her forehead. A doctor asked if I would like to do it.

'No probs,' I said.

He asked me whether I had sutured before, and I told him that I had never stitched a person but had practised on slabs of pig skin. The doctor's eyes bulged and he politely said he would take care of this one. Later that evening, a drunken, abusive man came in with a busted nose. He also required stitches; this time, my pig-skin qualification was sufficient.

≡

After returning from my first operational deployment, in February 1998 – an anti-poaching task in the southern Indian Ocean – I was keen to gain more medical experience.

I decided to organise a trip of my own. At the time, SAS soldiers were encouraged to venture overseas in what were known as 'Amelio' deployments. The primary aim was for soldiers to gain additional knowledge and experience, thus enhancing the capability of the Regiment.

In the 12 months that the project had been active, only one other soldier had made a submission. Although I was still a relatively junior member of the unit, I was confident I would gain approval for either a medical deployment to Chole Island, a small island 20 kilometres east of Tanzania, or a trip to Johannesburg, where I'd be attached to a hospital casualty ward. The prospect of treating gunshot wounds in Johannesburg was enticing, but I chose Chole Island as I believed I would learn more under the supervision of a former SAS Regimental Medical Officer (RMO) who had established a small medical clinic on the island.

I have always been drawn to positive people who aren't afraid to put themselves out there. The Doc was one such person. To be selected as our RMO was a feat in itself, as the position is always one that attracts much competition. Not content with this, the Doc decided to complete the selection course so he could better understand what it was like for the soldiers who took part. He received no favouritism and I'm sure that like everyone else, he learnt a lot about himself along the way. He passed the course and hobbled back to work.

I typed up an Amelio proposal and submitted the paperwork to my squadron commander. It came back later that day covered in red ink. I worked through his suggestions and submitted version two. This version copped an even bigger hammering than the first. After three or four knockbacks I was starting to regret making the application. As it was, I was only asking for $815 to pay for my accommodation and the flights from Dar es Salaam to Mafia Island, and that I be exempt from our compulsory week of med training the following year. With the amount of red pen my proposal received, anyone would think I was asking for a fully funded Contiki tour around Europe.

My troop commander sensed my frustration. 'Hey, Fenno,' he said. 'If it makes you feel any better, I don't think I've ever handed the Boss a piece of paperwork that he hasn't hammered. He loves his red pen.'

I didn't realise it at the time, but my squadron commander was doing me a favour. Besides testing my perseverance, he was nurturing me through the process because he wanted me to attain maximum growth. I was thinking about medical work in Africa – small picture – he was thinking about the process of organising such a trip – big picture.

I resubmitted my proposal again and soon learnt that I would have to present my plan to half a dozen senior officers, including the commanding officer of the SAS. *You've got to be shitting me*, I thought. *Just writing it was bad enough, and now I've gotta sell the freaking thing to the main man?*

I knew there was no way I could pull my submission without looking like a pussy, so I went home and asked my wife if she could give me a hand with a PowerPoint presentation. At the time, my computer skills were pretty much non-existent. I acknowledged the shortfall and within four months was touch-typing at 60 words per minute.

The presentation Colleen put together was probably a decade ahead of its time. It was so slick it bordered on ridiculous. When it was over, the commanding officer made a point of saying it was one of the best presentations he'd ever seen. My smug smile vanished when my troop commander enlightened the group that it had been my wife who had put the masterpiece together.

But the commanding officer approved my proposal. I was off to Africa.

The Doc and his wife had invited Colleen to join me, and she didn't have to be asked twice. We flew to Dar es Salaam and searched for a taxi. After 20 minutes we took our chances and threw our packs in an old banged-up station wagon. It was white and had a piece of mauve carpet glued to the dash. With not a lot of cash to throw around, we'd chosen to stay at the Safari Inn. For US$15 we weren't expecting anything flash.

Our taxi driver appeared genuine, and his face was full and smooth. But when he veered off the main road and began taking way down a couple of poorly lit alleys, I looked at Col and shook my head. 'If this dude tries to pump us over then I promise I'll snap his bloody neck.'

I felt a little foolish. Although I knew there wouldn't be a lot I could do if a group of his mates were waiting around the corner, I felt better knowing that he'd also have a pretty shitty night. We continued on. The sides of the alley were lined with corrugated iron, and the street narrowed to the point where it was impossible to open both left and right doors at the same time. Our vehicle headlights illuminated the dusty, potholed road.

The driver stopped the car and pointed to a building with barred windows. 'Safari hotel over there. I go check.'

I was tempted to follow him. There were many dull glows hidden behind drawn curtains. An armed guard approached the driver, they had a conversation and the driver returned. He looked relieved and told us everything was arranged. It was only the second time I had seen him smile; the first had been when he offered us a ride. I paid him and asked if he would pick us up the following morning. For this we scored smile number three.

Our room was surprisingly spacious, with two single beds set on opposite sides.

'This is cool,' said Colleen as she jumped onto her bed and unravelled the mosquito net.

I checked my bed and felt like Poppa Bear – someone with sandy feet had been sleeping in my bed. 'Do you want to go out for a look around?'

'No way,' said Col.

'Come on, we're in Africa.'

With an armed guard downstairs, Col was happy to stay in the room while I went for a walk. I removed everything from my wallet except for $10. Not far from the hotel I met a couple of locals who offered me some weed. I declined, so they asked if I would like a beer instead. I nodded and opened up my wallet nice and wide. They checked the contents and one of them signalled for me to give him two dollars.

With this in hand, he ran off down the road while his mate patted the kerb, encouraging me to take a seat. He smiled and sucked hard on his joint. I wasn't expecting to see the man who ran off with my two dollars again, and I didn't expect that Mr Weed was going to hang around either.

A couple of minutes later, the man returned with three bottles of beer, from which the caps had already been removed. I offered them both a bottle but they shook their heads and pointed to their joint. I was sceptical about drinking from a bottle that had been opened so I was adamant they joined me. They agreed to take one bottle between them; the other two were for me.

Before I had finished my second beer, Mr Weed signalled for my wallet, opened it, took out another two dollars and handed the money to his mate, who once again ran off down the road. He returned my wallet to me and smiled.

An Italian man wearing a white shirt and safari pants soon joined us, and so did three Masai men, their skin as dark and rich as chocolate. They were dressed in traditional red robes, wore sandals and carried spears. They were cool guys, and the Italian was able to smooth the boundaries between English and Swahili. Over the next two hours Mr Weed opened and closed my wallet three more times. The Africans preferred to smoke pot, while the Italian and I drank beer.

Colleen, wondering where I had got to, tiptoed out of her room and followed the laughs that bounced through the corridors. She was confused: she recognised my laughter but had no idea where it was coming from. She pressed her ear against several doors before returning to her room and going to bed. Not long afterwards, I opened the door, all smiles. Not even the grit between my sheets annoyed me that night.

The next morning, dressed in black pants and a white collared shirt, the driver waited eagerly by his cab. He looked like he was dressed for church. I wasn't surprised; he'd charged us $50 the day before. To him, we were easy money.

We spent the morning at the airport, arguing with a local travel agency. First they tried to tell us that our flights to Mafia Island had not been paid for, then they said there were no flights that day, and finally, after nearly six hours of waiting and heated negotiation, we were escorted to a dodgy plane, an old six-seater Cessna, out the back.

The plane had been double-booked, and it was obvious that our fares were supplementing a few of the locals'. Little wonder they didn't want us on the plane – there wasn't room. But I was adamant we were getting on, so we squashed our packs in the outside luggage compartment and boarded.

Col was petrified and refused to sit up the front near the pilot. She preferred to sit behind me, where she could close her eyes and pretend she was somewhere else. With just three seats remaining, seven other people piled on board; one guy was carrying a cage with a couple of chickens. The turbulent flight from Dar es Salaam to Mafia Island took 45 minutes, and I don't know who hated it more – Col or the chickens.

We retrieved our packs and were met by the Doc's wife, Jackie. She was a tall, attractive woman with a tremendous work ethic and keen sense of adventure. The Doc's boyish smile juxtaposed his powerful physique, which was well suited to playing rugby. They both were strongly motivated people, not by money but to provide the residents of Chole with sustainable primary health care. We rattled across

Chole Island, East Africa.

Mafia Island in an old four-wheel drive, which only took about 40 minutes. Then we bundled our packs and supplies onto a wooden sailing boat and enjoyed the 20-minute ride to Chole Island itself.

Chole forms part of the Mafia Island group, located south of Zanzibar. Largely surrounded by mangroves interspersed with quaint stretches of beach, the island has a tropical climate that is perfect for an assortment of palm and baobab trees. Thick rainforest dominates the centre. There are two rainy seasons: the short rains from November to December, and the long rains from March to May. Eighty per cent of the island's 2000 mm of rainfall each year comes during the latter season.

No vehicles are permitted on the island, and with no power Chole remains a reminder of what life was once like for millions of Africans. When the light fades, a hush envelopes the island as the locals retreat into their mud-brick huts, with sleep not too far away.

Besides the medical clinic, which the Doc and Jackie established in late 1997, an eco-tourism lodge was also being constructed. The owners have since done a wonderful job establishing a series of stunning treehouses that add to, rather than detract from, the island's natural beauty.

The 800 predominantly Muslim locals who lived on Chole Island appeared happy, their lives uncluttered and their days filled with fishing and subsistence farming. The Doc's residence had a biblical feel; a gravel path bordered by white coral led to a brilliant white building. Two red bougainvilleas dominated the entrance. The place looked so clean and so pure that for a moment I thought I might be refused entry unless I wiped the dust from my boots. But the goat shit that littered the front steps made me feel more at ease.

We arrived on 10 January 1999. The following morning I accompanied the Doc to the medical clinic, a 600-metre trek through the rainforest. By the time we reached the clinic my trousers and shirt were damp, my forehead shiny with perspiration. The clinic, small and clean, comprised two examination rooms, a birthing suite, laboratory, undercover waiting area, toilet and several storerooms. The floors, even in the waiting area, were concrete. The examination rooms had a couple of chairs, a wooden desk and a long examination table, which had been sanded smooth and painted with lacquer.

The staff were well trained and friendly. Although they only had a fairly limited grasp of English, what they did know was sufficient when translating between us and the locals.

Training for the local staff, Chole Island.

My first patient, a man aged in his mid-thirties, complained of numbness in his legs. The Doc waited until I'd asked a series of questions before telling me he was suffering from a disorder, Guillaine-Barré syndrome, which affected his bowels and limbs.

'Fenno, as you'll see, we're only able to provide limited treatment on the island. This man might never regain full sensation in his lower limbs. The main problem is infection, as he'll most likely cut his foot at some point and won't feel it.'

We gave the man a course of multivitamins and told him to regularly check the soles of his feet. There was nothing else we could do.

My next patient was a fisherman who had stepped on a nail. I cleaned and dressed the wound and sent him on his way. The next man, wearing a sarong and a loosely buttoned white shirt, hobbled into the examination room, propped himself up on the table and spread his legs. *A regular*, I thought.

The man smiled and revealed a dressing on the inside of his upper right thigh. What had begun as a minor graze had now degenerated into a deep tropical ulcer. I removed the dressing and held my breath as I inspected the wound. The stench, like a rotting mouse, was vile. A thin piece of sterile cloth – a wick – protruded from the wound.

'With something like this, it's better to allow the wound to drain,' the Doc said. 'We inserted a wick four days ago and he's come back to have it replaced. Even minor cuts can turn into deep ulcers in the tropics. Unless it's a clean cut, the best way to treat them is with either secondary healing or delayed primary closure.'

I took the end of the wick with a set of tweezers and slowly removed it from the wound. Like a multicoloured scarf being pulled from a magician's pocket, the pus-filled wick kept on coming. I cleaned the injury and picked up a fresh wick with a pair of forceps. Holding the wound open, I carefully pushed the forceps into the man's leg, my eyes flicking up to his face as I tried to ascertain how deep the sore penetrated. It wasn't until the forceps were at least three inches inside the man's thigh that he offered a wince.

'Keep going, mate, you can go a bit deeper,' said the Doc.

If I go any deeper I'll be through the other side, I thought.

I pushed until the man flinched again. I then began the tedious process of threading the wick into the wound. When it was done I removed my gloves and took a deep breath. 'That was pretty full-on . . . you're a tough guy,' I said, nodding my head. I didn't bother to ask the

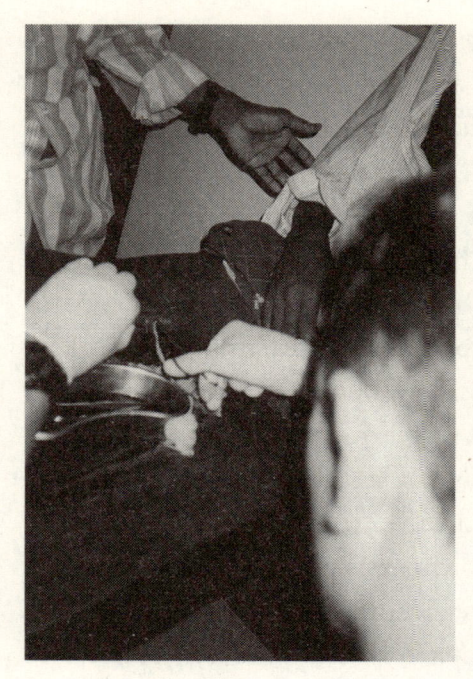

Inserting a sterile wick into a man's leg.

translator to spell it out; the man could see I was impressed.

That day I treated about a dozen patients, from prescribing half an Asprin to thin the blood of a woman with high blood pressure, to treating otitis externa (pus-filled ears), a fungal infection, food allergies and mastitis. The most difficult patient to diagnose suffered from an array of problems: difficulty breathing, swollen feet and clubbing of fingers (thickening of flesh underneath the fingernails). He also had an enlarged liver and spleen.

'It's highly likely this guy has HIV that may have progressed into AIDS, but without a blood test there's no way to be sure,' said the Doc. 'All we can do is treat the symptoms and try to make him feel more comfortable.'

The true extent of HIV on the island was unknown, but according to reports in Dar es Salaam, 60 per cent of all donated blood in the capital was infected with the virus. Because there was no way of determining whether or not someone on Chole Island was HIV positive, it was likely the virus was spreading at an alarming rate. The key was education.

There was one young man who came into the clinic with fluid-filled lungs, a large abdominal tumour and a severe rash over his stomach and lower chest. The lymph glands in his neck, under his arms and in his groin had become so enlarged that two of them had ulcerated the skin and burst.

'Fenno, what's your diagnosis for this guy?'

'By the size of his lymph glands, it looks like he has a major infection,' I said, frantically flicking through my *Patrol Med Aide Memoir*.

'What about the rash?'

I consulted my handbook. 'I don't know...it fits the description for herpes.'

'Yeah, it's called herpes zosta. It's a painful rash that can be triggered by a low immune system – a strong indicator that he has AIDS.'

'Can we tell him we think he has AIDS?' I asked.

'No, not without confirmation. I would say he has less than three months to live.'

As I looked at the man, my chest felt heavy. I asked him if I could take his picture, and he smiled and nodded his head. He stood still, his hands by his sides, his head tilted slightly to the right. I have since analysed this photo many times and wondered when it was that he died. My eyes are drawn to the burst lymph node on the left side of his neck. I then look at his eyes, which have the stare of someone who has just died. This man knows something pretty bad is going on inside him.

He would have passed away nearly 10 years ago. To most, he is just another statistic, another African nobody who has succumbed to the virus. But during

178 **WARRIOR TRAINING**

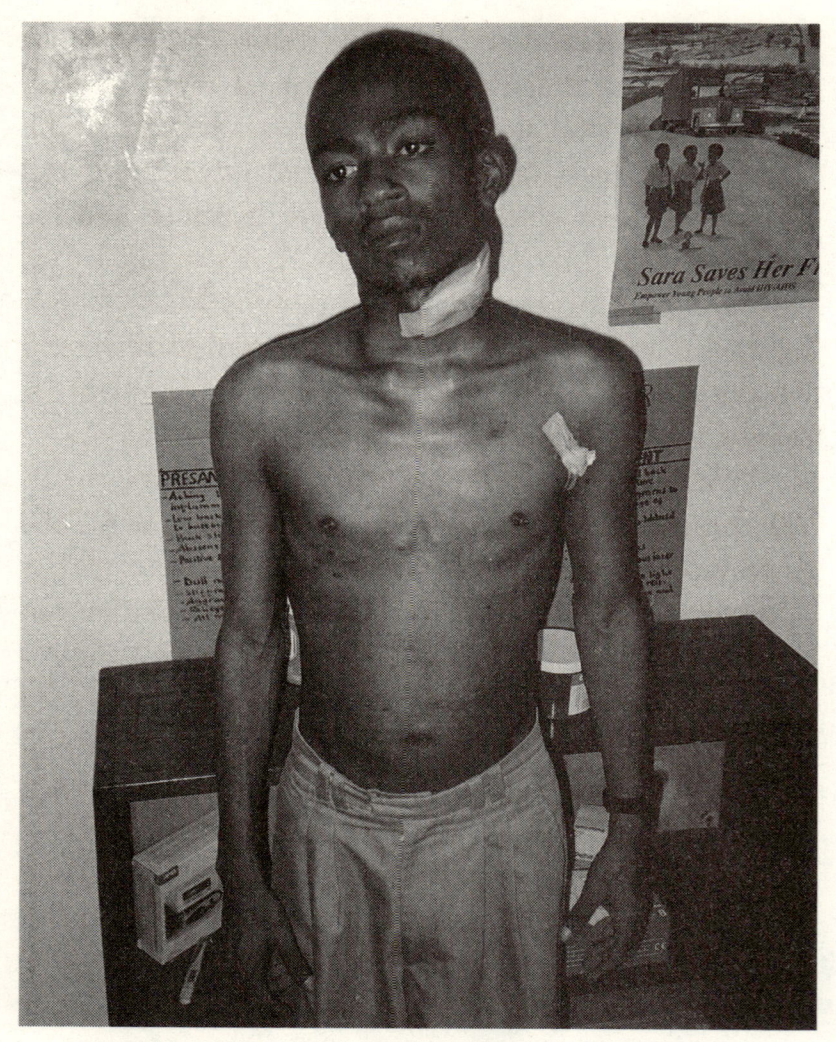

This man knew something pretty bad was going on inside him.

his examination, I saw a cheeky side to his persona that I liked. For me, this man was real, as real as death. Sometimes when I think I'm having a shit day I recall this sort of experience, which enables me to put things in their right perspective. A shit day, in reality, is usually still a pretty good day.

That evening, Col and I went for a walk around the island. We climbed through the remains of what appeared to be an old German garrison. Just a few walls remained, swallowed by the forest and covered with vines.

=

The next morning a man came to the clinic with two puncture wounds on his left ankle. He was in the water when he was bitten by a snake. I immediately applied a pressure immobilisation bandage and informed the Doc.

'Does he feel nauseated or have any stomach cramps?'

'Not that I'm aware of. He looks fine.'

'Then it's probably not poisonous. If it was then there's not a lot we could do. He'd be dead before we got him to the mainland.'

'What, there's no antivenom, not even on Mafia Island?' I asked, almost horrified.

'Nah, mate, depending on the type of snake and the amount of venom, it will either kill him or it won't. Was the wound bleeding?'

'No, it was dry.'

'That's a good sign,' said the Doc. 'Just keep an eye on him and see how he goes.'

I asked the man to wait outside but when I returned he was gone.

Many children on the island were anaemic and had swollen stomachs. We treated them for worms and prescribed Mebendazole. Malaria was also prevalent. We took a blood sample which we analysed under the microscope. Although the Doc explained it several times, I was flat out focusing the thing, let alone making an accurate diagnosis. Children were treated with chloroquinne and liquid paracetamol.

One woman regularly came in complaining of seeing smoke in her eyes. It was bizarre but I think she liked me. Her eyes were fine but she did have high blood pressure. We gave her some tablets to lower her blood pressure. *I'm sure I'll see you in a couple of days*, I thought. She was back the next day.

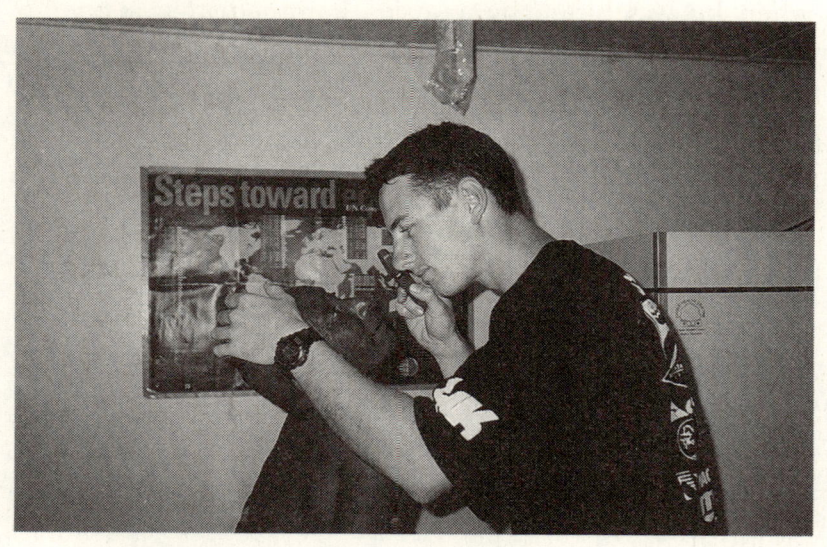

'I think she likes me.' A woman who complained of smoke-filled eyes.

When I arrived at the centre on 16 January, I saw an elderly man seated in the waiting area. His feet were swollen to an enormous size. *What the freak is going on there?* I thought. The Doc told me the man had elephantiasis. It is caused by a parasite that blocks up the lymphatic system, preventing it from draining.

'If you catch it early, it's reversible,' said the Doc.

'What about this guy?'

'Unfortunately, for him it's too late.'

Running a children's clinic, Chole Island.

It must have been a day for feet, because my next two patients both had deep gashes on their insteps. The first man had been struck by a machete, while the second had had an outboard motor dropped onto his foot. There didn't appear to be any broken bones so we cleaned the wounds and applied steri-strips.

On our second last day the Doc asked if I would like to run a children's clinic.

'Sure,' I said. 'It'll be a good way to finish off.'

Mothers and their babies were lined up all over the place. For them it was a special day, and they'd dressed their babies in their brightest, most flamboyant outfits. They looked gorgeous, but after I'd examined 85 of them I shot Col a look that said: *Is 25 too young to get a vasectomy?*

My initial motivation for wanting to go to Chole Island was two-fold. I hoped to increase my medical knowledge in order to become a better soldier, and I was after adventure. A deep desire to help others really hadn't entered my mind. But after spending a couple of weeks with the Doc and Jackie, their sense of humility and service had a big effect on me.

I'm a believer in the saying 'Hang around what you wish to become'. If you want to be a happy person, stick with people who make you laugh. If you aspire to be a back-stabbing arsehole who never has a good word to say about anyone or anything, then I'm sure there are plenty of people out there who can show you how to get there. The Doc and Jackie were two amazing people who were having an enormous impact on the lives of many. Everyone has goals and dreams for their future, but I don't know too many people who are more driven to help others instead of themselves.

=

On 23 January Col and I left the island and began our journey north to Arusha. Trying to find the right bus was tough – there were at least 50 jammed in a depot, all parked at different angles with hundreds of people running around yelling. A large African man offered me a challenge.

'Hello, mister, do you box?'

'Do I box,' I said with a smile, as I looked at Col and tried to work out what the guy was on about.

'Yes, boxing. Fitness.'

He began to throw a few punches and dance around.

'Only a little,' I said.

'You look strong. You want to come to boxing gym and train fitness?' He grabbed my upper arm and squeezed it. 'Ooh, very nice!'

Colleen laughed but I knew the guy was serious. He

called over a few of his friends and encouraged them to grab my arm. They were a little less exuberant and just stood there smiling.

'We like fitness and we train very hard,' said the man.

'Yeah, you look fit,' I said.

He flexed his bicep and signalled for me to touch it.

What the hell, we're in Africa, I thought. *If he gets an erection I can always boot him in the balls.* 'We're trying to find the bus for Arusha,' I said.

'Arusha,' he said, excited. 'Come!'

He grabbed my arm and, after a bit of frantic running around, proudly directed us to the right bus.

We thanked him; he smiled, flexed his bicep and left.

We'd paid for three seats – an entire bench seat – but a young African man had squirmed his way between Col and the window. Col looked uncomfortable so she and I traded places. Having the man's sweaty skin pressed against mine was a little irritating.

A woman with a box containing bananas and bottled water tapped on the window.

'How much for two bananas and two bottles of water?' I asked. I had no intention of negotiating; I just wanted to know how many Tanzanian shillings to dig out of my bumbag.

The man next to me took it upon himself to translate and said 3000, the equivalent of US$5. I handed him some money to pass to the woman, and then three bananas and bottles of water were coming our way! The man next to the window kept one of each for himself.

I looked at Col and shrugged my shoulders. *He must have slipped the lady some cash*, I thought. At the next stop

I ordered two ice-creams. Once again, three items were passed back through the window. This time I was laughing. 'How's the hide of this guy?' I said to Col. By the time I had unwrapped my ice-cream, the man had already wiped his lips and thrown his empty stick out the window.

When we arrived at Arusha we were swamped by scores of African men, from overzealous tour guides and hotel workers to men selling local ornaments. I was busy refusing offers when I heard Col scream. I turned around and saw three or four guys with their hands all over her. One was holding a maroon tea towel over her face while another had unzipped her bumbag and was helping himself. I launched into them and sent a couple reeling. I pointed to the man who'd had his hands in her bumbag and told him something that he'd definitely understand: 'You – fuck off!'

He returned the compliment: 'Fucking Americans,' and he walked away.

Col was rattled by the experience so I told her to walk in front of me so I could keep an eye on her. I pulled a map out of my bumbag and we headed off to the YMCA Hotel.

That evening we caught up with Alex and Eliza, friends from Australia who were joining us on a trek up Mount Kilimanjaro. They had flown into Nairobi but had missed their connecting bus to Arusha, so they'd organised a lift with some locals. While squashed in the back of a big black sedan, with several thousand dollars in their pockets, they began to realise how vulnerable they were. There were no streetlights, just a dark road, a car, several men and them – two trusting Aussies.

Eliza is usually pretty controlled but she'd been angry with Alex for their situation, repeatedly referring to him as a 'c—'. She was pissed off that Alex would, most likely, have been killed quickly, leaving her to deal with what followed on her own. She's an attractive young woman and her long, reddish-blonde locks often grab the attention of both men and women. Once a few years earlier when the four of us were in Sydney, a woman handed her a card with a contact number, saying: 'Don't worry, darling, heterosexuality is curable.'

After dinner we relaxed with a couple of drinks. Al and Liz's account of the drive was now hilarious. We sat at a table with a well-dressed African salesman who wore a big shiny watch. I asked him what he sold; I was thinking diamonds.

'Soap,' he said.

'Are you coming to bed,' Col asked me.

'Nah, I think I'll hang around and watch the cricket for half an hour.' Australia was playing South Africa.

'We're out of here,' said Al.

'See you guys tomorrow,' said Liz.

They were barely around the corner when the African man leant over the table and said: 'I think I'll retire too.'

Well, thanks for letting me know, I thought.

Then he dropped his room key into my hand. 'I'm staying in room 16 if you would like to join me.'

I dropped his key on the table and pretended that I didn't understand what he was on about. 'Nah, I'm watching the cricket,' I said, flicking my head back towards the small, fuzzy screen.

'As you wish.' He picked up the key, grabbed his briefcase and calmly left the room.

=

186 WARRIOR TRAINING

Early the next morning, from the first floor of the YMCA Hotel, Col and I saw Mount Kilimanjaro for the first time. The ice-capped volcanic rim sat above the clouds, and the round dome glowed in the morning light. We were excited to get going and make it to the top.

With a summit of 19,340 feet – or 5895 metres – above sea level, Kilimanjaro doesn't rate a mention for the serious mountaineer, but of the 30,000 people who attempt to summit it each year, many thousands fail due to a lack of preparation and altitude illness. On average, 10 Western climbers are killed annually on the mountain.

Treks to the north or south base camps of Mount Everest (at 17,600 feet and 17,090 feet respectively) take between 11 and 13 days. To summit Kilimanjaro, depending on the route, budget and tour company you use, only takes between 72 and 96 hours. Trekking from 4000 feet to nearly 20,000 feet in a couple of days is difficult as you

Mount Kilimanjaro from a distance.

have very little time for acclimatisation. Some people are more susceptible to altitude illness than others.

Since joining the Regiment, I had been pushed to the verge of my limitations several times. SAS soldiers must be able to keep going when their body is screaming to stop. But physical fitness and strength will only take you so far. It is the mind – your ability to hold it together when things get really tough – that can give the greatest rewards.

In the weeks before we'd departed Perth, Col had been so excited about the trek that she showed some of her work colleagues a miniature Aussie flag she intended to pull out on the summit.

'Providing you make it to the top, that is,' said a guy named Steve.

Up to that point, Col had assumed that making the summit was a formality. Steve's comments upped the ante for her. She started training even harder, squatting up to 70 kilograms and stomping up and down Jacob's Ladder, a mad set of stairs in central Perth, with a daypack. She also played touch football and worked on her upper-body strength. She could pump out seven chin-ups.

Eliza had also done some training. She and Al had been for a walk the day before they left.

We decided to climb the Machame route; it was steep and a little more expensive, but was regarded as one of the most beautiful routes and would get us away from the masses. There were no huts, though, so we had to hire tents. The locals referred to the Machame as 'Route Whiskey' because it was difficult. One guide and three porters were required per couple.

Alex treks through the rainforest on day one, Mount Kilimanjaro.

The most popular route was the Marangu, or 'Coca-Cola' route, which was slightly longer but far less severe. Dozens of people – up to 70 – travelled the Marangu every day.

We began the trek wearing shorts and T-shirts, as we pulled and stepped our way through a maze of vines and slippery tree roots. The humidity thinned as we negotiated the alpine country, where long grasses, moss and needle-leaf trees replaced the rainforest. We walked approximately 15 kilometres that day, ascending from 6500 feet to 10,000 feet. Camp One was damp and cool.

On day two we left the alpine country and arrived at Shira Hut, a flat rocky plateau sparsely covered with grass and small bushes. We were now perched at 12,500 feet and had covered another nine kilometres. A thick fog had swallowed the mountain.

That night Eliza had a severe headache and began to vomit. I was concerned that she was suffering from altitude illness, but by the following morning both Col and I were also feeling pretty average so it was most likely a stomach bug. I had a word to our guides and asked them to ensure they boiled our drinking water for at least 10 minutes.

Day three was always set aside for acclimatisation, so for most of the day we remained inside our sleeping bags, tucked up in the foetal position, and tried not to shit ourselves. Eliza, Col and I had lost our appetites, so Alex, who was the only one feeling okay, consumed a ridiculous number of hard-boiled eggs.

With each egg he popped into his mouth, he smiled and said: 'Mmm, more protein for me.' I knew eggs and altitude weren't a good mix but I decided to let Al find out for himself. Within a couple of days he too began shooting caramel milkshakes out his arse.

Day four was brilliant. The morning sun was warm, and the air cool and thin. We began climbing again, and by midday there was very little vegetation around us. The landscape was nothing more than rocks and scree. We passed a group of 14 climbers who had established camp at the Lava Tower, a large rocky outcrop that stuck out like a big wart. For most of the day we saw no one else, which was just the way we liked it. We arrived at the base of Arrow Glacier, 16,000 feet above sea level. The late afternoon sun doused the landscape in contrasting shadows. It was cold and beautiful.

'Is anyone keen to walk to the snowline?' I asked. I'd only seen snow a couple of times before and I wanted to touch it.

'Nah, I'm not walking all the way over there,' said Al.

'We'll watch you,' the girls said.

It took me about 20 minutes to reach the base of the cliff. Before I had even touched the ice, I heard a sharp cracking sound followed by distant screams. I didn't bother looking around; the roar of a massive boulder – the size of a small car – bouncing towards me had my undivided attention. I maintained a constant visual as I shuffled to my

A perfect day for trekking on Mount Kilimanjaro.

left. As it gained momentum, the frightening sound of rock slamming into rock intensified. I stopped when I realised I was no longer in its direct path, and I watched it thump by no more than 20 metres to my right.

I stood there a moment and examined the cliffs, my heart beating hard. The weight and speed of that rock was one of the most powerful things I'd ever witnessed. I felt okay so I walked back to the ice and touched it.

Yep, the ice is hard and cold, I thought. *No different from the stuff in the freezer. You're an idiot.*

Access to the summit via the Arrow Glacier was closed for several months in 1996 after three Western climbers were killed by a rockfall. Sometimes people contribute to their own demise, but sometimes, despite the utmost planning and care, Mother Nature just wins out.

We went to bed early as we knew we'd have to set off in the middle of the night. With the sun gone, the temperature had dropped to well below freezing. Col had to go to the toilet, but venturing outside meant throwing on several layers of clothing.

'Just hang your bum outside the tent,' I said. 'There's a fly, so no one will see.'

'You reckon?'

'Yeah, go for it.'

I waited until I heard the trickle of fluid hitting gravel before calling out to one of our guides: 'Hey, Thomas, can you come here, please? Colleen wants to show you something.'

Col was mortified and the casual trickle soon turned into a fire hydrant as she forced the fluid out and dived into her sleeping bag.

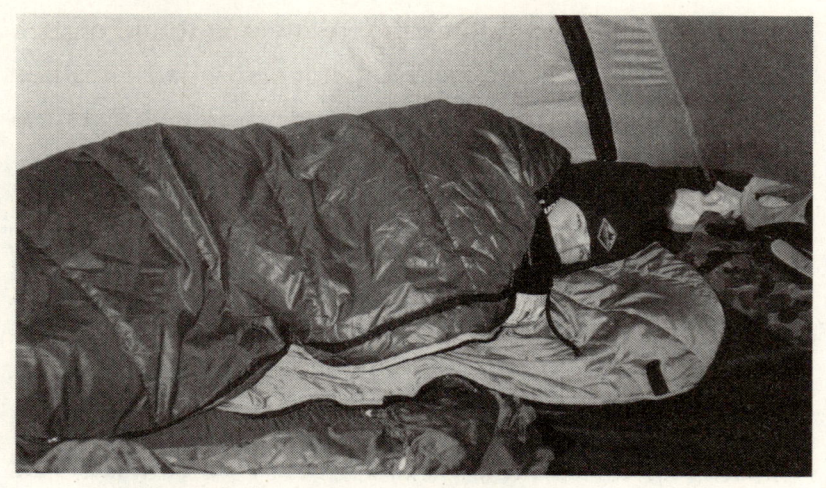

Colleen dived back into her sleeping bag after our guide, Thomas, nearly caught her in a compromising position.

'What's up, Mr Keith?' said Thomas.

'Nothing, Thomas,' said Col. 'Mr Keith's just being an arsehole.'

I laughed and pulled my head inside my sleeping bag.

Throughout the night a strong wind lashed our tents. None of us was able to sleep; I was checking my watch constantly. We rose just after midnight, slowly got dressed and readied our gear. It was cold, but by 0050 we were on our way. We'd been walking for a couple of hours when Col needed a toilet break.

Alex became frustrated because he was cold.

'Why don't you put your Gortex jacket on?' I asked.

'I don't have one.'

'What do you mean? Liz showed me the jacket she bought you — it was perfect.'

'I took it back,' said Al. 'I thought 400 bucks was a waste.'

'You tightarse. Is that all you've got, a $30 spray jacket?'
'Yeah.'
'You dick.'

Al had been sweating underneath his spray jacket, so when we stopped moving he was crippled by the cold. Col was missing, Al and the guides had the shits because they were cold, and Liz was crying because she was afraid of heights. Adventurous holidays with friends and loved ones can be such fun.

I went to look for Col so we could get going. Not knowing that she had diarrhoea and stomach cramps, she took offence with my tone and lashed out with a left. I offered her a drink of water but my camelback hydration pack was frozen. We laughed and shared a Mars Bar instead.

From that point on, Col set a cracking pace. Despite the thin air, she was powering up the mountain. By 0515 we had reached a plateau and began skirting around a large glacier. Al and Liz had been suffering from altitude illness for a couple of hours and both had severe headaches. As we scaled the final 200 metres, my brain also felt like it was being cut in half.

By the time we reached 19,000 feet, all of us except for Col were dizzy. We could only walk 20 to 30 paces before having to sit down. My heart was pounding as if I had just completed a running race, and our lungs had to suck hard for air. There never seemed to be enough oxygen to go around. The air was cold, the coldest my lungs had ever inhaled. The guides said it was somewhere between −15 and −17 degrees Celsius.

As we approached the summit, Col started jumping up and down. *Where in the hell is all this excess energy coming from?* I wondered. To our right was a thick glacial wall rising above a frozen body of water. To our left was a brown box with three metal poles jutting out of the top. The rock beneath our feet was uneven but not slippery.

As we got closer we noticed the box was covered with stickers. There was also a brown piece of timber, a metre

Colleen as the highest person in Africa.

long and 20 centimetres wide. Carved into the wood in yellow letters were the words: *YOU ARE NOW AT THE UHURU PEAK, THE HIGHEST POINT IN AFRICA. ALTITUDE 5895 METRES A.S.L.*

It was a euphoric moment, and we were the first to summit that day. No one was more excited than Colleen. She had trained hard and was ecstatic to have achieved her goal. In fact, she was so excited that she insisted that she sit on my shoulders and get a photo – proof that she was, at that moment, the highest person in Africa.

10

PHYSICAL TRAINING

Six months after joining an SAS sabre squadron, I was given the task of coordinating the physical training (PT) for a troop of 20 SAS soldiers. I was offered this task during my first year in the troop because of my passion for physical fitness.

Intense physical training has always been an integral part of my life. When I'm training hard, I feel there's nothing in life that I cannot achieve. I feel in control, in charge of my own destiny – proactive, rather than reactive. The endorphin rush that comes from an arduous workout gives me an addictive natural high that I would struggle to live without. It makes me feel alive. My senses sharpen and life's stresses become less significant. They don't disappear, but they are re-categorised – refiled in order of their real priority.

Running the PT for a troop of SAS soldiers was hardly a challenge, as all the guys were highly motivated – many already were at an elite level of fitness. My job was to ensure we achieved a balance between cardiovascular fitness, strength and endurance, and that the sessions were controlled; in an SAS water troop, where alpha males dominate, physical training could easily become a testosterone-charged dick-pulling contest. In writing this, however, I know I've been guilty of running my fair share of sessions like that, especially during my first couple of years in the troop.

≡

Seeing the way my three children approach exercise takes me back to the type of child I was growing up. Children are motivated by what they see and hear, but if a child has no interest or desire to do something, then it's not going to happen. Our eldest daughter, Tahlie, who is eight, often rises early, throws on her swimmers and a jumper and sits next to the garage door in the dark to ensure I don't leave for a session down at the beach without her. When she was seven she conned me into letting her paddle her

Tahlie doing what she loves most: catching waves on her paddle board.

nipper board from our local beach to a distant headland – a return trip of 3.5 kilometres. Colleen wasn't happy and said, 'If she doesn't come back then it's probably best that you don't either.'

The journey saw us negotiate some deep sections of water about 500 metres from the coast. On the way back I noticed that a lot of the time Tahlie's forehead was nestled on the front of her board – her neck wasn't strong enough to cope with the demands of such a long paddle. At one stage she peered at me through her stringy fringe and I saw that her forehead was chafed. I smiled to myself. *Bet you won't be bugging me to do this again for a while*, I thought.

What came out of her mouth surprised me: 'Dad, can we do this every Sunday?'

Her younger sister, Sian, aged seven, is no different. When she was six we went for a jog; I was thinking she'd be content with a couple of laps around the oval. After the first lap she told me we'd be doing it 20 times. And as for our son, Reyne, who has recently turned five: he's yet to start school but has asked his mum, Colleen, if she will train him for the school cross-country races.

So when did my passion for training begin? My parents weren't really into it. Ma played tennis and Dad played a little touch football. He also curled a piece of steel he kept in the garage, which gave him a set of arms that intimidated all my friends. I was probably nine or 10 years old when I told my organ teacher about an impending sports carnival. He was a young guy who didn't care about teaching music, and I was a kid who had potential but didn't wish to learn – perfect! Our 30-minute session was usually filled with him talking about girls and cars while I played

'Can we go for a run, Dad?'

a song or two. I told him that I wanted to beat a guy called Jamie in the 100-metre sprint as I was sick of coming second. He told me I needed to do sprints on the road to strengthen my legs.

The next day I rose early, threw on a pair of sneakers that probably had very little padding, and sprinted up and down the road, from lightpole to lightpole. Apparently, my shoes slapping against the bitumen made quite a racket as my neighbours soon asked my parents what I was doing. Not one to do anything in moderation, and having no clue about recovery, I pounded the asphalt every day for a couple of weeks.

After smoking Jamie, I ran to my ma, who was watching from the hill, and blurted out: 'Mum, I did it! I beat Jamie!'

Her face instantly changed colour. 'Keith, this is Jamie's mum . . .'

Then my face changed colour. Although I'd beaten him, the poor bastard had been suffering from a chest cold so shouldn't even have been running. At the time I attributed the victory to my preparation on the road, rather than acknowledging the wheezing chest of my adversary. Nevertheless, this is one of the earliest memories I have of setting a goal and following through.

About a year after that I started martial arts. As I progressed through the belts, my interest and enthusiasm began to soar. My taekwondo instructor, Charlie, was a good man who took a keen interest in my progression. I didn't have any more natural ability than my friends, but Charlie identified in me a sense of determination like his own. I would rarely miss a class, which is something that I have maintained to this very day – consistency. I refuse to let things such as the weather dictate how or when I train.

My general fitness level has barely changed over the last 15 years. Besides spiking for the occasional event, I maintain a regular and diverse training program – a sound base to launch from – because it is far less violent on the body and minimises injury and illness. My most severe injury – a knee reconstruction – was the result of overtraining and fatigue after a deployment overseas.

By age 13 I had decided to commit the next 12 months of my life to preparing for my black belt in taekwondo. Physically, I would be expected to perform the same board breaks as men who were aged in their twenties and thirties. Weighing in at less than 50 kilograms, I couldn't rely on brute strength or body mass, so I worked on my speed and technique. I regularly began to kick the back of the house, leaving grimy heel-marks all over the white bricks. Besides the noise, Dad gave me a serve for soiling the bricks and said I would crack the house, so I moved to the barbecue area and continued to slam the wall there. This lasted a day before Dad brought home half a dozen car tyres, sliced them down one side and looped them around a tree near the railway line at the back of the house.

After achieving a black belt in taekwondo I soon became restless. I wanted to study something more effective, so I began wing chun kung-fu. At age 16 I was driving my shins into those tyres most afternoons, only stopping when the bruises, welts and cuts made it too painful to train. I probably would have been well suited to hanging out in a monastery with a shaved head and an orange robe, and training seven days a week.

A year later I was preparing for my wing chun level one instructor grading – black belt equivalent – when I decided to vary my training to enhance my fitness. I included a couple of weekly circuits at the gym. At 17, after passing my grading, I was running my own kung-fu branch twice a week, and travelling to Sydney three times a week for my own training. I also used to get together with a few mates and spar two or three times a week.

I maintained this demented level of intensity until I was 19, when my enthusiasm began to fade. I was hoping to join the police force, so I began resistance training in order to put on a few kilograms. I gave up martial arts a year later – I was burnt out – to concentrate on weights training and general fitness.

My occupation as a motor mechanic was beginning to wear thin. In fact, it was driving me insane. I wanted a job that was exciting, and where I would be challenged. Each morning I struggled to get out of bed; the thought of putting a van on the hoist, dropping the oil, changing the spark plugs and painting the tyres made me want to pick a fight with my father in the hope he would put me out of my misery and sack me. My old man was an excellent mechanic. I was flat-out just popping the bonnet. I put all of my hopes on making it into the police force, but when I found out there was a 12-month freeze on applications, I decided to look elsewhere.

In the Regiment, from the second I opened my eyes my body became excited with the thought of going to work. Not everything we did in the Regiment was exhilarating – I'd rather mow the lawns than wash boats, de-service engines or clean weapons, as that was too much like a mechanic's work for me. But in nine years I never felt like rolling over and taking the day off – never! I would rise from bed, do the obvious, get dressed and have something to eat. My heart rate would be slightly elevated as I thought about the physical training session that would begin at 0745.

When employed as a motor mechanic, I probably never arrived 10 minutes early; I usually scurried in the door at the same time the radio announcer said it was 8 am. I wouldn't look at Dad – there was no point. I could feel his frustration burning holes in my back as I slipped on my boots. Sometimes he'd tap his watch, other times he'd look at the spark-plug clock before glaring in my direction. *Give me a break*, I thought. *I'm stuck here for the next eight hours, so there's no way I'm getting here any earlier than I have to.*

In the Regiment, if I wasn't seated in the troop office gobbing off at least 15 or 20 minutes early, then something was wrong. I was never late, but on one occasion it was close.

I pulled up at a set of lights on a Kawasaki ZXR 750 motorbike wearing the usual: a pair of rugby shorts, a

T-shirt and joggers. My reluctance to wear appropriate attire was the reason I eventually sold the bike. At the lights a white Commodore pulled up alongside me and revved its engine. Underneath my visor I just rolled my eyes and didn't even bother looking at the guy. *What a goose*, I thought. The light turned green and I accelerated up the hill.

After 400 metres, I checked my rear-vision mirror and was surprised to see the Commodore having a real go. Rather than letting him drive past, I kicked down a couple of gears and accelerated hard. As my bike revved through the power band I looked in my mirror and felt satisfied – I had opened up a 100-metre lead. However, this ceased when I saw a blue light flashing through the windscreen. *Shit!* I pulled over, got off my bike and removed my helmet. I had no idea how fast I was going.

'Have you even got a license for that thing,' yelled the officer.

I nodded and presented my motorbike license, which was snatched from my hand.

'You better have a bloody good reason for riding like that.'

'I am running a little late, but that's not why I accelerated up the hill,' I said.

Bip, bip, bip, bip sounded a horn as one of the SAS boys drove past. I didn't wave.

'Where do you work?' the officer asked.

'Swanbourne,' I said.

'Campbell Barracks?'

'Yes.'

The officer returned my license. 'Slow down, mate,' he

said. 'Next time, if someone pulls up alongside and revs their car then at least take the time to have a look. It may also be worth throwing on a pair of jeans and a jacket. If you do come off there'll be nothing left of you.'

I've owned several motorbikes, and I did many irresponsible things between the ages of 17 and 21. That sudden rush of blood can change your life in an instant. Many young men feel invincible and have little thought of self-preservation. This is an attitude that diminishes with age, although I still struggle with it. My mother never attempted to talk me out of buying a motorbike as she knew it'd be futile to try. Instead, she sent a top-of-the-range Shoei helmet to me in Perth.

So how should we encourage young males to drive or ride in a sensible manner? This is a challenge I'm sure I will be confronted with when my son, Reyne, turns 17. For me, the most effective motivation is to make a young man aware not of what he might do to himself, but of how his actions might impact on others. The more graphic television advertisements in which young men drive recklessly and kill innocent people have had a far greater effect on me than the doubling of fines did. And if that doesn't work, then I'll buy Reyne a clapped-out Datsun and remove a spark plug or two.

=

For SAS soldiers, having a high level of physical fitness, strength and endurance is not simply desirable; it is essential for our very survival. My experiences in the Regiment taught me that. From scrambling up the side of a mountain in Afghanistan, to trying to control our breathing while being hunted by militia forces in East Timor, to negotiating heavy seas while diving from oil platforms – the fitter and stronger the soldier, the greater his contribution to the team.

In the Regiment I rarely felt the need to look for excitement after I knocked off. It was the perfect job for someone with my personality. We were taught how to drive correctly, from seating and hand positions and vehicle dynamics, to braking, steering, cornering and acceleration skills. The training took place under stringent safety procedures at forgiving locations, such as racetracks and skidpans. I had no need to find a dirt road on my time off and throw a car sideways. Then there was the parachuting, climbing, roping, working with explosives, shooting and diving. We were also challenged intellectually, with medical, language, signals and computer skills. It was a brilliant combination that met our intellectual and physical desires.

As good as the specialist training was, I still looked forward to our morning PT sessions the most. On Monday mornings we would run the cross-country, an eight-kilometre soft-sand run. We'd slow-jog to the range sentry gate before stretching. At this stage there was usually still some talking, but most guys would fall silent as they began to psyche themselves up for the run.

If I was coordinating the session, I would attempt to control the speed until we reached the pumphouse near the beach. Trying to restrain 15 or 20 competitive guys who were keen to unleash was always difficult. We all wanted to be at the front. After reaching the pumphouse we would slow-jog along an orange gravel track before hitting the most challenging section of the course – two kilometres of sand dunes.

Not even a medic with an unlimited supply of valium-charged syringes would be able to calm the guys down from this point on. It simply became a race. The troop was so competitive that it was rare for any one person to dominate. If the guy in front maintained a cracking pace, then the next three or four guys would make use of his footsteps and wait for their own chances to pounce. If Kane, Charlie, Mick or the Boss led the pack, then that chance may never come. However, if a pretender – someone who had let his ambitions get ahead of his ability – tried to sneak into the lead – he might hear something like 'Knew you'd fade, pussy!' as a group of up to half a dozen men churned up the sand around him.

The lead pack would run hard but just within their limits, holding back a little for the monster sand dune known as 'the bowl'. At the top of each hill we would try to maintain our stride – quite a feat when your legs are heavy and burning with lactic acid. Our lungs fared no better. The front group would remain tight until the track swung west into the bowl. No one paced himself from here on in. Quite often it would be Kane who took the lead through the lower bowl, with the rest of us jostling for position. Then it was on. The gradient was perfect – steep. Kane would always go hard early but we'd often claw him back with five metres to go. He sometimes held on to win, but any one of three or four guys would hit the summit within half a metre of each other.

We'd then jog back to the rear gate, although sometimes this would become a second race.

Many guys would do their own strength work in the afternoons, so the morning PT sessions were a mix of running, swimming and circuit-training. A Tuesday might include a boxing circuit, or the guys might grab a 17-kilogram pipe and spend an hour curling, pressing and squatting the thing. We usually worked in pairs; one man would do 50 bicep curls before handing the bar to his partner. The second set would be 40 reps, followed by 30, 20 and then 10. With this complete, we'd pyramid back up to 50. The last two sets usually aroused a little grunting, as the guys maintained a balance between good form and racing each other.

A typical Wednesday included a transition session in the pool. It would begin with a 300-metre swim followed by a one-kilometre run. Without resting, the guys would then complete swims of 250, 200, 150, 100 and 50 metres, each separated by another one-kilometre run. This is a fantastic way to train. Just as the body begins to find a rhythm, it's thrust into a contrasting activity. Your blood is shunted from your legs to your upper torso. These sessions slightly favoured runners over swimmers.

A pool session often concluded with some underwater work to boost lung capacity. Everyone in the water troop had to be capable of swimming 25 metres underwater. The top guys, when fresh, could push double this – up to 60 metres. Carrying out a 'free ascent' – swimming from a tie-off line to a target vessel or oil platform with a single breath – always turned me on. I loved the challenge of trying to swim underneath a ship, especially in dark or murky conditions.

I've since taken an interest in breath-hold training

and am blown away by what some free-divers are able to achieve.

I realised the importance of remaining calm underwater when I lost my board in eight- to 10-foot storm swell and was caught in the impact zone. Sucked to the bottom over and over again, I had to force myself to remain calm.

'Static apnea' is an underwater discipline that requires a participant to hold their breath for as long as possible while their face remains underwater. After my first couple of attempts I managed three minutes and 10 seconds. I increased my preparation time, and four weeks later I held my breath for five minutes. I thought this was okay until

Underwater training: a 55-metre run, carrying two 32-kilogram kettlebells.

I viewed footage of a French guy holding his breath for 10 minutes.

With just a few weeks training, my lungs seemed stronger and more efficient. I don't do a lot of running – one track session and a mountain run each week – but within three weeks I had lowered my one-kilometre track time by 20 seconds.

The guys I train in the ocean with – Chris, Perry and Brett – are hard chargers who are also keen to increase their lung capacity. We began breath-hold training in a sand-bottom ocean pool. While carrying two 32 kilogram kettle-bells, we'd run 55 metres underwater. Running with a combined weight of 64 kilograms sees our lungs screaming for air before we're even halfway. To push the entire length of the pool and beyond is mentally and physically challenging. To work our upper bodies, we pull ourselves along a rope that is secured with kettle-bells to the bottom of the pool. Within a couple of sessions we were able to make 90 metres with a single breath. After 90 metres, I'd return to the surface dizzy and then float on my back as my lungs suck hard for air. I noticed that Chris was standing beside me, ready to pluck me out of the water if I pushed it a little too far.

Underwater training is dangerous and can be unforgiving. If someone panics or extends beyond their limits, there is a chance they can experience an underwater blackout. The training must be controlled and never performed alone. I always take the time to give a safety brief, which covers actions on something going wrong.

When we're finished I usually run a modified session for our children, who are eager to dive to the bottom and pull their way along the rope. It's great for their water confidence. On a recent trip in the car, Tahlie's best friend, Kate, asked me a question: 'Keith, are we doing breath-hold training tomorrow?' A nine-year-old girl enquiring about breath-hold training sounded tough. I looked at Colleen and we both laughed.

Sometimes I run sessions in rivers. I had the opportunity to train three hard-hitting corporate clients. By the end of the session each person was dragging a 24-kilogram kettle-bell across the bottom of a sandy river. To take a breath, they had to make it the 10 metres to the other side. Considering that one of these people wasn't comfortable in water, it was an amazing effort. I took as much inspiration out of the session as they did.

Underwater training: a 90-metre rope traverse.

Another exercise I do with non-military clients is to put a set of blacked-out goggles on one person and have another person guide them out the back of a surf zone without touching them. It is an excellent activity for communication and trust. You have to be clear and concise with your commands. This activity is dependent on surf conditions and one's ability.

I also sometimes conducted an exercise that I learnt from the US Navy Seals. If the participant is confident enough, he or she wears a blacked-out set of goggles and has their hands restrained behind their back with a thick elastic band. In a pool with a depth of at least 2.5 metres, you have to sink your body by exhaling quickly and firmly. When your feet touch the bottom, you crouch and drive towards the surface. Once your head breaks the surface, naturally, you take a breath. Then you repeat the exercise any given number of times. Someone who is uncomfortable might only manage five repetitions, while a person who is fit and confident can continue for several minutes. If you don't blow the air out quickly enough, you'll sink too slowly, or you might only sink a foot or two, and so you have to kick to reach the surface. If you're tentative when driving off the bottom then you'll also have to kick to the surface, burning up valuable oxygen. This type of training is hugely beneficial for confidence in the water, and over time it will give you a set of lungs like a whale.

Depending on the intensity of our previous three sessions, on Thursdays we would often do an interval session. This could include five one-kilometre sprints, fartlek training or – my last troop sergeant's favourite – the seven peaks.

We used to jog around Swanbourne and, every few minutes, select a hill and race to the top. The winner would receive gold, second place silver and bronze for third. The others were given a bowl of milk and told to try a little harder. The key to this was making your efforts at the right time. You shouldn't give 100 per cent on every hill, but rather decide when to go for it and when to conserve your energy. No one ever won two hills in a row. At the end of the session, the person with the most gold, silver and bronze was the winner. There was no second place – just 19 losers.

During those sessions there was always a lot of banter. On one occasion a strong sprinter and road-runner named Charlie said: 'Hey, let's all work together so Fenno doesn't get any gold medals.'

Why single me out, ya' bastard? I thought. I waited for the second sprint and yelled out: 'Fuck you, Charlie!' before taking off on my quest for gold.

Training hard together builds an esprit de corps. We were tight, a critical constituent for soldiers who might be sent to war at any time.

On Saturday mornings a few of us would meet at the Regimental gymnasium. Once a month we would go berserk and shock-load our bodies to test ourselves. Kane and I used to do a heavy chin-up/push-up session – 300 of each in 30 minutes. When Newy, a mate from another troop, heard about this, he asked to join in. We decided to up the ante to 400 chin-ups and 400 push-ups in 45 minutes. At the start of each minute we'd jump onto the heave bar and pump out 10 chin-ups. As soon as we were finished that we'd drop to the floor for 10 push-ups. This would have taken around 22 to 25 seconds, and we'd use the remainder of that minute to rest. After 30 continuous sets we would stop for a two-minute break.

'What do you think, Newy – you like it?' I asked at the break, trying not to laugh.

'It's a cracker! You fuckers are sick!'

Newy was a hyper-positive soldier who radiated energy. If someone was having a bad day, all they'd have to do was spend 10 minutes with Newy – then they'd be bouncing off the walls like he was, feeling stoked to be alive. He had a witty sense of humour and would often crack one-liners that Raymond Chandler would be proud of. He was also tall, exceptionally fit and one of the strongest swimmers in the Regiment. Kane and I looked forward to hurting Newy.

We completed another five sets before taking a further minute to rest. Our backs were beginning to cramp. Newy and his long arms were still hanging in there, but only just.

'Five sets to go, big guy,' I said.

'Is that all,' he said, bending over and shaking his arms.

After 350 chin-ups and push-ups, our arms felt like they were going to burst. We rested after sets 37 and 39. On the penultimate set, our form had well and truly gone to shit. We flicked our hips like a dog having sex as we tried to get our chins over the bar. Just hanging on was an effort.

'Good effort, boys,' said Kane.

'Yeah, thanks for that, fellas,' said Newy. 'If my arms weren't so useless I'd punch you both in the face.' He slumped down on the bench.

A few weeks later it was Buzz's turn. He was my first team leader and always keen for a challenging hit-out. The aim of the session was to complete five consecutive exercises without a rest, before taking a 90-second break and repeating the whole thing another four times. The first exercise was 10 chin-ups with a 10-kilogram plate slung around our waists. Then we'd jump onto the bench press and pump out 20 repetitions of 60 kilograms. From there we'd walk to the squat rack and complete 20 deep squats with 60 to 80 kilograms, before completing another 10 chin-ups and finishing off with 30 push-ups.

The first set is okay – you finish feeling pumped and your heart is beating hard. The second set starts to bite. By the third, you start to doubt whether there is enough blood and oxygen in your body to get the job done. During the fourth set, your body gets a little freaked out – a combination of rising nausea and dizziness – as you struggle to complete the reps. During our final 90-second rest, no one was talking and no one was sitting. We were all collapsed on the benches or the floor, hyperventilating and trying to summon the courage for the final set.

The chin-ups are a rest compared to the bench press, which is the most challenging activity. For me, the final two reps of the fifth set are always a struggle. The final trip to the squat bar is like trying to walk in a straight line after you have spun around 10 times with your eyes closed. If you're not dizzy when you start the squats, you might well be hallucinating by the time you get off. Then it's back on the chin-up bar before pumping out one final set of push-ups.

Buzz finished the workout – with no build-up training, we were impressed that he completed all the reps – then he walked outside and fertilised the garden. Now that's what we were hoping for.

=

Despite this type of training, trying to pull yourself out of a violent, windswept ocean in Bass Strait while burdened with 15 to 20 kilograms of equipment – body armour, a climbing harness, safety vest, weapons, ammunition, a radio and a sledge hammer – is still hugely taxing.

After completing a dive and establishing a 30- to 40-foot caving ladder, the final climb is always gruelling as blood is shunted between your legs and arms. If the water is cold – and it always is – then even hanging on to the ladder can be challenging.

The same goes for trying to remain coherent when scrambling up the side of a mountain in Afghanistan while carrying in excess of 65 kilograms.

The years we spent physically preparing and extending ourselves in training allowed us to perform during exacting operational deployments. In the SAS, being physically fit and strong is not about ego; it's about being able to get the job done and embrace tasks that are beyond the scope and capabilities of conventional military units.

It's different now. I no longer train for survival, but for sanity and enjoyment.

Although I consume a fairly balanced diet (one that does include pizza, Diet Coke and chocolate), my love of training does not extend to excessive protein consumption, which can trigger more than one sitting on a toilet per day, or to counting calories, hanging out in front of the mirror or balancing on scales. I like to train hard primarily because of how it makes me feel.

For the most part, I enjoy training with other like-minded people, but when I need to get back to basics, gather my inner thoughts and centre myself – as I did after SAS selection – I train alone. Taking on a heavy, wind-battered ocean; having a rigorous session on the kettlebells; or running up a densely wooded mountain, where I have nothing but the sound of my own laboured breathing to keep me company – these activities strengthen my soul.

They enhance my self-belief, as during those times I have no safety net. The only person I have for motivation – the only person I can rely on – is me.

Going solo against nature is as humbling as it is invigorating, and in more ways than purely the physical. The mental strength that enables you to conquer an extreme workout can be carried over to all other facets of life. For me, it's simple; a testing workout builds my self-esteem and self-belief, but also keeps my feet on the ground and promotes humility.

These days, I do most of my training in the ocean with a few mates, and I've started competing for our local surf

A mountain workout.

club. My whole family is into it too. Having the time to train for an event, and then actually being around long enough to go in it, has opened up my eyes to life after the Regiment. It was always there but it took me a while to find it. I've also met some remarkable people. When I first started training on a paddle board, an elderly gentlemen named Ross would regularly kick my arse. I'm 35 and he's 64; he's not double my age but he's close enough. This man and several others like him are inspirational.

≡

The fourteenth of January 2009 started off a little more exciting than most days. I arrived at the beach at 0600. The sun was not yet fully round, its arse still below the horizon. There was a slight breeze out of the north-west. *Excellent – the winds are offshore*, I thought.

I said g'day to Chris, a mad surfer mate who, like me, is now addicted to intense training on racing paddle-boards. I've met a great crew of guys who don't mind training hard. On this day, there were just three of us – Chris, myself and Brendon, a tenacious older guy in his mid to late forties. We decided to paddle 1000 metres around the rocks to the next beach, where we completed some beach and pool sprints before heading back. We'd been training for 50 minutes, so I decided to conclude the session with some interval training.

We consolidated at a buoy about 150 metres from the shore, where I explained to the guys how it would work. The aim of the training was to work through the phosphate and into the lactic acid energy system. In simple terms, we'd paddle hard around an opposite buoy in 45-second bursts – flat-out – to develop our power and speed. Since there were three of us, while one man was paddling the other two would rest. I normally prefer 1:1 rest when doing interval training, but the additional time off meant we could pull ourselves through the water a little harder.

'This will be the last one, mate,' I said to Chris, angling my board towards the buoy, waiting for Brendon to arrive back. He, as usual, was throwing his heart and soul into the session. When he was 10 metres away I began paddling towards him. I grabbed my side rails and prepared to jump onto my knees and get going, but a second later I noticed a large black shape breach the swell about three metres behind him. There was a distinctive wake, and the shape – the shark's head – was heading straight towards him, its speed at least double his. It's well known that sharks generally attack from below or behind.

It was bizarre. Before me was a perfect demonstration of a shark's final approach before an attack. Brendon was two or three metres from me when the head sank beneath the water. It turned right, revealing a shadow of considerable girth and at least three metres long.

Brendon's board glided past mine as I said: 'Oy, guys, there's something in the water, and it's fucking big.'

Brendon, who should by then have been recovering and enjoying his well-deserved rest, spun around towards Chris, his flushed face redder than his hair. Some people might have been overwhelmed by the thought of something big feasting on their body, and filled with panic. But these guys were the complete opposite – I was impressed.

'Hey, hold on, Keith saw something in the water,' said Chris.

'It had a bloody big head,' I said as we lay on our boards – with none of our appendages dangling in the water. We signalled to a dozen surfers 60 metres up the beach, then cautiously paddled up to them to spread the word.

'Guys, we're not trying to freak anyone out, but a decent-sized shark surged towards one of our boards. It was big. Just wanted to let you know.'

'Cheers, mate,' one said. They were cool. Some guys stayed, some paddled in.

I've read that sharks have no apprehension about approaching something if they are twice its size. Perhaps that's why this one didn't follow through. It was lining up the back of Brendon's board when it would have sensed two other shadows – Chris and I – moving its way. I guess it didn't expect that. Either that or, as Brendon said, it changed its mind when it noticed that he was a ranga – a redhead – and that his white legs were a little too raw for consumption.

On the beach, a fisherman told me that he was out there last week in a 22-foot boat when a 15-foot great white shark came alongside for a look.

'Yeah, they're out there,' I said.

'Sure are – it's where they live,' he replied.

I returned home and was met by Tahlie and one of her equally impatient friends, Kate. 'Dad, how was the surf – is it big?'

'Nah, it's just okay,' I replied.

'Can we go now?' asked Tahlie.

During the summer holidays, I usually run a bit of training for the children who are competing at the NSW Surf Life Saving state titles. The kids are amazing. At just eight or nine years of age they have already developed a deep love of the ocean. Depending on the conditions, they usually paddle around the buoy half a dozen times and then finish off with a few waves.

At 0800 we were back down at the beach. Bob, Kate's dad, sent the dozen or so kids on a warm-up run while I told their parents about what I'd seen. No one was too concerned, but we ran a modified session. Chris volunteered to hang out the back on a rescue board and provided water safety while the kids practised ins and outs in the surf zone. At the end of the session, a few of the kids hung around to catch waves. Jake, a keen 14-year-old, asked if he could paddle out the back.

'If you want – just be careful,' I said.

'You coming?' he asked. 'You don't have to.'

I laughed. I knew there was something I liked about this kid.

'Yeah, I'll come with ya.' Chris and I joined him out the back and caught a few waves.

'Hey, Chris,' I said. 'We never did finish that session. We've still got one more to go. Can't let a shark interfere with our training – gotta get back on the horse!' I said.

'Yeah, we do. No point delaying it,' replied Chris, grinning.

Although I was a little apprehensive, I was determined to get back out to the buoy as soon as possible. It had been two hours since the incident. *That's long enough*, I thought. The three of us paddled to the buoy, had a look around, then paddled back in.

'You training Friday?' asked Chris.

'Yeah, same time. See you then.'

We thought that would be the end of it, but later that day someone called the local paper and I was invited down to the beach for an interview.

'Look, nothing really happened,' I said over the phone. 'A large head broached the surface next to a few of us and an hour later we were down there with the kids.' I declined to do an interview because I didn't want to add to the exaggerated media frenzy and discourage people from enjoying the ocean.

The next day, on the front page of the local paper was a picture of a great white leaping out of the water. The story was titled 'Thirroul Surfers' Close Encounter: Great White Shark Scare'. All of a sudden, the story read, a '3.5 metre white pointer menaced surfers ... [and] flashed its pearly whites.' The beach was also 'cleared within minutes'.

I hadn't seen any teeth, and half a dozen surfers continued to catch waves. Now that's quality investigative journalism. I was also quoted as saying: 'It sort of jumped out of the water right next to one of the guys, had a look around and then dived down and swam off.' My nan picked up the paper, read the article and nearly had a heart attack when she saw my name.

Although the article was an extreme example of poetic license – in other words, bullshit – I was impressed by how Chris and Brendon remained calm after we learned about what was lurking beneath us. For me, and obviously for them, fear of letting our mates down well surpassed our fear of being eaten.

=

Life in the SAS was both mentally and physically challenging. I thrived on this combination. I also knew that my decision to leave such a lifestyle so I could be a dad had left me vulnerable; I missed the camaraderie, the action and the intellectual stimulation. If I was to have any chance of breaking away, it was vital that I looked forward and set myself new challenges.

11

DEALING WITH TRANSITION

Very little, if anything, that lives lasts forever. In some ways it would be nice to know the precise moment when we will draw our last breath. Armed with this knowledge, we might well get on with living, rather than thinking about what was, or what could have been.

When I was employed as a special-operations advisor in the United Arab Emirates, my boss, a former British special-forces soldier, offered some advice when he realised I was struggling with my transition away from the Regiment.

'Keith, we all think about going back. Most guys struggle for at least two years, but I think it'll take you three.'

In fact even he was wrong. For almost six years I wrestled with thoughts of returning to the Regiment. Even in the two years since leaving the private security industry, I've battled hard to remain at home. I missed the camaraderie, the rush of adrenaline and that feeling you get when you're being challenged under extreme conditions. When job offers arrived, I often deleted the emails without opening them, so as to not be tempted back into the fray. I didn't trust myself, so I kept busy writing, studying, training and looking after our three children.

When SAS soldiers leave the Regiment – often to spend more time with family or to seek new challenges – they usually feel as if life has lost its spark. You wake up in the morning and, for the first time in years, struggle to crawl out of bed. Even for those who are gainfully employed, their new jobs just don't cut it compared to life in the Regiment. It takes time for a soldier to detune, to wind down and to appreciate the other things life has to offer.

These are normal feelings that many people experience. When professional athletes retire, when mothers or fathers take time out to raise their children or when people leave the workforce, there is always a period of transition that they must negotiate. Leaving something that you're good at is difficult. You might have thoughts – insecurities – that you'll never reach that level of achievement again. Walking away can be an even greater challenge than getting there in the first place. Initially, there is a void, a chasm so deep and so wide that constructing a bridge over it to a new life seems impossible.

After I gave an interview last year following publication of *Warrior Brothers*, a psychologist approached me and said: 'Keith, after listening to some of your experiences, I must say that you sound surprisingly normal.'

I laughed. *You really have no idea*, I thought. He asked me if I'd ever received professional counselling, as he dealt with many former special-forces soldiers who were finding the transition to a civilian lifestyle unbearable.

'No, I haven't,' I said.

'That's interesting. Many soldiers who experience

combat are wound super-tight. They wake up in the middle of the night with elevated pulse rates. With no release, they struggle to come back down. I would like to know how you did it.'

'Writing my book was cathartic,' I said, 'but it was the new challenges and intense training sessions that kept me grounded when I was vulnerable to that. I'd sometimes grab a piece of paper and write down what I most wanted out of life. Having a relationship with my kids was right up there, and I set about making sure that happened. I think the attributes that helped me to get into the Regiment were the same ones that helped me to walk away. I also realised that, first and foremost, I was a person, a man. I didn't define myself by my job title.'

'What do you mean?' asked the psychologist.

'Well, being an SAS soldier was what I did for a job. To be honest, it was more than that – it was a lifestyle. But just because I left the SAS, it didn't mean that I was anything less than what I was. For example, if you're a company CEO and you define yourself by your position, you could struggle with a loss of identity when you leave the job. It's the same for a sports star. I wouldn't call Roger Federer simply a tennis star – he's much more than that. He's a man with strengths and weaknesses. He's a man who is committed and has worked hard to become one of the best tennis players in history. But if he didn't play tennis, then he most likely would have excelled at something else.'

'That's true, Keith, but negotiating the middle ground, from one life to another, is where most people struggle.'

'I think it's where everyone struggles. I had to set myself new and realistic goals. I had to concentrate on where I wanted to go rather than where I had been. But I still find it difficult.'

≡

For me, a divided loyalty is a hell of a thing to live with. Leaving my family for an operational deployment always felt similar to not being there with the boys when they suffered casualties. The latter has an even greater effect on me.

Colleen and I had every intention of returning to Perth for the Regiment's fiftieth anniversary celebrations in 2007. We had even booked our flights, but I didn't get on the plane. I knew it was still too early to go back. If I caught up with the boys and heard their stories, then the chances were good that I'd be straight back in. But I'd also be single and the next time I took a breath I'd be 40, maybe even 50. At best I'd have a mediocre relationship with my children, as I have an 'all or nothing' personality. If you're a former alcoholic, there's no such thing as drinking in moderation. It's the same for a soldier. To perform, I would have to throw myself into the job with total commitment. Total commitment would mean my family once again came second. It was time to move on.

How does one transition from an adrenalised lifestyle as an SAS soldier and security contractor, working in some of the world's most hostile locations, to a life as a husband and home dad?

I left the SAS in 2002 and moved with my family to the United Arab Emirates, where I was employed as a special-operations advisor. With no chance of being deployed, I felt like a young man in an old man's job. Most of my colleagues were at least a decade my senior, while some were even older than my parents. Although I was with my family, I was plagued by a gnawing feeling that never went away. For a soldier, watching others deploy is like having a rat in your stomach. No matter how much you feed the fucker, it's always hungry. I lasted 16 months before I caved in and disappeared into Iraq.

In a lifestyle that many would consider to be selfish and narcissistic, I met some of the most selfless men I had ever known. Some men delayed their leave by three months or volunteered for the most dangerous tasks not because they had a death wish, but because they wanted to be there to support their mates if things went wrong.

I spent 30 months running operations all over Iraq and Afghanistan, deploying hundreds of consultants on thousands of road moves as part of the reconstruction effort. I was proud that, during that time, we did not suffer or inflict one single casualty. Because I felt uneasy deploying the guys I led most of the road moves. I'm sure my wife – and my mother – would have questioned this decision, but I was genuinely torn between being a proactive husband and father, and supporting my mates who were in harm's way.

In time, I made the decision to leave and return permanently to my family so I could get to know my children. I thought that leaving my action-filled lifestyle would be relatively easy. I was wrong. The transition – like two cars colliding – was chaos. My first day as a home dad was a disaster.

'Where are the nappies?' I asked Colleen as she hurried out the door to work.

'You'll work it out,' she replied, blowing me a kiss. A large smile was plastered across her face. Our three children, Tahlie, Sian and Reyne – aged six, four and two – must have thought: *Who's this pretender? He has no idea.*

My first goal was to get Tahlie to school on time. 'Tahlie, what would you like in your lunch?'

'I don't know,' she replied.

Where is there to go from there? At first I was nice, thinking up half a dozen options. But Tahlie remained undecided. After 10 very frustrating minutes, I made a decision and smothered her sandwich with Vegemite. The result – tears.

'I don't like Vegemite,' she cried.

'Then what *would* you like?' I asked.

'Nutella.'

I threw the Vegemite sandwich in the bin and made one with Nutella. I thought this resolved the whole issue, but as it turned out I had cut the sandwich into squares rather than triangles. More tears, another wasted sandwich, and then it was time to do the girls' hair.

'I want piggies,' said Sian.

'Me too,' said Tahlie.

I gave it a go but no matter how hard I tried, one pigtail always seemed to look twice the size of the other. I settled on ponytails instead and accepted the obvious – more tears. I then heard the radio say it was 10 minutes to nine.

'Quick, kids, brush your teeth, we've got to go,' I yelled.

I bundled Reyne and Sian into the sports pram. We had four minutes to get to school. It was going to be close but I was confident we could make it.

'Dad, Reyne's done a poo in his nappy,' said Tahlie.

'Oh well, he'll just have to sit in it for now – we're not going to be late for school.'

'But it's coming out the sides.'

I peered into the pram and was mortified. *How could such a small child make such a vile mess?* I thought. There was shit everywhere.

I yelled at the kids to come back inside as I quickly put Reyne into the bath. With this complete, and much to Tahlie's disapproval, I squashed all three kids into the pram and, like a man possessed, ran down the hill, the kids hanging on for their lives.

We arrived several minutes after the bell. I didn't bother going to the office to fill out a late note. I preferred denial and definitely didn't need a piece of paper telling me I had screwed up.

We arrived home to a ringing telephone. *I bet it's Colleen checking up on me*, I thought. *Doesn't she know I was in the SAS?*

'Hi, babe, just wanted to let you know that you have mothers' group at 9.30. The kids need the stimulation.'

'Stimulation? I've never been more stimulated in my entire life. I've just spent the last 10 minutes squashing little faecal nuggets down the plug-hole after Reyne defecated in his jumpsuit.'

'Not you, the kids. It's not all about you.'

I threw Sian and Reyne back into the pram and we descended the hill once again, albeit at a much slower pace this time. I didn't mind being late for this one.

That evening, while I was standing at the sink scrubbing burnt chicken from the frypan, Colleen bounced through the door, all smiles.

'How was your day?' she enquired.

I wanted to lie and tell her that it was easy, but all these other words came out: 'I wanted to strangle the little bastards. It was hideous. What did you do to relieve the stress?'

'What do you mean?' she said, laughing.

'I don't know. Do we have anything to drink?'

'Like what?'

'Methylated spirits...Something strong to numb my brain,' I spluttered.

After a couple of weeks, I stopped burning the chicken and enrolled at uni. At the end of my first semester, I began to write. I was also employed on a four-day performance training camp for the Australian rugby union team, the Wallabies. Besides catching up with a few of my mates from the Regiment, it was rewarding to work with such highly committed and tough athletes. I was particularly impressed by Phil Waugh, the modest warrior. These men were already high-performing so our aim was to further build their sense of teamwork, and to offer guidance on leadership and decision-making under stress. After six months hanging out with my kids, I felt I was more than qualified for that.

The six members of my team had a tremendous esprit de corps and were committed to taking it to another level. On one afternoon, sitting atop a ridgeline in south-eastern Queensland, the guys were encouraged to share something personal with their mates. This was one of the most moving experiences of my life. I was humbled by the Wallabies' honesty and commitment to each other. There was much more to these guys than brawn.

Negotiating an obstacle with George Gregan and Phil Waugh during a training camp in south-east Queensland.

As a member of our local surf club, I found it equally rewarding to challenge young children and help them gain confidence in the ocean. By the following year, a couple of us established a performance program that catered for the kids who were keen to compete. The initial group of half a dozen young people soon grew to more than 30. At times, watching these eight-year-old children take on three- or four-foot waves left me speechless. Some of these kids were fortunate to be rewarded for their commitment with state medals. But a far greater reward was the ability they gained to conquer their fears. For many, the ocean was once intimidating, but this strength will support them for the rest of their lives.

With Reyne, who's ready to receive a baton during a beach relay.

A few months later, a guy I was training several times a week, a mate by the name of Karl, asked if I would be keen to do some motivational or keynote speaking.

'What do you have in mind?' I asked.

'We might start off with a group of 10 people or so. Have a think about it. I'll try to set something up next year if you're keen.'

Considering that next year was a couple of months away, I confidently said: 'Yeah, why not.' A few days later I received a phone call.

'Hey, mate, I've got you a gig.'

Shit! I thought. 'Really?'

'The guest speaker for an awards ceremony has just pulled out and they're after a replacement.'

'When's it on?' I asked.

'Next week. Can you talk about logistics?'

'Logistics?' I repeated, feeling slightly rattled.

'Yeah, logistics. You'll be addressing 150 people.'

So much for starting off nice and easy. I wanted to say no, but I had a problem: I had recently run a session for Karl that was framed around mental strength.

'Hey, mate,' I'd told him, 'we're doing five sprints up that nasty hill.' The road in question was hideously steep and extended for 400 metres. It offered beautiful views but I knew that after two sprints, taking in the scenery would be the last thing on Karl's mind. 'On one of the runs, I'll give you a head start – I want you to beat me to the top. If you fail, then we're heading straight to the pool and you'll swim 25 metres underwater.' This was something Karl was yet to achieve. 'If you puss out and don't make it all the way, I'll give you one more shot. If you fail again, you can find a new training partner. Any dramas?'

'Jesus, I'm nervous already,' he'd said, laughing.

Although he'd given it a good crack, there had been no way I would have allowed Karl to beat me to the top of that hill. The aim was to fatigue him and burn up his nervous energy. Really, I wanted him to overcome the underwater challenge, which he had struggled with. He was a tough man. I enjoyed training with him and I'd known he could do the underwater swim. Not only did he nail it, but he was so pumped that he'd done it a second time for good measure.

But speaking to such a big audience made me think twice. 'Mate, I don't know. Six days doesn't give me a lot of time to square myself away as a keynote speaker. I'll obviously need to write a speech and put a presentation together. Is there a format I need to follow?'

'You just need to link your experiences back to business. I can give you a few tips.'

You bastard! I thought. 'What do you reckon?'

'You can either take your opportunities or you can let them go.' The tone of his voice said something more: *If you turn this down, you're a freaking pussy.*

I accepted the job and vowed to make him vomit on our next training session.

This led to numerous speaking opportunities. I was surprised by how fragmented a lot of companies were, so one of the themes I often addressed was teamwork. There seemed to be so much internal competition — state versus state, branch versus branch. Rather than working together as a team to outperform their real competitors, people were keeping new and innovative ideas to themselves so they would be recognised for outperforming their own workmates. I knew very little about business, but to me this didn't make sense. Rather than rewarding internal conflict, companies ought to develop a sense of team purpose. If members of a company find a better or more efficient way to do something, they should share the knowledge with their mates.

My new life was busy and I was definitely being challenged, but I still craved the excitement and adrenaline of the SAS. I wondered whether this desire for my past life would ever abate. Was soldiering my destiny, or was I some sort of pretender who wanted to be a dad yet wasn't really capable of sticking it out?

≡

Three weeks before Christmas in 2008, I received an offer to deploy on an anti-piracy task in the Gulf of Aden. Colleen was on holidays at the time and my tertiary commitments wouldn't resume until February. *Perfect timing*, I thought. But I was nervous, and it had nothing to do with the threat. I knew I was someone who struggled with moderation. Many soldiers who leave the Regiment return later. I didn't want to be one of them. Had I really accepted my new life or was I living a lie? There was only one way to find out. I sent off my CV and asked for further information.

During 2008, the year of the economic meltdown, there had been over 100 reported pirate attacks in the waters surrounding Yemen, Oman and Somalia. The hijacking of the Saudi Arabian oil tanker, the MV *Sirius Star*, on its way to the United States with two million barrels of oil was one of the more daring and successful raids of 2008. For Somali pirates, business was booming. In order to safeguard their crews, vessels and cargo, scores of merchant shipping companies sought maritime security.

After receiving further details, I asked Colleen what she thought about it.

'Is it dangerous?'

'Nah ... It'll be like a cruise, except we get to carry weapons,' I said.

'You're full of it,' she replied, smiling. 'Why do you want to do it?'

'Mick's going ... It will be great to catch up. And I think there are 15 ex-Regiment guys on the task. It will be a mini SAS reunion.'

'Is that it?'

Negotiations are always fun, I thought. 'It's somewhere different, a new adventure ... I'm feeling a little restless and I'll get to earn some cash so I can stop bludging off you,' I laughed. 'Seriously, though, it's been almost two and a half years. I want to prove to myself that I'm over going away.' I felt like a little kid begging to go to the shop to buy some lollies.

'How long's it for?'

'Seventeen days, max. I'll be back before Christmas.'

Colleen agreed, I said yes to the offer, and I left for Singapore without even confirming the pay and conditions. The alcoholic licked his lips. I had promised Colleen and the kids that I'd be home before Christmas. This was a test – to see if I could drink in moderation.

≡

I arrived in Singapore on the evening of 6 December 2008 and caught a cab to the hotel. I love the aroma of tropical rain. The air's so thick you can taste it. I got out of the cab and sucked in a couple of deep breaths. I felt alive.

'Good evening, Mr Fennell,' said the receptionist. 'You're sharing a room with Mr Wynne. He has already arrived.'

I was stoked. I probably hadn't seen Wynnie for seven years. I first met him in the Battalion before we both joined the Regiment. We got along well.

I opened the door to my room and saw a massive set of feet hanging over the edge of the bed. They definitely belonged to Wynnie. He's a big man – six-foot-three and 108 kilograms. Not many guys of Wynnie's size pass the selection course, as they usually struggle with endurance. Wynnie was different. He could run, swim and stomp as well as anyone. But the gym was his domain, and when he threw on a set of gloves, the punching bags got nervous.

Wynnie is the perfect guy to share a room with. There's always a steady stream of food flowing through the door, the conversation is interesting and he loves to sleep. I thought Kane was strong in this area, but Wynnie makes Kane look like he's a dieting insomniac. Those two worked together in Bali, running resort security during the high season. I'm sure they came home well rested.

Wynnie is also a deeply reflective and philosophical man. He isn't a fan of city life and prefers the tranquillity of the country, where he lives with his wife. When Wynnie talks about his property – the stream that never runs dry, the old-growth trees that reach upwards forever and the native wildlife that abounds – his large shoulders relax and his face softens. It is his sanctuary.

The next morning I caught up with several of the boys for breakfast. The main reason I accepted the task was to see the guys. For that alone, it was worth it. There were no pauses in the conversation. After breakfast we were taken to the operations room and briefed on the task.

The company's director, a dynamic ex-Regiment soldier who loves to surf, asked what we knew about the task. The answer was: not much.

'Good,' he said, before telling us that we'd be sailing into the Red Sea, where we would rendezvous with several vessels. An armed security team would then be assigned to each vessel before they would move through the Gulf of Aden to Oman, our final destination. It sounded a simple mission, but there were many moving parts. We were all keen to get going.

Wynnie and I, together with a large switched-on Kiwi named Sonny, were sent to Yemen for a meeting with a contact to secure weapons. I initially thought the travel advisory for Yemen was a little ridiculous, giving the impression that any Westerners entering the country would immediately be whisked away by terrorists and never seen again. I had never been to Yemen and was excited to see the place.

But the 2009 slaying and mutilation of a group of aid workers — a British man and his South Korean wife, two German nurses, a German doctor, his wife and three children — reinforced that the threat to Westerners in Yemen was very real.

The airport at Sana'a reminded me of Kabul: primitive, chaotic and tense. We purchased visas, were stamped into the country and exited the terminal. We were unarmed so had to rely on our situational awareness to identify any threats.

'Guys, we'll grab a taxi to the Sheraton,' I said.

We had already discussed what we would do if a vehicle with armed men forced us off the road and attempted to take us hostage. We would simply smile, wave and calmly walk away. If things became hostile we would all break together in the opposite direction — one in, all in. If we became separated we would meet at a designated rendez-

In Sana'a, Yemen, with Wynnie.

vous point. If they started shooting, then they would have done it anyway, we thought. Copping a bullet in the back of the head would be more pleasant than having your head hacked off.

We remained alert. Those who hesitate or fail to react allow others to decide their fate. We were in charge of our lives and were determined to keep it that way. It felt good to be operating again.

We found a driver rather than letting one find us. His car wasn't a taxi – there was no meter or distinctive markings. In broken English, our driver told us there were two decent hotels in Sana'a. The Sheraton was, apparently, number two. Our driver, aged in his mid-fifties, wore glasses and carried a large traditional knife on his chest. We soon learned he had a family. He appeared genuine and I tried to keep him talking so we could assess him. I asked him to tell us where the hotel was – how far and in what direction. If he became tense, began driving erratically, in a different direction or tried to make a phone call, we would increase our vigilance. While I questioned him, Wynnie and Sonny searched for additional triggers, such as suspect vehicles trailing us. These observational skills were engrained in us from years of close-quarter battle (CQB), close personal protection (CPP), surveillance and counter-surveillance training.

We checked in to the Sheraton, completed a visual security assessment of the hotel and nominated emergency rendezvous points – both internal and external. It was a large hotel with many rooms. If we were inside and there was a bomb blast or sounds of rifle fire, we would move to a pre-designated room on the fifth floor. Once we had all been accounted for, we would barricade the alcove leading to the door with pieces of heavy furniture, then establish communications with our operations people and wait it out. There was a large military presence in Sana'a. If there was an incident, soldiers would be at the hotel within minutes. Without weapons, our aim was to remain concealed and out of the way – curiosity can be a killer.

If the hotel caught fire and we were threatened, we would make a rope out of the curtains, sheets and blankets. It wouldn't be long enough to reach the ground, but jumping from the second floor was far more appealing than jumping from the fifth. There was also a large tree five metres from our window. Leaping into that would definitely be a last resort, but if we were forced to get out fast, we'd have to take it.

Except in Iraq, Afghanistan, parts of Africa or in international waters, security consultants are rarely armed.

Former SAS soldiers are often employed to complete security surveys and provide close personal protection for VIPs because of their ability to identify threats and implement effective security procedures. If there's a bomb blast, security consultants with the SAS skill-set won't just run with everyone else in the opposite direction, as they are aware that the exits could be channelling people towards a secondary device. The bombing of the Sari Club in Bali was a tragic example of how devastating a secondary explosion can be.

An SAS soldier who has been in the Regiment for six years would have cycled through the counter-terrorism squadron twice and spent at least 24 months 'online'. During this time, he would have made tens of thousands of high-stress decisions, from target recognition and identifying booby traps to assessing doorways and how to react during a single- or double-weapon stoppage. To further develop their skills, it is common for several SAS soldiers to act as the enemy, especially during 'handover training', where one squadron is passing responsibility to another.

In a bomb blast, the first reaction of someone who is well trained will be to assess the situation rapidly, scanning for secondary threats or anything unusual: a truck laden with gas cylinders parked on the sidewalk, a fruit cart with no one selling fruit, an unsecure bicycle with a basket, or even a person acting differently from those around them will stand out to the trained eye. One must think like a terrorist. *If I was going to plant a secondary device, where would it wreak the most carnage?*

Once we had settled into the hotel, I arranged for us to meet a contact in the early afternoon to discuss purchasing weapons. The meeting went well, so I asked to inspect the weapons. Our contact appeared a little reluctant but agreed. We travelled through the city to an affluent neighbourhood. A large set of gates opened, granting us access to a private villa.

Our contact was clearly a busy man – his phone was running hot. We waited in his lounge room while he answered a call. The furniture was basic and practical. There were no decorations or ornaments, just a lounge, television, table and chairs. It was the residence of someone who was busy, someone who didn't have the time or inclination to add warmth or style. The place lacked emotion – it was a bachelor pad that was set up for business.

'Are you ready to see the weapons?' our contact asked after finishing his call.

'Let's do it,' I replied.

We walked into a large room and saw a couple of black pistol cases sitting on a table.

'May we check the weapons?' I asked.

'Of course,' he replied.

The pistol I picked up was a 9-mm Taurus. They were old but well oiled and clean; the slides moved freely. As secondary weapons they would be fine. Leaning against the wall were four AKS-47 assault rifles. Anyone with comprehensive weapons training would never store weapons that way. We cocked the rifles and fired the actions. They weren't ideal, but if our contact couldn't source AK-47s then these would have to do.

'Do you have access to normal AK-47s?' I asked.

'What do you mean normal?'

'These weapons have short barrels, which are good for fighting in confined spaces but they are only accurate to about 100 metres. We'd prefer normal AKs, which have a longer barrel and triple the maximum effective range.'

He wasn't a weapons guy but he understood our concerns. 'Yes, I can get anything.'

He agreed to source AK-47s, but it was no surprise when his guys turned up with more AK-shorts. He also offered to source two RPKs, a long-barrelled derivative of the AK-47 with a bipod, and a couple of 100-round drum magazines, but these didn't eventuate either. Instead he delivered two PKM medium machine guns. Only one of these weapons was serviceable – the second was filthy and corroded. The boys gave them a decent clean and got them singing.

A few days later we had coffee with a large Somali man in Djibouti, northern Africa. He had strong pirate connections and said he was able to source weapons and vessels for our subsequent tasks, but he wanted me to travel with him to Bombasso in Somalia to speak with his contacts as a sign of trust. I was fine with this, as he was business-oriented and appeared to be a man of integrity. He also told us that we wouldn't have any problems with Somali pirates over the next

Sourcing weapons in Sana'a, Yemen.

two weeks – apparently, they would be on holidays. As ridiculous as this sounded, there were religious celebrations taking place.

On the evening of 15 December 2008, 18 of us set sail for the Red Sea in a dodgy dhow. I didn't take any sea-sickness tablets as the Gulf of Aden was like a lake. This, however, would soon change.

At the rendezvous, Tony, Mick and I were allocated to the second vessel, a new tugboat bound for Kuwait. We were all former SAS water operators and had been in the same team – the lead water counter-terrorism assault team – and Tony had commanded it from 2000 to 2002. We had spent many months living in each other's pockets during numerous operational and training deployments. It was refreshing to be hanging out again.

Like me, both Tony and Mick had struggled with their departure from the Regiment. Mick spent over a year in Iraq, and not even a near-death encounter with a roadside bomb could persuade him to give the lifestyle away. But with the breakdown of his marriage, Mick's priorities had

Our dhow in the Red Sea.

changed. Over the next 18 months he dedicated his life to his two young sons, Hunter and Carden. They were his cure and are now his everything.

Tony had been assigned to a training role just prior to the first SAS deployments to Afghanistan. When injury also kept him out of the later deployments, he snapped and got out. Tony stopped socialising with mates who were still in the Regiment. Listening to their experiences had become excruciating, so much so that even attending one mate's funeral was impossible. Tony was not alone in this – there were many others with identical feelings. I was one of them.

Tony is an intellectual man, often consumed by his thoughts. He was aware that his family, especially his five children, needed him. But he also knew they needed a dad who felt fulfilled and challenged. After two brief deployments to the Gulf of Aden, his craving for action settled.

Although there was a significant international naval force patrolling the area, the high-threat zone included some 2.5 million square miles, making it virtually impossible to secure. The Somali pirates were becoming increasingly bold because of their success and the large ransoms they were being paid. They generally operated with the support of a mother craft disguised as a fishing boat. When a target vessel was identified, one or more skiffs – pirate speed boats – would be sent to intercept it. On some of the more complex attacks, they used up to 70 pirates and 20 skiffs.

We weren't permitted to carry weapons aboard our vessel, so we were issued with an LRAD 500 – a non-lethal, directional acoustic hailing device. The hexagonal LRAD

248 **WARRIOR TRAINING**

was white and sat atop a tripod. If a rapidly approaching vessel did not heed warnings to change course, the LRAD could be used to send a continuous acoustic tone to deter the attackers. If the vessel closed to within 500 metres, the intensity of the soundwave could be turned up to extremely irritating levels. If a suspect continues to close in, the acoustic tone could reach excruciating levels, to the point where an attacker might receive permanent hearing loss.

Mick and I rehearsed with the LRAD, moving it to numerous locations, to ensure we were able to respond to threats in any direction. While I untied the ropes securing the tripod, Mick disconnected the 240-volt power supply and ran it through the bridge to the opposite side of the vessel. I'd then carry the LRAD to the next location while Mick followed with the tripod. As he reconnec-

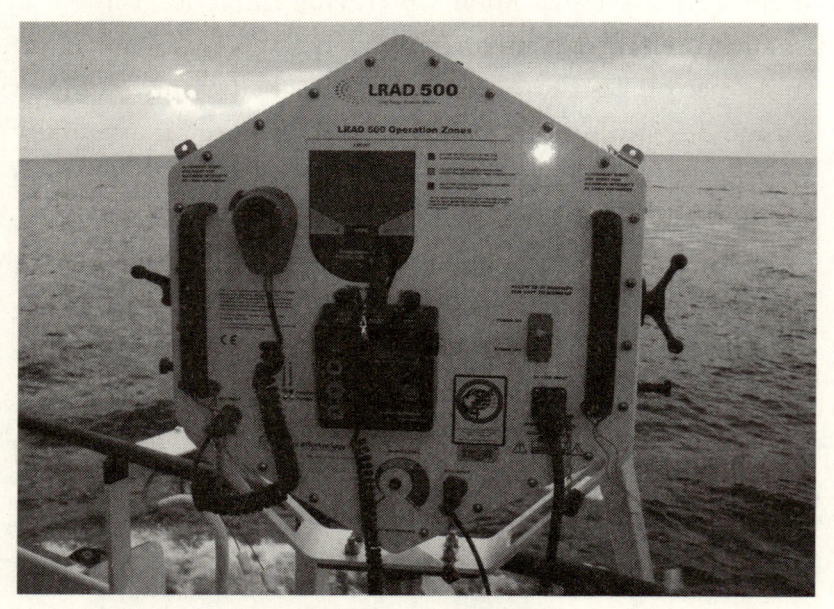

The LRAD 500, an acoustic hailing device.

ted the power supply, I donned hearing protection. We rehearsed until we were able to complete the task in less than 30 seconds. With the 20 seconds it took for the device to warm up, this meant we could be operational within 50 seconds.

Tony would remain in the bridge in order to direct the skipper and maintain communications with the flotilla commander, who was located on the lead vessel. Other craft were always positioned to be able to afford mutual support if we were attacked; they had access to automatic weapons, including PKM medium machine guns.

The next morning, we also tested the water cannon and ran rehearsals for the crew. We identified suitable ambush positions where we would be able to disarm the lead attacker with ASP batons. With one of us playing enemy, we adjusted our positions and rehearsed striking an attacker's head as we simultaneously controlled his weapon.

Preparation and planning are instrumental to success. Many years earlier, when I was a junior trooper in the Regiment, Tony had offered me some invaluable advice. I was tasked to run a lesson for the squadron in the lecture theatre. When Tony asked how my rehearsals were going, I said, 'I'm not going to worry about a rehearsal – I know the piece of kit. I'll cuff it.'

His reply: 'Mate, it's easy to tell when someone is cuffing it. If you want to be able to stand up and deliver, then I suggest you do a rehearsal or two. But I'll leave the decision up to you.'

Mick, Tony and I maintained a 24/7 security piquet and increased our vigilance during high-threat times of dusk and dawn. At 0621 on 17 December, a suspect boat was

Observing a suspect vessel in the Gulf of Aden.

identified off our vessel's port side. We readied the LRAD and were operational within 25 seconds. We remained alert until the threat subsided.

By 19 December, the seas had turned angry, battering our convoy with a relentless easterly swell. *So much for the Gulf being like a lake*, I thought. The sea-state, just like the tomatoes I had for breakfast, was on the rise. I could taste the brine in my mouth. *Damn it!* I thought. I knew I had passed the point of no return. I struggled down the stairs and just managed to get my head over the side when the violent contractions commenced. After clearing my stomach, I looked up at the bridge to see if anyone noticed. Mick was standing there laughing. But when the seas reached sea-state six, it was his turn.

The crew, concerned that we had lost our appetites, pressed us to eat. There was no chance – just walking past the galley made me want to throw up.

'*Saya tidak mau makan, aduh, sakit perut,*' I said with absolute conviction, telling them I didn't want to eat because I had a sick stomach. They expressed their sympathy by laughing.

After completing my shift, I went to the bathroom to brush my teeth. *Surely that will make me feel better,* I thought. As the vessel pitched and rolled, I held onto the basin to prevent being thrown about. The air-conditioning wasn't working so the bathroom was hot and stuffy. But it was the dreadful stench that wafted from the toilet that pushed me over the edge. I flicked off the lid of my toothpaste, held the tube close to my nostrils and sniffed like a coke addict. This only accentuated my desire to vomit. It was pathetic and I laughed in between contractions.

The following morning we learned that several guys on the other vessels had been vomiting. When I was asked how we were going, I decided to be up-front and honest. 'No dramas here,' I replied. But the next 36 hours were torturous. We were aboard a tugboat that was designed to operate in harbours. A sea-state six made things rather uncomfortable.

The following day we closed in on the coast of Oman. Late that afternoon, we observed two vessels moving across our front. We slowed down to assess the situation and readied the LRAD. The conditions were atrocious. The boats were heading towards Oman, possibly trying to escape the weather. We continued on.

At last we reached our destination, the port of Salalah. The hotel we checked in to was filthy – my bed looked like someone had been sleeping in it. The next day I flew home, arriving on the morning of 23 December. I had only spent 17 days away – almost nothing in comparison to years past – yet it was definitely long enough. I really missed taking the kids down to the beach.

≡

I knew my transition was complete when I had the opportunity to deploy at short notice to Afghanistan with the reserve Commandos over Christmas. It wouldn't be the same as going with the Regiment, but it was still an operational deployment. There were several reasons why I wanted to go, the strongest being to deploy with Al, one of my closest brothers. Al and I have been mates since primary school.

When Al had asked me to be his best man, he handed me a bottle of beer. The brand read:

Alexander
Keith's

'Why's your name first?' I asked, grinning.

'Yeah, but your name's written in larger letters.'

'That's true. Cheers, big guy.'

Al is a part-time Commando and is also studying medicine. For someone with a ridiculously high IQ, he's pretty funny, coordinated and surprisingly normal.

Al had his reasons for wanting to deploy, and although he asked for my opinion, he knew his decision had to come from within. As for me, after much deliberation I turned the opportunity down. I didn't want to spend another four months away from my family, especially over Christmas. Unless my circumstances changed, I would only contemplate short tasks. I had spent more than a decade going away; now that I knew what it was like to be a dad, I wasn't prepared to give that up. Perhaps people do change.

The week before Al left, I threw him off a 45-metre bridge into the ocean. He was attached to a rope. The abseil was spectacular. We also went for a fast run.

Al serving in Afghanistan.

'I'm going to set a cracking pace, mate,' I told him. 'This is similar to the speed an SAS troop runs when they're going hard. I want you to beat me to the other end of the bridge.'

He did. It was obvious Al had trained hard. Physically and mentally, he was ready to go to war.

Since Al's deployment, two Australian soldiers have been killed in Afghanistan. I heard about the first incident on the news, and I immediately thought of him. Al wasn't just a mate, he was a brother. A day later I found a message on my mobile from a voice I didn't recognise. I listened to it at least five times, then played it to Colleen.

'Who do you reckon this is?' I asked her.

'Don't know. I've never heard the voice before,' she replied.

I played the message again. 'Do you think it could be Al?'

'Nah, it's definitely not Al.'

I listened again, trying to connect some part of the

message to the guy I had known since I was five. 'You're right. It's not him,' I said.

But it had been Al. He'd been out on patrol when a soldier 15 metres in front of him tripped an improvised explosive device and disappeared. For this man, death was instantaneous, but for his family his death lingers forever. You can try to justify a death like this to those who are grieving, but in the end, when someone you love dies, it's just fucking sad.

Al's voice had carried the tone of a much older man. It was a lifeless voice – serious, distant and vague. We spoke later that day.

'You alright, mate?' I asked.

'Yeah, I'm fine. It's sad – he was a good guy.'

'I was hoping it was you so I could have your motorbike,' I said with a laugh.

Al laughed too. 'Yeah, well, you'll have to wait.'

Phone calls from soldiers on deployment are always guarded and a little weird, as they can't speak freely. I never asked Al what he'd been up to and he didn't discuss anything operational. I knew what it was like, so I spent the time telling him that he was missing out on a great summer.

Two weeks later a 107-mm rocket passed within 40 centimetres of Al's head. One of his mates wasn't so lucky. Although they had been struck by a violent hand, the Commandos' commitment to each other only intensified. For years Al had heard my stories; now it felt strange to be on the receiving end. But I was proud of him. Not a condescending, big-brother proudness. He was a mate and a soldier who had handled himself well under testing conditions.

I'm not sure how Al will find the transition from war to civilian life. The sounds, smells and images of war will remain etched in his long-term memory, but so too will the camaraderie that was forged during adversity.

One day we'll chat about it.

EPILOGUE

History provides a rich collection of stories of soldiers and armies who have displayed something special — those who have blended brains, courage and brawn. When I read about the Battle of Thermopylae, I was so impressed by the commitment and loyalty of King Leonidas' men to each other that I used their actions for motivation when working with the Auckland Warriors rugby league side in the lead-up to the team's 2008 NRL finals campaign.

The Auckland Warriors were an impressive outfit of men who displayed a wonderful combination of the warrior's spirit and humility. For me, it was an honour to have been invited to work with such a fine group of men. Their sense of teamwork and mateship was on par with that of my brothers in the Regiment, and like many SAS soldiers, they were heavily inked with meaningful tattoos.

Ahead of the team's vital match against the Melbourne Storm on 14 September 2008, I sent an email to their conditioning coach, Craig Walker, who pinned my message on the boys' lockers:

In 480 BC, King Leonidas of Sparta led 300 Spartans and 2000 Thespians and other Greek allies against a Persian army of 80,000 men. King Leonidas was offered control of Greece if he surrendered. His answer was, 'If you had any knowledge of noble things in life, you would refrain from coveting others' possessions; but for me to die for Greece is better than to be the sole ruler over the people of my race.' He was then asked to surrender his arms, to which he replied, 'Come and get them.'

During the first Persian assault, the Spartans cut their adversaries to pieces. Over the next two days, 10,000 Persians attacked the Spartans and failed. Another 50,000 Persians joined the battle. They also failed. The 300 Spartans were eventually defeated, but not before they destroyed 20,000 of their enemy.

All you have to do is defeat 13 other men. It doesn't sound that difficult when you think about what some other warriors have achieved throughout history.

Men are made up of blood, bone, meat and brain. Nothing more! No man or team is invincible. Take their measure and then take some more.

In the history of the NRL, no team in eighth position had defeated the minor premiers in the first round of finals. The Auckland Warriors, just like the Spartans, fought as a team and punched well above their weight. The Warriors were victorious while the Spartans eventually lost their lives, but both had self-belief and were not intimidated by the strength of their opponents.

Giving advice to others is one thing, but I also realise the value of self-criticism. I regularly reflect on my own shortfalls. Unless you're aware of your weaknesses, how can you possibly become stronger?

I have been addicted to adrenaline and the rush associated with working in dangerous locations. The time when you're fighting for survival is also the time when you feel most alive. It is near-on impossible to recapture this feeling in regular life. Trust me – I have nearly drowned trying.

When soldiers return from war, especially if they have had near-death experiences, they sometimes develop an attitude of invincibility – a bit like adolescent males who are charged with testosterone. Having been there, I know the feeling. I'm also aware that this mindset can be more perilous than bullets or bombs. Your ability to acknowledge danger can be more relaxed than that of someone who hasn't experienced such things. What others consider to be dangerous, returned soldiers sometimes view as acceptable, or even as desirable.

I have done some crazy shit in my time, including leaping off a bridge into water in the middle of the night without assessing the risk. After having a large quantity of salt water forced into my arse at high-speed and bruising my tailbone, culminating with six weeks of discomfort, I realised that there is a fine line between seeking adventure and making bad decisions.

Although I like to challenge myself in the ocean, especially when it gets a little nasty out there, I work hard on my fitness and skills, which gives me the ability to extend myself. My training includes underwater work, a combination of both high- and low-heart-rate breath holds.

I was recently stuck in the impact area of a large surf after losing my board. For over 15 minutes I was repeatedly sucked to the bottom and held under for 10 to 20 seconds at a time. The water was so aerated that I was unable to swim to the surface. Every time I needed a breath, I had to dive to the bottom and launch off the sand. I was rarely able to steal more than one breath before being sucked through the next wave and driven back down. I was telling myself to calm down and relax – drowning on my local beach would be bloody embarrassing. The three large bluebottles that were wrapped around my neck were the least of my concerns – I'm sure they hated the experience as much as me. I eventually made it in, 350 metres down the beach. When I got to the car I noticed my lips were blue; I was hypoxic.

I'd be a liar if I said the experience didn't rattle me a little. The next day I jumped in the pool with a couple of mates and did some underwater work. Training and preparation are critical for anyone who likes to push the limits.

Sadly, a young male exchange student from Saudi Arabia also ventured into the surf that night; he had been celebrating his 25th birthday with a group of friends. It was late, he was a poor swimmer, the surf was treacherous and he had been drinking. I knew how difficult I had found the conditions – the poor guy didn't stand a chance.

For people like me, my mates, young adolescent males and soldiers who are trying to negotiate their way back to a more banal lifestyle, I try to remember this: if we must fall, then let it be the hand of fate, not waste, or while doing what we love; our fleeting moments of madness should not remain forever.

Over the last couple of years I have heard of soldiers from several countries who boast about taking life, as if the experience should give them special status or joy. For me, such comments either show a false bravado or belie far deeper problems: that they have been desensitised to the point that they are out of touch with society. Killing may be integral to war, but it is not a sport. In war, there are no trophies and there are no winners.

Some guys pretend they are winners – a false ideal that is usually accentuated when in the presence of others and alcohol. But I challenge these men to rise from their beds in the middle of the night, walk to the bathroom, face the mirror and peer deep into the eyes before them. When there is no one to challenge their ego, when the night is as quiet as a corpse, what sort of man do they see? When they close their eyes and picture the faces and bodies of those who breathe no longer, do these indelible images give them the same uplifting feelings as watching children play?

For me, catching a wave, having a laugh with a few mates or hanging out down at the beach with my family gives me joy. And like any parent, I'm definitely guilty when it comes to bragging about the exploits of my children. Taking life does not define who I am: it is something I have had to do and it brings me neither guilt, pride nor joy. It was a requirement of war, and the memory of it gives me a hollow, dead feeling that I don't like to think about.

In the lead up to Anzac Day this year, I spoke with a number of World War II veterans who, to this day, still harbour a deep hatred for those who they met in battle. But these men were usually subjected to horrors that we may not fully understand. Despite this hatred, I have never heard one of these vets speak of taking life as if they had just hit the cricket ball over the fence for six. That is one thing I love about the elderly: they are more inclined to tell it how it is, rather than try to be perceived as something they are not.

Throughout my life I have gained inspiration, knowledge and guidance from many people, from family and friends to martial arts instructors and SAS patrol commanders. I have also drawn strength from people I barely know. Whenever I meet someone special, I try to ascertain what it is that makes them unique. It could be the way they have dealt with adversity, or how they have reached the top of their chosen field, or how their actions have had a positive effect on the lives of others. I find myself analysing them and hoping that a small piece of them will rub off on me.

But I don't gauge my success by comparing myself to others. Those who do so are often left bitter and fail to reach their potential. I compete with myself, because then the potential for growth is infinite; I am not bordered by those above and below.

My experiences, training and relationships have shaped my life, but the way I reflect on these things allows me to grow and progress with confidence. Not everything I attempt works out, but I give everything I attempt the same level of commitment.

Acknowledgements

Those who have had the greatest impact upon my life are those who have been the most generous with their time. Sincere thanks.

I would also like to thank my editor, Julian Welch, for his vision, efficiency and attention to detail. You're a legend, mate!

In memory of our warrior brother, Danny G

1969–2009

IF YOU LIKED THIS BOOK, THERE'S HEAPS MORE STUFF TO CHECK OUT AT

www.randomhouse.com.au

- ▶ Author interviews
- ▶ Videos
- ▶ Competitions
- ▶ Free stuff
- ▶ Games

▶ Sign up for newsletters and be the first to get news on your favourite books and authors

▶ Fantastic teachers' notes and reading guides

▶ Details on where you can meet authors

BOOKS ARE JUST THE START!

www.randomhouse.com.au